PARENTAL CHILD ABDUCTION TO ISLAMIC LAW COUNTRIES

As the world becomes smaller, family law is becoming truly global, giving rise to more and more questions for private international law. This book looks at the sensitive and complex question of child abduction, with a unique child rights perspective. Taking Islamic law as its case study, it delves into child abduction in key jurisdictions from Iran to Saudi Arabia and Libya to Pakistan. Rigorous doctrinal analysis is enhanced by empirical insights, namely interviews with abductees, parents and professionals. It is an excellent guide to a complicated field.

Volume 33 in the series Studies in Private International Law

Studies in Private International Law

Recent titles in the series

Cross-Border Litigation in Europe
Edited by Paul Beaumont, Mihail Danov, Katarina Trimmings and Burcu Yuksel

Forum (Non) Conveniens in England: Past, Present, and Future
Ardavan Arzandeh

Commercial Issues in Private International Law: A Common Law Perspective
Edited by Vivienne Bath, Andrew Dickinson, Michael Douglas and Mary Keyes

Jurisdiction and Cross-Border Collective Redress: A European Private International Law Perspective
Alexia Pato

Rethinking Judicial Jurisdiction in Private International Law
Milana Karayanidi

Economic Sanctions in EU Private International Law
Tamás Szabados

Clawback Law in the Context of Succession
Jayne Holliday

Place of Performance: A Comparative Analysis
Chukwuma Okoli

Private International Law in Nigeria
Chukwuma Okoli and Richard Oppong

Planning the Future of Cross Border Families: A Path Through Coordination
Edited by Ilaria Viarengo and Francesca Villata

The Private International Law of Authentic Instruments
Jonathan Fitchen

The Hague Judgments Convention and Commonwealth Model Law: A Pragmatic Perspective
Abubakri Yekini

A Guide to Global Private International Law
Edited by Paul Beaumont and Jayne Holliday

Parental Child Abduction to Islamic Law Countries
Nazia Yaqub

Parental Child Abduction to Islamic Law Countries

A Child Rights Analysis of the Legal Framework

Nazia Yaqub

•HART•
OXFORD • LONDON • NEW YORK • NEW DELHI • SYDNEY

HART PUBLISHING

Bloomsbury Publishing Plc

Kemp House, Chawley Park, Cumnor Hill, Oxford, OX2 9PH, UK

1385 Broadway, New York, NY 10018, USA

29 Earlsfort Terrace, Dublin 2, Ireland

HART PUBLISHING, the Hart/Stag logo, BLOOMSBURY and the Diana logo are trademarks of Bloomsbury Publishing Plc

First published in Great Britain 2022

A catalogue record for this book is available from the British Library.

A catalogue record for this book is available from the Library of Congress.

ISBN: HB: 978-1-50993-911-4
ePDF: 978-1-50993-913-8
ePub: 978-1-50993-912-1

Typeset by Compuscript Ltd, Shannon

This book is for my family; Othman, Zara, Aboudy and Daoud, for all their support.

SERIES EDITOR'S PREFACE

I have had a very longstanding interest in the civil aspects of international child abduction. I co-authored the first monograph on the *Hague Convention on the Civil Aspects of International Child Abduction* with Peter McEleavy that was published by Oxford University Press in 1999 and I gave my first set of lectures at the Hague Academy of International Law on 'The Jurisprudence of the European Court of Human Rights and the European Court of Justice on the Hague Convention on International Child Abduction' (2008) 335 *Hague Collected Courses* 9-104. As the Series Editor for the Hart Studies in Private International Law I am proud that the Series has made a major contribution to the subsequent literature on the topic. Rhona Schuz produced the second major monograph on the Convention – *The Hague Child Abduction Convention A Critical Analysis* (Hart, 2013) which is a must read for anyone interested in the field; Katarina Trimmings dealt with the EU aspects in *Child Abduction within the European Union* (Hart, 2013); Sarah Vigers produced an excellent short book on mediation in the context of child abduction cases which is still highly relevant – *Mediating International Child Abduction Cases The Hague Convention* (Hart, 2011); and Thalia Kruger wrote a thought provoking book based on empirical research into the views of parents affected by international child abductions in Belgium – *International Child Abduction The Inadequacies of the Law* (Hart, 2011). Recently Maria Caterina Baruffi and Jayne Holliday have produced a very up to date and stimulating chapter on 'Child Abduction' in Paul Beaumont and Jayne Holliday (eds) *A Guide to Global Private International Law* (Hart, 2022) 481–495 which defends the appropriateness of the Hague Child Abduction Convention to primary carer abductions.

This book by Nazia Yaqub takes the study of parental child abduction in six directions. First, it focuses on abductions of children from the UK to Islamic Law countries – many of which are not Parties to the Hague Child Abduction Convention 1980. However, it builds on the works referred to above on the Hague Convention because it does analyse situations where the child is abducted to an Islamic Law State that has become a Party to the Hague Convention (notably Morocco). Second, it explicitly adopts a child's rights framework of analysis of the law on parental abductions. This direction builds on the work of Rhona Schuz in her monograph in this Series referred to above. The book takes the opportunity to reflect on how the Hague Guide to Good Practice on Article 13(1)(b) of 2020 helps to ensure that children's rights are upheld by an appropriate use of the Article 13(1)(b) exception to the duty to return the child to the country of their habitual residence in cases where there is a grave risk of physical or psychological harm or where return would otherwise cause an intolerable situation and of the

Article 13(2) exception where the child objects to returning to their habitual residence. Third, it records the empirical research conducted by the author in relation to children who have been impacted by parental child abductions from the UK to Islamic Law countries. This direction builds on the empirical approach of Thalia Kruger in her monograph in this Series referred to above (which did include abductions between Belgium and some Islamic Law countries and interviews with left-behind and taking parents) but takes it in a new direction by getting the views of a small number of abducted children, and by making the focus of the study abductions from the UK to Islamic Law countries. Fourth, it examines how the criminal offence of child abduction is applied in international cases in the UK. Fifth, there is a detailed analysis of how the child's voice can best be heard from a child's rights perspective in parental abduction cases leading to a clear preference for children to be separately represented in Hague Convention return proceedings. Sixth, the book gives a detailed analysis of the risks associated with gender discrimination in cases of parental child abduction involving Islamic Law countries and concludes that the Hague Child Abduction Convention has the tools to deal with this issue appropriately through Articles 13 and 20 of that Convention.

The book is an invaluable resource on how Islamic Law countries deal with parental child abduction cases. From a child's rights perspective it critiques the existing Islamic Law and the Hague Child Abduction Convention. It rightly concludes that Islamic Law countries should be encouraged to become Parties to the Hague Child Abduction Convention and that non-Islamic Law countries should accept the accession of those States to the Convention. On this last point the UK and EU should improve their record of doing so.

Paul Beaumont
University of Stirling

PREFACE

Globally, thousands of cases occur each year where children and young people are taken to another part of the world by a parent. When this occurs without the consent of the left-behind parent or a court, the situation in law is termed abduction. While parental child abduction disputes are played out by disagreeing parents, the impact of those decisions often falls upon the children who are at the centre of the conflict. The removal can require a tremendous amount of adjustment by the abducted young person to his or her new environment, with little knowledge of how long the situation will continue.

To what extent children have a say in such matters is complex. In International Law, the United Nations Convention on the Rights of Child 1989 ('CRC') grants children the right to express a view in judicial proceedings affecting them (Article 12), to have their best interests treated as a primary consideration (Article 3) and the right to non-discrimination (Article 2). It is from this viewpoint the research examines how the child's rights are upheld in the context of cross-border parental abduction proceedings.

The analysis focuses exclusively upon parental child abduction disputes to Islamic law countries. The approach is taken because the majority of Islamic law countries are not signatory to the international law treaty designed to address the phenomenon, the 1980 Hague Convention on the Civil Aspects of International Child Abduction ('Hague Convention'), and consequently such cases are decided in domestic Islamic (shari'a) law proceedings. The parallel legal provisions allow the opportunity to evaluate how the abducted child's CRC rights are facilitated in the range of processes designed to respond to parental child abduction.

The research highlights how the effects of the law are perceived by young people abducted from the UK to Islamic law countries. The project examines 29 cases of abduction to Islamic law countries, involving 54 children, and includes interviews with young people, some of whom remain in the abduction situation. The aim is to contribute to a clearer understanding of what abducted young people consider to be in their interests in a parental abduction situation and whether this perspective differs from how the law operates.

In July 2016, for the first time ever, the UK entered into Hague Convention treaty obligations with an Islamic law country when it accepted Morocco's accession to the Hague Convention. The development presents an ideal opportunity in which to evaluate whether other Islamic law countries should accede to the Hague Convention, in order to advance children's rights. The legal development with Morocco also necessitates analysis of how the English courts will reciprocate the return of abducted children to the jurisdiction of Morocco's Islamic (shari'a) law courts, in light of the differences between English and Islamic custody law.

The empirical study referred to throughout this text was carried out between 2016–2019.

The law is stated up to 1st January 2022.

CONTENTS

ABBREVIATIONS

GC5	General Comment Five
GC12	General Comment Twelve
GC14	General Comment Fourteen
GC18	General Comment Eighteen
GC28	General Comment Twenty-Eight
CRC	United Nations Convention on the Rights of the Child
ECHR	European Convention on Human Rights
ECtHR	European Court of Human Rights
FCDO	Foreign, Commonwealth and Development Office, UK
FOIA	Freedom of Information Act Request
Hague Convention	The Hague Convention on the Civil Aspects of International Child Abduction 1980

TABLE OF CASES

England and Wales

European Court of Human Rights

USA

Pakistan

Malaysia

Other Jurisdictions

TABLE OF LEGISLATIVE INSTRUMENTS

Treaties

1

Introduction

Millions of children migrate across the world in various circumstances, seldom being consulted or having the authority to decide whether or not to travel.[1] The focus of this analysis is on cross-border parental child abduction, where one parent takes their child to another legal jurisdiction or retains the child after an agreed visit, without the consent of the left-behind parent or a court. The incidence of parental abduction is reportedly on the increase[2] due to the ease of foreign travel, inadequate screening at ports, increasing rates of divorce and subsequent child custody disputes.[3] Its impact on children and families is documented to cause significant distress to all concerned,[4] particularly as legal responses vary globally. The cross-jurisdictional nature of the phenomenon necessitated the development of an international treaty to recover abducted children. Negotiations began during the 1970s, which eventually led to an international convention: the Hague Convention on the Civil Aspects of International Child Abduction 1980 ('Hague Convention').[5]

[1] See Louise Ackers 'From "Best-Interests" to Participatory Rights – Children's Involvement in Family Migration Decisions' (2000) *Child and Family Law Quarterly* 167.

[2] It is reported that more than 100,000 children around the world are victims of cross-border parental child abduction due to cross-border marriages and the changing nature of families; Alessandra Cancedda and others *Missing children in the European Union: Mapping, Data Collection and Statistics* (Luxembourg Publications Office of the European Union, 2013); See also Christopher Paul and Sybillie Kiesewetter *Cross-Border Family Mediation: International Parental Child Abduction Custody and Access Cases* (Wolfgang Metzner Verlag, 2011); Mark Simmonds 'New FCO figures show parental child abduction cases on the rise' (Foreign and Commonwealth Office, 12 December 2013).

[3] Helen Stalford, 'Crossing Boundaries: Reconciling Law, Cultures and Values in International Family Law Mediation' 32 (2010) 2 *Journal of Social Welfare & Family Law* 155, 163.

[4] Marilyn Freeman, *Parental Child Abduction: The Long-Term Effects* (International Centre for Family Law, Policy, and Practice, 2014); Thalia Kruger, *International Child Abduction: The Inadequacies of the Law* (Hart Publishing, 2011); University of Antwerp, *Bouncing Back: The Wellbeing of Children in International Child Abduction Cases* ('eWELL') (Missing Children Europe, 2017); Mary Gibbs and others, 'The Consequences of Parental Abduction: A Pilot Study with a Retrospective View from the Victim' (2013) 21 (3) *The Family Journal* 313–317; Geoffrey Greif, 'A Parental Report on the Long-Term Consequences for Children of Abduction by the Other Parent' (2000) 31(1) *Child Psychiatry and Human Development* 59–78; Geoffrey Greif, 'The Long-Term Aftermath of Child Abduction: Two Case Studies and Implications for Family Therapy' (2009) 37 *The American Journal of Family Therapy* 273–286; Geoffrey Greif, 'Ambiguous Reunification: A Way for Social Workers to Conceptualize the Return of Children After Abduction and Other Separations' (2012) 93 (4) *Families in Society: The Journal of Contemporary Social Services* 305–311; Geoffrey Greif & Rebecca Hegar, 'Impact on Children of Abduction by a Parent: A Review of the Literature' (1992) 62 (4) *American Journal of Orthopsychiatry* 599.

[5] A second convention was also developed, the European Convention on Recognition and Enforcement of Decisions Concerning Custody of Children and on Restoration of Custody of

Islamic law countries have been reluctant to accede to the Hague Convention, and for three decades none were a party to the Hague Convention. Morocco changed the landscape when it acceded in 2010 and presented an ideal opportunity in which to evaluate whether accession to the Hague Convention should be undertaken by other Islamic law countries to advance children's rights. Subsequently, Iraq, Pakistan and Tunisia have also acceded. There are still many Islamic law countries that are not members, however, and cases of children abducted to an Islamic law country will be decided according to domestic law in Islamic law countries.

The focus of this analysis centres on abduction to Islamic law countries and in undertaking this examination, analyses cases of parental child abduction from the UK. The analysis aims to fill a gap in the literature while building on the scholarly work of the other publications on cross-border parental child abduction.[6] English law has no jurisdiction in Islamic law countries, and so the most the English courts can do once an abduction occurs is to make an order for the child to be made 'a ward of court' and returned to the UK.[7] While the English court will readily grant a wardship order, the order is unenforceable in the Islamic law country and so is ineffective. The lack of a legal solution has prompted calls by State authorities like Canada[8] and the United States[9] for Islamic law countries to accede to the Hague Convention and extend the Convention's protections to children abducted to that part of the world. Accession to the Hague Convention by Islamic law countries raises all sorts of questions and expectations, however, on whether or not membership will advance the rights of the abducted child. This text presents the first comprehensive socio-legal analysis of abduction from the UK to Islamic law countries, and in particular, it seeks to respond to the following questions:

(1) How does the legislation in Islamic law countries respond to cases of parental abduction from the UK?

Children 1980. In a European context the Conventions are supplemented by the Brussels IIA Regulation: Council Regulation (EC) No 2201/2003. Only the Hague Convention applies to non-European/Islamic law cases, however, and so will be the primary focus of this text.

[6] Paul Beaumont and Peter McEleavy, *The Hague Convention on International Child Abduction* (OUP, 1999); Kruger (2011) (n 4); Sarah Vigers, *Mediating International Child Abduction Cases: The Hague Convention* (2011); Rhona Schuz, *The Hague Child Abduction Convention* (Hart Publishing, 2013).

[7] The inherent jurisdiction of the court, of which wardship forms part, derives from the duty of the Crown to care for individuals who are unable to care for themselves. Only the High Court has jurisdiction in such proceedings and once a child is made a ward, the court holds responsibility for that child. Thereafter, the consent of the court is required for all important decisions concerning the child, such as with whom and where the child shall reside; For a discussion on wardship and the court's inherent jurisdiction see Kate Standley, *Family Law* (Palgrave Macmillan, 2010).

[8] Mobina Jaffer and Salma Ataullahjan, *Challenges and International Mechanisms to Address Cross-Border Child Abduction*, Report of the Standing Senate Committee on Human Rights (Canadian Government, July 2015) 16, 278, available at https://sencanada.ca/content/sen/Committee/412/ridr/rep/rep13jul15-e.pdf.

[9] USA Government, '*Investigation into Abductions of American Children to Saudi Arabia. Hearings before the Committee on Government Reform*' House of Representatives. 107th Congress. Second session. (United States Government Publishing Office, 2002).

(2) What are the outcomes for children abducted from the UK to Islamic law countries?
(3) Are children's rights upheld in domestic parental abduction law in Islamic law countries?
(4) Do children abducted to Islamic law countries consider that the law upholds their rights?
(5) Would accession to the Hague Convention by Islamic law countries improve outcomes for abducted children and advance their rights in comparison to the domestic Islamic law regime?

In answering these questions, the principal objective of this text is to identify what legal developments are needed to uphold the rights of children abducted to Islamic law countries. In order to do so, the analysis adopts a child-rights based approach underpinned by doctrinal analysis and empirical work.

I. Islamic Law Countries as a Focus

While there has been a great deal of research undertaken on the problem of cross-border parental child abduction ('parental abduction'), very little empirical work has been conducted internationally on abductions to Islamic law countries. Existing empirical research concentrates predominantly on cases involving states that are members of the Hague Convention,[10] except for the 2011 survey by Thalia Kruger.[11] Kruger's research analyses abduction cases to and from Belgium and abductions to Islamic law countries feature amongst the 667 cases analysed as part of that study.[12] The topic of Islamic country accession has also raised some academic interest, as part of enquiries for the Hague Conference on the feasibility of Islamic law countries becoming members.[13] Now that Islamic law countries are starting to accede, there is increasing interest on whether Hague offers a better framework and better outcomes for children.

The number of children abducted by a parent without the left-behind parent's consent have remained steady in the last two decades. It is difficult to provide a precise figure, and the closest estimate is taken from the most recent global

[10] Empirical investigations in the UK have been undertaken by Freeman (2014) (n 4); Marilyn Freeman, *International Child Abduction: The Effects* (Reunite, 2006); Marilyn Freeman, *The Outcomes for Children Returned Following an Abduction* (Reunite, 2003); Trevor Buck, *An Evaluation of the Long-term Effectiveness of Mediation in Cases of International Parental Child Abduction* (Reunite, 2012).

[11] The cases examined are files that were 'opened' (ie reported by a parent) in 2006 and 2007; Kruger (n 4) 4–8.

[12] Kruger (n 4) 108–111.

[13] Anver Emon and Urfan Khaliq, *Islamic Law, Private International Law & Cross-Border Child Abduction* (Hague Conference in Private International Law, 2014) available at https://assets.hcch.net/docs/5eb980b4-d9b2-4020-935f-4c91aff1319c.pdf; Emon A and Khaliq U. '*Jurisdictional Exceptionalisms: Islamic Law, International Law and Parental Child Abduction*' (CUP, 2021); Zaleha Kamaruddin, *Islamic Legal Perspectives on Cross-Border Family Disputes Involving Children* (Hague Conference in Private International Law, 2014) available at https://www.hcch.net/en/publications-and-studies/details4/?pid=6172.

Survey[14] which specifies that in 2015 'at least 2997' children were the subject of court applications for their return. The Survey only provides a snapshot of cases in that year, however, and does not include the numbers of children who cannot be located, or cases in which the left-behind parent does not have the resources to instruct lawyers and issue court proceedings in another country.[15] The figure also does not include details of children abducted to states not party to the Hague Convention, which includes Islamic law countries.

There is very little data available on the incidence of parental abduction from the UK to Islamic law countries. Parental abduction cases that do not fall under the Hague Convention are assigned to the government department, the UK Foreign, Commonwealth and Development Office ('FCDO', formerly known as the 'FCO'). The information from the FCDO is that the number of non-Hague Convention cases doubled in the last decade from approximately 272 cases reported to the FCDO in 2003–04 to 580 cases in 2012–13.[16] The FCDO says it dealt with 493 new non-Hague Convention cases in 2014–15 and 445 new cases in 2015–16.[17] The figures are not disaggregated further, however, to identify what proportion of these cases concern abduction to Islamic law countries. A Freedom of Information Act request made to the FCDO revealed some disaggregated detailed statistics: between January 2009 and July 2014, there were 179 reports of parental abduction made to the UK FCDO involving Pakistan alone.[18] There were a further 20 cases involving Pakistan in the latter half of 2014, bringing the total of cases to Pakistan in 2014 to 39 cases.[19]

The FCDO has since made the data publicly accessible without requiring specified Freedom of Information Act requests.[20] Consular data is available for each country which specifies the number of reports made to the FCDO for a range of matters, including parental child abduction. The information made available only specifies the number of cases reported and does not provide detail on the status of the case (as is published in the USA).[21] The UK data confirms that there were at least 56 reported cases of abduction from the UK to an Islamic law country in

[14] Lowe N and Stephens V, *A Statistical Analysis of Applications Made in 2015 Under the Hague Convention of 25 October 1980 on the Civil Aspects of International Child Abduction – Global Report* (Hague Conference, 2017); For statistics of cases to and from Belgium, see Thalia Kruger, *International Child Abduction: The Inadequacies of the Law* (Hart Publishing, 2011).

[15] The statistics also only relate to those Hague member states that elect to participate in the Survey of Hague Convention cases, ibid.

[16] Simmonds (n 2).

[17] After enquiries were made for the author's study.

[18] The Freedom of Information Act 2000 request is in the public domain: FCDO FOI request made in 2014 available at https://www.gov.uk/government/uploads/system/uploads/attachment_data/file/382997/FOI_ref_0851_parental_child_abduction.pdf.

[19] FOI request dated June 2016 available at https://assets.publishing.service.gov.uk/government/uploads/system/uploads/attachment_data/file/540319/FOI_0503-16_International_parental_child_abduction_-_India___Pakistan.pdf.

[20] Consular data by country: https://www.gov.uk/government/collections/consular-data.

[21] For example the USA compiles an annual report listing every case of abduction to and from the USA. It further separates the number of cases for each country and sets out details on cases resolved. An extract provides: 'During 2015, the Department had 25 reported abductions to Egypt. Of those, nine

2017, 21 reports were received concerning Pakistan, 12 reports concerning Egypt, seven for Tunisia, six for the UAE and fewer than five reports[22] for each of Algeria, Bahrain, Iran, Iraq, Jordan, Kuwait, Lebanon, Malaysia, Qatar and Saudi Arabia. In 2018 there were at least 48 reported cases of abduction from the UK to an Islamic law country: 22 cases were reported in relation to Pakistan, 18 reports with regard to the UAE and fewer than five reports for each of the states of Iraq, Iran, Egypt, Lebanon, Malaysia, Oman, Qatar and Tunisia.

The data further illustrates that there were at least 58 reported cases of abduction from the UK to an Islamic law country in 2019. There were twenty cases reported in the context of Pakistan, 20 concerning abductions to the United Arab Emirates and seven cases of abduction reported to Iraq. There were fewer than five cases reported for each of Bahrain, Bangladesh, Egypt, Iran, Malaysia, Morocco, Oman, Qatar, Saudi Arabia and Tunisia. Data of abduction cases reported to the FCDO in 2020 and 2021 will not feature as part of this analysis because of the unclear picture emerging during this time as a result of the travel restrictions prompted by the global coronavirus pandemic. It is, however, noteworthy that reports of parental child abduction from the UK were still received by the UK FCDO in relation to the Islamic law countries during 2020 and 2021. Cases of parental child abduction were reported during this period to the Islamic law countries of Algeria, Bahrain, Egypt, Iran, Malaysia, Pakistan, Qatar, Saudi Arabia and the United Arab Emirates.[23]

While the incidence of the cases reported is not high, the statistics reveal cases reported only, and not the actual number of children abducted per family. Moreover, data from the empirical investigation reveals that many left-behind parents decide not to report the abduction to the authorities and resort to other methods to return the child, such as counter-abduction. The offence of parental abduction is a criminal offence in the UK, carrying a prison sentence of up to seven years[24] which the Law Commission has recommended should be increased to 14 years.[25] The risk of a lengthy term of imprisonment of a former partner may be a reason why some left-behind parents may decide not to make an official

were newly reported during the calendar year. In 2015, 20 applications for return that the Department had submitted to Egypt were pending; the Department submitted eight of these applications during 2015. By December 31, 2015, two cases with pending applications (10 per cent of cases open during 2015) had been resolved, one was resolved by a voluntary agreement between the parents that resulted in the child returning to the United States, the other was resolved when the left behind parent did not pursue the return any further. Three other cases closed prior to submission of applications for return. By December 31, 2015, 20 reported abductions remained open. At the end of 2015, ten cases (50 per cent of cases open during 2015) were unresolved.' Annual Report (United States Department of State, Bureau of Consular Affairs, 2016). Available at https://travel.state.gov/content/dam/childabduction/complianceReports/2016%20IPCA%20Report%20-%20Final%20(July%2011).pdf.

[22] The FCDO representative explained during interview the data is recorded as '<5' where there were fewer than five cases that year to the country in question to ensure individual cases/children are not identified.

[23] n 20.

[24] Child Abduction Act 1984.

[25] Law Commission, *Simplification of Criminal Law: Kidnapping and Related Offences* (Law Com No 355, 2014).

complaint to the authorities. It would seem, therefore, that there are likely to be many more cases of parental abduction which do not feature within the statistics.

The statistics available indicate that there are a steady number of cases of parental abduction to Islamic law countries. The impact of parental abduction on families is reported in studies to have severe adverse effects,[26] which might be exacerbated in the case of abductions to Islamic law countries, where international abduction law does not apply. Indeed, although the study by Kruger does not focus specifically on Islamic law countries, she notes the difficulty in cases where the Hague framework does not apply. Citing a biography by one left-behind mother whose children were abducted from Bali to Saudi Arabia,[27] Kruger observes 'mothers who struggle to have contact with their children in countries where the legislation gives them very little rights fight a very hard battle. They might not be the majority, but their stories speak of such distress that their voices must be heard.'[28] The appraisal by Kruger prompted the author to also gather data from parents affected by parental abduction to Islamic law countries, both left-behind and abducting parents. A literature review of the published studies in this area led to a reflection on whether the impact of abduction might be greater on children abducted to Islamic law countries, due to the lack of an international legal framework to respond to such cases. The decision was therefore made to prioritise the focus of this analysis on children abducted to Islamic law countries.

II. The Abducted Child as a Focus

Children are at the heart of this issue and yet so far very few projects have engaged directly with abducted children. Freeman undertook a qualitative study in which 33 adults who were abducted as children reported their experiences of child abduction.[29] Another qualitative study by Freeman involved ten abducted children aged between ten and 18 years old at the time of the interview.[30] One further study has since been published, which engaged with nineteen abducted children, aged between 12 and 19. The University of Antwerp undertook a project involving partner agencies[31] entitled 'Bouncing Back: The Wellbeing of Children in International Child Abduction Cases' ('eWELL').[32] The report comprises an analysis of the views of parents; children's perceptions of the abduction experience (interviewed in Belgium, France and the Netherlands); and a review of the case

[26] See studies cited above at n 4.

[27] See Helle Amin, *Reunited in the Desert* (John Blake, 2008). Where the left-behind mother explains the difficulties she experienced trying to leave Saudi Arabia with her children.

[28] Kruger (n 4) 151.

[29] Freeman (2014) (n 4).

[30] Marilyn Freeman, *International Child Abduction: The Effects* (Reunite, 2006).

[31] University of Antwerp, Child Focus, Centrum IKO, CFPE-Enfant Disparus, and in collaboration with the French Central Authority and Missing Children Europe.

[32] University of Antwerp, eWELL (n 4).

law. The analysis covers five stages of the abduction process: pre, during, end, and post-abduction, while the fifth stage is that of legal proceedings. Consideration is given in the report to how the child's wellbeing is affected by the abduction so that adults can reflect on how the decisions made for children can impact the child. None of these studies relates specifically to the situation of abductions to Islamic law countries, however, and so this analysis seeks to advance existing knowledge as it provides a deeper understanding of how parental abduction to Islamic law countries affects children and the enforcement of their rights. It argues that abduction to Islamic law countries is distinct from other abduction contexts, both because of the unique cultural, religious and legal framework in place and because most Islamic law countries are not signatories to the Hague Convention.

III. A Children's Rights-Based Approach

A children's rights-based approach applies to this research and findings, grounded in the United Nations Convention on the Rights of the Child 1989 ('CRC').[33] An essential feature of such an approach is ascertaining the views of children on their experience of parental abduction. As Stalford highlights, up until the 1990s child and family laws and policies were generally constructed based on adult presumptions regarding children's interests.[34] Since then, there has been a wealth of research undertaken on participatory methods with young people as an effective means of informing law, policy and practice.[35] Yet despite the developments there has been a minimal attempt to apply this to the issue of parental abduction and, as far as the writer is aware, no attempt at all to consider this in the context of abduction to Islamic law countries.

A children's rights-based approach builds upon the earlier established human rights-based approach, which is underpinned by principles of human dignity, moral respect,[36] and those found under the Universal Declaration

[33] Adopted and opened for signature, ratification and accession by General Assembly Resolution 44/25 of 20 November 1989, with entry into force 2 September 1990. The development of the CRC is explained in detail in chapter 2.

[34] Helen Stalford, *Children and the European Union: Rights, Welfare and Accountability* (Hart Publishing, 2012) 93.

[35] See the work of Carol Smart, 'From Children's Shoes to Children's Voices' (2002) 40 3 *Family Court Review* 307; Nicholas Wilson, "The Ears of the Child in Family Proceedings" (2007) September *Family Law* 808; Priscilla Alderson and Virginia Morrow, *Ethics, Social Science Research and Consulting with Young People* (Barnardo's, 2004) 22; Nigel Thomas, 'Towards a Theory of Children's Participation' (2007) 15(2) *International Journal of Children's Rights* 199–218; Laura Lundy and Lesley McEvoy, 'Children's Rights and Research Processes: Assisting Children to (In)formed Views' (2012) 19(1) *Childhood* 116.

[36] For an in-depth discussion on the issue of morality and dignity underpinning human rights, see Ronald Dworkin, *Taking Rights Seriously* (Harvard, 1978) 198; Francesca Klug, *Values for a Godless Age: The Story of the UK's New Bill of Rights* (Penguin, 2000); Jack Donnelly, *International Human Rights* (Westview, 2007); Philip Alston 'The Universal Declaration in an Era of Globalization' in Barend van der Heijden and Bahia Tahzib-Lie (eds) *Reflections on the Universal Declaration of*

of Human Rights.[37] These notions are given additional prominence under the rights-based approach, as it places obligations on duty-bearers to uphold and further the rights of rights-holders,[38] and demand change.[39] A children's rights-based approach also builds upon rights established in a range of pre-CRC human rights instruments, including the 1924 Declaration of the Rights of the Child, the European Convention on Human Rights and Fundamental Freedoms 1950 (ECHR), the 1959 Declaration on the Rights of the Child, the International Covenant on Civil and Political Rights 1966, the International Covenant on Economic, Social and Cultural Rights 1966, and a number of International Labour Organisation Conventions.[40] Children's rights are upheld in a number of post-CRC conventions too, which include the African Charter on the Rights and Welfare of Children, private international law instruments of the Hague Conference,[41] and other European conventions.[42] Lundy and McEvoy adopt principles of the human rights-based approach from the UN Statement of Common Understanding, along with the CRC to develop a broad children's rights-based framework.[43] They regard the Statement as a 'practical articulation of the concepts central to the human rights discourse,' and that essential to the implementation of a rights-based approach are the children's rights standards contained in the CRC.[44] Lundy and McEvoy develop their children's rights-based approach directly from the three principles contained within the Statement, suggesting a children's rights-based approach must ensure: (i) the process furthers the realisation of children's rights, (ii) the aims and process should be informed by and comply with CRC standards, and (iii) outcomes should build

Human Rights: A Fiftieth Anniversary Anthology (Martinus Nijhoff, 1998); Jack Mahoney, *The Challenge of Human Rights: Origin, Development and Significance* (Blackwell Publishing, 2007) 146.

[37] The principles of universality and inalienability; accountability; indivisibility; inter-dependence and inter-relatedness; non-discrimination and equality; participation and inclusion; accountability and the rule of law.

[38] Michael Freeman, *Human Rights* (Polity, 2002) 61; Charles Beitz, *The Idea of Human Rights* (OUP, 2009); Donnelly n 36, 28.

[39] Jack Donnelly, *Universal Human Rights in Theory and Practice* (Cornell University Press, 2003) 12.

[40] For a discussion of the various international children's rights instruments, see Philip Veerman, *The Rights of the Child and the Changing Image of Childhood* (Martinus Nijhoff, 1992); Philip Alston and John Tobin, *Laying the Foundations for Children's Rights* (UNICEF Innocenti Research Centre, 2005).

[41] See for instance the Hague Convention of 29 May 1993 on Protection of Children and Co-operation in Respect of Intercountry Adoption; the Hague Convention of 19 October 1996 on Jurisdiction, Applicable Law, Recognition, Enforcement and Co-operation in Respect of Parental Responsibility and Measures for the Protection of Children; and the Hague Convention of 23 November 2007 on the International Recovery of Child Support and Other Forms of Family Maintenance.

[42] See for example the European Convention on the Exercise of Children's Rights 1996, ETS No 160; the revised European Social Charter 1996, ETS No 163; The 1999 ILO Convention on the Worst Forms of Child Labour (Number 182); the 2006 UN Convention on the Rights of Persons with Disabilities.

[43] United Nations, *Statement of Common Understanding on a Human Rights-Based Approach to Development Co-operation* (United Nations, 2003). The statement outlines the UN agencies commitment to rights-based approaches www.undp.org; see also Laura Lundy and Lesley McEvoy, *Getting it Right for Children: A Practitioners' Guide to Children's Rights Programming* (Save the Children, 2007).

[44] Laura Lundy and Lesley McEvoy, 'Childhood, the United Nations Convention on the Rights of the Child and Research: What Constitutes a Rights-Based Approach?' in Michael Freeman (ed), *Law and Childhood* (OUP, 2012) 78.

the capacity of children, as rights-holders, to claim their rights and build the capacity of duty-bearers to fulfil their obligations.

The framework of analysis in this text builds upon these three broad concepts and adds more specific detail from the legal framework of the CRC. UNICEF affirms that 'a children's rights-based approach is grounded in the CRC,[45] which Stalford et al highlight is characteristically the first port of call when seeking to apply a children's rights-based approach to decision-making.[46] They explain a comprehensive framework of rights is provided by the substantive provisions of the CRC, the accompanying guidance of the Committee on the Rights of the Child,[47] and the CRC's general principles.[48] These sources are utilised here to give effect to the children's rights-based approach. Firstly, three of the CRC's general principles of the best interests of the child, participation and non-discrimination will guide the examination of the rights of abducted children. Secondly, the analysis will employ the guidance issued by the UNCRC Committee in the form of General Comments (General Comment 5, 12, 14 and 18). The General Comments establish processes by which to prioritise children's rights[49] and so are adopted here to measure the degree to which the rights of abducted children are upheld in the law. Thirdly, the CRC Committee's Concluding Observations on reports by Islamic law countries are relied upon to substantiate the analysis.[50]

Stalford and Hollingsworth further identify five indicators of a children's rights-based approach, to evaluate how salient children's rights are in law, and in published judgments in particular.[51] Judgments for cases of parental abduction are not publicly available in Islamic law countries,[52] and so it is not possible to

[45] See UNICEF, '*A Child Rights-Based Approach: Seven Principles Grounded in the UN Convention on the Rights of the Child*' available at www.unicef.org.uk/child-friendly-cities/child-rights-based-approach/.

[46] Helen Stalford, Kathryn Hollingsworth and Stephen Gilmore (eds), *Rewriting Children's Rights Judgments: From Academic Vision to New Practice* (Hart Publishing, 2017) 18–19.

[47] Derived from its General Comments and the Concluding Observations on reports by state parties.

[48] Note that the CRC's general principles have been adopted as child-rights based approach in themselves by Collins, a PhD student of Geraldine Van Bueren. Collins' adaptation of the children's rights-based approach to her topic of monitoring CRC rights is to apply the CRC's four guiding principles as a framework for analysis: non-discrimination (Article 2), best interest (Article 3), maximum survival and development (Article 6), and views of the child (Article 12); Tara Maeve Collins, *The Monitoring of the Rights of the Child: A Children's Rights-Based Approach* (PhD text) (Queen Mary & Westfield College, University of London, 2007).

[49] CRC Committee, General Comment No 5: *General Measures of Implementation of the Convention on the Rights of the Child* CRC/GC/2003/5 para 9.

[50] It is recognised here that the CRC framework is not an uncontested perspective through which to examine rights. The methodology is arguably the most appropriate in the child abduction context however and the competing views are explored throughout the text. Emon and Khaliq (2021); see also K Valentin and L Meinert, 'The adult North and the young South: Reflections on the Civilizing Mission of Children's Rights' 2009 25 (3) *Anthropology Today* 23–8, who view the CRC as imposing the views of the Global North on the Global South and U Narayan, *Dislocating Cultures, Identities, Traditions and Third-World Feminism* (Routledge, 2007).

[51] Kathryn Hollingsworth and Helen Stalford, 'Towards Children's Rights Judgments', chapter 3 in *Rewriting Children's Rights Judgments*, n (46) 53–4.

[52] The inaccessibility is confirmed by Lynn Welchman, *Women and Muslim Family Laws in Arab States: A Comparative Overview of Textual Development and Advocacy* (Amsterdam University Press, 2007) 14.

apply the five indicators without adaptation.[53] As a result of the inaccessibility of judgments, the indicators are modified here to a legislative context and analyse: (1) whether or not the legislation responding to parental abduction (domestic Islamic law and the Hague Convention) upholds children's rights; (2) whether the legislation grants the judiciary discretion to interpret parental abduction law in a manner consistent with children's rights and (3) the developments in the law that are needed to centralise the rights of the child in a parental abduction context.

IV. Methodological Approach

This analysis seeks to implement a qualitative approach in order to explore the experience from the perspective of children and adults affected by parental abduction to Islamic law countries. The findings from the empirical work are drawn upon throughout the text and statistical data is also applied to contextualise and complement the more qualitative examples where available.

The discussion above identifies that children are generally missing from research on parental abduction and with the added dearth in research on abductions to Islamic law countries; children are practically invisible in this context. Thus it was considered important to facilitate the involvement of children in the design of the project, as research about children, without involving children, could be undermined.[54] Alderson identifies that adults generally hold beliefs or theories about what children will or will not think and so part of implementing a children's rights-based methodology involves confronting the assumptions held about what children might wish to discuss or are comfortable discussing.[55] The issue was addressed by allowing young people with direct experience of abduction to an Islamic law country to assist in the design of the research from the outset.

The doctrinal analysis is supported by documentary analysis of CRC Committee reports and Concluding Observations together with an empirical investigation to gather new qualitative data. Alongside the doctrinal and theoretical analysis, the text will also use empirical 'case studies' from interviews with ten abducted

[53] The five indicates are: whether parental abduction law explicitly adopts a child-rights approach by drawing on the CRC? Does parental abduction law (and the judiciary) draw on scholarly insights to address theoretical tensions which hinder the resolutions of cases in ways which best protect the rights of abducted children? Do the legal processes in abduction cases maximise children's participation by conforming to child-friendly procedures? Does the narrative used in the legislation and cases relating to parental abduction centralise the child's perspective and voice? Are children acknowledged as one of the audiences for legal judgments?

[54] Sharon Bessell, Research with Children: Thinking About Method and Methodology in *Involving Children and Young People in Research* (ARACY and the NSW Commission for Children and Young People, 2009).

[55] Priscilla Alderson and Virginia Morrow, *Ethics, Social Science Research and Consulting with Young People* (Barnardo's, 2004) 22; Beazley, H and others, 'How Are the Human Rights of Children Related to Research Methodology?' in Invernizzi, A and Williams, J (eds), *The Human Rights of Children: From Visions to Implementation* (Ashgate Publishing, 2011) 164.

young people. The case study approach aids the analysis at several levels. Firstly, introducing the young people abducted to Islamic law countries allows them to tell their life stories in their own words. Secondly, the case studies are helpful to illustrate how the law under examination applies to real-life cases. Thirdly accessing published judgments in this specialised area of law can prove difficult,[56] and is further complicated by the fact that judgments in Islamic law countries are not published as they are in the UK.[57] The case studies provide information on the pertinent issues in such cases, also providing detail on how the law is applied and the decisions of the Islamic courts. While the sample size of ten case studies of abducted young people is small, data is more broadly gathered from 48 participants. This sample does not claim to present a representative picture of the overall experience of individuals affected by abduction to Islamic law countries, but to provide insights into the experiences of some of those affected, to broadly corroborate impressions gleaned from other critiques of child abduction, and to tease out the distinctive features of the Islamic context. This form of qualitative research takes many forms and means different things to different people.[58] Silverman describes the work of qualitative researchers as; 'Using multiple methods to collect rich, descriptive, contextually situated data to seek understanding of the experience of human experience or relationships within a system or culture.'[59] Obtaining this type of qualitative data from individuals with first-hand experience of parental abduction to Islamic law countries creates scope for an evaluation of the law.[60]

Dataset

Interviews were undertaken with various categories of individuals with experience of parental abduction to Islamic law countries. The author's empirical study comprises twenty-nine cases of abduction, involving fifty-four abducted children. A total of 48 individuals participated: 23 left-behind parents, 4 abducting parents, 10 young people (aged 16–24) abducted as children, and 11 professionals. The professionals, whose daily work involves cases of parental abduction to Islamic law

[56] A study which highlights the difficulty in accessing published judgments on parental abduction cases in European states highlights: 'Accessing Belgian and French case law however was more challenging, as many judgments are not published online or made publicly available elsewhere.' Sara Lembrechts, 'Hearing Abducted Children in Court – A Comparative Point of View from Three Countries (Belgium, France & the Netherlands)' in *The Child's Voice – 15 years later. The Judge's Newsletter on International Child Protection* (Hague Conference on Private International Law, 22 (2018) 28 ('The Child's Voice – 15 years later').

[57] Confirmed by Welchman. Though note the formerly colonised Pakistan and Malaysia have a form of law reporting available on Lexis and their relevant international parental abduction judgments are considered in the analysis where available. Lynn Welchman, *Women and Muslim Family Laws in Arab States: A Comparative Overview of Textual Development and Advocacy* (Amsterdam University Press, 2007) 14.

[58] Chris Mann and Fiona Stewart, *Internet Communication and Qualitative Research: A Handbook for Researching Online* (Sage Publishing, 2000) 2.

[59] David Silverman, *Doing Qualitative Research: A Practical Handbook* (Sage Publishing, 1999) 2.

[60] Julia Brannan, *Mixing Methods: Qualitative and Quantitative Research* (Routledge, 1995).

countries and who have experience of work both in the UK and across Islamic law countries include members of the judiciary, lawyers, mediators, representatives of parental child abduction charities and their staff, civil servants of the Foreign Office dealing with non-Hague Convention cases and the Central Authority offices dealing with Hague Convention cases. While the professionals interviewed have experience of working with hundreds of cases, for the sake of precision, the only cases included in the sample are those 29 cases where first-hand accounts are provided by the abducting parent, left-behind parent or abducted young person. Studying the phenomenon from more than one perspective helped explain more fully the richness and complexity of human behaviour.[61] Moreover, comparing perspectives from professionals of different disciplines who bring different perspectives further triangulated the data.[62]

The 54 abductees whose cases are examined were abducted to; Algeria (3 children), Egypt (4), Iran (2), Jordan (5), Libya (17), Oman (2), Pakistan (5), Syria (1), Saudi Arabia (9), Tunisia (3) and the UAE (3). Data in relation to other Islamic law countries was provided by professionals as part of the empirical investigation.

Diversity of Islamic Law Countries

Cross-national research in its most basic sense is identified by Kohn as 'any research which transcends national boundaries.'[63] This research explores how differently the law responds to cases of parental abduction in different Islamic law countries as compared with the UK, and in this respect, the research is cross-national. The study further falls within the definition of cross-national research as provided by Hantrais and Mangen: 'examining one or more units in two or more societies, cultures or countries are compared in respect of the same concepts and concerning the systematic analysis of phenomena, usually with the intention of explaining them and generalising from them.'[64] Islamic law countries are generally concentrated in parts of Africa, Asia and the Middle East. Equally so, Muslim families have migrated and settled across the world and this subsequently results in an examination of cases that are geographically dispersed. Countries with Muslim majority populations have diverse legal systems; Nigeria, for example, has distinct regions where Islamic law applies and other regions where it does not.[65] It is for this reason that only countries where Islamic family law applies exclusively are included in the sample, ie Algeria, Bangladesh, Bahrain, Jordan, Indonesia, Iran, Iraq, Kuwait, Libya, Malaysia,

[61] Louis Cohen and others, *Research Methods in Education* (Routledge, 2017) 254.

[62] Mwaniki Celestine Ndanu and Mue Jacinta Syombua, 'Mixed Methods Research: The Hidden Cracks of the Triangulation Design' (2015) 4 *General Education Journal* 46–67, 49.

[63] Melvin Kohn (ed), *Cross-National Research in Sociology* (Sage Publishing, 1989) 20.

[64] Linda Hantrais and Stephen Mangen (eds), *Cross-National Research Methods in the Social Sciences* (Pinter, 1998) 2.

[65] See Isaac Sampson, 'Religion and the Nigerian State: Situating the de facto and de jure frontiers State–Religion Relations and its Implications For National Security' (2014) 3 (2) *Ox J Law Religion* 31

Morocco, Oman, Pakistan, Qatar, Saudi Arabia, Syria, Tunisia, UAE and Yemen. Within these countries there exist some variations in custody/abduction law, which are examined further in chapters 3 and 4.

In electing how to frame the research, Redmond observes that cross-national methodologies have matured and now encompass greater diversity. The diversity includes, as is illustrated in this text, through choosing to not limit examination exclusively through a comparative law lens, but also examine the socio-legal focus.[66] Thus, while the findings do not produce a comparative indicator of the legal response to parental abduction cases in each of the 11 Islamic law countries included, the data does illustrate how the law is implemented in practice. Indeed, the interview data reveals the varying approaches adopted by the courts in different Islamic law countries, such as on the topic of children's participation in proceedings examined in chapter 4. Interviewing research participants with experience of abduction to the eleven Islamic law countries involved interviewing participants in several different countries. Some were still resident in the Islamic law countries, whilst others had moved away or returned to the UK. Participants were interviewed while in Algeria, Egypt, Jordan, Libya, Malta, Oman, Pakistan, Syria, Saudi Arabia, Tunisia, the United Arab Emirates, and the UK. Interview data from participants of such different nations encompass multiple cultural and linguistic variants to which the methods have to be sensitive.

There is a cultural context to the data collected, with potentially different meanings and actions specific to the communities from which the research participants derive.[67] The majority of interviews were undertaken through technological means, with vast geographical distances. Efforts were made to avoid assumptions about Islamic societies, with an awareness that a community of individuals does not mean class, cultural, religious, and political homogeneity.[68] Attention is paid to meanings attached to terms such as 'primary carer' and 'parental abduction,' which required engagement with the concept and not a literal translation. Crossman highlights that this involves 'peeling away layers of personal cultural assumptions so that the intercultural implications can become accessible to others unfamiliar with the context under study.'[69] In this way, an attempt to engage with each participant's culture was made with notes to contextualise the data collected, such as how the abducted young people perceived the issue of the mother's religion.[70] Reflection was necessary before, during and after the interview on the possible 'non-Western' complexities that might arise, and the impact these might have

[66] Mark Redmond, 'Cultural and Ethical Challenges in Cross-National Research: Reflections on a European Union Study on Child and Youth Migration' (2003) 2(4) *International Journal of Qualitative Methods*.

[67] Kathy Charmaz, *Constructing Grounded Theory* (Sage Publishing, 2014) 330–1; Corrine Glesne, 'Research as Solidarity' in Norman Denzin and Michael Giardina (eds), *Ethical Futures in Qualitative Research: Decolonizing the Politics of Knowledge* (Routledge, 2007) 169–78.

[68] Vera Sheridan and Katharina Storch, 'Linking the Intercultural and Grounded Theory: Methodological Issues in Migration Research' (2009) 10(1) *Qualitative Social Research*.

[69] Crossman, J cited in Charmaz (n 66) 332.

[70] Kathryn Roulston, *Reflective Interviewing: A Guide to Theory and Practice* (Sage Publishing, 2010).

upon participants' accounts and perceptions.[71] Long-standing civil conflict is one such example, and this emerged in volunteer discussions about parental abductions to Libya and Syria.

The Limitations of this Methodology

The study draws on the use of a sample of interviews, which might limit the generality of the results. It is also noteworthy that the abductees were young (aged between 2–10 years old) at the time of the abduction and were reporting their recollections years later. While the reflections assist in understanding how the abductees view parental abduction law impacted them, it may be helpful to also interview younger abductees in the future, to examine whether children's views on the abduction change as children mature.

V. The Parameters and Overview of this Text

The following chapters of the text set out to explore how the legal frameworks responding to parental abduction – domestic law in Islamic law countries and the Hague Convention – uphold the rights of abducted children. The analysis will contribute to answering the overarching question this text seeks to respond to: whether accession to the Hague Convention by Islamic law countries will advance the rights of children abducted to Islamic law countries.

This text engages with the subject of parental abduction to Islamic law countries specifically from the perspective of the abducted child. As highlighted above, the perspective of abducted children is an under-researched area and geographical, cultural and language difficulties make children and young people abducted to Islamic law countries a hard-to-reach group of participants. In addition, this analysis seeks to make sense of a broad and complex area of Islamic law and to analyse its effectiveness through the lens of specific CRC principles. As a result, this text had to stop short of considering some broader issues of relevance in the interests of engaging in a focussed legal analysis of children's rights in the domestic legislation in Islamic countries. and the Hague framework. The data integrated is only that which is relevant to the discussion surrounding the child's rights and specifically Article 2 (non-discrimination), 3 (best interests) and 12 (participation) CRC rights.

Having explained why there is a specific need for research in relation to the literature, and the theoretical approach that will underpin the analysis, the following chapters aim to evaluate the extent to which children's rights are upheld in

[71] Anne Ryen, 'Exploring or Exporting: Qualitative Methods in Times of Globalisation' (2011) 14 (6) *International Journal of Social Research Methodology* 439.

parental abduction law. A case-study approach is adopted, drawing on the empirical data, and the accounts provided by participants are integrated throughout the analysis to highlight the impact of the law upon the very children affected by parental abduction.

Chapter 2 critically reflects on the children's rights-based scaffolding in Islamic law countries and their Article 11 CRC obligations to take measures to address parental abduction. In order to undertake the evaluation, both the CRC and the Hague Convention are examined to understand the relationship between both treaties and the commitments states make when committing to each. Morocco, as the only Islamic law country for which Hague Convention data is available, is adopted as a case study. The discussion evaluates Morocco's commitment to children's rights and whether it has the structures in place to give effect to a children's rights application of the Hague Convention.

Chapter 3 moves the analysis from a context-setting to a review of the legal framework that regulates cases of parental abduction in Islamic law countries. In doing so, it seeks to analyse whether the legal process promotes children's rights, as per the obligation of Islamic law countries under the CRC. Chapter 3 examines explicitly whether the best interests of children abducted to Islamic law countries are a primary consideration in parental abduction law, and which of the two legal regimes under examination – domestic law in Islamic law countries or the Hague Convention – gives greater effect to the child's Article 3 CRC right. In doing so, the discussion explores the interplay between the CRC and the Hague Convention; between the CRC and Islamic law; and between Islamic law and the Hague Convention.

Chapter 4 builds upon the analysis in chapter 3 and argues that a child's best interests cannot be determined without first hearing the child's views. In doing so it examines children's participatory rights in abduction proceedings pursuant to Article 12 CRC. The chapter comprises an investigation of how both legal frameworks give effect to the child's right to be heard through examining the processes by which children's views are ascertained and the weight given to the child's views by the courts. The chapter examines the developments in child abduction law, reflecting upon whether the legal reforms enhance or infringe upon the participatory rights of abducted children.

Chapter 5 builds upon the analysis undertaken in earlier chapters with a focus on children's right to protection against discrimination as enshrined in Article 2 CRC. It highlights, in particular, the gender discrimination emerging within the legislative framing, procedural protocols, and substantive outcomes for children abducted to Islamic law countries. The chapter then examines some opportunities by which to respond to gender discrimination in child abduction law, through applying a human rights framework broader than the CRC, addressing the cultural context of gender discrimination, and applying relational theory, to examine how the rights/interests of the mother can be linked with those of the abducted child. The chapter also reflects upon how the English courts might address the problem of gender discrimination in cases involving abduction to Islamic law countries.

The concluding chapter 6 draws together the analysis on the rights of abducted children examined against the children's rights indicators introduced in chapter 1. The chapter reflects on how Islamic law countries might respond to cases of abduction from the UK and suggests achievable and measurable children's rights-based developments for Islamic law countries and Hague Convention States more generally. Finally, the chapter offers a perspective on potential avenues for future research in this area.

2

The Importance of Children's Rights to the Regulation of Parental Child Abduction

Islamic law countries have for many years chosen not to accede to the Hague Convention on the Civil Aspects of International Child Abduction 1980 ('Hague Convention'). While existing research looks at the possibility of accession;[1] this research examines whether Islamic law countries can – if it is decided that the Hague Convention upholds the rights of children abducted to Islamic law countries – implement the Hague Convention in a children's rights-compliant way. The argument presented in this chapter is that if a state does not have a real commitment to children's rights, implementation of the Hague Convention by an Islamic law country will not necessarily achieve better outcomes for children.

In developing the argument, the first section of this chapter will explore the children's rights priorities of the Hague Convention before moving on to examine, in the second section, the methods by which states could incorporate children's rights to give effect to the Hague Convention. The discussion in section three moves on to apply the methods identified to the example of Morocco, to evaluate whether such methods of incorporation are achievable in Islamic law countries. Morocco is the first Islamic law country to accede to the Hague Convention and has had the longest period in which to cultivate its relationship with the Hague and CRC provisions. The examination of Morocco is a testing bed to assess if other Islamic law countries can assume the responsibilities arising from accession to the Hague Convention, in a manner consistent with the children's rights-based approach.

Before looking more closely at the specific children's rights-based principles in the context of Islamic country accession, it is necessary to examine the legal regulation of cross-border parental abduction and children's rights more generally.

[1] Abdul Hamid and others, 'The Applicability of the 1980 Hague Abduction Convention in Muslim Countries: Particular Reference to the Malaysian Position' (2018) 32 *Arab Law Quarterly* 99.

I. A Children's Rights-Based Approach Requires the Hague Convention to be Interpreted as a Children's Rights Instrument

The premise of this analysis is that as children are central to any parental abduction dispute, any resolution to a case should be considered from a children's rights perspective.[2] Though several instruments exist which give effect to children's rights,[3] the focus here is exclusively on the CRC for three reasons. First, because of the CRC's specific reference to parental abduction.[4] Secondly, because the children's rights-based approach derives from the CRC,[5] and thirdly due to the fact that all Islamic law countries are a signatory to the CRC. Several children's rights concerns arise from any one case of cross-border parental child abduction. These include the child's CRC right to have his or her best interests taken into consideration,[6] to participate in decisions affecting him or her,[7] to maintain regular contact with both parents,[8] to exercise and maintain his or her cultural identity,[9] to education,[10] to the highest attainable standard of health[11] and freedom of association.[12]

The most explicit right related to cross-border parental abduction under the CRC appears under Article 11, which has the effect of enshrining the child's right to be protected from the harm of cross-border parental abduction. It provides:

> 1. States Parties shall take measures to combat the illicit transfer and non-return of children abroad.
> 2. To this end, States Parties shall promote the conclusion of bilateral or multilateral agreements or accession to existing agreements.

The Article 11 reference to multilateral and existing agreements is accepted as referring to the Hague Convention. The view is adopted because the Hague Convention predates the CRC and a perusal of the resolutions drafted during the

[2] The reasons why have been set out in literature by Leena Alanen, 'Taking Children's Rights Seriously' (2010) 17(5) *Childhood* 5; Jane Fortin, *Children's Rights and the Developing Law* (Butterworths, 2003); John Eekelaar, 'The Emergence of Children's Rights' (1986) 161 *Oxford Journal of Legal Studies* 170–1; Michael Freeman, 'Why it Remains Important to Take Children's Rights Seriously' (2007) 15(1) *International Journal of Children's Rights*, 5–23.

[3] The Declaration of the Rights of the Child 1924, the European Convention for the Protection of Human Rights and Fundamental Freedoms 1950 ('ECHR'), the 1959 Declaration on the Rights of the Child, the International Covenant on Civil and Political Rights 1966, the International Covenant on Economic, Social and Cultural Rights 1966, and the International Labour Organisation Conventions. The UN Convention on the Rights of Persons with Disabilities, the UN Refugee Convention 1951, the African Charter on the Rights and Welfare of Children 1990.

[4] In Article 11.

[5] See chapter 1, III.

[6] Art 3 CRC.

[7] Art 12 CRC.

[8] Arts 9(1), 9(3) and 10(2) CRC; and Art 8 ECHR.

[9] Art 8 CRC.

[10] Art 28 CRC.

[11] Art 24 CRC.

[12] Art 15 CRC.

working group sessions reveals that discussions on the phrasing 'accession to existing agreements' cited the Hague Convention by name. This assumption is further supported by the fact that consideration was given during the drafting process as to whether Article 11 should adopt language similar to the language adopted in the Hague Convention.[13] This analysis, therefore, proceeds on the basis that Article 11 CRC requires states to accede to the Hague Convention, or a treaty having the same effect. If this duty is translated into the language of children's rights, then it shall be expressed here as the child's right to be protected from the harm of cross-border parental abduction. As why else would a *children's rights* treaty require states to accede to the Hague Convention, if not to protect *children* from the harm arising from cross-border parental abduction and to uphold their rights. Indeed that was the very purpose stated during the meetings that occurred as part of the CRC's drafting process.[14]

The language of the Hague Convention aligns with Article 11, although is expressed more in the language of children's welfare than children's rights. This is observable in the Preamble to the Hague Convention, which provides:

> The States signatory to the present Convention,
>
> Firmly convinced that the interests of children are of paramount importance in matters relating to their custody,
>
> Desiring to protect children internationally from the harmful effects of their wrongful removal or retention and to establish procedures to ensure their prompt return to the State of their habitual residence, as well as to secure protection for rights of access,
>
> Have resolved to conclude a Convention to this effect …

Alongside the Preamble to the Convention, the Explanatory Report to the Hague Convention highlights that the underlying objective of the Convention is to protect the best interests of children.[15] The divergence in language adopted in both

[13] *Legislative History of the Convention on the Rights of the Child* (Vol 1, Office of the United Nations High Commissioner for Human Rights, 2007) available at www.ohchr.org/Documents/Publications/LegislativeHistorycrc1en.pdf, 63, 202, 375–6, 449. See 28th plenary meeting of 7 May 1982 where the Economic and Social Council resolution 1982/39 on the 'Protection of the rights of children and parents in cases of removal or retention of children' was adopted; CRC *Legislative History* ibid 100, 434–6. For discussion on the interpretation of Article 11 see John Tobin, Nigel Lowe and Elliott Luke, 'Article 11' in John Tobin (ed) *The UN Convention on the Rights of the Child: A Commentary* (Oxford University Press, 2019) 370–396

[14] See CRC *Legislative History* ibid 158, during which Mr Colliard (the representative for France) stated 'the fate of children torn between two parents separated by a frontier was particularly distressing. Geographical distance often led to despair on the part of mothers and fathers hoping to fulfil their role as parents and educators. Distance was also heart-rending to children, who needed both a maternal and a paternal stabilizing influence and who were entitled not only to the affection of their fathers and mothers and their paternal and maternal families, but also to the benefits of two distinct cultures. With the possible exception of special cases, those children also had a right to freedom of movement between the two countries.'

[15] Elisa Perez-Vera, *Report on the 1980 Hague Child Abduction Convention* (Translation of The Permanent Bureau, 1981) paras 24–5. See also para 72 which provides 'The Convention put its emphasis on protecting the right of children to have the stability which is so vital to them respected. In other words, the Convention protects the right of children not to have the emotional, social etc. aspects of their lives altered.'

Conventions is attributable to what is described by Schuz as the 'children's rights revolution.'[16] The children's rights revolution occurred during the period between the Hague Convention in 1980 and the CRC in 1989. During this time, Schuz explains the focus shifted from protecting the welfare of children and upholding parental rights, towards reflecting more upon the child's rights.[17]

The closely related history and relationship between the CRC and the Hague Convention are attributable to the fact that many of the same states were involved in the negotiation of both instruments.[18] The parties to the Hague Conference on Private International Law are also of the view that the best interests of the child lies at the heart of both Conventions, and so no further protocol or amendment is needed to give effect to the children's rights aspirations of the Hague Convention.[19] Thus as the notion of children's rights develop, there exists a greater recognition of children's rights within Hague proceedings than existed previously.[20]

Despite the closely aligned history of both Conventions, there are concerns that automatic return under the Hague Convention can in some ways impede, rather than promote, children's rights. These concerns arise from the manner in which the policy of automatic return under the Hague Convention requires the court to order a child's return to the state of habitual residence, without considering the child's circumstances if the Hague Convention criteria are satisfied. The criteria are that a return application is lodged within 12 months of discovering the child's whereabouts and it is demonstrated that the child was habitually resident in the contracting state to which return is requested immediately before the breach of custody rights.[21] Once it is established the removal or retention

[16] Rhona Schuz 'The Hague Child Abduction Convention and Children's Rights' (2002) 12 *Transnational Law & Contemporary Problems* 393, 396–7.

[17] For a discussion on the developments around this time, see Philippe Lortie and Frederic Breger, *The Child's Voice – 15 Years Later* (Permanent Bureau of the Hague Conference on Private International Law, Judges' Newsletter Vol XXII) 4–5.

[18] See Stalford and Hollingsworth who explain the discussions that informed the 1980 Hague Convention inspired several provisions of the CRC, and in turn, the CRC provided the basic principles around which subsequent private international law instruments of the Hague Conference were constructed: Kathryn Hollingsworth and Helen Stalford, 'Judging Parental Abduction: What Does It Mean to Adopt a Children's Rights-Based Approach?' in Gillian Douglas and others (eds), *International and National Perspectives on Child and Family Law Essays in Honour of Nigel Lowe* (Intersentia Publishers, 2018) 3; Adair Dyer, 'The Contribution of the Hague Children's Conventions to the Protection of Human Rights' [2012] *International Family Law* 7; William Duncan, 'The International Family Law Lecture 2010: Is It Time For A Protocol?' (2010) 1 *Journal of Family Law and Practice* 4.

[19] Report on the Fifth Meeting of the Special Commission to Review the Operation of the Hague Conventions, (March 2007) available at https://assets.hcch.net/upload/wop/abd_2006_rpt-e.pdf.

[20] See *Re E (Children) (FC)* [2011] UKSC 27; although see analysis below on how much more can be achieved.

[21] Pursuant to Article 4 Hague Convention. If the applicant fails to do so, the abduction is not considered wrongful under the Hague Convention and the child will not to be ordered to return. The legal interpretation of habitual residence in Hague proceedings has therefore resulted in much case law (see for example *Re F (A Minor) (Child Abduction)* [1992] 1 FLR 548, CA) and academic commentary; Ruth Lamont, 'Habitual Residence and Brussels II bis: Developing Concepts for European Private International Family Law' (2007) 3 *Journal of Private International Law* 277; Schiratzki JL, 'Friends at Odds – Construing Habitual Residence for Children in Sweden and the United States' (2001) 15 (3) *International Journal of Law, Policy and the Family* 4.

was wrongful,[22] Article 16 Hague Convention provides that the courts must order the child's return.[23] The policy of automatic return and the six-week timeframe for the court does not, in some cases, allow time for the courts to check whether return could be harmful to the child, and this could ultimately fail to protect the child's right to protection, survival and development.[24] The aspects of the Hague Convention that raise concern in the context of children's rights will be the subject of analysis in the chapters below. But that is not to say the Hague Convention is not a children's rights instrument; only that the manner in which the courts apply it can serve to derogate children's rights. Application and interpretation of the Hague Convention, it is argued, should take account of the CRC's affirmation of children's status as independent rights holders. Decisions made under the Hague Convention must, therefore, be made in accordance with children's rights.

The fact that the Hague Convention can aspire to be a children's rights instrument is further demonstrated by Schuz,[25] who highlights several areas where the courts could more clearly interpret the Hague Convention from the perspective of children's rights, rather than those of parents. She suggests that courts should ascertain the child's place of habitual residence from the perspective of the child concerned, allow the child greater rights of participation in abduction proceedings, prioritise the child's right to maintain contact with both parents, and more broadly interpret the defences to return.[26] This text develops the work of Schuz by extending the children's rights-based analysis of the Hague Convention, specifically to an Islamic country context.

On this basis, for Islamic law states to be able to interpret and apply the Hague Convention in a children's rights compliant way, it is important that they have children's rights incorporated within the fabric of their legal systems. Debate does arise on whether universal standards are necessary to ensure all children are treated the same or whether account should be taken of the diverse conceptions of childhood across the globe.[27] And whilst this issue is addressed in the thematic

[22] Article 3 Hague Convention specifies 'the removal or retention of a child is to be considered wrongful where it is in breach of rights of custody attributed to a person, an institution or any other body, either jointly or alone, under the law of the state in which the child was habitually resident immediately before the removal or retention and at the time of the removal or retention those rights were actually exercised, either jointly or alone, or would have been so exercised but for the removal or retention.'

[23] *Re M (Abduction: Psychological Harm)* [1997] 2 FLR 690 at 694; unless one of the exceptions to return apply under Articles 12, 13 and 20 Hague Convention, examined in detail in the chapters below.

[24] Articles 3(2) and 6(1)(2) CRC.

[25] Schuz, 2002 (n 16) 393, 400; Rhona Schuz, *The Hague Child Abduction Convention* (Hart Publishing, 2013).

[26] Schuz (2013) ibid 437–9.

[27] Discussed below. See also the body of work in this area: A An-Na'im, *'Muslims and Global Justice'* (Penn State University Press, 2010); K Valentin and L Meinert, 'The adult North and the young South: Reflections on the Civilizing Mission of Children's Rights' 2009 25(3) *Anthropology Today* 23–8; U Narayan, *Dislocating Cultures, Identities, Traditions and Third-World Feminism* (Routledge, 2007); see also WJ, Talbott, '*Which Rights Should be Universal?*' (OUP, 2005); Nico Brando, 'Universalism, embeddedness and domination: an analysis of the Convention on the Rights of the Child' 2019 (15) 3 *Journal of Global Ethics* 270–286, 271.

chapters below, it does not distract from the analysis in this chapter for two reasons. First, when considering the situation of a child abducted from the UK, for example, to an Islamic law country, the arguments on whether a different interpretation of childhood based on local cultural norms need not apply. This is because the child is recognised as being habitually resident in the country abducted from, in our example, the UK, and is therefore regarded as being connected with the UK cultural context, rather than the cultural environment of the Islamic law country the child is abducted to by the parent. Secondly, incorporation of CRC rights is indeed another layer of the children's rights-based approach. The children's rights-based approach underpins the methodology of this analysis and therefore an examination of the extent to which children's rights are incorporated within legal jurisdictions is essential. It is on this basis that the analysis begins in this chapter to reflect upon how children's rights can be embedded within the legal framework, to enable states to respond to cases of parental child abduction in a manner consistent with the children's rights approach.

II. Embedding Children's Rights to Correctly Apply the Hague Convention

In the determination of a parental abduction dispute, the CRC's articles serve as a reminder of the child's right to a relationship with both parents, the child's right to have his or her best interests taken into consideration and the child's right to participate in decisions that affect him or her. Accordingly, contracting states are encouraged to give effect to the children's rights aspirations of the Hague Convention and have the processes in place to achieve outcomes which uphold the rights of abducted children.

There exist three methods by which a state can incorporate children's rights cultures and systems within its legal system. These methods are (i) constitutional incorporation, (ii) legislative incorporation and (iii) incorporation by the judiciary. Whilst the methods can be applied in a variety of contexts, the focus here is on a state's legal system as this text examines children's rights within the context of abduction proceedings. The specific methods are considered here before this chapter moves on to identify whether such methods of incorporation are possible in Islamic law countries. Measuring the degree of incorporation of children's rights is indicative of whether Hague accession will make any difference to children abducted to Islamic law countries.

Of the three methods by which incorporation is achievable, this chapter looks first to constitutional incorporation. The impact of constitutional incorporation is evaluated in research by Tobin,[28] who affirms that a state's commitment to

[28] John Tobin, 'Increasingly Seen and Heard: The Constitutional Recognition of Children's Rights' 21:1 (2005) 86 *South African Journal on Human Rights* 94.

children's rights is identifiable by a state's reference to children within its constitution. Tobin arrives at this conclusion by examining how states have addressed their commitment to the CRC.[29] He categorises the state's efforts by identifying where children are either invisible within the state's constitution, accorded special protection or granted specific rights. Constitutional incorporation is not requisite under the CRC, as its Article 4 imposes only a general obligation for States Parties to 'undertake all appropriate legislative, administrative and other measures for the implementation of the rights recognised.' While Article 4 CRC allows states parties discretion, the CRC Committee's General Comment No 5 (2003) on the General Measures of Implementation of the Convention ('GC 5') 'welcomes the incorporation of the Convention into domestic law … Notwithstanding incorporation, this does not avoid the need to ensure that all relevant domestic law, including any local or customary law, is brought into compliance with the Convention.'[30] The General Comment makes clear that while direct incorporation is not compulsory, a state's laws must comply with CRC provisions.

The work of Lundy et al[31] develops the method for CRC incorporation. Their research into 12 countries[32] demonstrates the variety of ways in which states have implemented the CRC at the national level. After evaluating the effects of the different methods of incorporation, they propose that for the CRC to be given full effect, it should be incorporated within the legislation of states. Their research demonstrates that states that have given effect to the CRC in domestic law can evidence greater practical application of the CRC and a firmer commitment to children's rights. The recommendations of Lundy et al extend more extensively than legislative incorporation; they identify other methods by which states can embed children's rights into their domestic systems and processes. These include promotion and awareness-raising of the CRC, the allocation of child-specific budgets, the undertaking of child impact assessments and child participation. They further recommend the creation of a Children's Rights Commissioner or Ombudsman and for states to establish comprehensive data on children. They suggest rather than just child development indicators; states should keep children's rights indicators to enable evidence base for policy development.[33] Any national

[29] Ibid 94.

[30] CRC/GC/2003/5 para 20.

[31] Laura Lundy and others, *The UN Convention on the Rights of the Child: A Study of Legal Implementation in 12 Countries* (Queen's University Belfast, 2012) available at https://www.unicef.org.uk/wp-content/uploads/2012/11/UNICEFUK_2012CRCimplementationreport-FINAL-PDF-version.pdf.

[32] Australia, Belgium, Canada, Denmark, Germany, Iceland, Ireland, New Zealand, Norway, South Africa, Spain and Sweden.

[33] Despite many similarities, human rights indicators and human development indicators have different emphases. A high human development ranking is not a guarantee of a faultless human rights record as the realisation of rights goes beyond average national performance. For a discussion on the differences between human development indicators and rights-based indicators see United Nations, *Human Development Report* (OUP, 2000) 89–93, Maria Green, 'What We Talk About When We Talk About Indicators: Current Approaches to Human Rights Measurement' (2001) 23 *Human Rights Quarterly* 1064.

plan needs to be kept current and should be accompanied by concrete action plans and targets. They specify that even where there is no explicit link between national plans and CRC implementation, an ambitious national strategy can drive CRC implementation.[34] To achieve more effective incorporation, the research of Lundy et al identifies three further drivers that support increased levels of implementation: a strong non-governmental organisation or voluntary sector; key children's rights advocates or supporters in government or public office; and the CRC periodic reporting process.[35] The discussion in the chapters below illustrates that implementation of these recommendations in all contracting states could improve the situation for abducted children, as more emphasis on children's rights would feature in decision making.

Notably, much of the improvements recommended require political support, but where that might be a barrier, Stalford et al[36] suggest CRC incorporation can be further effective through judicial incorporation. They too note the need for a political commitment to embedding children's rights into domestic legislation and the investment of ample resources in the structures and processes that give effect to the law.[37] Where the CRC is not incorporated at domestic level, they suggest the judiciary should step in to incorporate children's rights provisions.[38] Judges can do this by developing their role from merely applying the law to interpreting the law in a way that advances children's rights. One way this can be achieved, Stalford et al suggest, is that judges can do their part to promote children's rights by drawing on the CRC in their judgments. More specifically, they recommend judges can draw on scholarly insights, maximise children's participation, and the judgment should be expressed in a child-friendly way, which centralises the child's perspective and voice.[39] Judicial incorporation of the CRC is particularly relevant in the case of cross-border parental abduction, as the phrasing of the Hague Convention is fairly rigid, drafted pre-CRC, and so it is only the judge that can properly give effect to the CRC in Hague Convention proceedings. In a focused analysis of Hague Convention cases, Stalford and Hollingsworth[40] recommend that judges can incorporate the CRC particularly in cases where one of the exceptions to return applies, where judges have a larger discretionary space within which to take account of children's rights.[41]

[34] Lundy and others (n 31) 5–8.

[35] Ibid.

[36] For further discussion on this see Helen Stalford, Kathryn Hollingsworth and Stephen Gilmore (eds) *Rewriting Children's Rights Judgments: From Academic Vision to New Practice* (Hart Publishing, 2017) 58; John Tobin, 'Judging the Judges: Are They Adopting the Rights Approach in Matters Involving Children?' (2009) 33 *Melbourne University Law Review* 580; John Eekelaar, 'Judges and Citizens: Two Conceptions of Law' (2002) 22 (3) *Oxford Journal of Legal Studies* 497; Mark Hedley, *The Modern Judge – Power, Responsibility and Society's Expectations* (LexisNexis, 2016).

[37] Stalford and others ibid 53–4.

[38] Ibid.

[39] Ibid.

[40] For a discussion upon precisely what judges can do to give effect to the children's rights aspirations of the Hague Convention, see Hollingsworth and Stalford (n 18).

[41] See for example the approach taken by Baroness Hale in *Re M and another (Children) (Abduction: Rights of Custody)* [2007] UKHL 55 para [46].

These are three very clear methods of integrating children's rights in the law, in keeping with the principle of incorporation under the children's rights-based approach; through embedding the CRC through the constitution, legislation and judicial determinations. Including children's rights within the legal framework of states can create a minimum threshold by which those operating the law must comply when making decisions relating to children. In the following section, this chapter applies the three methods of CRC incorporation to the situation in the Islamic law country of Morocco. The purpose of this is to ascertain whether Islamic law countries have the constitutional, legislative and judicial scaffolding to give effect to the children's rights aspirations of the Hague Convention.

III. Morocco: A Case Study

The factor of religion cannot be ignored when examining the position of children's rights in Morocco, or indeed any Islamic law country. The majority of Islamic law countries have declared themselves to be Islamic states,[42] or as is the case with Morocco, specify Islam is the state religion. Such declarations mean that religious law applies in their legal systems and so religious law is a factor that will permeate any discussion relating to children's rights within Islamic law countries. There exists vast literature asserting that Islamic law promotes children's rights[43] and it is, in fact, the political disposition of Islamic law countries, not their religion that leads to a failure of some Islamic law countries to fully engage with universally agreed rights.[44] Of course, the extent to which this is accurate will vary from country to country, as Islamic states are diverse.[45] For ease of understanding, Islamic law countries can be identified as three distinct categories: the first category of countries is secular, where religion does not play a role in the legal system. The countries that fall under this category are signatories to the Hague Convention: Turkey, Turkmenistan, Uzbekistan and Kazakhstan.[46] The second category follows Islamic law exclusively, in both criminal and civil law. The countries that fall under this category are, for example, Saudi Arabia and Iran. The final group of Islamic law countries falls somewhere in between. The vast majority of Islamic law countries fall under this category and include, for example, Malaysia, Pakistan, Egypt,

[42] Afghanistan, Bahrain, Brunei, Iran, Maldives, Mauritania, Oman, Pakistan, Saudi Arabia, Yemen.

[43] See the works of Nisrine Abiad *Sharia, Muslim States and International Human Rights Treaty Obligations: A Comparative Study* (British Institute of International and Comparative Law, 2008); Abdullahi Ahmed An-Na'im, *Muslims and Global Justice* (University of Pennsylvania Press, 2010); Javaid Rehman, 'Religion, Human Rights and the Rights of the Child: Complexities in Applying Sharia in Modern State Practices' (2011) 2 *Northern Ireland Legal Quarterly* 62, 153.

[44] Ibid.

[45] See the survey examining 38 Islamic Family Law states by Abdullahi Ahmed An-Na'im, *Islamic Family Law in a Changing World. A Global Resource Book* (Zed Books, 2002).

[46] Note there exists debate on the extent to which religion pervades family law in secular states; see for example Ihsan Yilmaz, 'Semi-Official Turkish Muslim Legal Pluralism: Encounters between Secular ficial Law and Unofficial Shari'a' in Adam Possamai, James Richardson and Bryan Tuner (eds) *ne Sociology of Shari'a: Case Studies from Around the World* (Springer, 2015) 51–65.

Morocco, Iraq, Kuwait, Jordan and Syria. These countries are governed by family law legislation referred to as 'Personal Status Codes' which whilst generally based on Islamic law, do not always follow one particular juristic school and in certain areas, legislation may borrow from the teachings of different schools or modify the traditional Sharia rules.[47] The finite differences between practices in Islamic states are examined below in chapter 4. Despite some differences between Islamic law countries, they have all ratified the CRC, whereas interestingly, they appear reluctant to accede to the Hague Convention. It is suggested here that this is because the CRC allows reservations to be entered against its obligations, whereas the Hague Convention does not allow such.

Morocco's children's rights commitments primarily arise from the CRC and domestic law provisions.[48] Morocco signed the CRC on 26th June 1990 and ratified on 12th June 1993. Despite taking objection to several articles during the drafting process,[49] upon ratification, the only article Morocco entered a reservation against was Article 14. Article 14 provides that state parties shall respect the right of the child to freedom of thought, conscience and religion. Morocco's reservation states: 'The Kingdom of Morocco, whose Constitution guarantees to all the freedom to pursue his religious affairs, makes a reservation to the provisions of Article 14, which accords children freedom of religion, given the fact that Islam is the State religion.' It was clear from the outset of the process of drafting the CRC that Article 14 would prove problematic for Islamic law countries.[50] During the process of drafting, Morocco, supported by other Islamic law countries, declared that the 'rule adopted in Moroccan legislation is that the child shall follow the religion of his father. In this case, the child does not have to choose his religion, as the religion of the state is Islam.' This standpoint of Islamic law countries was ignored, and Article 14 was included within the CRC. As a consequence of the inclusion of Article 14, most Islamic law countries entered reservations against their commitment to the CRC. Some reservations were made more broadly against any aspects of the CRC in conflict with Islamic law,[51] while others were exclusive to Article 14. Notably, there is no specific objection raised by Islamic law countries to those provisions of the CRC that relate to Article 11 CRC and cross-border parental abduction.

[47] Zaleha Kamaruddin, *Islamic Legal Perspectives on Cross-Border Family Disputes Involving Children* (Hague Conference in Private International Law, 2014).

[48] Whilst there are other children's rights instruments that could be examined, only the CRC is relevant to Morocco. Morocco is not a member of the EU and so European law does not apply. It also has not ratified the African Charter on the Rights and Welfare of the Child 1990.

[49] CRC Legislative History (n 13) 63, 202, 375–6, 449.

[50] On this topic, see Philip Veerman and Caroline Sand, 'Religion and Children's Rights' *The International Journal of Children's Rights* 7 (1999) 385–7; For a broader discussion, see Sharon Detrick, *A Commentary on the UN Convention on the Rights of the Child* (Martinus Nijhoff, 1999) 243–256 and Sharon Detrick (ed) *The United Nations Convention on the Rights of the Child* (Martinus Nijhoff, 1992) 238–248.

[51] See for example the reservation by Pakistan: 'The provisions of the Convention shall be interpreted in the light of the principles of Islamic laws and values.' UNCRC, *Reservations, Declarations and Objections Relating to the Convention on the Rights of the Child – Note by the Secretary-General* (CRC/C/2/Rev 3, 11 July 1994); see also Tobin (2005) (n 28) 98.

The UN Committee on the Rights of the Child ('Committee'), the independent body of experts monitoring the implementation of the CRC, criticises the broad nature of reservations. According to GC 5, reservations that limit respect for the Convention by reference to a state's existing constitution or legislation, including religious law, breach the CRC.[52] More specifically, the Committee has repeatedly raised concerns on the reservations based on religion.[53] The Committee's recommendation has resulted in Morocco subsequently withdrawing its reservation against Article 14. The withdrawal cannot be celebrated as an advancement in children's rights, however, as Morocco replaced the reservation with an interpretative declaration which states that 'Moroccan law guarantees freedom of worship for all and stipulates that parents owe their children the right to religious guidance.'[54] What is the effect of such a declaration? Well, it is evident from the Committee's comments that the interpretive declaration has the same effect as the reservation. The Committee states 'While welcoming the withdrawal of the State party's reservation to Article 14, the Committee regrets that this reservation has been replaced by an interpretative declaration, which continues to affect the implementation of the rights guaranteed in this Article. The Committee, in light of the 1993 Vienna Declaration and Programme of Action, encourages the State Party to withdraw its interpretative declaration regarding Article 14.'[55] The interpretative declaration undoubtedly adds to the confusion of Morocco's position with regards to this right. Particularly as, according to an NGO report, some judges and lawyers working with children in Morocco are not aware of the reservation's withdrawal and sources say that restrictions are still in force vis-à-vis this section.[56]

The comments of the CRC Committee appear to be having some effect, as twelve Islamic law countries have withdrawn their reservations against the CRC. These withdrawals have led to the summation by some authors[57] that there appears to be a growing culture of children's rights within Islamic law countries. While this is promising and is illustrative of Islamic law countries taking note of the CRC

[52] General Comment No 5: *General Measures of Implementation of the Convention on the Rights of the Child* (CRC/GC/2003/5) Article 51(2) states: 'A reservation incompatible with the object and purpose of the present Convention shall not be permitted.'

[53] See for example Concluding Observations for Djibouti (CRC/C/15/Add131, 28 June 2000) para 9 expresses concern that the broad and imprecise nature of the declaration made by the State party, … which amounts to a reservation, potentially negates many of the Convention's provisions and raises concerns as to its compatibility with the object and purpose of the Convention. Similarly observed in the Concluding Observations Syrian Arab Republic (CRC/C/15/Add212, 10 July 2003) para 7; Concluding Observations Saudi Arabia (CRC/C/15/Add148, 26 January 2001) para 7.

[54] Concluding Observations Morocco (CRC/c/MAR/CO/3-4, 14 October 2014) 8–9.

[55] Ibid.

[56] Manara Network, *Country Profile of Morocco: A Review of the Implementation of the UN Convention on the Rights of the Child.* (Save the Children Sweden, 2011) available at www.ibcr.org/wp-content/uploads/2016/07/Country-Profile-Morocco.pdf, 19 and 31.

[57] See research by Shaheen Sardar Ali and Sajila Sohail Khan, 'Evolving Conceptions of Children's Rights: Some Reflections on Muslim States' Engagement with the UN Convention on the Rights of the Child' in Nadjma Yassari and others (eds), *Parental Care and the Best Interests of the Child in Muslim Countries* (TMC Asser Press, 2017) 309–10.

Committee's recommendations, Morocco's replacement of the reservation by an interpretative declaration instead suggests otherwise. It indicates that Morocco, and possibly other Islamic law countries are merely complying with the basic requirements of the CRC reporting process, and in embracing children's rights, are only prepared to do as much as Islamic law doctrine allows. It further confirms Islamic law countries will not breach religious laws for the sake of CRC commitments because Islam is central to countries like Morocco, whose constitution declares Islam to be the state religion, and who have religious advisory bodies guiding the government.[58]

A. Morocco's Incorporation of Children's Rights

Having explained the reservations entered against the CRC based upon religion, this chapter returns to the three modes of incorporation of children's rights introduced above; constitutional, legislative and judicial incorporation of the CRC, and apply these to evaluate the approaches to CRC incorporation in Morocco.

Prior to the reforms that resulted in Morocco's renewed Constitution in 2011, there was no reference to children within Morocco's Constitution. The 2011 Constitution has, in some ways rectified this gap, as it dedicates Article 32 to the rights of the family through pledging equal legal protection for all children. It also establishes a Consultative Council of the Family and Childhood, though notably, there is no explicit incorporation of CRC.[59] While the English translation of the 2011 Constitution specifies in its margin that Article 32 relates to children's rights, this analysis considers how the Constitution's limited reference embeds children's rights in Moroccan law. Firstly, as Tobin identifies,[60] the constitutional recognition of children's rights offers no guarantees concerning the enjoyment of their rights, but at a minimum, it legitimates political discourse on children's rights, allowing children to be seen and heard. By this standard, at the very least, Morocco's reference to children in its 2011 Constitution should increase the likelihood of political discourse on children's rights.

In examining the standards for legislative and systemic incorporation identified by Lundy et al[61] against Morocco's efforts, it is notable that Morocco's implementation of the CRC within its domestic law is sparse. Morocco does not have a specific law or code relating to children. Instead, the legal framework for the protection of children comprises of the Penal Code, the Penal Procedure Code, the Code of the Family and the Kafala Law. Morocco does not have a Children's Commissioner or Ombudsman. It has over the years allocated the responsibility for children's welfare

[58] As per Article 41 of Morocco's 2011 Constitution. The English translation of the 2011 Constitution is available at www.constituteproject.org/constitution/Morocco_2011.pdf; for a discussion on the nature of religious advisory bodies, see Yassari ibid.

[59] Morocco's 2011 Constitution ibid.

[60] Tobin (2005) (n 28) 94.

[61] Lundy and others (2012) (n 31) 4–8.

and rights to various branches of government. An NGO report of 2011[62] states the Government created a non-ministerial decision-making body under its control, the 'National Observatory for Children's Rights.' The observatory, chaired by Layla Meryem, the sister of Morocco's King Mohammed VI, was to monitor the implementation of the CRC, acting as a coordination and support tool to assess actions implemented for children nationally, regionally and locally.[63] After the Moroccan Government's 2013 initiative to address its children's rights commitments,[64] it allocated the responsibilities of CRC implementation to the Ministry for Solidarity, Women, the Family and Social Development.[65] The Ministry is intended to be the central core of the coordination among the different ministries (education, justice, health, etc) responsible for the implementation of national policies and action plans aimed at protecting children. The ministry aims to coordinate the Integrated Public Policy for Protection of Children in Morocco (PPIPEM), the implementation of the National Action Plan for Children (PANE), The Code of the Child, and a children's strategy document. UNICEF confirms that none of these had been developed two years later at the time of its published report in 2015 and no further information is available at the time of the publication of this text.

Conversely, Morocco has acceded to the Hague Convention, and so while it does not have a Children's Code in place, or legislation giving effect to the Hague Convention, there is an obvious process in place which gives effect to the automatic return process under the Hague Convention. Statistical analysis of the cases received by Morocco in 2015 demonstrates that of the eight cases of cross-border parental abduction it received, the Moroccan courts returned children in seven out of the eight cases.[66] Whether the cases were determined in accordance with children's rights is to be explored in the following chapters, but it will suffice to say here that Morocco can, it has demonstrated, implement and give effect to an International Law treaty if the political will exists.

On the topic of the three drivers identified by Lundy et al to support increased levels of CRC implementation,[67] it is seen below that Morocco appears to be engaging with the CRC periodic reporting process. Moreover, among the nearly 40,000 organisations working on the ground, there are reportedly over one hundred advocacy groups for the defence and the promotion of children's rights in Morocco.[68] Nonetheless, it is evident from the progress thus far, that this alone is not resulting in the ideal advancement of children's rights. For the CRC to be implemented more effectively, based upon the suggestions of the CRC Committee

[62] Manara Network (n 54).

[63] National Observatory for Children's rights, Bylaws available at www.ondemaroc.org/francais/_aboutfr.php?filename=200604281657340.

[64] Morocco Third and Fourth Periodic Reports (CRC/C/MAR/3-4, 2013).

[65] Child Notice Morocco (UNICEF, 2015) available at www.unicef.nl/media/4646666/cn-marokko-eng-def.pdf, 17.

[66] Nigel Lowe and Victoria Stephens, *A Statistical Analysis of Applications Made in 2015 Under the Hague Convention of 25 October 1980 on the Civil Aspects of International Child Abduction – Global Report* (Hague Conference, 2017) ('Hague Survey 2015').

[67] Lundy and others (2012) (n 31) 5–8.

[68] Manara Network (n 54) 25.

and the indicators identified by Lundy et al, it appears that there is not a firm commitment by the Moroccan government to the CRC, nor are there sufficient supporters in public office, or sufficient budgets allocated to achieve progress.[69]

With respect to judicial efforts to incorporate the CRC as suggested by Stalford et al, Morocco falls under the category of countries that have a dual system, where human rights instruments have not been incorporated into domestic law, and the judiciary is required to evaluate the responsibility of the state when deciding a case.[70] Granted, Morocco's 2011 Constitution stipulates that international law supersedes domestic law. Yet judges who must give effect to that commitment may not feel confident in asserting children's rights when these might go against other priorities of the state. The separation of powers of the legislative branches of government is not as clearly defined in all Islamic law countries. This situation can become further obscured as not all Islamic nations have an independent judiciary, as an independent judiciary is the first victim of any non-democratic state.[71] Thus the judge's position in Islamic law countries can be complex when considering children's rights and cross-border abduction cases.

What is more, in some Islamic law countries, as transpires in the analysis below, the judiciary opts to apply a more conservative interpretation of the law where legislation allows for judicial discretion. A judge will make a determination based upon his or her values and philosophy,[72] on his role as a judge, his role with the legislature, his role with the state and, as Stalford et al identify, the judge's own characteristics, experience and values.[73] Bordat and Kouzzi highlight the way in which judges are able to apply their own values in the context of Morocco.

> Given the difficulty of raising awareness of women's rights in a religiously conservative society, and the lack of institutions to monitor the judiciary's performance, it is clear that the passage of the reforms marks a step forward for women's rights, not the conclusion of the struggle.[74]

Another commentator has highlighted that with a predominantly male judiciary in Morocco, there is a risk that judges who adhere to the former traditional Islamic laws may be susceptible to corruption, resulting in the inaccurate application of Morocco's liberalised law.[75] Judicial activism here can be seen to erode not enhance rights. Thus the judicial response in Islamic law countries to politics can work against rather than in favour of children's rights.

[69] Morocco Concluding Observations (2014) (n 53) para 10.

[70] Stalford and others (n 36).

[71] On this topic, see Danny Boggs, 'Remarks on the 1980 Hague Convention on the Civil Aspects of International Child Abduction' (2000) 33 *NYU J Int'l L & Pol* 43, 48, 47–8.

[72] On this topic see also Robert Mnookin, *In the Interests of Children: Advocacy, Law Reform and Public Policy* (WH Freeman, 1985) 16–17.

[73] Stalford and others (n 36) 41.

[74] Stephanie Wilman Bordat and Saida Kouzzi, 'The Challenge of Implementing Morocco's New Personal Status Law', (2004) 2 (No 8) *Carnegie Endowment for International Peace Arab Reform Bulletin*.

[75] Laura Weingartner, 'Family Law and Reform in Morocco – The Mudawana: Modernist Islam and Women's Rights in the Code of Personal Status' (2005) 82 *University of Detroit Mercy Law Review* 687, 711.

Constitutional, legislative and judicial incorporation of the CRC is not ideal in Morocco, and other processes created to embed children's rights have not fared much better either. To address the absence of an independent mechanism concerning the rights of the child, Morocco suggested within its 2012 report to the CRC Committee that it was drafting a law to implement the CRC. It proposed a mandate of the National Human Rights Council to create an independent child-sensitive monitoring mechanism with a clear mandate to receive and address individual complaints of alleged violations of children's rights,[76] which in comparison to efforts of other (non) Islamic law states is commendable. According to UNICEF, however, this is another organisation that is promised but has not yet transpired.[77]

Legislatively, Morocco has taken great strides in developing a new Constitution, one which now refers to the rights of children and specifies that international law supersedes domestic law. However, many of the initiatives proposed by Morocco have not been developed. The lack of progress has meant that the CRC has not been incorporated into domestic law and has not made its way into judicial decision-making.[78] Morocco is delivering on ideas, yet the initiatives have not yet followed through. The 2011 Constitution created a Consultative Council for Childhood which appears to be a role similar to a Children's Commissioner or Ombudsman elsewhere. Several years after the 2011 Constitution, the Consultative Council for Childhood has not been realised. Morocco's communications to the CRC Committee suggest the role of the Council is replaced by the (seemingly broader) Ministry for Solidarity, Women, the Family and Development. The removal of children from the title is not a positive development; it seems that children's rights have once again become swallowed up by broader family agendas. The national plan and children's code that are supposed to be implemented by this Ministry have also not been developed. The failure to get any of the ideas off the ground suggests the rhetoric surrounding children's rights is all that is on offer, and few of the proposals makes it past paper.

The implications of these failings on abducted children are not positive. If Morocco does not incorporate children's rights within the law and its legal system, children will be at worst, invisible, and at best, subject to a welfarist approach[79] rather than an approach based on children's rights. Failure to implement effective children's rights processes also has implications for the application of the Hague Convention. Hague accession by Islamic law countries is not merely about returning children, but ensuring children's rights are respected during abduction proceedings. If the appropriate institutional and procedural structures do not exist in Morocco that are needed to give effect to the Hague framework provisions, a children's rights application of the Hague Convention is near impossible. In the following section the impact of the CRC in Morocco is evaluated.

[76] Morocco 2014 Concluding Observations (n 53) para 18.
[77] Child Notice Morocco (n 63) 17–18.
[78] See further discussion in chapters 3 and 4; see also Child Notice Morocco (n 63).
[79] For further details, see discussion below in chapter 3.

B. CRC Impact in Morocco: By Reference to the CRC Reporting Process

This section looks at the effects of Morocco's efforts to embed children's rights, by reference to the CRC periodic reports. The CRC periodic reports are used as a reference point as they set out Morocco's own submission on its efforts, and the time periods of developments are also recorded. The discussion establishes that Morocco's commitment to children's rights is not as firmly scaffolded as it could be.

One of the drivers identified by Lundy et al which supports increased levels of implementation is the CRC periodic reporting process.[80] The reporting process requires States Parties to update the CRC Committee on progress made in implementing children's rights every five years. By this reference point, Morocco has participated in the reporting process and could also be said to be engaged in the process, by making efforts to respond to recommendations. Morocco's first two reports on compliance with the CRC were submitted almost on time in 1995 and 2000. Morocco, in its 1995 report,[81] itself made the correlation between children's rights and compliance with the Hague Convention. It confirmed it had entered into some bilateral agreements to respond to the cross-border parental abduction and was negotiating accession to the Hague Convention. In doing so, Morocco appears to recognise that accession to the Hague Convention is to promote children's rights, and application of its provisions must also honour those children's rights commitments. In its observations, the CRC Committee[82] commented upon the difficulties regarding custody and visitation rights for Moroccan children where one parent lives outside Morocco and for foreign children where one parent is Moroccan. The Committee recommended Morocco strengthen dialogue with countries it had signed an agreement with regarding custody or visitation rights, and accede to the Hague Convention.

The third and fourth reports were not submitted until 2012,[83] three years after the fourth was due, and were not examined by the Committee on the Rights of the Child until September 2014, 11 years after the previous examination. By that time, Morocco had acceded to the Hague Convention, and the King of Morocco had ordered a new Constitution in response to public demands for reform which gave greater recognition to universal human rights. In 2012 Morocco signed the Optional Protocol to the CRC, allowing children or their representatives to bring violations of their rights directly before the CRC Committee if no national legal remedy is available, but as yet Morocco has not ratified the Protocol.

In its Concluding Observations to the 2012 report, the Committee did not comment on Morocco's accession to the Hague Convention or Morocco's

[80] Lundy and others (2012) (n 31) 5–8.
[81] Morocco CRC/C/28/Add.1 (19 August 1995) at para 148–151.
[82] Concluding observations Morocco (CRC/C/15/Add. 211,4, 10/07/2003).
[83] Morocco Reports Submitted (2013) (n 62).

interpretation of the Convention in accordance with children's rights. The Committee expressed concern about '(a) The lack of progress in adopting a comprehensive Children's Code, which was first proposed in 2003; (b) The numerous provisions of the Family Code that continue to discriminate against girls and to maintain severe gender discrimination; and (c) The lack of effective enforcement of existing legislation relating to children, due mainly to the lack of resources, capacities and supervision.'[84] The CRC Committee expressed concern over the 'various shortcomings of the National Action Plan for Children; particularly that no budget is allocated for its execution.[85] Each of the issues raised by the Committee directly affects how Morocco will apply the Hague Convention and how children abducted to Morocco will be affected by cross-border parental abduction. Failure to address gender discrimination within the law and a lack of resources to uphold children's rights will undoubtedly filter through to the way in which children's rights are exercisable in abduction proceedings, and this is explored in chapter 5. If Morocco is unable to develop processes to give effect to children's rights, how will other Islamic law countries fare, those that have similar problems with resources, capacity and supervision? Dialogue on these issues is needed when States decide to accede to the Hague Convention to ensure accession is not tokenistic and an appropriate framework is in place to give effect to the Hague Convention in a manner sensitive to the rights of abducted children.

IV. Conclusion

A children's rights-based approach requires that states embed children's rights into the legal regulation of their states. The analysis of the Islamic state of Morocco illustrates continuing efforts to incorporate the CRC but, unfortunately, few measurable outcomes are demonstrated. According to the most recent 2015 statistics,[86] Morocco is applying the Hague Convention provisions in that it is returning abducted children to their state of habitual residence. The extent to which Morocco – and other Islamic states – can apply the Hague Convention in a children's rights compliant way is to be explored in the following chapters.

The discussion now moves on from considering the broader children's rights framework in Islamic law countries in this chapter to a more focussed analysis of whether the rights of abducted children are given effect to in the legislative framework of Islamic law countries. The wide range of CRC articles relevant to this area means that there is insufficient scope within this text to undertake a broader

[84] Morocco Concluding Observations (2014) (n 53) para 3.
[85] Ibid para 12.
[86] Hague Survey (2015) (n 64).

right-by-rights analysis of applicable CRC provisions.[87] The children's rights analysis for this text is therefore grounded in the CRC's general principles, those on the best interests of the child (Article 3), the voice of the child (Article 12) and non-discrimination (Article 2).

The analysis begins in the next chapter on the child's Article 3 CRC right to have his or her best interests taken into consideration. The chapter will examine what place this CRC principle of best interests takes in cross-border parental abduction proceedings, to answer, ultimately, the question of whether Hague Convention accession by Islamic law countries can advance the rights of abducted children.

[87] For example, Article 5 (parental guidance and a child's evolving capacities); Article 9 (separation from parents); Article 10 (family reunification); Article 18 (parental responsibilities and state assistance).

3

In the Best Interests of the Abducted Child

This chapter examines the extent to which the two legal regimes – domestic Islamic law and the Hague Convention – uphold the child's Article 3 CRC right to have his or her best interests treated as a primary consideration. In accordance with the adopted children's rights-based approach,[1] the framework of analysis in this chapter is the guidance issued by the CRC Committee in its General Comment No 14 on the Right of the Child to Have His or Her Best Interests Taken as a Primary Consideration ('GC14').[2] The Committee establishes in GC14 that the expression of the best interests of the child is a threefold concept; it is a right, a principle and a rule of procedure. The three concepts are distinct and necessitate separate requirements of State parties. For example, as GC14 explains, as a substantive right, an obligation is created to which States must adhere. As an interpretive legal principle, the interpretation which most effectively serves the child's best interests should be chosen. And as a rule of procedure, the decision-maker is required to assess the impact of a decision on a child and ensure that such impact is given due importance. The three dimensions are adopted here as a measure by which to evaluate if, and how, the child's best interests are articulated in both the domestic law in Islamic law countries and the Hague Convention.

The chapter begins by introducing, in section I, the four participants whose case studies will help to analyse the law in this chapter. Sections II–V then examine both legal frameworks under the scope of the GC14 guidance, to evaluate the extent to which they each uphold the Article 3 CRC right of the abducted child. The evaluation will contribute to answering the overarching question in this analysis of whether Islamic law countries accession to the Hague Convention will advance children's rights.

The use of case studies in this text is valuable for a number of reasons. First, the case studies provide detail on the outcome of proceedings before the Islamic law courts, making accessible information which is not readily available from other sources. Secondly, it is extremely valuable to the analysis to hear the views of the parties affected and, more significantly, the views of the actual children affected by the decision under examination. Thirdly, the discussion reflects on what the

[1] See chapter 1.
[2] CRC/C/GC/14 (2013).

abductees believe to have been in their best interests and so also provides socio-legal insight into how the law affects the very children it is designed to protect.

I. Introducing Samir, Yasmin, Jamal and Daniel

A. Samir[3]

Samir was born in England and lived with his parents until they separated. After his parents separated, Samir lived with his mother and siblings. During a Saturday contact visit with his father, Samir's father took him and his siblings to his father's home country of Libya without his mother's consent. Samir was aged four at the time. Samir says people in Libya speak about his father as a hero for saving his children. Growing up, Samir missed his mother very much, wishing to be with her and have a normal life. Samir recalls his mother visited him for two weeks in the summer as part of a group visit organised by Colonel Gaddafi's Government, which granted the mothers of abducted children visas and access to their children. The visits stopped when Gadaffi's government was overthrown in 2011.[4]

On reflection, speaking at age 21, Samir says he understands why his father abducted him. Samir says that his mother 'left Islam' after separating from his dad and was living with another man. His dad 'had no control over them' and wanted to make sure they were raised as Muslims. After the abduction, his mother married again and had other children. Samir is of the view that there is no ideal solution but believes his parents should not have had children together if they could not stay together.

Samir feels at a disadvantage in Libya because of the economic circumstances and thinks he would have had a better life and better opportunities in the UK had he not been abducted. Samir has never returned to the UK, although he can legally leave Libya as a male adult. He says there is no British Embassy in Libya at which to obtain a British passport, but in any event, he does not have the money to travel and does not feel able to ask his mother if he can visit.

B. Yasmin[5]

Yasmin's parents separated and she lived with her mother. Also living in the household were Yasmin's sisters and later her step-father. During a contact visit, Yasmin

[3] Participant 28C, interview 21/04/16 (on file with the author).

[4] The information about the annual group contact visit to Libya is confirmed by a member of the organising body, Children and Families across Borders.

[5] Participant 31C, interview 12/06/16 (on file with the author).

was abducted by her father to the UAE, at the age of six. Shortly after the abduction, Yasmin recalls an incident where her mother and step-father were arrested in the UAE trying to re-abduct Yasmin. Yasmin recalls being taken to the police station to say goodbye to her mother.

Yasmin was only able to return to the UK after running away shortly before her 16th birthday. Yasmin's mother arranged for a British passport to be issued and given to Yasmin at the British Embassy in the UAE as she approached her sixteenth birthday. Speaking at age 21 Yasmin says tourism in the UAE made it easier to leave from there. Yasmin has not seen her father since her return to the UK.

C. Jamal[6]

Jamal's parents separated and he lived with his mother, having regular contact visits with his father. When Jamal was aged seven, his father took him to Jordan to visit his father's home country during the school holidays. The trip was not unusual, as he had enjoyed a trip like this previously with his father and returned to his mother in England. During this trip, however, Jamal's mother arranged for divorce papers to be sent to his father. When his father received these, he was upset that the separation would be permanent and so decided to keep Jamal in Jordan with him.

His mother made some visits to his grandparents' home in Jordan to see Jamal, but these stopped after a few years. Jamal is now aged 24 and, as a male adult, Jamal is free to leave Jordan. He remains living with his father's family, however, as he feels too estranged from his mother to ask to return to the UK to live with her.

D. Daniel[7]

Daniel's parents were living together when he was taken to Saudi Arabia by his mother without his father's knowledge. Daniel was aged two at the time and his sister, then aged five, was also taken. Daniel's understanding of the situation is that his mother had no choice but to leave. He says that after he was born, his father's other children came to live with them and one of the children 'his brother from another mother' was a drug addict. His father worked away a lot, and his mother did not feel she and her children were safe. His father ignored his mother's concerns, and so his mother returned to her home country of Saudi Arabia, where she would receive support from her family to look after the children. At age 16, Daniel says he has had a good life in Saudi Arabia and has recently begun having contact with his father.

[6] Participant 35C, interview 29/05/16 (on file with the author).
[7] Participant 34C, interview 21/07/16 (on file with the author).

II. The Principle of the Best Interests of the Child and the Law on Cross-Border Parental Abduction

The best interests principle is enshrined in Article 3(1) CRC and provides that 'in all actions concerning children, whether undertaken by public or private social welfare institutions, courts of law, administrative authorities or legislative bodies, the best interests of the child shall be a primary consideration.'[8]

This chapter evaluates the different approaches the law takes when deciding what should be in the best interests of children abducted to Islamic law countries. The differing approaches are made possible by the simple fact that the legal interpretation of what is deemed to be in the best interests of an abducted child is vague and lacks consensus.[9] As Stalford highlights:

> Notwithstanding the global influence of best interests, it remains a highly contested concept on a number of levels. First, long-standing criticisms as to its vagueness and indeterminacy and its vulnerability to highly subjective and variable interpretations remain persuasive today. Specifically, it has been contended that such interpretations inevitably reflect the value preferences and, indeed prejudices of the individual making the decision. Moreover, it has been claimed, that the UNCRC's expression of this principle – with its universality aspirations – is steeped in a narrow predominately western vision of child welfare which can be odds with the experience and attitudes towards children from non-western countries and cultures.[10]

The ambiguity is further exacerbated in an international parental abduction context by the fact that any one case can include different legal jurisdictions and thus different interpretations of what is in the best interests of children.[11]

[8] The principle also finds expression in: Principles 2 and 7 of the 1959 Declaration on the Rights of the Child; Art 5(b) and 16(d); the 1979 Convention on the Elimination of All Forms of Discrimination Against Women; General Comments 17 and 19 of the Human Rights Committee in relation to the International Covenant on Civil and Political Rights 1966; Arts 7(2), 23(2), and 23(2) and (4) of the UN Convention on the Rights of Persons with Disabilities.

[9] The definition of best interests suggested by Michael Freeman is 'basic interests, for example to physical, emotional and intellectual care developmental interests, to enter adulthood as far as possible without disadvantage; autonomy interests, especially the freedom to choose a lifestyle of their own;' Michael Freeman, 'Article 3: The Best Interests of the Child' in André Alen and others (eds), *Commentary on the United Nations Convention on the Rights of the Child* (Brill, Nijhoff, 2007); Robert Mnookin 'Child-Custody Adjudication: Judicial Functions in the Face of Indeterminacy' (1975) 39 *Law and Contemporary Problems* 226, 260; Stephen Parker, 'The Best Interests of the Child: Principles and Problems' (1994) 8 *International Journal of Law, Policy and the Family* 26; Helen Stalford, 'The Broader Relevance of Features of Children's Rights Law: The "Best Interests of the Child" Principle' in Eva Brems and others (eds), *Children's Rights Law in the Global Human Rights Landscape: Isolation, Inspiration, Integration?* (Routledge, 2017) 37.

[10] Helen Stalford, 'Children's Rights under EU Family Law: Custody, Access and Parental Child Abduction' in *Children and the European Union: Rights, Welfare and Accountability* (Hart Publishing, 2012) Chapter 4.

[11] Philip Alston (ed), *The Best Interests of the Child: Reconciling Culture and Human Rights* (Innocenti, 1994) 13; For further discussion in the context of abduction cases see Adair Dyer, 'A Report on International Child Abduction by One Parent "Legal Kidnapping"' (The Hague Conference, 1978) 22–23; Elisa Perez-Vera, *Report on the 1980 Hague Child Abduction Convention* (Translation of The

The variables result in different approaches to assessing the best interests of the abducted child and, as a consequence, can result in different outcomes for the child depending upon the subjective assessment and which legal framework is applied.

III. How the Domestic Islamic Law Framework Responds to Cases of Parental Child Abduction from the UK

The relevant law in this area is Islamic child custody law, as there is no legislation in Islamic law countries which responds to cases of 'incoming' abductions.[12] An Islamic court will, therefore, respond to a case of parental abduction before it as a custody matter and so the following discussion on custody law should also be read as parental abduction law.

The Islamic law provision on child custody is founded upon historical religious interpretations of what is in the best interests of children generally. The law is expressed as 'rules of custody' which were developed by Islamic scholars and jurists earlier in Islamic history, pre-15th century,[13] based upon the interpretation of what was in the best interests of children in that era. The rules were not set out in legislation and so decision-makers had the discretion to apply the regulations as appropriate in each case, based upon the individual circumstances of the child and family.[14] Fast-forward hundreds of years and those very rules are still in use today.[15] In the last 40–50 years, the common law rules have been fixed into legislation, however, and in many countries, no adaptations have been made to reflect changes in society and perceptions and experiences of childhood since the

Permanent Bureau, 1981) paras 20–24; See also Beaumont and McEleavy who highlight that it allows courts to arrive at any conceivable measure, although 'often influenced by the moral or social values prevailing in the society in question'; Paul Beaumont and Peter McEleavy, *The Hague Convention on International Child Abduction* (OUP, 1999).

[12] While some Islamic law countries have legislation criminalising the removal of children from their own borders, there is no legal regulation for incoming abduction cases. See further Abdul Hamid and others, 'The Applicability of the 1980 Hague Abduction Convention in Muslim Countries: Particular Reference to the Malaysian Position' (2018) 32 *Arab Law Quarterly* 99, 110 and 120.

[13] Ibrahim writing on this topic identifies the different periods in Islamic legal history, identifying the pre-modern period as being pre-15th Century and the early modern period extending from the 1500s to the 1820s. He explains that while many important social and legal changes took place during these different periods of Islamic legal history, much of the discourse of child custody law remained largely unchanged throughout these different periods; Ahmed Fekry Ibrahim, *Child Custody in Islamic Law: Theory and Practice in Egypt since the Sixteenth Century* (CUP, 2018) 26.

[14] Ibrahim ibid 6–8; Ahmed Fekry Ibrahim, 'The Best Interests of the Child in Premodern Islamic Juristic Discourse and Practice' (2015) 63 *The American Journal of Comparative Law* 859.

[15] Mahdi Zahraa and Normi Malek, 'The Concept of Custody in Islamic Law' (1998) 13 *Arab LQ* 155, 156–7; For further discussion of how the rules are applied in different countries, see Lynn Welchman, *Women and Muslim Family Laws in Arab States: A Comparative Overview of Textual Development and Advocacy*. (Amsterdam University Press, 2007) 13.

rules were initially developed.[16] What is more, the discretion previously granted to decision-makers no longer exists, and so the legislation is often applied rigidly.[17]

The current best interests of the child assessment in Islamic law is therefore based upon what was deemed as 'best' for children centuries ago. The patriarchal view that historically prevailed across the world Centuries ago still exists in many parts of the Islamic world.[18] Children in Islamic law countries are raised with the knowledge that the mother is responsible for the day-to-day care of the children and the father, as the legal guardian, is responsible for providing financially and making decisions about the children's education, travel and finances.[19] This arrangement continues even if the parents separate until such time as children are considered mature enough to make decisions themselves about their welfare and where they wish to live.[20] This age of maturity is set in legislation and differs from country to country, ranging between ages seven to fifteen. It is explored in greater detail in the following chapter.

As the Islamic courts respond to a case of parental abduction as a custody dispute, when deciding with which parent a child shall live, Islamic law presumes it is in the best interests of a child that she or he (i) lives with a Muslim parent; (ii) lives with a mother who has not remarried; and (iii) lives near the father. These factors are set out in statute in most Islamic law countries, and so there is no opportunity for a judge to assess the best interests of a child abducted from the UK to the Islamic law country if the three fundamental criteria are not satisfied.

The requirement for the parent with custody of the child to be Muslim is intended in Islamic law to ensure that the child is raised as a Muslim.[21] A child of a Muslim father must be raised a Muslim, irrespective of the Article 14(1) CRC right that 'States Parties shall respect the right of the child to freedom of thought,

[16] Lynn Welchman, '*A Husband's Authority: Emerging Formulations in Muslim Family Law*' (2011) *25 Int'l JL Pol'y & Fam.*

[17] See Nadjma Yassari (ed), *Changing God's Law: The Dynamics of Middle Eastern Family Law* (Routledge, 2016); Imen Gallala-Arndt, 'Negotiating Parenthood in Muslim Countries: Changing Concepts and Perceptions' (2015) 63 *The American Journal of Comparative Law* 847; Welchman (2007) (n 15); Welchman (2011) (n 16).

[18] For further discussion see Welchman (2007) (n 15); Welchman (2011) (n 16).

[19] Lena-Maria Möller, 'An Enduring Relic: Family Law Reform and the Inflexibility of Wilaya' (2015) 63 *The American Journal of Comparative Law* 847, 910–11; An example of the law in Morocco is Morocco Law No 70.03 of 2004, articles 231, 238.

[20] Note the interesting observation of O'Donnell, that while the rules appear arbitrary, the views of the wishes of adult duty-bearers are also of no relevance; Daniel O'Donnell, *The Right of the Child to be Heard: Children's Right to Have Their Views Taken Into Account and to Participate in Legal and Administrative Proceedings* (Innocenti Working Paper, UNICEF, 2009) 18.

[21] Emon and Khaliq clarify the need for this rule stemmed from the licence Muslim men had to marry women who were not Muslim. Muslim jurists presumed the children would be Muslim given the prevailing presumption that the child's faith followed the father's. But where a Muslim father and non-Muslim mother divorce, jurists were concerned about the effect of the non-Muslim mother's different faith on the Islamic faith of the presumably Muslim children. Anver Emon and Urfan Khaliq, *Private International Law, Islamic-law, and Cross-Border Child Abduction: A Historic-Legal Analysis* [Online] (Ontario, 2016) 48; Emon, A, & Khaliq, U, *Jurisdictional Exceptionalisms: Islamic Law, International Law and Parental Child Abduction* (CUP, 2021).

conscience and religion.' In order to comply with the requirement that the parent with custody of the child must be Muslim, the left-behind parents interviewed provide insight into the various methods deployed to persuade the Islamic court in abduction proceedings that they were in fact Muslim. Left-behind parents obtained documentation confirming their 'conversion' to the Islamic faith and, as a precaution, left-behind mothers outwardly dressed and presented as upstanding Muslim women, also ensuring their social media accounts reflected this image. As one left-behind mother who initiated proceedings in Algeria for the return of her abducted child explains: 'I had to pretend I was a Muslim to have any chance of winning. I'm not proud of it, but they gave me no choice.'[22] Another left-behind mother explained this was not enough to persuade the courts: 'My ex told the court I didn't provide a suitable environment my children needed to be brought up in their religion, that I am a false Muslim and that I wear the headscarf to trick people.'[23]

The Islamic law requirement for a child to be raised by a Muslim parent is seen in the case of Samir. Samir was aged four at the time of the proceedings in Libya. He recalls being told about the court's decision later by his siblings whenever he asked about his mother. The court accepted the information provided to the court by Samir's father about Samir's upbringing in England. Samir's mother 'left Islam' after separating from his dad and at the time of the abduction was living with another man. He explains:

> When we were in England, my father couldn't see us every day, so he decided to take us to Libya to save us, that's what he thinks he did. He can't control us in England; he wanted us to be Muslim. I can't say that I agree and I can't say that I don't agree because I don't know what the best solution was. I wish they fixed the problem and stay together because it's hard to stay away from one of them.

The Libyan court determined that it was in Samir's best interests that he remains in Libya with his father in an Islamic environment.

The requirement for the child to live with a Muslim rather than non-Muslim parent applies irrespective of the parents' gender, it seems, from examining the case of Daniel. Daniel's case is different from the majority in the sample as the abduction to the Islamic law country was carried out by Daniel's mother and not his father. After proceedings for Daniel's return were initiated, the Islamic court decided that it was in Daniel (and his sister's) best interests that they remain living with their Muslim mother in Saudi Arabia, and not with their non-Muslim father outside of the Kingdom. Daniel's case is illustrative of the significance of the child's religious upbringing in the Islamic law best interests assessment, over all other factors, including the patriarchal rights of the father as the child's legal guardian.

The patriarchal view that prevailed at the time the rules were developed pre-15th century saw a mother who marries again 'enter the household' of her

[22] Participant 14M, interview 29/05/16 (on file with the author).
[23] Participant 21M, interview 23/09/16 (on file with the author).

new husband, which it was thought could be a hostile environment for a step-child. In addition to concerns about the child's place within a new household, it was believed that the mother might be unable to meet the child's needs while also having to fulfil her wifely obligations serving her new husband. As a consequence, it was decided by scholars that it was in the best interests of a child that a mother who remarried was prevented from retaining custody of the child, unless the mother remarried someone to whom the child was already related, such as the child's paternal uncle, as it was presumed that he would naturally care for the child. Emon and Khaliq writing on this issue identify that the presumptions of the child's best interests described here are products of a certain culture – social, economic, historic and legal – and highlight that the pre-modern doctrines on child custody are often criticised for their inegalitarian nature and as a poorly hidden critique of the now well-known patriarchy in Islamic family law.[24] Though the situation of step-families is more common in the 21st century than it was pre-15th century, the Islamic courts are bound by legislation specifying that custody will not be awarded to a mother who has remarried. Empirical data collected illustrates that the court will accept the father's evidence of the mother's new relationship: A mother whose two daughters were retained by their father after an agreed holiday to an Islamic law country explains: 'It was because I remarried. He said if I divorced my new husband, he would send the girls straight back. He was worried about the girls living with another man. He didn't mind the boys being with me; it's different for girls.'[25]

The application of the law is illustrated in the case study of Yasmin. The Islamic court decided that Yasmin should remain with her father in the UAE. The decision was based on the fact that after divorcing Yasmin's father, Yasmin's mother married again, this time to a non-Muslim man. Yasmin explains her father was unhappy about another man living with his daughter:

> For my dad, it was why should another man be around my daughter, and I think that's what he couldn't deal with, I don't think it was a love thing taking me. Things got bad when we moved into my step-dad's house. I remember when he'd pick me up, he'd ask lots of questions. If I'd been to a birthday party the week before he'd be like who took you there? And I'm like, oh my friend's mum came and picked me up, and he'd be like you're lying to me, he [step-father] took you didn't he? He was just paranoid about him, I think I started to like him a lot more than my dad, and I think it made my dad quite jealous and angry.

The situation was confirmed to the Islamic law courts when Yasmin's mother and step-father travelled to the Islamic law country to re-abduct Yasmin. The re-abduction attempt was unsuccessful, and Yasmin's mother and step-father returned to England without Yasmin.

Another presumption of the child's best interests in Islamic law is that the mother lives near the father to allow the father to fulfil his guardianship

[24] Emon and Khaliq (2016) (n 21) 46–7.
[25] Participant 13M, interview 10/09/16 (on file with the author).

responsibilities towards the child.[26] The distance was specified historically by jurists as within 48 miles, to enable the father to visit the child and return home the same day[27] and it seems the distance has not been revised to reflect advances in technology and modes of travel. The application of this rule is seen in the case study of Jamal. After the abduction, Jamal was living with his father's family in Jordan. Jamal's mother persuaded the court that she was Muslim and successfully obtained a custody order confirming Jamal could live with her in Jordan. Jamal was never 'handed over' to his mother, however, and instead Jamal's father's family insisted that Jamal's mother could live near them and see Jamal as often as she wished. When Jamal's mother sought legal advice, she was advised by her lawyer that enforcement of family law orders is carried out by the police in Jordan and that no police officer would remove Jamal from his father's home in the patriarchal construct of their society:

> The lawyer told me exactly what I needed to do to get custody; to convert to Islam and get papers in an order stating I had lived there [in the Muslim country] for six months and had a stable job there. But then she told me even if you get custody; it doesn't mean you can take your child home because that's still the father's decision and she said even though you win in court, no authority's going to make the family hand over the child.[28]

Enforcement of the order proved impossible. Instead, Jamal's mother was allowed visits with Jamal at his grandparents' home. She hoped for Jamal to live with her but as the family were anxious she would abduct him visits were only allowed inside their home:

> When I used to do the visits we were just locked into a room, the house was locked, we couldn't go out of the gates together, we couldn't do anything except be in a room together and guarded.

Without any hope of Jamal returning home with his mother, Jamal's mother managed as many visits with Jamal as she could in that situation, but after some months left Jordan:

> When I'd gone to the lawyer's office, and both of them had tried, they told me to go to the family, stay with them as long as you want, as long as they will let you, and you know just enjoy your child there. So I went to the house, I did not want to stay there, I was feeling so bad, I was scared for what was going to happen if I stayed. I still believed that

[26] Or if the father passes, his paternal relatives who will be responsible for the child's financial upbringing, to provide education and decision-making on matters such as travel.

[27] Sahih Al-Bukhari (English Translation by Muhammad Muhsin Khan), *The Book of Funerals* (Maktabah Dar-us-Salam, 1994) cited in Shabnam Ishaque and Muhammad Mustafa Khan, 'The Best Interests of the Child: A Prevailing Consideration within Islamic Principles and a Governing Principle in Child Custody Cases in Pakistan' (2015) 29 *International Journal of Law, Policy and The Family* 78, 171–2; Khaliq and Young confirm the exact distance varies between jurisdictions, and some courts have become more lenient in this respect (see Pakistan case of *Hina Jilani v Souhail Butt* NLR (1995) SD 387); Urfhan Khaliq and James Young, 'Cultural Diversity, Human Rights and Inconsistency in the English Courts' (2001) 21 *Legal Studies* 192, 211.

[28] Participant 14M, interview 29/05/16 (on file with the author).

> I had this piece of paper, I had the right to see my child by myself. I went to visit and they let me talk to my son alone and I gave him a mobile phone, and we had tea. Ever since the day, I perceived him as broken, or something had happened, he never spoke to me again by telephone. When I saw him he never spoke to me, he only answered yes or no or smiled, so even though I spent like one or two hours alone with him, he hardly spoke. I talked to him, I took pictures of us together, I gave him this phone and you know he was like a big kid by then. Then after a couple of hours it was time for me to leave because I had decided not to spend the night there so I told him I was coming back to get him and then the family tried to stop me, saying 'why all this' and my son he started to cry which was a horrible thing to see, like a big boy like that just sitting like this and crying. And I left, you know I was really upset because I did not know if what I was doing was the right thing or not but just I cried in the car and said please God help me. I still believed that I had this piece of paper you know; I could have somebody help me see my son. So I went back to the lawyer and I found out that it would be impossible, nothing could be done so I just went back home.

Jamal's case demonstrates how the best interests of the child assessment in Islamic law places great emphasis on the child living near the father, as his legal guardian. The onus is on the mother and not the father to move to enable the child to see both parents.[29]

A. Best Interests as a Substantive Right in Islamic Law?

As a substantive right, GC14 affirms that the right of the child to have his or her best interests assessed and taken as a primary consideration is guaranteed. The ratification of the CRC by Islamic law countries creates a legal obligation to uphold Article 3. If however, a state has incorporated the CRC or the best interests principle into its domestic law, Article 3 can also be invoked before a court.[30] As identified in chapter two, no Islamic law country has yet incorporated the CRC into its domestic law,[31] and so a child abducted to an Islamic law country cannot invoke his or her Article 3 CRC right before the Islamic courts as a separate application. The abducted child still, however, has the Article 3 CRC right to have his or her best interests treated as a primary consideration by the court in any proceedings before it, and so the Islamic courts are required to ensure the child's Article 3 right is upheld when deciding a case of parental abduction. The majority of Islamic law

[29] The Moroccan system offers some scope for a mother to apply to the court to travel with the child, though according to Article 179 of the 2004 Moroccan Family Code 'permission shall not be granted until the judge has ascertained that such travel is temporary and that the child will be returned to Morocco.' Thus it is exceptionally difficult, if not impossible, for a mother to persuade the Islamic court that the child should be taken to live in another country.

[30] GC14 (n 2) paras 6–7, 39.

[31] John Tobin, 'Increasingly Seen and Heard: The Constitutional Recognition of Children's Rights' (2005) 86 *South African Journal on Human Rights* 21:1; Laura Lundy and others, *The UN Convention on the Rights of the Child: A Study of Legal Implementation in 12 Countries* (2012) available at www.unicef.org.uk/wp-content/uploads/2012/11/UNICEFUK_2012CRCimplementationreport-FINAL-PDF-version.pdf.

countries are also signatories[32] to the Vienna Convention on the Law of Treaties, which was adopted on 23rd May 1969 and entered into force on 27th January 1980. The Vienna Convention establishes rules of interpretation of international treaties such as the CRC and the Hague Convention. Article 31 of the Vienna Convention requires that 'A treaty shall be interpreted in good faith in accordance with the ordinary meaning to be given to the terms of the treaty in their context and in the light of its object and purpose.' Article 3 is, therefore, very much an obligation for Islamic law countries.

It may be argued that the interpretation of what is in the child's best interests in Islamic law countries is intended to uphold the rights of the child, ie the requirements for the parent with custody to be Muslim, and for the mother to live near the father and not remarry, all ensure the child's interests are accorded greatest priority. From the perspective of Islamic law, these requirements will ensure the child has a good moral upbringing, maintains regular contact with both parents and is not exposed to any hostility from a step-father. Arguments along these lines support the idea that the child's Article 3 CRC rights are upheld by an Islamic law perspective on the child's best interests. The support for this view is also seen by some English court decisions, particularly when the courts are justifying a decision to return abducted children to Islamic law countries. Peter Hughes QC (sitting as a deputy High Court judge) states in the case of *B v EL-B (Abduction: Sharia Law: Welfare of Child)*:[33]

> The approach to welfare and upbringing of children is very different in Muslim countries from our own approach. It does not necessarily follow, though that it is not child-centred. Simply that Muslim countries, which apply Sharia law, have different philosophies, customs and practices to our own. It would not be right to conclude that it is not concerned with the welfare of the child.[34]

It was also stated by Phil LJ in *Re E (Abduction: Non-Convention Country)*:[35]

> The application of Muslim law to this Muslim family is appropriate and acceptable … these are Sudanese children. Their welfare may be well served by a decision in accordance with Sudanese law, which may be taken to reflect the norms and values of the Sudanese society in which they live. A solution in accordance with local law is capable of being in the interests of the child.[36]

The trouble is that this assessment results in discrimination towards the mother,[37] and as is illustrated in chapter 5, can also adversely affect the child. Up until 2005,

[32] See list of member states at https://treaties.un.org/Pages/ViewDetailsIII.aspx?src=TREATY&mtdsg_no=XXIII-1&chapter=23&Temp=mtdsg3&clang=_en.

[33] [2003] 1 FLR at 811.

[34] Ibid at 816–7.

[35] *Re E (Abduction: Non-Convention Country)* [1999] 2 FLR 642 Phil LJ at 651.

[36] Ibid.

[37] Note that whilst the law in other Contracting States can also serve to restrict parents relocating to another jurisdiction with the child, those provisions are intended to apply equally to both mothers and fathers. See further M Hayes, 'Relocation Cases: Is The Court of Appeal Applying the Correct

there were conflicting judgments from the English courts on the effect of Islamic custody law and whether the Islamic law presumptions were in the best interests of the child.[38] The inconsistent approach was addressed by the then House of Lords in *Re J*,[39] in a case where a Saudi mother refused to return her child to Saudi Arabia after a period of study in England. The House of Lords examined the effect of the Islamic custody law provisions and determined that these were indeed discriminatory towards mothers, and the impact of the potential separation of the mother and child if returned was not in the best interests of the child. The House of Lords affirmed the viewpoint on Islamic custody law in a later case, where a mother fled Lebanon to England because Islamic custody law would separate her from her child. The House of Lords, in this case, describes Islamic law on child custody as 'arbitrary, discriminatory and incompatible with human rights.'[40]

The concerns about domestic Islamic law impacting upon children and family life are echoed by the European Court of Human Rights ('ECtHR'), which too has expressed that Islamic law is incompatible with human rights law. While the case in question looked at the freedom of association rights of a political party, the ECtHR made its views clear on the application of Islamic law in modern times:

> sharia, which faithfully reflects the dogmas and divine rules laid down by religion, is stable and invariable … It is difficult to declare one's respect for democracy and human rights while at the same time supporting a regime based on sharia, which clearly diverges from Convention values, particularly with regard to its criminal law and criminal procedure, its rules on the legal status of women and the way it intervenes in all spheres of private and public life in accordance with religious precepts …[41]

The fact that Islamic law presumptions of children's best interests are at odds with the provisions of the CRC has been stressed on numerous occasions by the UNCRC Committee. For example, in the Concluding Observations for Algeria,[42] the country to which three children in the sample were abducted, the CRC Committee highlighted concerns about the child's best interests arising from Algerian custody law:

> The 2005 Family Code still prohibits the marriage of Muslim women to non-Muslims, which has an obvious negative impact on the rights of children born of such marriages.

Principles?' [2006] CFLQ 351; J Herring and R Taylor, 'Relocating Relocation' [2006] CFLQ 517; F Judd and R George, 'International Relocation: Do We Stand Alone?' [2010] *Family Law* 63; S Gilmore, 'The Payne Saga: Precedent and Family Law Cases' [2011] *Family Law* 970; R George, 'Reviewing Relocation?' [2012] CFLQ 110; R George, *Relocation Disputes: Law and Practice in England and New Zealand* (Hart Publishing, 2014).

[38] *Al Habtoor v Fotherington* [2001] EWCA CIV 186; *Re JA (Abduction: Non-Convention Country)*[1998] 1 FLR 231, CA; *Re M (Abduction: Peremptory Return Order)* [1996] 1 FLR 478, CA; *Osman v Elasha* [2000] Fam 62; *Re E* ibid; *Re S (Minors) (Abduction)* [1994] 1 FLR 297; See also the analysis by Khaliq and Young (n 27).

[39] *Re J* [2005] UKHL 40 at 45.

[40] In *EM (Lebanon) v Secretary of State for the Home Department* [2008] UKHL 64.

[41] Case of *Refah Partisi (the Welfare Party) and Others v Turkey* (App Nos 41340/98, 41342/98, 41343/98 and 41344/98) judgment of 13 February 2003, para 123.

[42] Concluding Observations Algeria (CRC/C/DZA/CO/3-4, 18 July 2012) para 48–54.

> In case of divorce, article 65 of the Family Code grants the mother custody of male children only until age 10 and of female children until they reach marriage age; In accordance to article 66 of the Family Code, women who remarry after divorce lose the custody of their children. The Committee recommends the State party to ensure that mothers and fathers equally share the legal responsibility for their children in accordance with article 18, paragraph 1, of the CRC.

The Committee urged Algeria to:

> Revise the 2005 Family Code and ensure that (a) all provisions that discriminate against women and negatively impact on their children, such as those which authorize polygamy, and repudiation be repealed; (b) To recognize by law the marriage between a Muslim woman and a non-Muslim (c) To review its legislation relating to the custody of the child with a view to ensuring that all decisions taken are based on the principle of the best interests of the child in line with articles 3 and 12 of the Convention and that children can no longer be withdrawn from their mother's custody if she remarries.

With regards to parental child abduction, referred to in the CRC Committee report as 'Illicit transfer and non-return of children abroad.':[43]

> The Committee reiterates its concern about the difficulty in implementing judicial decisions regarding custody and visitation rights for Algerian children with one parent living outside Algeria and the prevalence of child abduction among children of mixed marriages. The Committee reiterates its recommendations (CRC/C/15/Add.269, para. 49) that the State party undertake all necessary efforts to prevent and combat illicit transfer and non-return of children and to ensure proper and expeditious implementation of judicial decisions made with regard to custody and visiting rights. It further recommends that the State party strengthen dialogue and consultation with relevant countries, notably those with which the State party has signed an agreement, regarding custody or visitation rights. The Committee also urges the State party to ratify the Hague Convention on Civil Aspects of International Child Abduction of 1980.

The Concluding Observations for Algeria, and incidentally for Morocco too, which has almost identical recommendations,[44] demonstrate that the interpretation of the best interests of abducted children in Islamic law is not as is envisaged by Article 3 CRC. But of course the Islamic law interpretation predates the CRC, and so the conflict in viewpoints was acknowledged at the time Islamic law countries ratified the CRC. Islamic law countries went so far as entering broad reservations against any aspects of the CRC that conflict within Islamic law and the Committee's response to these reservations are discussed above in chapter 2. With this in mind, it is apparent from reading the Concluding Observations of the CRC Committee that it hopes Islamic law countries will work on reforming their custody laws to align more closely with the ambitions of the CRC. The Committee's recommendations have been responded to by the Islamic law countries that have since acceded to the Hague Convention: Morocco, Tunisia and Pakistan. The following section

[43] Ibid para 50–51.
[44] Morocco Concluding Observations (CRC/C/15/Add.211, 10 July 2003) para 40–41.

identifies the efforts thus far by these countries to work with the CRC to uphold the best interests of the child as a substantive right under their domestic law.

B. Analysis of the Language of the Child's Best Interests in Morocco, Tunisia and Pakistan

Decades of dialogue between the CRC Committee and Islamic law countries began a slow move towards adopting the language of the best interests into domestic custody law.[45] The analysis for this project identifies that merely inserting the language of best interests into legislation will not suffice, however, if the proper effect is not given to the expression of best interests as a right and a principle.

Analysis undertaken of the situation in three Hague Islamic law countries is illustrative of this fact. Morocco acceded to the Hague Convention in 2010, Iraq in 2014[46] and both Tunisia and Pakistan in 2017. Morocco's reform of its custody law in 2004 arose as a result of significant compromise. The religious scholars in Morocco and the conservative sections of Morocco's Islamic society were not ready for an overhaul of its family laws, because of the impact this would have on the patriarchal rights of the heads of Muslim households.[47] So although the reforms resulted in Moroccan custody law adopting the language of the best interests of the child,[48] the child's best interests are not assessed as a primary consideration the way in which is anticipated by the CRC. This is because Morocco's custody legislation continues to specify factors which prevent a mother from retaining custody of a child, irrespective of whether or not this is in the best interests of the child concerned.[49] Prior to the reforms, a mother's remarriage was an automatic bar to her retaining custody in Morocco. The compromise in the law now is that the mother can retain custody after her remarriage if the father does not object within 12 months of discovering the mother has remarried, if the child is aged below seven, if the child will be harmed by the separation, or if the child has a health condition which will render the custody of the non-mother extremely

[45] See for example Concluding Observations Morocco (CRC/c/MAR/CO/3-4, 14 October 2014) para 10; see also Concluding Observations Morocco (2003) ibid para 40–41: 'The Committee is deeply concerned at the existence of difficulties in the implementation of decisions of the courts regarding custody and visitation rights for Moroccan children one of whose parents live outside Morocco and for foreign children one of whose parents is Moroccan. The Committee recommends that the State party ratify the Hague Convention 1980.' After which Morocco did take steps to accede.

[46] The analysis of developments in Iraqi law is not included in this analysis, due to the ongoing political instability in Iraq.

[47] For a discussion on reform see Laura Weingartner, 'Family Law and Reform in Morocco – The Mudawana: Modernist Islam and Women's Rights in the Code of Personal Status' (2005) 82 *University of Detroit Mercy Law Review* 687, 693.

[48] Article 171 of the Moroccan Family Code 2004 provides that the court can decide 'in view of what would serve the interests of the child, to award custody to the most qualified of the child's relatives.'

[49] Zakia Salime, 'Revisiting the Debate on Family Law in Morocco: Context, Actors, and Discourse' in Kenneth Cuno and Manisha Desai (eds), *Family, Gender and Law in a Globalizing Middle East and South Asia* (Syracuse University Press, 2009) 145, 161.

burdensome.[50] It is remarkable that while the objection to the mother's remarriage arises from concern about the child's welfare, the language of the legislation focuses upon the interests of the adults. This is a prime example of how the child's best interests are intended to be the primary concern in Islamic law,[51] but the way in which the law is expressed and applied results in the child's interests being hijacked by the interests of the father. This text argues, through highlighting the example of Moroccan law, that merely adopting the language of the best interests of the child in legislation is not sufficient to conform to the child's CRC rights and that the best interests' assessment in Moroccan law does therefore not meet the CRC criteria.

The legal developments in this area within different Islamic law countries vary, dependent upon how conservative the views are of the State's leaders and populations.[52] The example of Morocco can be contrasted with nearby Tunisia and Algeria. In both these Islamic law countries, the law allows the mother to be appointed as legal guardian alongside the father, which subsequently grants the mother the authority to make decisions relating to a child's travel.[53] Tunisia too acceded to the Hague Convention, and whilst its legislation does make reference to the mother's religion, remarriage and residence,[54] the stipulations are, it is documented, not strictly enforced in Tunisia.[55]

Pakistan also acceded to the Hague Convention in 2017 after a period of liberal interpretation of Islamic custody law in abduction cases.[56] Pakistan's law does not appear to require comprehensive reform like in other Islamic law countries, as the legislation that is in operation (introduced by the British in 1890)[57] does not

[50] Art 175-6 of the Moroccan Family Code 2004.

[51] For a detailed discussion, see Shaheen Ali, 'Comparative Perspective of the Convention on the Rights of the Child and the Principles of Islamic Law: Law Reform and Children's Rights in Muslim Jurisdictions' in UNICEF, *Protecting the World's Children: Impact of the Convention on the Rights of the Child in Diverse Legal Systems* (Cambridge University Press, 2007) 142.

[52] For a detailed discussion, see Abdullahi Ahmed An-Na'im, *Toward an Islamic Reformation of Civil Liberties in Human Rights and International Law* (Syracuse University Press, 1990); Ziba Mir-Hosseini and others (eds), *Men in Charge? Rethinking Authority in Muslim Legal Tradition* (One World Publications, 2015).

[53] Algeria Decree No 05-02 of 2005, art 87; Tunisia Code of Personal Status, art 154–155. Though see case of *AB v AB* [2015] EWHC 2422 (Fam) before the English court that illustrates whilst the law exists, mothers in Algeria are still unlikely to be granted consent to relocate.

[54] Tunisia Code of Personal Status 1956, art 154–155.

[55] See publication by the UK Tunisian Embassy which explains the rules on remarriage and religion are not strictly applied: 'Although these articles are not strictly applied by courts, the Code of Personal Status provides these rules that should be known by the spouses.' Also on Guardianship and the child's travel the publication confirms, 'the judge may entrust the powers of guardianship *to the mother* if the guardian who holds custody of the child displays abusive behaviour, neglects to fulfil his obligations, or is absent from his home or becomes homeless, or is detrimental to the best interest of the child. In such a case, the mother can freely travel outside of Tunisia without any threat to her custody rights.' *Tunisian Family Law* (British Embassy, Tunis) 15, available at https://assets.publishing.service.gov.uk/government/uploads/system/uploads/attachment_data/file/797548/Tunisian_Family_Law_-_Print_Version_Final_Document.pdf.

[56] See analysis of the case law by Ishaque and Khan (n 27).

[57] Specialised Family Law courts have jurisdiction in custody matters as per Pakistan's Family Courts Act 1964.

apply religious rules, but rather provides for consideration of the child's welfare. A welfare test operates under the Pakistan Guardian and Wards Act 1890, which is similar to the best interests standard followed in English law, although applied of course by the judiciary in accordance with the Pakistani cultural context. The legislation provides the judiciary discretion when undertaking individualised best interests assessments in cases concerning children's welfare. Some examples exist of parental child abduction cases before the Pakistani courts, where children were abducted from Scotland,[58] France[59] and Canada.[60] In these cases, the courts have granted custody to a mother in an abduction case, irrespective of the mother's religion, remarriage and the fact that she intends to live in a different country to the father.[61] The judiciary in these cases used principles of Islamic law to stress the child's best interests require the child is returned to his or her mother's care, establishing that Islamic teachings place greater emphasis on the relationship between the child and his or her mother than the mother's religious beliefs. Yet it seems from the available evidence that the application of Islamic custody rules by the Pakistani courts varies between domestic custody cases in Pakistan, and international cases of abduction heard by the courts.[62] It is therefore suggested[63] that this shift in approach has more to do with the diplomatic nature of Pakistan's relationship with the West than to more principled developments in Pakistan's assessment of the child's best interests. The manner in which Pakistani courts interpret domestic custody law suggests that Islamic custody law does have the inbuilt latitude to uphold children's rights as envisaged by the CRC and that the interpretation of the child's Article 3 CRC right is one of political motivation, rather than religious law exclusively.[64] Notwithstanding the peculiarities of Pakistan's approach, the discourse surrounding children's rights within Islamic law points to the fact that there is sufficient flexibility in Islamic law to ensure leaders do not violate children's rights in their failure to interpret Islamic law provisions appropriately,[65] and so the future aspirations of the CRC Committee appear achievable.

[58] *Louise Ann Fairley v Sajjad Ahmad Rana* 113 PLD 2007, Supreme Court 292.

[59] *Peggy Collins v Muhammad Ishfaque Malik* (2009) PLD 48, Lahore High Court.

[60] *Roshni Desai v Jehanzeb Niazi* (2011) PLD 423, Lahore High Court.

[61] In the case concerning the child abducted from Scotland, Pakistan's Supreme Court reversed the decision based upon the child's views (which will be explored in more detail in chapter 4): *Fairley v Rana* (n 58).

[62] In the case of *Shabana Naz v Muhammad Saleem* (2014) SCMR 343 the court prioritised factors such as a child's religious upbringing.

[63] Ishaque and Khan (n 27) 87–88; Helen Pidd, 'How Colonel Gaddafi Helped to Get My Daughter Back (*The Guardian*, 09.02.2013); Helen Pidd and others, 'Abducted Atiya Anjum-Wilkinson Returns to UK From Pakistan' (*The Guardian*, 28.12.2012).

[64] Javaid Rehman, 'Religion, Human Rights and the Rights of the Child: Complexities in Applying Sharia in Modern State Practices' (2011) 62 *Northern Ireland Legal Quarterly* 2, 153; For a detailed discussion, see An-Na'im (n 52); Mir-Hosseini (n 52).

[65] See Ali (2007) (n 51) 142; Kamran Hashmi, 'Religious Legal Traditions, Muslim States and the Convention on the Rights of the Child: An Essay on the Relevant Documentation' (2007) 29 *HRQ* 194.

C. Islamic Law Best Interests as a Fundamental Interpretative Legal Principle

General Comment 14 requires that the expression of the best interests of the child is to be applied as an interpretive legal principle, and as a mediating principle assisting in resolving conflicts between different rights.[66] As an interpretive legal principle, the best interests expression is also developed to limit the unchecked power over children by adults.[67] The CRC Committee explains in GC14: 'If a legal provision is open to more than one interpretation, the interpretation which most effectively serves the child's best interests should be chosen.'

The analysis above illustrates that when determining what is in the best interests of the child in a parental abduction case, 'the interpretation which most effectively serves the child's best interests' is not chosen in domestic law in Islamic countries but rather the interpretation that serves the rights and interests of the father. Such observations are supported by the interviews with the abductees when asked to reflect on whether they felt the courts in Islamic countries upheld their right to have their best interests treated as a primary consideration. The following discussion reflects on what the abductees believe to have been in their best interests. In reflecting on the court's decision, the two main themes that emerge are (i) that the abductees disagree with the court's determination that it was in their best interests to live without their mother, and (ii) the court did not take into account the impact the decision would have upon their educational and future prospects.

i. The Requirement to Stay in the Islamic Law Country Meant I Missed Out on a Mother

The nine abductees who were ordered by the court to remain with their father disagreed with the court's assessment of their best interests. They did not view separation from their primary carer as being in their short or long-term best interests, and consider being impaired by the court's assessment:

> I missed my mum. They were hard years for me. I felt sad all the time and felt different from others. (Jamal)
>
> Sometimes I don't even want to see his [abducting father's] face. As a child, you have to grow up with your parents. When I came to Libya, I was four years old, and I forgot how to speak English. I can't speak with my mother normally. (Samir)

[66] Michael Freeman, 'Article 3: The Best Interests of the Child' in Andre Alen and others (eds), *Commentary on the United Nations Convention on the Rights of the Child* (Brill Nijhoff, 2007) 32.

[67] Jean Zermatten, 'The Best Interests of the Child Principle: Literal Analysis and Function' (2010) 18 *International Journal of Children's Rights* 483, 485; see also Meda Couzens, 'The Contribution of the South African Constitutional Court to the Jurisprudential Developments of the Best Interests of the Child' in Alison Diduck and others (eds), *Law and Society: Reflections on Children, Family, Culture and Philosophy: Essays in Honour of Michael Freeman* (Brill, 2015) 525.

> I was angry at my dad for a long time, you know, but he had to do what he had to do. What he did wasn't right, but since all that happened, what can you really do as a child? When I started to grow up, I wanted to know why it happened and did my mum do something? When I did eventually start to ask questions, I was told to shut up and get on with life. It has had a huge impact on my life. Not only missing out on a relationship with my mother but also, now years later, it's difficult to build our relationship. (Ryan)[68]

> Of course I knew they [father's family] were not my mother and I only have one mother and I missed her. But I couldn't do anything about it, just accepting the situation. [It had] a big impact on my relationship with them [parents], I rarely speak with my father, never call him, not because I'm angry with him, I just think I don't have anything to tell him except how are you, good, ok. With my mother, it's better, we don't really talk to each other, and I don't know much about her, but I'm always happy to see her. It's not really a child and mother relationship, I guess, but it's okay. (Aidan)

> I get depressed quite a lot. It's not as if I sit there and think about everything and get depressed. I think I'm just prone to depression now so I take anti-depressants which I've taken since six months ago. But I do wonder whether or not if I'd be prone to depression if what happened hadn't have happened. I don't know whether that's an effect, but it's something that I have now. I have a lot of resentment. I have a lot of resentment for a lot of people in my family. (Sara)[69]

Nine of the ten participants abducted as children perceived the event as an abduction. The remaining child Daniel, who was abducted by his mother, and was aged sixteen at the time of the interview, did not view his move to the Islamic law country as abduction. Although he does appear to say his ability to trust what his parents say about each other is affected by the abduction:

> And I trust no one. Yeah about this, since the two most important people in my lives keep making a devil of each other really affected me trusting people. But the whole thing didn't emotionally affect me in any way other than 'trusting'. (Daniel)

The left-behind mother is somewhat of a stranger to those children who were unable to remain in contact during the period of abduction:

> When I came back to England, I realised even though I spoke to my mum, I didn't know her at all. Like it took me a while to reach out, like I knew that I loved her and I knew that I was happier to be here, but I didn't know her, it took me a while to get to know her, and we've got a good relationship. She's quite an obsessive person, so she's really annoying me but I think she's been quite damaged from this herself, and I think that's stuck with her, but I just want to get over it and move on. (Yasmin)

This feeling was reciprocated by left-behind mothers, who felt there was a barrier in the relationship. As one left-behind mother states:

> I think it sort of put a barrier between us, we're not as close as obviously, we would be if I'd have brought them up because they weren't with me, I haven't seen them grow,

[68] Participant 30C, interview 17/03/16 (on file with the author).
[69] Participant 32C, interview 18/06/16 (on file with the author).

> I mean every year I used to go and see them bigger or their hair was longer, face was a bit fatter, and that used to break my heart.[70]

This is an issue raised repeatedly by the left-behind parents:

> Yes she tells me that she loves me and she's quite warm at times towards me, it's not like we have an awful relationship, but it's not, you know I could be her friend or an aunt, I could be just someone she knows well. I don't think that there is a maternal relationship with her, in her view anyway. I'm just somebody at the fringes of her life.[71]

In being forced to grow up in the Islamic environment, some children became less accepting of the left-behind mother's lifestyle choices:

> When I came back when I was thirteen years old, I did not know anything about my mum, it took me a long time to get used to her and we didn't get along at all. Because I was definitely a different person, I grew up with different traditions, and the culture shock of seeing her live with another man, the differences in school, the accents it was all different. It was hard for a couple of years I was so depressed. (Aliyah)[72]

Other than the one child abducted by his mother, the nine abducted participants interviewed reported feeling somewhat estranged from both parents after the abduction. The feeling of estrangement is also observed in the research undertaken by Marilyn Freeman of child abduction cases between Hague Convention states[73] as a psychological barrier that develops, resulting in both losing faith in their reciprocal need. Sara explains:

> My mum gives a biased view of how she was a victim, but the fact that she went on holiday when dad took me is always is left out of the story. Anything she might have done to make the situation worse is always left out. When I first came back, I put my mum on a pedestal. But over the last few years, I've realised both my parents made mistakes. There's a lot of things she did that I look back on and I think it wasn't really fair that you did that, and it has had an effect on our relationship. I'd never openly speak to her about it, but I think I'm closer to my sisters now than my mum. It sounds terrible considering everything my mum's been through. But she's difficult sometimes. (Sara)

Despite the feeling of estrangement, the abducted participants are able to maintain a relationship with both parents, if only minimal to remain on speaking terms, once they become old enough to access social media. In only two of the overall 29 cases examined, the abducted children decided not to retain contact with the abducting father. In one case a child attempted to re-establish contact three years after returning to the UK:

> I wanted to know what he had to say for himself, surely he must know he's done something wrong now. And I wouldn't want him to die and me not have spoken to him. So I contacted him, and he had nothing to say for himself, he didn't apologise. I decided

[70] Participant 10M, interview 05/07/16 (on file with the author).
[71] Participant 09M, interview 22/06/16 (on file with the author).
[72] Participant 33C interview 01/06/16 (on file with the author).
[73] Marilyn Freeman, *Parental Child Abduction: The Long-Term Effects* (International Centre for Family Law, Policy, and Practice, 2014) 28.

> not to speak to him after that, and I just said I don't really like him, I don't need him in my life. (Sara)

In the second case, the other child, aged ten, was ordered by the English court to have contact with her father but refused to do so, despite her younger siblings enjoying contact. Greif identifies the differing reaction of siblings is attributed to their age when abducted, how much they can recall of life prior to the abduction and their experience during the period of abduction.[74] Greif also highlights that refusing to connect with the estranged parent could be as much to do with children reaching young adulthood, needing less frequent contact with parents, as it has to do with the abduction.[75] And so it is difficult to really say whether the level of contact between older children and the parent not living with the child would be the same if the child had not been abducted.

Abducted children discovered the truth about being abducted as they matured; two of the children discovered letters sent to them by the left-behind parent, hidden away by the abducting parent. It was a surprise to the children the abductor had retained these. Children also heard 'things' from relatives, enlightening them that the person caring for them was not their biological mother, and their mother lived in the UK. In their research on the effects of parental child abduction, Sagatun and Barrett[76] identify that children can be terrorised through the lies they are told by abducting parents, with children feeling their childhood has been stolen from them as a result.

Older abducted children that did remember the left-behind parent were equally confused about how to feel about the abduction. Aidan[77] explains: 'I think this event had a very negative effect on me as a child, because my desire as a child to go play outside, do sports, do creative things like drawing or anything has gone. I was always at home didn't really want to make friends at the beginning and I think I am more introvert than I would have been if I stayed there [UK].' A left-behind mother reports the effect of the abduction on her daughter. In an effort to have some form of control of her circumstances she resorted to taking sleeping tablets and controlling her food intake, leading to a long-term eating disorder:

> He's never kissed and cuddled his children or nothing like that, he's always been a sergeant major, always controlled what they ate and whatever. I believe this is why, she [daughter] did say she had an eating disorder because she had no control over her life in Libya, but she realised that she could control what she was eating so that was the only way of having some control over her life. She said whilst she was in Libya she didn't

[74] Geoffrey Greif and & Duane Bowers, 'Unresolved Loss: Issues in Working With Adults Whose Sibling Was Kidnapped Years Ago' (2007) 35 *American Journal of Family Therapy* 203.

[75] Geoffrey Greif 'A Parental Report on the Long-Term Consequences for Children of Abduction by the Other Parent' (2000) 31(1) *Child Psychiatry and Human Development* 59, 67.

[76] Inger Sagatun and Lynn Barrett, 'Parental Child Abduction: The Law, Family Dynamics, and Legal System Responses' (1990) 18 *Journal of Criminal Justice*, 433, 440.

[77] Participant 35C, interview 29/05/16 (on file with the author).

know what eating disorders were. She didn't know she had an eating disorder until she actually came back to the UK and started reading and hearing things about it.[78]

Some of the findings in the author's study are similar to those experienced by children abducted by a parent to a non-Islamic law country, ie anxiety and resentment, the inability to trust, depression, and anger about what happened to them.[79] Gibbs et al[80] identified that the impact on abductees included loss of trust, trouble making and keeping friends, and trouble recalling important aspects of the abduction. It is noteworthy here that some of the effects specific to abductions to Islamic law countries are unique, in that when abducted by their father, the abductees were not cared for by the abducting parent (in 27 of 29 cases considered). The father's relatives cared for the abducted children, and the father in some cases moved to yet another country for employment purposes, leaving the child with his relatives. As a result, some of the children abducted at a very young age did not comprehend who the left-behind mother was until much older. One left-behind mother reads from a diary entry of her abducted daughter: 'I remember thinking who is this nice lady who comes to visit us, she stays for a little while and then she'd go. I didn't really know who she was, but people told me that it was my mum. I didn't feel that connection until my teenage years.'[81]

Of the ten abductees interviewed, four remain living with the abductor at the time of the interview, three returned to the left-behind mother, and the remaining three live independently. The abducted participants in this study have not been returned from the Islamic law country long enough to compare the 'long-term' effects with the studies by Greif[82] and Freeman.[83] Of the five abductees who returned to the UK at the time of the interview, three had not been back in the UK for five years. In comparison, Greif's study examined the effects of abducted children who had returned ten years earlier and Freeman's study was able to compare the impact of the abduction on the abductee up to 50 years after the abduction. Their findings describe abducted children as experiencing difficulties with intimate relationships decades after the abduction, a constant sense of insecurity, problems with attachment and loss of self-worth. Very significant effects were reported by 73.53 per cent of Freeman's sample, revealing a high level of mental health problems. Greif identifies significant problems continue for as many as 42 per cent of abducted children in his sample. It is possible, therefore, that as the abductees in this study 'age out', they may begin to experience different thoughts about the abduction experience, on how the separation from their mothers impacted upon them and whether the Islamic courts' assessment was in fact in their best interests.

[78] Participant 06M, interview 14/06/16 (on file with the author).
[79] Freeman (2014) (n 72) 28.
[80] Mary Gibbs and others, 'The Consequences of Parental Abduction: A Pilot Study with a Retrospective View from the Victim' (2013) 21(3) *The Family Journal* 313.
[81] Participant 08M, interview 01/07/16 (on file with the author).
[82] Greif (2000) (n 74) 67.
[83] Freeman (2014) (n 72) 28.

Analysis of the long-term impact on children abducted to Islamic law countries would, therefore, be helpful if explored and compared in the future.

ii. The Requirement to Stay in the Islamic Law Country Affected My Future Long-Term Interests

The abductees interviewed describe the impact of the court's decision on their future best interests. Notably, the view the abductees express on whether the court's decision was positive or not relates to their perceived educational achievement. The educational and employment opportunities available in the Islamic law country to which the child is abducted appear to be a factor, and whether the opportunities are the same for girls as they are for boys. This gendered issue is explored in detail in chapter 5.

> I think it had like a massive effect on my childhood. I think like the positive side is that I understand my dad's culture. Had I not gone there, I wouldn't have understood, and I'd always be curious about it. I understand my dad's religion which I would never have understood, and even though I don't believe in any religion really I'm glad that I do understand. (Sara)
>
> He [father] mainly took us to have a good education. (Aidan)
>
> The university here is rubbish, there is no practising, and after you graduate, there are no jobs, but if I were there [England] things could have been different. (Jamal)
>
> I've lived a really comfortable and happy life so far. Growing up here [in the Islamic law country], I think, was better than growing up in the West. (Daniel)
>
> I believe in being my own woman, I like working, I like having my own money, I like being free and honestly if I had stayed over there [Islamic law country] right now I don't know I possibly would have been married you know with kids. Education wise I'm better off here [UK] other than that you know I love them they're my family but you know life wise I think it's best for me to be here [UK]. (Aliyah)

A left-behind mother whose daughters were abducted to Libya speaks of the different opportunities her daughters have in Libya in comparison to the UK: 'They've got no independence, they're reliant on their husbands, they don't drive, they've never worked a day in their life. Their lives just revolve around having babies, looking after their husbands, staying in the house and cooking.'[84] Helpless observing, a left-behind father describes the way in which his daughter has been raised in the Islamic law country: 'She doesn't even choose her clothes each day there; her stepfather chooses them for her. I'm worried about her education, and I'm not happy with the chances she's got there. She had a really interesting conversation with me saying that she doesn't even get why women have the chance to vote. These are challenges that I've got to be really careful with; I don't want to have a cultural battle with her saying this system [UK] is better than your [Islamic law] system.'[85]

[84] Participant 06M, interview 14/06/16 (on file with the author).
[85] Participant 03M, interview 19/04/16 (on file with the author).

Both Aidan and Yasmin mention the outcome of the Islamic court assessment was perhaps in their best interests as they benefitted from a good education. 'When I visited [the UK] last year I saw some of my old friends, none of them are in university, and they don't have jobs, so I realised that maybe it was not so bad for me.' (Aidan). 'I did get a good education while I was over there and in a way, I'm sort of grateful for it [abduction] in the respect that I wouldn't be me if that hadn't have happened.' (Yasmin). Nonetheless, as one left-behind mother whose sons were abducted to Libya points out, benefitting from a good education for some abducted children did not necessarily lead to their overall happiness:

> He had a bad life bless him, and he really suffered. I mean he's 34 today; he's a very, very successful young man you know. He's a senior medical physicist, and he's just an inspiration, he's a wonderful person. But if we, the two of us sit and talk about this it all comes back, and he'll be in floods of tears, and he's 34 now. He carries a heavy burden, and that will never go. I've always hoped it would, but he's kept so much inside, he had a very, very, very traumatic time and life.[86]

Abductees spoke of how the abduction impacted upon them, which played out in their behaviour, and subsequently the educational opportunities available to them:

> I wasn't ready to be at uni after everything that had happened; I didn't really go to any of my classes. I had such a sheltered upbringing I then went too much to the opposite; I drank a lot, did drugs. I'd be on a night out, and I'd start crying, and I wouldn't be able to move, and people would have to like carry me home. I was a weird person for ages after. (Sara).

Younger children have also demonstrated the impact of the abduction upon them with troubling behaviour. A left-behind mother describes the behaviour of her child who returned from the Islamic law country aged ten:

> She was so aggressive they were going to put her into care, hitting us, tried to stab us, there was one time when I was driving she tried to get the wheel and tried to drive the car into a lorry. She came back and no one would tell her off because of what she's been through. She was hanging out of car windows shouting 'sexy' to all the men walking past. She wouldn't settle at school, so got put in a special school. She didn't settle into the new one either because the children are a lot older. That school is for pregnant schoolgirls and one of the boys in her class, speaks like a zombie. Her attendance is only 27 per cent.[87]

The left-behind mother was concerned about the impact of the abduction on her child's schooling and subsequent prospects. This type of behaviour is also identified by Greif, in his study of abducted children;[88] he found 27 per cent of parents stated their child was prone to self-destructive behaviour after return. The more recent study by eWELL also affirms 'Children who receive psychological assistance upon their return show significantly better wellbeing as compared to children who

[86] Participant 07M, interview 16/06/16 (on file with the author).
[87] Participant 13M, interview 10/09/16 (on file with the author).
[88] Greif (2000) (n 74) 66.

did not receive such assistance.'[89] In the current study, some of the children who returned to the UK and received therapy responded differently. Aliyah's perception was:

> Counselling wasn't helpful for me. Instead, I had loads of support from people around me and who cared for me. I just needed time to figure it out in my own head.

Depression was cited by several participants in the author's study as an effect of abduction and this was confirmed in research by Senior, Gladstone, and Nurcombe[90] who found depression among the abducted children they treated. Abductees discovered methods of overcoming the effects in their own way, sharing experiences with abducted siblings or others who could empathise. One abductee, for example, now a doctor, later chose to return to Libya to marry someone who was also a doctor. His wife too had been abducted by her father as a child from the UK and taken to another part of Libya.[91]

The accounts provided by abductees illustrate an appreciation of the complex nature of their future-orientated best interests assessment by the Islamic courts. The abductees recognise that the Islamic courts decided it was better for the children that they remain with the abducting parent, who would raise them as a Muslim. This factor was more important than their opportunities for education, employment, or to live with their mother. The Islamic courts decided in all ten cases that the children would remain in the Islamic law country with the abducting parents, based on the Islamic law assessment of what is presumed to be in the best interests of children generally. Whilst it would be helpful to undertake a direct comparison of the data with other sources, this is not possible at the present time. Decisions of abduction cases decided in the Islamic law courts are not published in law reports. Data from studies relating to abducted children is also limited in the Islamic law country context. The only other data that makes reference to abductions to Islamic law countries is a study of cases of parental abduction from Belgium, examining cases decided under a Belgian bilateral treaty with Tunisia and Morocco.[92] A further published report also examines the ineffectiveness of the bilateral agreements and protocols.[93] Neither of the two studies directly engage with children

[89] University of Antwerp, *Bouncing Back: The Wellbeing of Children in International Child Abduction Cases* ('eWELL') (Missing Children Europe, 2017) 38.

[90] Neil Senior and others, 'Child Snatching: A Case Report' (1982) 21 *J Amer Acad Child Psych* 579.

[91] Participant 07M, interview 16/06/16 (on file with the author).

[92] Thalia Kruger undertook a survey of Belgian cases open in 2007 and 2008. These provide quantitative and qualitative analysis of 667 abduction files at the Belgian Central Authority, the Belgian Ministry of Foreign Affairs and the organisation, 'Child Focus.' The survey collates statistics for incoming and outgoing abductions, analysing the legal instruments applied in seeking the children's return (whether the Hague Abduction Convention, Brussels II bis, or the Protocols involving Morocco or Tunisia; Thalia Kruger, *International Child Abduction: The Inadequacies of the Law* (Hart Publishing, 2011) 108–111.

[93] Caroline Gosselain, *Child Abduction and Transfrontier Access: Bilateral Conventions and Islamic States* (Hague Conference, Permanent Bureau, Preliminary Document No 7, 2002) available at www.hcch.net/upload/abd2002_pd7e.pdf; Marilyn Freeman, 'When the 1980 Hague Child Abduction Convention Does Not Apply: The UK-Pakistan Protocol' [2009] September IFL 181.

abducted to Islamic law countries to ascertain their views on how the abduction affected them. Equally, as none of the cases analysed in the author's study were decided under the legal provisions of a bilateral treaty,[94] a direct comparison of the two sets of data cannot be undertaken.

The decisions of the Islamic law courts are at direct odds with what the abductees themselves consider to have been in their best interests. Nine of the ten abductees think a return to their left-behind mothers, and return to the United Kingdom, was in their best interests. This is irrespective of the mother's religious affiliation and remarriage. The abductees' views on what they consider to be in their best interests appear to more closely align with the Hague framework. An analysis of how the Hague Convention operates and whether it would better uphold the Article 3 CRC rights of these young people is undertaken in the following section.

IV. How the Hague Regime Fares as an Alternative to Upholding the Article 3 CRC Right of Children Abducted to Islamic Law Countries

In order to undertake a comparative analysis between the two legal frameworks, the Hague Convention and domestic law in Islamic law countries, the discussion here focuses upon if and how the Hague Convention upholds the child's Article 3 CRC right to have his or her best interests treated as a primary consideration.

The closely aligned history between the Hague Convention and the CRC is discussed above in chapter 2. The Hague Convention was explicitly referred to during the drafting of Article 11 CRC.[95] And although the final Article 11 CRC only refers implicitly to the Hague Convention, it does so 'unequivocally',[96] encouraging States parties to the CRC to ratify or accede to the Hague Convention. The ongoing

[94] Countries experiencing high volumes of abduction to the particular Islamic law countries sought to address the problem through the mechanism of bilateral treaties. The bilateral agreements that exist appear to have been entered into in or after 1980. The agreements addressing international parental child abduction are: (1) Belgium-Morocco 1981; (2) France-Tunisia 1982; (3) France-Egypt 1982; (4) Belgium-Tunisia 1982; (5) France-Morocco 1983; (6) Sweden-Tunisia 1994); (7) Sweden-Egypt 1996; (8) Spain-Morocco 1997; (9) Canada-Egypt 1997; (10) France-Algeria 1988; (11) France-Lebanon 2000; (12) Australia-Egypt 2000; (13) Canada-Lebanon 2000; (14) USA-Egypt 2003; (15) Switzerland-Lebanon 2005; (16) UK-Pakistan 2003; (17) UK-Egypt 2005.

[95] For specific references to the Hague Convention, see the *Legislative History of the Convention on the Rights of the Child*, Vol 1 (Office of the United Nations High Commissioner for Human Rights, 2007) available at www.ohchr.org/Documents/Publications/LegislativeHistorycrc1en.pdf 158; Conversely as the Hague Convention predates the CRC, the discussion surrounding the draft of Article 3 CRC does not refer to the Hague Convention. This is likely to be because the CRC is intended to apply to a variety of situations much broader than parental child abduction. See pp335–48 of the CRC's legislative history documenting the discussions relating to Article 3 CRC from the First Polish draft convention and comments (1978) through to the developments leading up to the second reading (1988–89).

[96] Adair Dyer, 'The Hague Convention on the Civil Aspects of International Child Abduction – Towards Global Cooperation its Successes and Failures' (1993) 1 *The International Journal of Children's Rights* 273.

relationship between the Hague Convention and the CRC is identified by Adair Dyer, the retired Former Deputy Secretary-General of the Hague Conference on Private International Law.[97] Dyer refers specifically to Articles 10, 11 and 12 CRC stating they echo the 1980 Hague Convention on the right of the child to maintain her or his relationship with a parent who resides in a different country, the right not to be wrongfully removed from his or her country of habitual residence, and the right to express views about decisions affecting him or her.[98]

Dyer asserts that the Hague Convention is compliant with children's rights and the CRC. The basis of his argument is that specific mention of the 1980 Hague Convention was made during the drafting of the CRC,[99] so the drafters of the CRC knew of the policy of automatic return at the time Article 11 CRC was concluded. In fact, by that time, the Hague Convention already had 14 States parties, many of who were also involved in the drafting of the CRC. Dyer sees the appropriate approach to the issue of the primacy of the child's best interests as being to find a place within the structure of the CRC both for Article 3(1) and for Article 11. He supports the assertion by referring to the preamble of the Hague Convention, which he says illustrates the preoccupation of its drafters with protecting the best interests of children.[100] Thus all countries that have joined the Hague Convention have expressed in the Preamble that they are '… firmly convinced that the interests of children are of paramount importance in matters relating to their custody' and that they desire 'to protect children internationally from the harmful effects of their wrongful removal or retention and to establish procedures to ensure their prompt return to the State of their habitual residence, as well as to secure protection for rights of access.'

Though the significance of the child's best interests is expressed within the Preamble to the Hague Convention, the following analysis considers how the actual wording and effect of the Hague Convention, may, in some respects, demonstrate otherwise. This chapter, as stated at the outset, reflects on the expression of the best interests of the child as a threefold concept, as is illustrated in GC14, as a right, a principle and a rule of procedure. The three dimensions are adopted in the following sections as a measure by which to evaluate if, and how, the child's best interests are articulated in the Hague Convention.

A. Best Interests as a Substantive Right under the Hague Convention?

The Hague Convention does not aim to assess the best interests of each individual child in Convention proceedings but presumes it is in the best interests

[97] Adair Dyer, 'The Contribution of the Hague Children's Conventions to the Protection of Human Rights' (2012) *International Family Law* 7, 9–11.

[98] Ibid, 9.

[99] Sharon Detrick, *A Commentary on the UN Convention on the Rights of the Child* (Martinus Nijhoff, 1999) 207–208.

[100] Dyer (2012) (n 96) 9.

of abducted children that they are returned as quickly as possible to their pre-abduction environment and that the courts in the child's usual place of residence, with the closest connection to the child, are best placed to decide where the child should live.[101]

The issue of whether the child's best interests should be investigated in Hague proceedings was a particular point of contention during the drafting process. The extent of the difficulty in reaching consensus is described by those involved in the Convention's development as almost being a 'deal-breaker.'[102] The problems arose as member states developing the Hague Convention, of mainly Western origin, all have legal systems in which the best interests of individual children are assessed in proceedings, albeit under the guise of 'welfare'.[103] The drafters of the Hague Convention were aware of the fact that the principle of the best interests of the child was far from uncontested, even in Western legal systems, and characterised by vagueness and subjective bias (see discussion above at II). To extend such a nebulous principle to one that could encapsulate the interpretations adopted by all parts of the world was not expected to be straightforward. There were, therefore, alternative proposals contemplated by the drafters to the Hague Convention to decide how best to resolve the situation of the child abducted by one parent. As alternative proposals, the drafters considered whether the new legal framework should seek to enforce existing custody orders, or whether the legal jurisdiction of all member states should be harmonised in abduction cases. There was no agreement on the alternative proposals, however, and so, after much debate, the format of the Convention and the approach to the child's best interests arose out of necessity as the other options were rejected.[104] The basis upon which the Hague Convention is founded therefore represents a compromise. The proposal agreed upon was that the purpose of the Hague Convention is to avoid any lengthy drawn-out proceedings. The detailed best interests assessment is to be undertaken after the child's return to his or her habitual residence, to avoid the child becoming further settled in the new environment.[105]

The reality of achieving political momentum and making concessions in return for a workable solution is recognised[106] as, without compromise, the Hague Convention may never have been completed. Notwithstanding this, to what extent should compromise affect individual children and their rights? Requiring the courts to automatically return children without an examination of the child's best interests does appear at odds with the child's Article 3 CRC rights. On the one hand, it can be argued that the Hague Convention upholds the child's Article 3

[101] Article 4 Hague Convention.

[102] Brigitte Bodenheimer, 'The Hague Draft Convention on International Child Abduction' (1980) 14 *Family Law Quarterly* 99, 102; Paul Beaumont and Peter McEleavy, *The Hague Convention on International Child Abduction* (OUP, 1999) 21.

[103] See for example English legislation, Children Act 1989, section 1.

[104] Beaumont and McEleavy (n 101) 21; Bodenheimer (n 101) 102.

[105] Conclusions and Recommendations of the Special Commission of March 1979 available at www.hcch.net/en/docs/05998e0c-af56-4977-839a-e7db3f0ea6a9.pdf.

[106] Beaumont and McEleavy (n 101) 21.

CRC rights by returning the child and restoring the status quo. But the presumption that return is automatically in the child's best interests does not uphold the Article 3 rights of abducted children in their various circumstances, such as in Daniel's case referred to above. Daniel was abducted by his mother fleeing a turbulent family life in the UK and returned to familial ties for support.

The manner in which the Hague Convention appears to satisfy the Article 3 CRC requirement is to examine the interests of the affected child through its use of the exceptions to return. In cases where an abducting parent responds to the Hague Convention return application by raising one or more of the defences to return, the court is obliged to consider that child's individual circumstances and in so doing conducts an interim assessment of the child's interests.[107] The defences to return are found under Articles 12, 13 and 20 of the Hague Convention. The Article 12 exception applies if more than a year has passed and the child is settled in the new environment. The Article 13 defence (examined in chapter 4) applies where the child objects to being returned and has attained an age and degree of maturity at which it is appropriate to take account of the child's views. Article 13(1)(b) (examined below) allows the courts to consider the child's best interests if it is claimed that an order for return will place the child at grave risk of harm or in an intolerable situation. The final exception, or defence to return, found under Article 20 (examined in chapter 5), states a child need not be returned if it would not be permitted by the fundamental principles of the requested state, relating to the protection of human rights and fundamental freedoms. Each of these defences allows the court to pause the requirement to automatically order the child's return and instead examine evidence of the child's situation. Thus, the court's power to refuse a return based upon a child's circumstances illustrates that there is scope to consider the child's individual best interests in Hague Convention proceedings.

This viewpoint was affirmed by the Grand Chamber of the ECtHR in *X v Latvia* where the court stated:[108]

> The Court reiterates that there is a broad consensus – including in international law – in support of the idea that in all decisions concerning children, their best interests must be paramount. The same philosophy is inherent in the Hague Convention, which associates this interest with restoration of the status quo by means of a decision ordering the child's immediate return to his or her country of habitual residence in the event of unlawful abduction, while taking account of the fact that non-return may sometimes prove justified for objective reasons that correspond to the child's interests, thus

[107] See discussion by Charlotte Mol and Thalia Kruger who analyse the use that judges make in their decisions on the concept of 'the best interests of the child'. They scrutinise abduction case law of the Netherlands and England and Wales. They confirm that the concept of the best interests of the child is often used without substance, and sometimes only to endorse conclusions that would have possibly been reached in any event. Charlotte Mol and Thalia Kruger, 'International Child Abduction and the Best Interests of the Child: An Analysis of Judicial Reasoning in Two Jurisdictions' (2018) 14 (3) *Journal of Private International Law* 421.

[108] Application No 27853/09, Grand Chamber 96–7.

explaining the existence of exceptions, specifically in the event of a grave risk that his or her return would expose the child to physical or psychological harm or otherwise place the child in an intolerable situation (Article 13, first paragraph, (b)).

The assessment by the Grand Chamber of the ECtHR affirms that the Hague Convention establishes circumstances when it may not be in the best interests of the child to be returned to the country of their habitual residence, which are set out in the exceptions to return. Similarly, commentators have argued[109] that the individual child's circumstances may therefore not require an independent assessment by the judge hearing the Hague return application to assess whether it is in the best interests of that child to return. This viewpoint is premised on the basis that States Parties to the Hague Convention comply with their obligations under Article 3 CRC by requiring their courts to examine whether any of the exceptions in Articles 12, 13 and 20 of the Hague Convention apply in the individual child's case. The interpretation suggests the premise underlying the Hague Convention does satisfy Article 3 CRC requirements, as the interim assessment of the child's circumstances can be construed as an assessment of the child's best interests. Analysis of the jurisprudence below demonstrates, however, that whilst the Hague Convention may satisfy the Article 3 CRC threshold, the way in which the exceptions to return are interpreted by the courts can, if not appropriately applied, fail to adhere to the child rights principles under the CRC.

Thus whilst the Hague Convention framework can be interpreted to uphold the abducted child's Article 3 CRC right, there are numerous examples where the courts have narrowly applied the exceptions to return,[110] to avoid the Hague Convention becoming a 'dead letter.'[111] Case law illustrates that sometimes very little regard is paid, for example, to the concerns raised by abducting parents of the risk of harm to a child under the Article 13(1)(b) Hague Convention exception if the child is ordered to return.[112] The courts have often disregarded claims that a mother is at risk of domestic abuse if forced to return with the abducted child,[113] or the child is at risk of harm through witnessing abuse against the mother. This

[109] Paul Beaumont, 'The Jurisprudence of the European Court of Human Rights and the European Court of Justice on the Hague Convention on International Child Abduction' (2008) 335 *Hague Collected Courses* 9, 102; Paul Beaumont, Katarina Trimmings, Lara Walker and Jayne Holliday, 'Child Abduction: Recent Jurisprudence of the European Court of Human Rights' (2015) *International and Comparative Law Quarterly* 39–63.

[110] The narrow interpretation of the Article 13(1)(b) exception was confirmed in *Re E (Children) (FC)* [2011] UKSC 27 where it was held the harm must have reached such a level of seriousness as to be characterised as grave, amounting to more than discomfort and distress.

[111] Elisa Perez-Vera, *Report on the 1980 Hague Child Abduction Convention* (Translation of The Permanent Bureau, 1981) para 34.

[112] Rhona Schuz, *The Hague Child Abduction Convention* (Hart Publishing, 2013) 273–89; Merle Weiner, 'International Child Abduction and the Escape from Domestic Violence' (2000) 69 *Fordham L Rev* 593, 637–39; Miranda Kaye, 'The Hague Convention and the Flight from Domestic Violence: How Women and Children Are Being Returned by Coach and Four' (1999) 13 *Int'l JL Pol'y & Fam* 191, 192.

[113] *Simcox v Simcox* 511 F 3d 594 (2007), para 17.

was affirmed in *Re M (Abduction: Intolerable Situation)*,[114] a case which concerned a Somali family living in Norway. The mother abducted the children to England after which the father initiated Hague Convention proceedings for the return of the children to Norway. The court accepted the evidence that the father had previously been violent towards the mother and had served a prison sentence in Norway for the murder of another Somali national with whom he suspected the mother had an affair. Despite concerns about threats made to the mother, the English court accepted the father's claim that the mother would be protected by the Norwegian authorities. The trial judge stated that an abducting parent who sought to argue that the authorities in the state of habitual residence would not be able to offer adequate protection should provide appropriate evidence to substantiate such submissions. As the mother was unable to evidence failure on Norway's part, the court ordered the return of the children.

While *Re M* was a case decided in England, case law demonstrates most major jurisdictions have adopted a strict approach to the application of Article 13(1)(b) to prevent it becoming a tool through which abducting parents evade the return mechanism; the exception has been restrictively interpreted in the USA[115] in Ireland,[116] Canada[117] and Scotland.[118] In narrowly applying the defences to return, courts have taken the view that the authorities in the requested state can offer protection to the child and mother and so have refused to engage in a broader best interests assessment of the child's circumstances nor addressed concerns that the child could be affected by harm to the mother (the gendered quality of parental abduction law is explored in chapter 5). Yet even in cases of harm against the abducted child by a left-behind parent, for example, where sexual abuse is alleged, the courts have upheld that the authorities in the requested state can protect the child and so the child must be returned.[119]

[114] [2000] 1 FLR 930; A similar decision was reached by the English Court of Appeal in *TB v JB (Abduction: Grave Risk of Harm)* [2001] 2 FLR 515 although in this case, the children refused to return despite being escorted by Court Officers (Tipstaff) to the airport and the court recognised that the return order became unenforceable.

[115] *Fredrich v Fredrich* 78 F 3d (6th Civ 1996).

[116] *AS v PS* [1998] 2 IR.

[117] *Thomson v Thomson* [1994] 3 SCR 551.

[118] In the case of *Starr v Starr* 1999 SLT 335 the mother abducted her 4-year-old daughter from the USA to Scotland in breach of a custody order in favour of the father. The mother's 16-year-old son from another relationship accompanied them. The mother claimed that as the child had been in her sole care since July 1997, and the older brother wished to remain in Scotland, ordering her daughter's return would place the child at grave risk of emotional harm. The mother also provided evidence of the intolerable situation she would encounter if forced to return as she would not be entitled to welfare benefits for the first 30 days or legal aid. The court did not accept the mother's argument that this satisfied the threshold and ordered the child's return. The court also observed the risk of psychological harm was created by the mother herself and so she should not be permitted to rely on that risk to bring the case within the Article 13(1)(b) grave risk exception.

[119] See *N v N (Abduction: Article 13 Defence)* [1995] 1 FLR 107 and *Re L (Abduction: Pending Criminal Proceedings)* [1999] 1 FLR 433 where the mother also feared being arrested at the airport if forced to return.

The principle of the Hague Convention to return children to their habitual residence is presumed to be in the best interests of children, and based on this analysis, the Hague Convention upholds the child's Article 3 substantive right more so than under domestic law in Islamic law countries. Nonetheless, the narrow application of the defences to return ensure that even under the Hague Convention, the fulfilment of the child's Article 3 CRC rights can be patchy;[120] the child's best interests are certainly not treated as a primary consideration *in all judicial proceedings* affecting children, as is required by the CRC. The concern this has raised in the context of the child and parent's right under Article 8 ECHR to a private family life is explored further in the following section, which reflects upon best interests as a 'fundamental interpretive legal principle'. It is however important to note here before moving on that there are some case examples in which the courts have, as is within their discretion, more broadly interpreted the Article 13(1)(b) exception to return. For example, in the case of *Re S (A Child) (Abduction: Rights of Custody)*[121] the UK Supreme Court ordered that the child abducted to England was not to be returned to Australia upon her father's request because the threshold under the Article 13(1)(b) exception was satisfied. In this case it was agreed that the father, who had previously been a heroin addict, had suffered a relapse prior to the mother's departure and the mother had been subjected to serious violent behaviour from the father. Whilst the court acknowledged the Australian authorities would provide adequate protection measures, it accepted the evidence presented on behalf of the mother that a forced return would result in the mother's anxiety affecting the child. The mother had suffered from 'Battered Women's Syndrome' whilst in Australia and the medical opinion was that there was a risk of relapse if the mother was forced to return. The decision of the highest court in the UK is expected to influence how the exception is interpreted by lower courts. Indeed, the wider interpretation is observed in the later case of *X v Y and Z Police Force, A, B and C (By Their Children's Guardian)*.[122] The father in this case abducted his three children from Australia to the UK and the mother applied under the Hague Convention for the children's return. The father, supported by his employing police force, claimed a return would place the children at grave risk of harm or otherwise place them in an intolerable situation. The father had been employed as an undercover police officer and, after being relocated to Australia, circumstances had arisen during the course of his employment which would render it unsafe for the family to return. The court accepted it was not safe for the children to be returned to Australia and refused the mother's application for the children's return. The two decisions of the English courts illustrate that where the evidence, such as expert opinion, is supportive of the claim that the children or indeed the parent accompanying the children will be harmed

[120] Michael Freeman, 'Article 3: The Best Interests of the Child' in Andre Alen and others (eds), *Commentary on the United Nations Convention on the Rights of the Child* (Brill Nijhoff, 2007).
[121] [2012] UKSC 10.
[122] [2013] 1 FLR 1277.

if ordered to return, the court will apply its discretion and refuse the abducted children's return.

Continuing the analysis of the expression of the best interests of the child as a threefold concept – as a right, a principle and a rule of procedure – the following section examines the principle of the abducted child's best interests as a fundamental interpretative legal principle under the Hague Convention.

B. Best Interests as a Fundamental Interpretative Legal Principle under the Hague Convention

General Comment 14 requires that the expression of the best interests of the child is to be applied as an interpretive legal principle, and so 'If a legal provision is open to more than one interpretation, the interpretation which most effectively serves the child's best interests should be chosen.'

It is identified above that the drafters of the Hague Convention argue that the presumption of return absolutely does serve the best interests of the child. Yet when deciding the outcome of abduction proceedings, the courts have announced that this is not the Hague Convention's only aim. Butler-Sloss LJ affirmed in the case of *C v C* that 'the welfare of the child as the paramount consideration is not the basis of the Hague Convention.'[123] This sentiment has been repeated by the courts on several occasions since, where it is stated that the best interests of the individual child are not the first and paramount consideration in Hague Convention cases,[124] despite some members of the judiciary being uneasy with the sentiment.[125] Indeed, there was even a period of uncertainty with the European Court of Human Rights (ECtHR) questioning the Hague Convention's interpretation of Article 3 CRC rights of the abducted child, in the case of *Neulinger and Shuruk v Switzerland*.[126] In this case, the mother abducted the child from Israel to Switzerland and the father sought the child's return. The lower Swiss court accepted the mother's claim that the Article 13(1)(b) exception was satisfied and the child would be at grave risk of harm or placed in an intolerable situation if ordered to return. The mother claimed the father had joined an ultra-orthodox religious sect and she was concerned he would remove the child from Switzerland to join the organisation. The Swiss Federal Court disagreed with the decision of the lower court, finding the Article 13(1)(b) threshold was not satisfied as the Israeli authorities could protect

[123] *C v C (Minor: Abduction: Rights of Custody)* [1989] 2 All ER 465, 471.

[124] See *Re N (Minors) (Abduction)* [1991] 1 FLR 413, 417; *Re A (Minors) (Abduction: Custody Rights) (No 2)* [1993] Fam 1, 14; *Re HB (Abduction: Children's Objections)* [1997] 1 FLR 392, 400.

[125] Baroness Hale, 'Child Abduction from the Child's Point of View' in *The Child's Voice – 15 Years Later*, (Permanent Bureau of the Hague Conference on Private International Law, Judges' Newsletter Vol XXII) 40.

[126] App no 41615/07 (Application No) IHRL 3717 (ECHR 2010).

the child and mother from any risk of harm. The mother appealed to the ECtHR claiming a return would violate the child and her right to a family life protected under Article 8 ECHR. The ECtHR determined by a 4:3 majority ruling that there had not been a breach of the mother and child's right to family life under Article 8 of the European Convention on Human Rights. After a request by the applicants for the Grand Chamber to hear their application, the eventual outcome was that the ECtHR held, by sixteen votes to one, that if the return order was enforced, some three years after it was made and five years after the abduction, the mother and child's Article 8 rights to family life would be breached.

The *Neulinger* decision raised concern as the court stated that to be compliant with Article 8 ECHR, before ordering a return, the domestic court must have conducted an in-depth examination of the family situation. It was, therefore, suggested the swift summary approach to Hague Convention proceedings was insufficient, and a full merits examination was necessary. The later abduction case of *Re E*,[127] heard by an English court, discussed the ECtHR decision in *Neulinger*. It was argued in *Re E* that the ECtHR strayed beyond its brief in *Neulinger*, for while it is clearly in the court's remit to comment on how the 1980 Hague Convention operates in individual states, it is not legitimate territory to critique the Convention and offer its own interpretation. Though the case of *Re E* confirmed the Hague Convention's compatibility with Article 3(1) of the CRC, Stephen and Lowe[128] writing at the time expressed concern that *Re E* did not resolve the problem created by *Neulinger*. They argued the conflicting decision could encourage abductors to delay return in the hope the ECtHR decision would apply, and this would undermine the effect of the Hague Convention. This is because an examination of the best interests of children in each case would create delays in Convention proceedings, which were designed to be dealt with expeditiously and to allow the best interests examination to be undertaken post-return by the courts of the child's habitual residence.

The *Neulinger* ruling resulted in much academic debate,[129] after which the ECtHR reverted to its prior acceptance of the compatibility between the Hague Convention and the ECHR in the case of *X v Latvia*.[130] In *X v Latvia* the Grand Chamber expressed the importance of an effective examination of the factors capable of constituting an exception to the child's return. The mother in this case

[127] *Re E (Children) (Abduction: Custody Appeal)* [2011] UKSC 27.

[128] Victoria Stephen and Nigel Lowe, 'Children's Welfare and Human Rights Under the 1980 Hague Abduction Convention – the Ruling in *Re E*' (2012) 34(1) *Journal of Social Welfare and Family Law* 133.

[129] Lara Walker and Paul Beaumont, 'Shifting The Balance Achieved by the Abduction Convention: The Contrasting Approaches of the European Court of Human Rights and the European Court of Justice' (2011) 7 *Journal of Private International Law* 2 231; See also later analysis of the effect of the courts' decision by Helen Keller, 'Protecting the Best Interests of the Child: International Child Abduction and the European Court of Human Rights' (2015) 84 *Nordic Journal of International Law* 270; Ruth Lamont, 'Free Movement of Persons, Child Abduction and Relocation Within the European Union' (2012) 34(2) *Journal of Social Welfare and Family Law* 231, 237.

[130] *X v Latvia* (App no 27853/09, Judgment (Grand Chamber) of 26 November 2013, Reports 2013).

had removed her child from Australia to return to the mother's home country of Latvia after her relationship with the child's father deteriorated. The Australian father made a Hague return application which the mother opposed, claiming the child would suffer harm if returned to Australia and separated from the mother. The mother claimed the father had mistreated her and had criminal convictions. The mother also had no employment in Australia and if made to return would not be able to financially support herself and the child. The Latvian court did not accept the mother's argument that the Article 13(1)(b) threshold was satisfied and ordered the child's return on the basis the protective measures in Australia law would sufficiently protect the child from any harm. The father visited Latvia and executed the return order himself, returning to Australia with the child. The Australian court granted the father custody of the child and the mother was permitted contact visits, which were to be supervised by a social worker. The mother made a complaint to the ECtHR under Articles 6 and 8 ECHR that the proceedings before the Latvian courts had not been fair, and the decision infringed her right to respect to a family life. In 2011, the ECtHR held (by a majority of five to two) that the applicant's Article 8 rights had been breached. The Latvian Government asked for the case to be referred to the Grand Chamber and the Grand Chamber subsequently held, by 9 votes to 8 that there had been a violation of Article 8 ECHR. The Grand Chamber found that the mother was subject to a disproportionate interference with her right to respect for her family life and the Latvian court had not correctly undertaken an effective examination of her allegations under Article 13(1)(b) of the Hague Convention. The mother had submitted evidence from a psychologist confirming the risk of trauma to the child if separated from the mother and the mother had also informed the court of the father's criminal convictions and ill-treatment on his part. The Grand Chamber took the view that the Latvian court should have undertaken checks to establish the existence of the risk of harm to the child in Australia, by requesting evidence of the father's criminal convictions from the Australian authorities. The Grand Chamber held that the refusal of the Latvian court to do so resulted in mother suffering a disproportionate interference with her right to respect for a family life.

The majority decision of 9 votes to 8 illustrates the difference in opinion on whether the Latvian court appropriately complied with the procedural requirements under the Hague Convention. The dissenting judges expressed the view that the Latvian court did take into consideration the evidence submitted by the mother and subsequently determined that the psychological evidence was relevant only to the issue of the child's separation from the mother, which was an issue relevant to the custody determination and therefore the Australian courts. They were also of the view that the mother's allegations against the father were dismissed by the Latvian court as these were not supported by any evidence and the Latvian court did appropriately consider the factor of the protective measures in Australia. The dissenting judges were also clear in their view that it was the parent opposing return, here the mother, that had the burden to provide evidence on the father's convictions and ill-treatment.

The differences in opinion, and the fact that the decision could so easily have fallen either way, demonstrates the tension in this area. In addressing the issue of the breach of Article 8 ECHR, the Grand Chamber clarified that in cases of child abduction, the Article 8 ECHR obligations must be interpreted as per the Hague Convention, the CRC and other international law principles relevant to the two states. The Grand Chamber stressed that it must be satisfied the decision-making process adopted by the domestic courts in Hague proceedings is fair and the best interests of the child are 'defended'.[131] The Grand Chamber in *X v Latvia*[132] clarified that whilst the *Neulinger* case was suggestive that the domestic courts were required to conduct an in-depth examination of the child's circumstances, the court's finding in *Neulinger*[133] did not set out any principle for the application of the Hague Convention by the domestic courts. Thus, whilst the ECtHR requires the domestic court to appropriately consider any factors capable of constituting an exception to the child's return under Articles 12, 13 and 20 of the Hague Convention, it confirmed it does not require an in-depth examination of the child's circumstances.

The Grand Chamber in *X v Latvia* expressed that in its view[134] a harmonious interpretation of the Hague Convention and the ECHR can be achieved if two conditions are observed. First, the domestic court hearing a Hague Convention application must undertake an effective examination of the factors that are capable of constituting an exception to return under Articles 12, 13 and 20 of the Hague Convention: these 'must genuinely be taken into account by the requested court'. The court must then make a decision that is sufficiently reasoned to enable the ECtHR to verify those matters have been examined. Secondly, the factors must be evaluated in light of Article 8 ECHR, which the Grand Chamber went on to explain as[135] 'due consideration of such allegations, demonstrated by reasoning of the domestic courts that is not automatic and stereotyped, but sufficiently detailed in the light of the exceptions set out in the Hague Convention, which must be interpreted strictly is necessary.'

The complexity of achieving the appropriate balance in upholding the child's right to have his or her best interests treated as a primary consideration is obvious from the jurisprudence of the ECtHR: whilst an in-depth examination of the child's circumstances is not necessary, the court must ensure the exceptions are 'interpreted strictly' and ensure that an effective examination of the factors capable of constituting an exception to return are 'genuinely taken into account by the requested court' to ensure there is no breach of Article 8 ECHR rights. Judge

[131] Ibid 102.
[132] Ibid 105.
[133] In the *Neulinger* judgment at para 139.
[134] *X v Latvia* (130) 106.
[135] Ibid 107.

Pinto de Albuquerque's dissenting opinion provides an interesting assessment of the relevance of an 'effective examination' of the best interests of the individual child over 14 pages. The assessment appears to support the argument presented in this analysis, that whilst the Hague Convention itself has the latitude to satisfy the Article 3 CRC requirements, the way in which domestic courts interpret the exceptions to return could go further to support this objective. Judge Pinto de Albuquerque states:[136]

> In the absence of any meaningful supranational review of the way in which the Contracting States implement, interpret and apply the Hague Convention, courts of Contracting States do as they please, sometimes ostensibly and one-sidedly ruling in favour of the national party. This inherent weakness in the Hague mechanism is magnified by the ambiguous and undefined legal terminology utilised in the Hague Convention and the lack of procedural rules on the conduct of judicial return proceedings, such as on evidentiary hearing, discovery, burden of proof, appeals, stay of orders pending appeals and interim measures. The damaging effect of differing, contradictory and confusing national case-law is further amplified by the fact that the enforcement stage of the return order is not regulated at all in the Hague Convention, and more specifically no legal basis is provided for stipulations, conditions or undertakings imposed on the parties or a system of judicial cooperation for the implementation of 'mirror orders'.

These difficulties in uniform interpretation amongst over 100 Contracting States will undoubtedly occur, and it is therefore hoped that the Hague Conference's 2020 Guide will assist domestic courts in this respect.[137] Judge Pinto de Albuquerque concludes:[138]

> Justice for children, even summary and provisional justice, can only be done with a view to the entirety of the very tangible case at hand, ie of the actual circumstances of each child involved. Only an in-depth or 'effective' evaluation of the child's situation in the specific context of the return application can provide such justice. In layman's terms, *Neulinger and Shuruk* is alive and well. It was and remains a decision laying down valid legal principles, not an ephemeral and capricious act of 'judicial compassion'.

These views expressed are, of course, only the view of one judge and the majority in the *X v Latvia* decision did not agree with this viewpoint. Yet despite the ECtHR reaffirming that the Hague Convention is compliant with Article 3 CRC, the concerns expressed in relation to the way domestic courts apply the exceptions to return in Hague proceedings which consequently fail to 'defend' the best interests of the child cannot be overlooked. The following section considers how the assessment of the child's best interests is affected in some cases by the domestic courts prioritising the Hague Convention's commitment to the two public policy factors of deterrence and comity with nations which, the analysis will demonstrate, can often be upheld as having equal importance to the interests of the individual child.

[136] Ibid pages 44–45 (no paragraph numbers provided).
[137] Guide to Good Practice on Article 13(1)(b) – available at https://www.hcch.net/en/publications-and-studies/details4/?pid=7059 – pp 73–74.
[138] ibid page 48–49.

i. Comity

The 'comity with nations' policy of the Hague Convention refers to the notions of 'reciprocity' and judicial courtesy.'[139] Schuz,[140] writing on the topic, notes that while the meaning of 'comity' is not agreed amongst scholars,[141] it is entirely relevant to the Hague Convention. Its relevance 'underlies' the whole Convention because Contracting States are only required to return abducted children to other *Contracting* States. The Hague Convention's public policy priorities are seen in action through the unquestionable acceptance that the State requesting the child's return is in a position to protect the mother from harm and in turn also the child's interests.[142] This prioritisation is seen in the United States Hague Convention case of *Blondin v DuBois*,[143] where it was stated that 'comity is at the heart of the Hague Convention.' The judge went on to explain that the United States urges its courts to have confidence in the ability of the French legal system to protect its own children as, in a reverse case, the United States would expect the French courts to have the same confidence in the United States Courts and system of child protection. Failure to accord such confidence to other states would, the court said, seriously erode the system of trust and cooperation essential to the functioning of the Hague Convention.[144]

The Hague Convention's commitment is also seen in its primary objective as set out in Article 1, to promote the prompt return of abducted children and to ensure the rights of custody and access under the law of one Contracting State are respected in other Contracting States. The Hague Convention seeks to uphold the rule of law, and seek justice between the parents by preventing the abducting parent from gaining an advantage from his or her wrongdoing.[145] Thus, as Baroness Hale set out, the court is entitled to weigh in the balance the general policy considerations underlying the 1980 Convention against the interests of the child in the individual case, which include not only the swift return of abducted children, but also comity between the Contracting States and respect for one another's judicial processes.[146] In this way, by forcing return without the best interests assessment, the Hague Convention is construed as parent-centred,[147] as the rights of custody

[139] For further detail on this topic, see Kristin Haugevik, 'Parental Child Abduction and the State: Identity, Diplomacy and the Duty of Care' (2018) 13 *The Hague Journal of Diplomacy* 1–21.

[140] Schuz (2013) (n 111) 126, 129–36.

[141] On the topic of comity, see Joel Paul, 'Comity in International Law' (1991) 32 *Harvard Journal of International Law* 1; James Fawcett and Janeen Carruthers, *Cheshire, North and Fawcett, Private International Law* (OUP, 2008) 36–7.

[142] *Re M (Abduction: Intolerable Situation)* [2000] 1 FLR 930.

[143] 189 F3d 240, 248 (2nd Cir 1999).

[144] Karin Wolfe, 'A Tale of Two States: Success and Failures of the 1980 Hague Convention on the Civil Aspects of International Child Abduction in the United States and Germany' (2000) 33 *New York University Journal of International Law and Politics* 317.

[145] Perez-Vera (n 110); See also Schuz (2013) (n 111) 97.

[146] Baroness Hale (n 120); Confirmed also by the House of Lords, in *Re M (Children) (Abduction: Rights of Custody)* [2007] UKHL 55 paras 42–43, 46.

[147] Schuz (2013) (n 111) 124.

of the left-behind parents appear to take more precedence than the rights of the abducted child. Of course, this issue is not solely attributable to the Hague Convention, as Article 3 CRC is worded to allow competing interests to supersede the best interests of the abducted child. The use of the expression '*a* primary consideration', rather than '*the* primary consideration', points to the fact that the best interests of the child are a 'consideration of first importance among other considerations, but do not have absolute priority among other considerations.'[148]

ii. Deterrence

The automatic return policy is intended to deter other abductions from occurring, and its significance to the overall aim of the Convention is discussed in the Explanatory Report to the Convention. The report states 'one effective way of deterring him [abductor] would be to deprive his actions of any practical or judicial consequences.'[149] In this way, the Hague Convention approves the automatic return of children, even though the effect of the deterrence objective is not measurable.[150] Schuz argues that on this basis the Hague Convention is not entirely children's rights friendly and is in some respects inconsistent with the CRC. She asserts:

> … a children rights approach would marginalise the objective of deterring child abduction because the public interest, even where it is designed to protect children as a class cannot as a matter of principle justify violating the individual child's rights. This point is strengthened by the fact that it has not been proven and probably cannot be proven that the Hague Abduction Convention or indeed any other mechanism actually deters potential abductors. Moreover, a summary return mechanism, which is the most likely method of successful deterrence, is difficult to reconcile with both protection and rights because it does not allow time for the courts to check properly whether the return is likely to be harmful to the child or to breach the child's rights in some other way.[151]

The argument is compelling, yet the data on the Hague Convention Islamic state of Morocco provides a possible contrary perspective. The 2015 review of Hague cases confirms that of the eight abductions to Morocco that year; the mother was the abductor in five cases (63 per cent) the father in two (25 per cent) and one case involved another family member.[152] Let us compare these statistics with existing data that affirms in abductions to non-Hague Convention Islamic law countries, fathers undertake the majority of abductions (80–89 per cent)[153] and, contrastingly,

[148] Detrick (1999) (n 98) 91.
[149] Perez-Vera (n 110) para 16.
[150] For a discussion on this topic, see AE Anton, 'The Hague Convention on International Child Abduction, 30 *Int'l & Comp LQ* (1981) 537, 543; see also Perez-Vera (n 110) para 25.
[151] Rhona Schuz 'The Hague Child Abduction Convention and Children's Rights' (2002) 12 *Transnational Law & Contemporary Problems* 393, 396–7.
[152] Hague Survey (2015) Annex 3.
[153] Kruger's survey reveals fathers are the main abductors to North and Central Africa and certainly to the Middle East, where they are responsible for 80% of the 25 abductions she examined to Middle

in abductions between Hague Convention states, it is mothers who undertake the majority of abductions (70 per cent).[154] It appears that the statistics on Morocco's Hague cases point to some potential deterrent effect of the Hague Convention, as where the Hague Convention overrides domestic Islamic law, the proportion of fathers abducting is lowered and potentially the incentive to abduct to Islamic law countries also diminishes. The finding is treated with caution, however, because (i) the sample size is small, (ii) this is only the first cycle of data in which information is available on Morocco's Hague cases and (iii) from the perspective of the abducted child's Article 3 CRC right, the rights of the individual child should not be disregarded in the hope that it might potentially deter other abductions.

The analysis above highlights that the criterion under GC14 to 'apply the interpretation which most effectively serves the child's best interests' is not entirely satisfied under either legal system, as both legal regimes prioritise the interpretation which serves the interests of others over the best interests of the child to some extent. It is noteworthy, therefore, that the Hague Conference issued guidance in 2020 on how domestic courts should apply the Article 13(1)(b) Hague Convention defence, 'The HCCH Convention of 25 October 1980 on the Civil Aspects of International Child Abduction – Part VI – Article 13(1)(b)'[155] ('2020 Guide'). The document provides guidance on the appropriate application of Article 13(1)(b) and explains[156] 'through the enumerated exceptions, the Convention recognises that the non-return of a wrongfully removed or retained child can sometimes be justified. The general concept that a prompt return is in the best interests of the child can therefore be rebutted in the individual case where an exception is established.' As there are now more than 100 Contracting States that are required to interpret the Article 13(1)(b) defence, clarification and guidance of this nature from the Hague Conference is likely to prove highly effective. This is particularly so on the topic of domestic abuse which is a feature in some of the cases discussed earlier in this chapter, in which domestic responses to familial abuse vary and are not always appropriately enforced (see discussion in chapter 5). On this issue, the 2020 Guide suggests that the courts can regard the protective measures in the requesting State as ineffective where the left-behind parent has repeatedly violated protection orders, which may place the child at grave risk of physical or psychological harm.[157] The 2020 Guide provides extensive recommendations

Eastern countries; Kruger (n 92) 78–79; Chiancone et al whose survey drew responses from ninety-seven parents, of which 25 per cent of abductions were to Muslim countries, found that mothers were more likely to take their children to Latin America, and fathers were more likely to take their children to the Middle East; Janet Chiancone and others, *Issues In Resolving Cases of International Child Abduction by Parents* (United States Department of Justice, 2001). These statistics are similar to those found in the author's study, where all 29 cases of abduction were undertaken by the Muslim parent and 26 of these by the father (89.65 per cent). The findings demonstrate that despite the changing statistics globally, the proportion of male abductors in relation to abduction to Islamic law countries remains consistent.

[154] Hague Survey (2015) 15–16.

[155] Available at https://assets.hcch.net/docs/225b44d3-5c6b-4a14-8f5b-57cb370c497f.pdf.

[156] Ibid para 23–24

[157] Ibid para 59.

to domestic courts seised with a Hague application and addresses some of the ECtHR's criticism (see discussion above) on how domestic courts respond to allegations raised within Hague Convention proceedings on matters that could fall within the exceptions to return.

The case law examined demonstrates that the Hague Convention has the scope to allow the domestic courts to uphold the abducted child's Article 3 CRC rights as intended by the CRC. The Hague Conference's 2020 Guide, which more clearly sets out the circumstances in which the defence to return is permitted, could provide the courts with greater confidence to appropriately weigh up the best interests of the abducted child against the Convention's aim to prevent the abducting parent from benefitting from his or her actions. The 2020 Guide provides specific examples of the defences most often raised by abducting parents in the Hague precisely with reference to case law via INCADAT. The recent guidance will provide domestic courts in the vast number of Contracting States the resources to apply the Hague Convention in conformance with child rights principles under the CRC.

The theoretical discussion in this chapter has challenged the presumption that the application of the Hague Convention will uphold the best interests of the abducted child. The 2020 Guidance will mitigate some of the problems identified in the analysis, once the guidance takes effect within the wide sphere of Contracting States. Before arriving at a definitive conclusion, it will be helpful to identify how Article 3 CRC would actually apply in practice. The next section, therefore, speculates on how the four case studies in this chapter are likely to have been resolved under the Hague Convention.

C. How the Four Case Studies Would be Resolved in Hague Convention Proceedings

The proceedings before the Islamic courts resulted in all four children being ordered to remain with the abducting parent in the Islamic law country. If the Hague Convention framework is applied to the case studies, the outcomes could differ in the following way:

i. The Policy of Automatic Return

So long as the left-behind parent initiates proceedings within 12 months of the abduction, the Hague Convention's policy of automatic return would apply.

Jamal's situation is legally termed as 'unlawful retention' rather than abduction. Jamal's father did not abduct him during a contact visit like Yasmin and Samir, but he was 'unlawfully retained' after a period of agreed contact. Notwithstanding the technical difference, the Hague Convention applies in cases of unlawful retention equally as it does to cases of abduction. In *Re H (Abduction: Custody Rights)*[158] it was explained that a wrongful retention occurs when a child is not returned at the end of a period of time which it has been agreed he will spend abroad, but can also occur when after a lawful removal there is a refusal to comply with a request to return the child made by a person who has acquired rights of custody subsequent to the removal. Thus it does not matter that Jamal's father was acting lawfully when he travelled to the Islamic law country with Jamal. The act of retaining Jamal after the agreed date makes the retention unlawful and the Hague Convention effective.

The abducting parents could seek to argue any of the defences to the return application. Based on the information provided on their abductions above, it is unlikely that any of the exceptions to return would apply. The abducting parents' concerns about Samir and Daniel not being raised as Muslims, Yasmin living with her step-father, or Jamal residing in another country, would not satisfy the Article 13(1)(b) or Article 20 criteria.

At ages four and two, Samir and Daniel would be presumed too young to express their views on whether or not they should be returned to the UK. Yasmin and Jamal, both aged seven, could be asked their opinions on return as part of Hague Convention proceedings. The case law in some countries illustrates that the courts in Hague Convention proceedings also consider children aged seven too young to express a view on such matters. The discourse surrounding the age of maturity and the process by which the children's views are ascertained is explored in more detail in chapter 4.

Based on the information provided, it is likely that an order for return would be made in respect of all four children to be returned to the United Kingdom. The courts in the UK could then undertake a detailed best interests assessment of the children's situation if any proceedings were initiated upon their arrival in the UK. Though the strict interpretation of the Hague Convention would result in return orders, individuals do respond differently to legal proceedings, and data illustrates that some abducting parents decide to settle cases outside of court, mediate or refuse to comply with court orders. Kruger's survey reveals that the Hague Convention was applied in 73 cases in which the child had been abducted from Belgium to another country. The outcome was known in 49 cases. Of these, the child returned in 33 cases (67.3 per cent), but did not return in 16 cases (32.7 per cent). In 19 cases (35.8 per cent) a settlement was reached, in one case (1.9 per cent) the applicant parent abandoned proceedings, and in seven cases (13.2 per cent) no solution was found.[159] Therefore while the Hague Convention aims to apply a legal solution to the abduction, it is noted that other factors such as the costs of funding litigation, engaging the abducting parent to participate in proceedings and difficulties in enforcing return orders are all factors that affect how the law is implemented.

[158] [1991] 2 AC 476.
[159] Kruger (n 91) 115.

ii. Primary Carer Abductions

Daniel would be ordered to return, irrespective of the fact that Daniel was abducted by his mother and, at age two, Daniel might suffer harm if separated from his primary carer. In *C v C (Minor: Abduction: Rights of Custody Abroad)*[160] the English court did not accept the argument that a child in a situation similar to that of Daniel's should not be returned if his mother is unable or unwilling to accompany him. The court took this approach in order to prevent the Article 13(1)(b) grave risk of harm exception from becoming an easy escape route from the Hague Convention's automatic return mechanism.

Daniel's mother could raise the Article 13(1)(b) defence, arguing that there was a grave risk that Daniel's return would expose him to physical or psychological harm or otherwise place Daniel in an intolerable situation. Daniel told us his mother was concerned for their safety after she was made to live with and look after his older half-brother, who was a drug addict. In this situation, the court may take the view that it is up to the authorities in the United Kingdom to protect Daniel, his sister and mother. Daniel's father could provide undertakings that he will provide financial support for Daniel's mother on her return, for food and accommodation. The undertakings are not always enforceable, however, and so Daniel's mother might not feel she can return to the situation described.[161] It is questionable whether Daniel's return to the United Kingdom, either with or without his mother, would serve his best interests. There is a degree of discretion afforded to the courts in Hague Convention proceedings (see above analysis in section A and the cases of *Re M* and *Re S*)[162] and so whether or not the court would accept Daniel's mother's Article 13(1)(b) defence is uncertain.

The way in which the Hague Convention determines it is in the best interests of Daniel to be returned, potentially without his mother, to a precarious situation, could be in breach of his Article 3 CRC rights, and it is on this issue of primary carer abductions that the Hague Convention is particularly criticised. While the proportion of the sample of this study of primary carer abductions is small, (below 11 per cent of cases examined), globally, the percentage of abductions undertaken by mothers between Hague Convention States is approximately 70 per cent of cases, and so this situation is more common than appears in this analysis. A more detailed exploration of primary carer abductions is undertaken in chapter 5.

[160] [1989] 2 All ER 465; See also *Starr v Starr* (1999) SLT 335.

[161] Butler-Sloss LJ explained undertakings are accepted to make the return of children easier and provide for the necessities such as a roof over their heads and adequate maintenance. They are intended however, to have a short life, ie until the court of the child's habitual residence becomes seized of the proceedings. The court should be careful not in any way to intrude upon the functions of the court of habitual residence, with undertakings being applied with care; In *Re M (Minors) (Abduction: Undertakings)* [1995] 1 FLR 1021, CA.

[162] *Re M (Abduction: Intolerable Situation)* [2000] 1 FLR 930 and *Re S (A Child) (Abduction: Rights of Custody)* [2012] UKSC 10.

iii. Imprisonment

If the abducting parent returns to the United Kingdom, she or he is at risk of imprisonment of up to seven years pursuant to the Child Abduction Act 1984. The risk applies in the case of Samir, Yasmin and Daniel. Jamal's case differs as his situation is legally termed as 'unlawful retention' rather than abduction and currently the criminal law does not apply to cases of unlawful retention. Jamal's father could, therefore, return to the United Kingdom without the threat of imprisonment. The anomaly in the law is identified by the Law Commission, which has made recommendations for the act of unlawful retention to also become a criminal offence, and for the term of seven years' imprisonment to be increased to 14 years to become a greater deterrent.[163]

There are three available defences to the criminal offence: (a) If the abducting parent can provide evidence, the left-behind parent consented to the travel; (b) If the abducting parent took all reasonable steps to communicate to the left-behind parent his or her intention to remove the child but was unable to do so; (c) The left-behind parent unreasonably refused consent although this defence does not apply if the left-behind parent had a Residence or Child Arrangements Order for the child. It appears that none of the three defences applies in the case studies. Daniel's mother could be imprisoned if she returned with Daniel, and the case of *Re L (Abduction: Pending Criminal Proceedings)*[164] confirms that this possibility in and of itself does not provide Daniel's mother with a defence in Hague Convention proceedings against returning Daniel. So the threat of Daniel's mother being imprisoned does not constitute a 'grave risk of harm' necessarily to satisfy the Article 13(1)(b) exception to return.

What is the likelihood of actual imprisonment for the abducting parents in the four case studies examined? The numbers of criminal convictions in the UK for cross-border parental abduction are not readily available.[165] Nonetheless, it is reported[166] that one-fifth of child abductions recorded by the police are committed by a parent or family member, almost a third of these (66 cases in 2011–12) are cases of international parental child abduction.[167] There are very few criminal law reports available to access concerning parental child abduction to Islamic

[163] Law Commission, *Simplification of Criminal Law: Kidnapping and Related Offences* (Law Com No 355, 2014).

[164] [1999] 1 FLR 433.

[165] Section 4(2) of the Child Abduction Act 1984 confirms no prosecution for this offence can be instituted except by, or with the consent of Director of Public Prosecutions, which could affect the number of prosecutions pursued. Though note the Law Commission's report affirms that the guidance not to proceed with prosecuting parents after the case of *Re C* [1991] 2 FLR 252, [1991] Fam Law 522 no longer stands since *R v Kayani* [2011] EWCA Crim 2871 and so it is anticipated more prosecutions will be initiated; Law Commission, *Simplification of Criminal Law: Kidnapping and Related Offences* (Law Com No 355, 2014) 44.

[166] Geoff Newiss and Mary-Ann Traynor, *Taken: A Study of Child Abduction in the UK* (PACT and the Child Exploitation Protection Centre, 2013).

[167] The study by PACT identifies 66 cases of international parental child abduction by 'crime type' involving 88 children, ibid.

law countries. The decisions of the lower (first instance) criminal law courts are not routinely published in the official law reports and only the decisions of the criminal law cases that are heard at the appeal level are available. A detailed judgment is, however, available in the law reports of two UK cases[168] that were joint appeals against custodial sentences for the criminal offence of parental child abduction. The first defendant, Kayani, took his two sons to Pakistan in 2000 and returned with them to the UK in 2009, waiting until they were aged 16 and 17. The children refused to have any contact with their mother upon return, the abduction clearly having had a detrimental impact upon their relationship. Subsequently, the father was sentenced to five years imprisonment for two counts of child abduction, being allowed a 20 per cent reduction to the sentence for an early guilty plea. The second defendant, Solliman, abducted his children for seven years: he took his three children to Egypt in 2002 and returned with them to the UK in 2009. Solliman was sentenced to three years' imprisonment for three counts of child abduction. In both cases the children were reported to be distressed by their father's imprisonment, and so the issue for the criminal appeal court was whether the interests of the children should lead to a reduction in sentence despite the fact that a serious offence had been committed and sentencing should serve as a deterrent. The appellate court determined that in both cases the mothers and children had suffered greatly as a result of abduction thus any further suffering caused by the prison sentence was a direct result of the father's actions and consequently did not justify a reduction in sentence. Both appeals were dismissed and the sentences of five years imprisonment for Kayani and three years for Solliman were upheld.

In a further case, involving abduction by a mother to a Hague Convention state, the court considered again whether it was appropriate to imprison an abducting parent. In the criminal law appeal case of *RH*[169] the parents had separated and their 8-year-old daughter lived with the mother. After a period of no contact with the father, the family court awarded the father a contact order. Soon after, the mother abducted the child from the UK, first to Cyprus, then on to Egypt, the UAE and finally the USA. After a request by the father, the mother was ordered by the English Family Court to return to the UK. The mother returned to the UK to participate in the family court proceedings without the child; the child was left in the care of the mother's relative in the USA. The mother was arrested upon her return to the UK and the child was later returned to the UK, having been away for three months. The mother pleaded guilty to the offence of parental abduction and the criminal court imposed a custodial sentence for a term of one year eight months. The mother appealed, claiming the sentence was excessive and her time in custody was adversely impacting the child's welfare. The court, taking into consideration the guidance on children's welfare when sentencing parents for any offence (guidance in the criminal law case of *R v Petherick*),[170] determined that there was

[168] A search for convictions under the Child Abduction Act 1984 identifies the cases *of R v Kayani and Solliman* [2011] EWCA Crim 2871 concerning imprisonment of fathers for abducting children from the UK to Pakistan.

[169] [2016] EWCA Crim 1754, [2017] 1 Cr App R (S) 23 (165).

[170] [2012] EWCA Crim 2214.

'nothing excessive about the sentence imposed, even when the interests of A [the child] are put into the scales'.[171]

Whilst the official law reports only detail cases heard by the senior appellate courts,[172] as part of this analysis the author also ascertains information through examining media reports for information on abducting parents being imprisoned by the English courts. Analysis of the media reports suggests that there are a greater number of abducting parents being imprisoned than appears to be the case from the official law reports. The media, for example, reports a father who abducted his then 3-month-old daughter to Libya during a contact visit was imprisoned in November 2014 for six and a half years when he returned to the UK without her.[173] Accomplices to the offence of parental abduction are also reported to be convicted under criminal law. In 2005 Mustapha Abushim was convicted of conspiracy to kidnap for his part in the abduction of children by their father, who took them to Libya during a contact visit.[174] The fact that the authorities now recognise the severity of the offence and the harm it can cause is illustrated in another case in 2014, in which the UK police arranged for the extradition of an abducting father from Norway to England, so that he could be tried at the Reading Crown Court. The man had abducted his two children from the UK to Pakistan in 1998, and the offence had been committed sixteen years earlier.[175] He was sentences to seven years imprisonment.

There are also cases where the abducting parent is imprisoned within the context of family law proceedings, suggesting there may be many more parents imprisoned as a result of the abduction than appears from criminal law reports.[176] Abducting parents who return to the UK without the abducted child can be imprisoned for contempt of court[177] for failing to abide by a family court order to return the child. For an individual to be found guilty of contempt, the left-behind parent must prove to the court that the respondent deliberately failed to comply with the return order issued by the family court. Despite the proceedings being issued in the family court, the evidential threshold that must be satisfied is the higher criminal law standard, ie, that the defendant is guilty beyond reasonable doubt, rather than the lower evidential threshold in civil (family) law proceedings which would require evidence that the defendant is guilty 'on the balance of probabilities.' This higher threshold was crossed in a case where a father who unlawfully retained his child in Egypt in

[171] *RH* (n 169) [26].

[172] And so cases decided by the lower English criminal courts that are not subsequently appealed by the defendant or the prosecution are unlikely to feature in the law reports.

[173] Simon Keegan, 'Dad Jailed for Kidnapping Daughter from her Mother and Taking her to Libya' (Mirror, 10.11.14) available at www.mirror.co.uk/news/uk-news/dad-jailed-kidnapping-daughter-mother-4605929.

[174] Dan Grimmer, 'Abduction torment of Norwich Mum' (Easton Daily Press, 03.11.10) available at: https://www.edp24.co.uk/news/crime/abduction-torment-of-norwich-mum-461912.

[175] Paul Miles, 'Father jailed for seven years after abducting his two children' (*Slough Express*, 05.09.14) available at www.sloughexpress.co.uk/news/slough/70485/Father-jailed-for-seven-years-after.html.

[176] See also Frances Gibb, 'Judges Using Contempt of Court Laws to Punish Parents Who Abduct Children' (*The Times*, 02.09. 2017).

[177] Contempt of Court Act 1981: interfering with the administration of justice can be criminal or civil and is punishable by imprisonment of up to two years or a fine of an unlimited sum.

2011 was imprisoned in January 2012 for a term of two years for being in contempt of court when he refused to abide by the family court order to return the child to the UK. At the end of that sentence period, Mr Justice Cobb ruled the father had committed fresh breaches of the family court order to return the abducted children to the UK and by failing to notify the court of the child's whereabouts. The court ordered that the abducting father would serve a further 12 months in custody.[178] Similarly, in a case of abduction to Pakistan, a father was imprisoned for contempt of court in April 2010 after repeatedly ignoring High Court orders to reveal the abducted child's whereabouts. The child was located by the police in Pakistan three years later and returned to her mother in the UK. Upon the child's return to the UK, the father applied to be released from prison. In hearing the father's application, the court ordered that the father could not take credit for the abducted child's return to the UK and so he must remain in custody.[179] A further contempt of court case was brought before the English courts concerning an abduction to Oman. In the application before the court, the judge heard that an eleven-year-old girl and her eight-year-old-brother had been taken to Oman by their father four years earlier.[180] The father returned to the UK without the children and refused to reveal the children's whereabouts to the left-behind mother or the authorities. The father was sentenced to a four-year prison sentence for the criminal offence of parental abduction, being required to serve two years in prison and the remaining two years on parole/licence in the community. Upon the father's release from prison for the criminal law offence, the mother made an application to the family court for the father's committal to prison for breaching family court orders to return the children to the UK. These decisions suggest that imprisonment does not always persuade the abducting parent to return the child. In fact, the data suggests the courts have had to resort to threatening to deport the abducting parent after the term of imprisonment ends, in the hope that this may encourage the abducting father to arrange for the abducted child's return to the UK.[181]

The data illustrates that the courts go to great lengths to secure the return of children abducted from the UK to Islamic law countries, whether that is through the criminal law process or the contempt of court provisions available to the family courts. Data from the author's study also highlights a further category of cases that do not result in conviction or imprisonment, notwithstanding efforts by the police to prosecute abducting parents on their return to the UK. Thus the prospect of a

[178] Author unknown, 'Fugitive dad in Leeds child-snatch case has jail term extended' (*Yorkshire Post*, 16.01.13) available at www.yorkshirepost.co.uk/news/crime/fugitive-dad-leeds-child-snatch-case-has-jail-term-extended-1873638.

[179] Author Unknown, 'Father Who Held Abducted Daughter in Pakistan For Three Years Ordered to Stay In Jail' (Standard, 14.01.13) available at www.standard.co.uk/news/crime/father-who-held-abducted-daughter-in-pakistan-for-three-years-ordered-to-stay-in-jail-8451519.html.

[180] Frances Gibb, 'Judges jail parents who abduct children for contempt of court' (*The Times*, 02.09.17) available at www.thetimes.co.uk/article/judges-jail-parents-who-abduct-children-for-contempt-of-court-28v52qzgq.

[181] Jenny Rees 'Cardiff Mum's Plea After Daughter Abducted By Dad In 2012' (BBC, 25.09.18) available at www.bbc.co.uk/news/uk-wales-45601290.

trial for returning abducting parents is very real. A left-behind mother reports that the father who abducted his daughter from the UK to Egypt was found not guilty of the offence in the criminal law courts;

> The Police lost the case at court because the evidence was not enough to prove dad guilty. The police made mistakes during the case because it was after two years and they'd been calling me for updates. They should have collected more evidence and not rely on me to provide all the details. They pressured me. I was not doing him for abduction; it was the police. I was just the witness and put in the stand. The jury believed the children's grandfather had cancer so that was the reason he took my daughters to Egypt. When the police called after the hearing and said we're sorry, we lost, it felt like the whole world was collapsing. I risked my life going to Egypt and nothing has gone from them [the Police].[182]

In reflecting therefore on the likelihood of criminal proceedings for the returning abducting parent, it is clear that parents who abduct their children to non-Hague Islamic law states risk prosecution on return to the UK, as do parents who have abducted children from the UK to other (non-Islamic law) Hague Convention states.[183] It is noteworthy that parents who have abducted their child from the UK to another Hague Convention state are also at risk of imprisonment, despite the return mechanism under the Hague Convention being available in those cases.[184] This is seen in the example of a father who abducted his son from the UK to Turkey.[185] Notwithstanding the fact that Turkey is a Hague Convention treaty partner with the UK, where the automatic return process was available to the left-behind mother, the father was sentenced to 20 months' imprisonment in 2013. The child was in Turkey for three and a half months before the mother was able to locate him and bring him back to the UK. The data also highlights that custodial sentences are imposed regardless of whether it is the father who abducts the child, or the mother. A mother was imprisoned for abducting her six-year-old daughter from the UK to Turkey. The child lived with her father in the UK, and during a contact visit, the mother travelled with the child to Turkey. The court accepted the abduction was 'planned' as the mother had sold her house in the UK and enrolled the child into a Turkish school. Two months after the abduction, the

[182] Participant 13M, interview 10/09/16 (on file with the author).

[183] An Indian father was sentenced to three years and four months for abducting his daughter from his former partner in the UK and leaving the child in a boarding school in India. The child had not returned to the UK at the time of the conviction in 2015. Press Trust of India, 'Indian-origin man jailed for abduction, cruelty of daughter' (*Business Standard*, 07.12.2015) available at www.business-standard.com/article/pti-stories/indian-origin-man-jailed-for-abduction-cruelty-of-daughter-115120701240_1.html; See also the committal case for the Hague partner State of Poland: *Sanchez v Oboz* [2015] EWHC 611 (Fam) where the child was made a Ward of court and the father ordered to return his daughter to the UK from Poland. The father was committed to prison for 12 months for his failure to return the child.

[184] See discussion above in case of *RH* [2016] EWCA Crim 1754, [2017] 1 Cr App R (S) 23 (165).

[185] Joe Nimmo, 'Man Jailed For Taking Son to Turkey in Custody Row' (*Oxford Mail*, 24.05.2014) available at www.oxfordmail.co.uk/news/yourtown/oxford/11234491.Man_jailed_for_taking_son_to_Turkey_in_custody_row/.

mother arranged a brief visit to the UK in order to organise her financial affairs and was at that stage arrested at the airport for the criminal law offence of parental child abduction. Overall the child had been retained in Turkey for a period of two months and for this offence the mother was sentenced to twelve months' imprisonment.[186]

It would be helpful to review the reasons for the court's decision in these cases, particularly as the child was reunited with the left-behind parent at the time of the criminal law proceedings. The imposition of a custodial sentence was not necessary to secure the return of the abducted child in these two cases concerning abductions to the Hague Convention state of Turkey. Unfortunately, the information is not available, as the media reports do not set out detailed legal reasoning as would be the case if reported in an official law report, and so it is unclear from the data collected why the court adopted the approach that it did. Access to a transcript of the judgments in these cases would be helpful to the analysis to identify whether (i) imprisonment was deemed necessary in each case because enforcement of a return order was made difficult, and (ii) if abducting parents who are not the child's custodial parent are routinely imprisoned, even in cases where the Hague Convention applies. The case of *RH* discussed above illustrates that the UK Court of Appeal does not differentiate between abductions undertaken by mothers or fathers. Nor does it make a difference that the abduction was for a period of three months only, or that at the time of the abduction, the mother was awarded an order from the family court confirming the child would remain living with her. The criminal court was also not concerned that the abduction had taken place between two Hague Convention states, and so there was a civil law remedy available to secure the child's return from the USA to the UK. The custodial sentence of one year and eight months' imprisonment was regarded by the appeal court as entirely proportionate, taking into account the child's welfare and, in fact, the court indicated that the sentence could have been longer. In this case, the mother was reported to have been dishonest with the authorities seeking the child's return to the UK and the mother had abducted the child to thwart the child's contact with the father. The decisions confirm that the sentences imposed are to serve as a deterrent to any would-be abducting parents. It is also worth reflecting on the discussion above on the individual and collective best interests of children. When the courts decide to imprison (primary carer) parents so the law can serve as a deterrent measure for would-be abductors, this situation, as is seen in the case of *RH*, results in the rights of individual children whose parents are imprisoned being sacrificed for the rights of children as a group. The idea will be considered further in the context of primary-carer abductions in chapter 5 below.

[186] Kelly Williams, 'Mum Breaks Down in Tears after Being Jailed For Abducting Her Daughter' (*Daily Post*, 04.06.19) available at www.dailypost.co.uk/news/north-wales-news/mum-breaks-down-tears-after-16375254.

With a high number of cases of parental abduction between Hague Convention States cases each year, it would be unlikely that imprisonment is ordered in every abduction case. Yet with long prison sentences for even short periods of abduction, it seems that the courts will imprison the abducting parent for the offence of abduction if there is a custody order in favour of the left-behind parent. The gaps in information highlight that further research is needed in this area, as imprisonment of a parent will impact upon the child's opportunity for contact with both parents, and consequently the child's Article 9 CRC rights.

It is also worth noting here that the risk of imprisonment does not, according to the Hague Conference's 2020 Guide,[187] satisfy the threshold of 'grave risk of harm' to the child. Consequently, in cases like Daniel's, the 2020 Guide affirms Daniel's mother is unlikely to be successful in pleading the Article 13(1)(b) exception to return based solely on the risk of imprisonment upon return, even if this will result in Daniels' separation from his primary carer.

iv. Post-Return Contact

Return under the Hague Convention is intended to reverse the effects of the abduction for the abducted child, but in this type of situation, where the abducting parent is at risk of imprisonment, the return might not achieve the desired outcome.

This risk of imprisonment is sufficient enough to deter an abducting parent from returning to the UK. The fact that Samir and Yasmin's father would possibly not return to the UK because of the risk of prosecution means that once the children return without their abducting parent, (a) no domestic proceedings are likely to be initiated post-return, and so the English court is not required to undertake an individualised best interests assessment as is envisaged by the Hague Convention, and (b) Samir and Yasmin's contact with their father will be affected. Contact in person will not be an option but, if accommodated, communication of sorts could be maintained through telephone/video call.

In the event proceedings are initiated by the abducting parent for contact with the abducted child post-return, the court will assess the risk of further abduction. Whether or not the courts think that contact is in the child's best interests depends very much upon the family circumstances and the child's experiences of the abduction. The courts also factor in the risk of a further abduction, particularly if the child's return was difficult to achieve. A case heard by the English court in 2017, *B and C (Change of Names: Parental Responsibility: Evidence)* illustrates the significance placed upon this risk by the court.[188] In this case, the father abducted the children from the UK to Iran. The mother was then able to clandestinely re-abduct the children from Iran, and as Mr Justice Cobb states 'she was assisted by

[187] n 155 at para 67.
[188] [2017] EWHC 3250 (Fam).

the abduction team of the Foreign and Commonwealth Office and by the British Embassy in Turkey.' The English court accepted the mother's concerns about the father's threats to re-abduct the children and ordered that the children live with the mother, and have no contact with the father. The court also decided that the children's names could be changed to prevent the father from being able to locate them in the future.

Though this case may not apply in the hypothetical application of the Hague Convention framework as it relates to a non-Hague Convention Islamic law country, the outcome indicates (a) the power of the domestic court to limit contact between the child and abducting parent post-return, (b) how the courts might view the risk of further abduction, and (c) the courts' concern regarding countries where enforcement of return orders might prove difficult because of the lack of procedures to give effect to the Hague implementation, discussed above in chapter 2.

Having examined the expression of the best interests of the child as a right and a principle, the analysis now turns to the final of the three concepts, to reflect on the principle of the best interests of the child under the Hague Convention as a rule of procedure.

V. Best Interests of the Child as a Rule of the Procedure

The expression of the best interests of the child being a primary consideration contains a rule of procedure which requires that the decision-maker assess the impact of a decision on a child or children and that such impact is given due importance.[189] General Comment 14 explains:

> Whenever a decision is to be made that will affect a specific child, an identified group of children or children in general, the decision-making process must include an evaluation of the possible impact (positive or negative) of the decision on the child or children concerned. Assessing and determining the best interests of the child require procedural guarantees. Furthermore, the justification of a decision must show that the right has been explicitly taken into account. In this regard, State Parties shall explain how the right has been respected in the decision, that is, what has been considered to be in the child's best interests; what criteria it is based on, and how the child's interests have been weighed against other considerations, be they broad issues of policy or individual cases.[190]

There are many similarities between the two legal processes examined – domestic Law in Islamic law countries and the Hague Convention – in how they both satisfy and fail to meet the criteria of Article 3 CRC. So while both regimes conform to the requirement in GC14 to explain how the best interests of children collectively

[189] Zermatten (n 66) 485; See also Couzens, (n 66) 525.
[190] GC14 para 6.

have been accommodated, neither legal framework has in place a process to assess the impact it will have on the individual child affected in every single case. The difficulty with both legal frameworks is that procedurally they are designed to consider and prioritise the interests of children as a homogenous group, rather than considering the interests and rights of the individual child, irrespective of the impact this can have on the abducted child. The Hague Convention presumes it is in the best interests of children that they return and Islamic law presumes that it is in the best interests of children that they live near the father. The extent to which Article 3 CRC permits the prioritisation of the best interests of children as a class, over and above the interests of the individual child is debatable. The reason for this is because while the language of Article 3 is content with children's best interests being 'a' and not 'the' primary consideration,[191] GC14[192] establishes more emphasis is to be placed by the Hague Convention upon the rights of the individual child:

> Potential conflicts between the best interests of a child, considered individually, and those of a group of children, or children in general, have to be resolved on a case-by-case basis, carefully balancing the interests of all parties and finding a suitable compromise. If harmonisation is not possible, authorities and decision-makers will have to analyse and weigh the rights of all those concerned, bearing in mind that the right of the child to have his best interests taken as a primary consideration means that the child's interests have high priority and not just one of several considerations. Therefore, a larger weight must be attached to what serves the child best.

Article 3 CRC, therefore, does not advocate the interests of individual children being compromised for the broader interests of abducted children as a group. Based on the GC14 requirement to assess their impact on individual children, it appears that both the Hague Convention and Islamic custody/abduction law have the mechanism in which to consider the individual child's circumstances. The Hague Convention defines how the abstract notion of the best interests of an individual child should be interpreted by the courts in Convention proceedings, ie, that it is in the best interests of the individual child to be returned to the country of their habitual residence for the courts there to decide on the child's custody arrangements unless, as in the case of Daniel discussed above, one of the exceptions in Articles 12, 13 or 20 of the Convention applies. Conversely, parental abduction cases are heard by the domestic courts in Islamic law countries as custody cases. And whilst Islamic custody law considers the best interests of the individual child concerned, the law is founded on presumptions about the interests of children generally – that children should be raised by a Muslim parent and live near the father. These assumptions of best interests do not satisfy the GC14 requirement for the impact of the legal framework on individual children to be assessed and would accordingly fail to apply the expression of best interests as a procedural rule within child abduction law. From the threshold of a children's

[191] For further discussion on this point see Schuz (2013) (n 111) 113.
[192] GC14 paras 37–40.

rights-based approach, the domestic legal framework within Islamic law countries does not convey the significance of the best interests of the individual child, such as in the case of Samir, Yasmin and Jamal discussed above.

VI. Conclusion

The analysis demonstrates that the domestic Islamic legal system sets out quite clearly what it presumes to be in the best interests of the child in domestic custody/abduction cases. The child's interests are pre-speculated, and while the law may be effective in a domestic setting, this is not the case when transposed to an international abduction context. In the global abduction context, the courts in Islamic law countries fail to consider the child's individual best interests, either as a substantive right, legal principle or procedural rule. In contrast, the Hague Convention at least allows for a best interests assessment to be undertaken in the courts of the child's habitual residence. And for some children, an interim best interests assessment occurs as part of the Hague proceedings if a defence to return is raised. The analysis in this chapter, therefore, demonstrates that it is better for abducted children that abduction proceedings occur under the Hague regime than under domestic law in Islamic law countries.

How the Hague Convention and domestic Islamic law articulate the best interests of the abducted child poses a problem for the young people in the sample. The courts in the Islamic law countries did not uphold the Article 3 CRC rights for any of the ten young people. The court could not undertake a best interests assessment as the criteria for the left-behind parent to be eligible for custody were not satisfied in any of the cases. All ten children were ordered to remain with the abducting parent in the Islamic law country as it was deemed to be in their best interests to continue living with a Muslim parent and raised in an Islamic environment, irrespective of what the young people themselves consider to have been in their best interests.

Conversely, the Hague Convention presumes return is in the best interests of all abducted children and would force the return of Daniel, aged two, if the defences to return his mother could raise were not accepted by the court. The juxtaposition of both legal processes is that they would achieve the exact opposite result. The only similarity is that the outcome under both legal frameworks leads to difficulty in the child maintaining contact with both parents.

The way in which the law on parental abduction assesses the best interests of the abducted child highlights the difficulty in deciding what is best for abducted children, and the factors that should be prioritised when making those decisions. The following chapter develops the discussion further, focuses on the voice of the child in abduction proceedings in Islamic law countries and considers the role of the child's views in determining his or her best interests.

4

The Child's Voice in Abduction Proceedings

Cross-border parental child abduction is a distinctive area through which to examine children's participation, as the terms 'child abduction' and 'child participation' appear contradictory and irreconcilable. In English law, a parent who takes a child to live in another country without the consent of a family court or the left-behind parent is treated in law as an abductor, *even if* the child consents to the travel.[1]

This chapter examines the extent to which the two legal regimes – domestic law in Islamic law countries and the Hague Abduction Convention – uphold the Article 12 CRC right of children to participate in cross-border parental child abduction proceedings. The analysis will contribute to answering the overarching question in this text of whether Islamic country accession to the Hague Convention will advance children's rights. The chapter will begin by setting out the Article 12 CRC right in a parental abduction context and then go on to critique if the right is upheld, first under domestic Islamic family law, followed by Hague Convention proceedings. The chapter will conclude with an analysis of which of the two frameworks is most likely to give effect to the voice of the abducted child.

I. An Abducted Child's Right to be *Heard*: Article 12 CRC

The right of the child to be heard in proceedings, and this includes abducted children engaged in abduction proceedings, is affirmed in Article 12 CRC which provides:

> 1. States Parties shall assure to the child who is capable of forming his or her own views the right to express those views freely in all matters affecting the child, the views of the child being given due weight in accordance with the age and maturity of the child.
> 2. For this purpose, the child shall, in particular, be provided the opportunity to be heard in any judicial and administrative proceedings affecting the child, either

[1] Child Abduction Act 1984.

> directly, or through a representative or an appropriate body, in a manner consistent with the procedural rules of national law.

The discussions during the drafting process of Article 12 highlight the significance placed upon this right by States,[2] where it was emphasised that the child's voice and the child's best interests are entwined.[3] In fact, at one stage, the right of the child to be heard and the right to have his or her best interests treated as a primary consideration were, in fact, drafted as one article.[4] After much debate on the technical effect of the language, the text for Article 12 was agreed as it is today. The concession resulted in the right to be heard expressed broadly, in that it does not specify the appropriate processes by which to hear the child's views, leaving this to national law: 'the child shall, in particular, be provided the opportunity to be heard … in a manner consistent with the procedural rules of national law.'

There is much debate about the facets of the Article 12 right, particularly relating to the age at which children's views should be heard, the process by which the child's views should be ascertained, and how much weight is to be accorded to the child's views.[5] The discourse surrounding the voice of the child has developed extensively since the introduction of the CRC. The developments in legal thought consider that the right should not be restricted to merely being heard, but should facilitate children's participation in proceedings in so far as the child wishes to engage. The UNCRC Committee recognises this development, expressing:

> A widespread practice has emerged in recent years, which has been broadly conceptualised as 'participation', although this term itself does not appear in the text of Article 12. This term has evolved and is now widely used to describe ongoing processes, which include information-sharing and dialogue between children and adults based on mutual respect, and in which children can learn how their views and those of adults are taken into account and shape the outcome of such processes.[6]

The right to participate, rather than merely being heard, is more in keeping with the children's rights-based approach, of which the principle of children's participation is an essential component.[7] A vast amount of research evidences the benefits arising from children's participation in matters affecting them, for both adults and children alike.[8] Children's rights academics argue that participation should not be

[2] *Legislative History of the Convention on the Rights of the Child* (Vol 1, Office of the United Nations High Commissioner for Human Rights, 2007) 437–44.

[3] See discussion by the CRC Committee in GC14 para 43–45.

[4] *Legislative History* (n 2) 437.

[5] Carol Smart, 'From Children's Shoes to Children's Voices' (2002) 40 *Family Court Review* 3, 307; Nicholas Wilson, 'The Ears of the Child in Family Proceedings' (2007) September *Family Law* 808; Judith Wallerstein and Tony Tanke, 'To Move Or Not To Move: Psychological and Legal Considerations in the Relocation of Children Following Divorce' (1996) 30 *Family Law Quarterly* 305.

[6] GC12 para 3.

[7] See discussion in chapter 1.

[8] Richard Warshak, 'Payoffs and Pitfalls of Listening to Children' (2003) 52 *Family Relations* 373; Judith Wallerstein and Joan Kelly, 'The Effects of Parental Divorce: The Adolescent Experience' in E Anthony and C Koupernik (eds), *The Child in His Family: Children At Psychiatric Risk* (Wiley, 1974).

limited to a tokenistic expression of the child's views but, instead, that Article 12 requires the child be allowed to participate meaningfully in proceedings,[9] or 'participation with a purpose' as is expressed by Liam Cairns.[10] Schuz suggests that any child-centred legislation requires separate representation for the child, to enable the child's interests to be represented separately to the parents'[11] and Daly goes further and argues that, where possible, mature children should be listened to and should determine the outcome, so long as it does not place them at risk of significant harm.[12] Daly takes the view that children should be assisted in making decisions themselves, to shift the focus from merely hearing children to actually seeking to uphold their autonomy, through what is referred to in Daly's discussion as a 'children's rights autonomy principle.' The principle would require that in legal decisions in which the child's best interests are the primary consideration, children should get to choose – if they wish – how they are involved in proceedings (process autonomy) and the outcome (outcome autonomy) unless it is likely that significant harm will arise from their wishes. So while there would still be room for adult discretion in a system that prioritises autonomy, Daly argues at least adults would have more explicit obligations to provide support to children, to clearly consider autonomy and to better justify overriding children's wishes. Daly's views demonstrate how the discourse on children's voice has developed since the introduction of the CRC, and the discussion below will demonstrate how the notion of children's autonomy in custody cases is analogous to the Islamic law viewpoint, in principle at least.

Participation in this context is viewed as being in the best interests of children, and correspondingly, a child's best interests cannot be determined without consideration of the child's views. Indeed the UNCRC Committee observes:[13] 'There can be no correct application of article 3 if the components of article 12 are not respected. Likewise, article 3 reinforces the functionality of article 12, facilitating the essential role of children in all decisions affecting their lives.' So building upon the discussion in the last chapter, it does not appear possible for children's best interests to be determined by a court, without first hearing from the abducted child in question.

A. General Comment 12 as a Framework for Analysis

The text of Article 12 has evolved as a result of the guidance issued by the UNCRC Committee in its General Comment No 12 on the right of the child to be heard in

[9] Helen Stalford, Kathryn Hollingsworth and Stephen Gilmore (eds), *Rewriting Children's Rights Judgments: From Academic Vision to New Practice* (Hart Publishing, 2017).

[10] Liam Cairns, 'Participation with Purpose' in John Davis and others, *Children, Young People and Social Inclusion: Participation for What?* (Policy Press, 2006).

[11] Rhona Schuz, *The Hague Child Abduction Convention* (Hart Publishing, 2013) 392 and see discussion on separate representation for abducted children below at III.D.

[12] Aoife Daly, *Children, Autonomy and the Courts* (Routledge, 2017) 14.

[13] General Comment No 12: *The Right of the Child to be Heard*, CRC/C/GC/12 (20 July 2009) para 74.

proceedings affecting him or her ('GC12').[14] GC12 develops Article 12 to recognise the child's right to participate, rather than merely be heard. The UNCRC Committee establishes in GC12 five stages states parties should adhere to in implementing the Article 12 right. The five stages are as follows: (A) *Preparation stage*: This stage asks states parties to ensure the child is given information about his or her right to express a view, and the option of communicating the view to the decision-maker directly or through a representative. It further recommends that the child is made aware of the consequences of any choice. (B) The *hearing stage* requires that the context in which a child is heard is enabling and encouraging. (C) The *stage of assessment* asks that the decision-makers practice of evaluating the child's capacity adheres to the guidance issued in GC12 (which is discussed below). At the *feedback stage* (D) states parties are expected to ensure the child is later informed of the weight accorded to his or her views. And finally, the *redress stage* (E) asks states parties to provide a remedy in legislation for children whose right to participate is disregarded or violated.

GC12 is not an uncontested provision, as it broadly specifies children's entitlement to participate, but equally restricts participation to an adults' assessment of a child's maturity. This perspective is criticised[15] by research that identifies that children of even very young ages can meaningfully participate in matters affecting them, and children of all ages can be assisted in understanding matters affecting them and expressing their views.[16] The interest and research in this area resulted in the development of other models of children's participation, alongside GC12. There is, for example, Roger Hart's 'ladder of participation'[17] and its adaptation by Harry Shier[18] as a model for enhancing children's participation. Shier labels his developed model as 'Pathways to Participation'. Sheir's framework enables organisations that seek to engage children to determine how effective their processes are through answering a series of questions.[19] The model illustrates how individuals and organisations can then progress to the next stage and so is a useful measure

[14] Ibid.

[15] Gerison Lansdown, *Promoting Children's Participation in Democratic Decision-Making* (UNICEF Innocenti Insight, 2001) 2–3; Ellen Garrison, 'Children's Competence to Participate in Divorce Custody Decision-Making' (1991) 20 *Journal of Clinical Child Psychology* 78; Gerison Lansdown, *Taking Part* (Institute for Public Policy Research, 1995); Gerison Lansdown, 'The Realisation of Children's Participation Rights' in Barry Percy-Smith, and Nigel Thomas (eds), *A Handbook of Children and Young People's Participation: Perspectives from Theory and Practice* (Routledge, 2009) 11; Gill Barn and Annie Franklin, 'Article 12 – Issues in Developing Children's Participation Rights' in Eugeen Verhellen (ed), *Monitoring Children's Rights* (Martinus Nijhoff, 1996).

[16] Priscilla Alderson and Virginia Morrow, *Ethics, Social Science Research and Consulting with Young People* (Barnardo's, 2004) 22.

[17] Roger Hart, *Children's Participation: From Tokenism to Participation* (UNICEF, Florence, 1992).

[18] Harry Shier 'Pathways to Participation: Openings, Opportunities and Obligations' (2001) 2 *Children & Society* 15, 107.

[19] Shier establishes five distinct stages of children's participation: 1. Children are listened to; 2. Children are supported in expressing their views; 3. Children's views are taken into account; 4. Children are involved in the decision-making process; 5. Children share power and responsibility for decision-making. From an organisational perspective, three stages of commitment are also identified at each level; these are openings, opportunities and obligations.

by which organisations/individuals can improve processes to enhance children's participation. The model developed by Laura Lundy[20] streamlines the process of children's participation further for those wishing to enhance children's participation by identifying the four pillars of 'Space, Voice, Audience and Influence.' Lundy's model of children's participation was developed to aid practitioners to meaningfully give effect to Article 12 CRC by focusing them on the four distinct but related elements of Article 12. In a child abduction context,[21] providing children with the necessary space to be heard would ideally require children to be in an environment where they feel comfortable to express their views. Voice focuses on the need to listen to children and put questions to them in a way that they can respond in their own voice. The third pillar is audience, requiring the listener to be an appropriate audience for the child, as children will respond to an audience which they feel understands and will listen to them. Finally, influence is important; children must know that what they say will have some influence on the outcome and that their views will be used respectfully.

Though each of the models has its own unique strengths, the analysis in this chapter will adopt the framework of GC12 as this is issued by the CRC Committee and is therefore in keeping with the children's rights-based approach adopted for this analysis.[22] This framework will be supported by Lundy's model, which guides how to give clear effect to Article 12 CRC, and reference shall be made to both throughout this chapter. The five stages of GC12 are adopted here as a measure by which to evaluate if, and to what extent, the child's right to participate is upheld in both the domestic law in Islamic law countries and the Hague Convention, and which of the two could most uphold the Article 12 right of the abducted child.

The chapter begins by introducing the three participants whose case studies will help to analyse the law in this chapter. Sections two to four then examine both legal frameworks under the scope of the GC12 guidance, to evaluate the extent to which they each uphold the Article 12 CRC right of the abducted child.

B. Introducing Sara, Aidan and Harris

i. *Sara*[23]

Sara's father is a national of an Islamic law country and her mother is English. After Sara's parents separated, the English court decided she would continue to

[20] Laura Lundy, '"Voice" is Not Enough: Conceptualising Article 12 of the United Nations Convention on the Rights of the Child' (2007) 33(6) *British Educational Research Journal* 927.

[21] See application of Lundy's model to the child abduction context by Mark Heneghan, 'The Voice of the Child in International Child Abduction Cases – Do Judges Have a Hearing Problem?' in *The Child's Voice – 15 years later: the Judge's Newsletter on International Child Protection* ((2018) 15 Hague Conference on Private International Law, 22) ('*The Child's Voice – 15 years later*').

[22] See chapter 1.

[23] Participant 35E, interview 29/05/16 (on file with the author).

live with her mother and have regular contact with her father. Sara's mother was fearful of abduction, and she asked the judge not to allow a long contact visit for fear Sara might be taken abroad. The English court did not accept the risk was sufficiently serious and granted Sara's father a contact visit for one week during the school holidays. During that week, instead of visiting a theme park as her father had promised, he took Sara (then aged ten) to his home country of Jordan. Sara explains:

> He [father] had me for a week, and my mum and my step-dad went on holiday abroad. He said we're going to go to a theme park, but we need to go onto a plane to get there. Which at the time I kind of thought – because you know like my mum always told me you should never get on a plane with your dad, but my dad was quite a, he wasn't like an angry man, he was quiet and hostile looking, but he was very stern. So even though I knew that I shouldn't be going with him on a plane I didn't know how to get out of that situation because, obviously, I was only ten so I just decided to believe him. We got on the plane, and he said that we were going to Jordon and I asked him how long we were going for, and he said just two weeks, and I was like okay and then next thing you know I was there.

Within a few months of the abduction, Sara's mother travelled to Jordan and applied to the Islamic courts for Sara's return to the UK. The application was unsuccessful based on the Islamic law best interests of the child assessment, as Sara's mother had re-married and consequently the court ordered that Sara remain in Jordan. Sara remained in Jordan with her father until she was aged 18 and she managed to persuade her father, over several months that she should be allowed to return to England to attend university. Sara's father agreed on the condition that she would return 'home' to him each summer in Jordan. Sara could not face the idea of returning after her first year at university, and so she did not return. Sara, aged 25, states she has severed ties with her father.

ii. Aidan[24]

Aidan's parents lived together, and during his school summer holidays, Aidan's father took Aidan aged ten to visit his father's home country of the UAE. It was intended to be a summer holiday after which he would return home. During the visit, his father decided to keep him in the UAE. Aidan recalls:

> They [parents] were living together, but they were always arguing, and I knew that they would not continue together.

When asked about the travel plans, Aidan explains:

> No he [father] didn't tell me clearly, and I didn't have the choice to decide because he thought that I was too young to understand and decide. He told me we were going to the UAE, but I didn't know that I could not come back. I don't remember that we talked about it before.

[24] Participant 35F, interview 29/05/16 (on file with the author).

Aidan's mother travelled to the UAE and applied to the courts there for his return to the UK. As a non-Muslim, Aidan's mother was unsuccessful in her application and the court ordered that Aidan remain living with his father in the UAE. Aidan explains he was left upset and confused about what his parents were doing to each other and always missed his mother. As a male adult, Aidan, aged 24, can leave the UAE, but he remains living with his father's family and feels too estranged from his mother to ask to return to live with her.

iii. Harris[25]

Harris's parents separated before he was born and he was living with his mother and step-father in England. Harris's father always lived in Algeria. When Harris was aged eight, his parents agreed that Harris would visit Algeria that summer with his mother, so that he could meet his father. During the trip, Harris spent time with his father and paternal relatives. By the end of the trip, Harris was staying with his father's family and was being visited for short periods by his mother. Harris's mother told him that Harris's father would not allow Harris to return to England with her. She was also unable to persuade the court in Algeria that Harris should be allowed to return to England because the law stipulates Harris should live near his father.

Harris's mother returned to Algeria when he was aged 10 to abduct him so they could return to England together. Harris, at age 24, recalls the incident:

> I remember the event: my mother tried to get me across the border somehow, and it didn't work. I was given a game-boy [hand-held games console]. Like the day when she came to collect me from school, I was given a new game-boy and stopped at the back of the car, and you know I just kept myself busy, just playing the game-boy and then after a day or two I was back at school like nothing ever happened.

He adds:

> I don't believe that a mum or a dad could abduct … I didn't think of it as abduction; I knew that my mum was in trouble, but I didn't really understand much.

Harris's mother was unsuccessful in trying to leave Algeria with Harris and was arrested. After some diplomatic negotiation Harris's mother was pardoned for the attempted abduction. She was unable to return to Algeria as a result.

Harris spent the following years with his father's family in Algeria and only returned to England at the age of fifteen after he ran away from his father's home and managed to board a flight to England. He has since travelled back and forth extensively between both parents' homes but says he feels disconnected from both parents.

[25] Participant 35G, interview 29/05/16 (on file with the author).

The analysis in this chapter begins by examining the extent to which the courts in Islamic law countries uphold the child's Article 12 participatory rights, before critiquing how this applies in the context of abduction proceedings.

II. A Child's Right to *Autonomy* in Decision-Making: Islamic Court Proceedings

Historic Islamic law provides that a child, upon reaching the age of autonomy, is mature enough to decide with which parent to live. The discussion in this section illustrates how this children's right has evolved since the 13th century. The established autonomy has since weakened because of the claims of mothers requesting that children be allowed to remain in their care for a longer period. The legal developments and how they affect children's Article 12 CRC rights are explored in the context of custody and international parental abduction.

The ruling on children's autonomy is found within one of the primary sources of historic Islamic law, the teachings of the Prophet Mohammed:

> A woman complained to the Prophet; her husband wished to take her son away from her, 'although he (the son) gives me comfort and brings me drinking water from the well.' Thereupon the husband appeared denying her claim over the child. The Prophet then said: 'Child! Here is your father and here is your mother; make a choice between the two whomsoever you want.' The son caught hold of the hand of his mother, and she went away with her son.[26]

As outlined in chapter 3, Islamic custody rules derive from the period between the 13–15th Century. The rulings were only fixed into legislation in past five or six decades,[27] and so for the intervening centuries, judges/scholars had discretion on how to apply the ancient rules in individual cases. As a consequence, there are significant variances in how the judges applied the rules.[28] The main differences relate to the age at which a child is considered mature enough to choose between the parents, with the two differing viewpoints (as is illustrated in the analysis below) being either the age of discernment, considered to be at age seven, or the age at which a child reaches puberty.[29]

[26] Goolam, N, 'Formulation of the Best Interests Principle in Islamic Law' (Children's Rights International 2005) 3, available at www.childjustice.org/index.php?option=com_edocman&view=document&id=183&catid=3&lang=en.

[27] Lynn Welchman 'First Time Codification in Three Gulf States' (2010) *Int'l Surv Fam L* 163, 173–4.

[28] Ibrahim writing on this topic identifies the different periods in Islamic legal history: the pre-modern period as being pre-15th century and the early modern period extending from the 1500s to the 1820s. He explains that while many important social and legal changes took place during these different periods of Islamic legal history, much of the discourse of child custody law remained largely unchanged throughout these different periods: Ahmed Fekry Ibrahim, *Child Custody in Islamic Law: Theory and Practice in Egypt since the Sixteenth Century* (CUP, 2018) 26.

[29] Lynn Welchman, *Women and Muslim Family Laws in Arab States: A Comparative Overview of Textual Development and Advocacy* (Amsterdam University Press, 2007) 135.

The differences are attributed to the varying jurisprudential viewpoints within Islamic law. Emon and Khaliq explain that as jurists developed their own interpretations, groups of students would rally around certain esteemed jurists and their corpus of doctrine. Gradually, these groups turned into what are now called 'schools' organised around a particular doctrine. There exist four main schools of Islamic jurisprudence: Shafi'is, Hanabalis, Hanafis and Malikis.[30] The distinction in jurisprudential viewpoints were not introduced in chapter 3, as the jurists do not differ so much on the issues discussed in chapter 3 (for the child's mother to be Muslim, live near the father and not remarry).[31] There are greater variances in scholarly opinion upon the age at which a child should be allowed to make decisions for him or herself, and these variances are examined in the following section.

A. Age of Autonomy in Islamic Law

Islamic law recognises three stages of childhood: it views children under the age of seven as lacking discretion; the age of discretion begins at seven years of age and ends at puberty, and the third stage begins at puberty and ends at full adulthood.[32] The age of discernment is generally assessed as the point at which a child has achieved some degree of independence and can feed, clothe and cleanse him or herself. The period after this stage is when the child no longer requires specific care from the custodian mother when he or she is already capable of managing him or herself and of distinguishing between right and wrong.[33] As Emon and Khaliq explain:

> The reference to a specific age served as a legal trope or proxy for juristic considerations about paternalism and autonomy in the case of children. Certainly, modern readers might baulk at the suggestion that a child of seven years can determine his or her own interests. But we must recall that in the pre-modern or medieval period, infant mortality

[30] These relate to the Sunni Muslims, as there exist other variations for Shi'a schools of thought which would apply for example in Iran (Ja'fari School), in Yemen, (Zaydi School) and in Canada and the UK (Ismaili School). See further, Anver Emon and Urfan Khaliq, *Private International Law, Islamic-law, and Cross-Border Child Abduction: A Historic-Legal Analysis* (Ontario, 2016) 40–41; Emon, A, & Khaliq, U *Jurisdictional Exceptionalisms: Islamic Law, International Law and Parental Child Abduction* (CUP, 2021).

[31] On the topic of the mother's religion, the main variation that exists is that the Hanafis and Malikis say a non-Muslim mother is only allowed custody of the child up until the child is aged seven, or earlier if the child is old enough to understand differences between the religions. Shafi'is and Hanbalis, on the other hand, specify that a non-Muslim mother should never have legal custody of the child, but unlimited contact with the child is permitted. See further Mohammed Zaharuddin Zakaria and others, 'Children's Participation in Custody Disputes Involving Interfaith Parents' (2017) Vol 23 *Advanced Science Letters* 4813.

[32] Ahmed Fathi Bahnassi, 'Criminal Responsibility in Islamic Law' in Cherif Bassioni (ed), *The Islamic Criminal Justice System* (Oceana, 1982) 192.

[33] Mahdi Zahraa and Normi Malek, 'The Concept of Custody in Islamic Law' (1998) 13 *Arab LQ* 155, 166; See also Roslina Che Soh, 'Children's Participation in Custody and Access Proceedings (2014) 22 IIUMLJ 53, 59–62.

> was high and the average life expectancy far lower than it is now. For children to reach the age of seven or older was an important marker of their capacity to survive the harsh conditions of life in those varying contexts.[34]

Children are therefore automatically placed with the mother until age seven, at which point the variances in jurisprudential viewpoints emerge. The Shafi'is and Hanbalis agree that the child has the right to choose which parent to live with at age seven, based upon the literal interpretation of Prophet Mohammed's teachings described above. The two jurists differ, however, on whether boys and girls should choose at this early age. The Shafi'is do not differentiate between genders, unlike the Hanbali's who limit such a right only to a male child. The reasoning provided in Islamic law for differentiation between genders is to be explored in chapter five.

The other two jurisprudential viewpoints, the Hanafis and Malikis, propose that children are not mature enough to decide between the parents, as they will naturally choose the parent to whom they are more attached or who would give them more freedom which could lead to choosing a parent who may not act in the best interests of the child.[35] These jurists require that once a child reaches the age of capacity (to be able to cleanse themselves) the custody of boys is automatically transferred to the father, as boys are 'in need of education; the cultivation of a masculine ethic"[36] Mothers retain custody of girls until the girl is ready for marriage.

In summary, the Hanafis and Malikis do not grant children a voice or a choice, and the Hanbalis only grant boys a choice, which leads to the contention that Islamic custody law is determined largely based on age/gender-based criteria. Most Islamic law countries have pledged allegiance to at least one of the schools of Islamic jurisprudence, which dictates the content of their custody legislation. The Ḥanafi School is predominant in South Asia and Turkey, the Maliki School predominates in North Africa, the Shafi School in Southeast Asia and Egypt and the Ḥanbali School in the Gulf region.[37]

While only a small proportion of Muslim countries will give children a voice in custody proceedings, for the category of children who are granted the right, the age-related criteria can be a further limitation. Assessing precisely when a child is mature enough to make a decision is clearly dependent upon when the child achieves the requisite level of independence and of course puberty, too, is individual to the specific child. This is where the lack of judicial discretion in some Islamic law countries is problematic. The process of codifying the custody rules into legislation, (discussed in chapter 3) has created a situation where the law makes generalisations about the ages at which children reach the developmental

[34] Emon and Khaliq (n 30) 54–5.
[35] Che Soh (n 33).
[36] Emon and Khaliq (n 30) 51.
[37] For a study of the practice of Muslim countries, see Aayesha Rafiq, 'Child Custody in Classical Islamic Law and Laws of Contemporary Muslim World: An Analysis' (2014) 4(5) *International Journal of Humanity and Social Science* 272–276; See also Emon and Khaliq (n 30) 51.

stages of discernment and/or puberty. The approach does not conform to the CRC Committee's guidance on assessing the capacity of individual children. The Committee specifies: 'Some jurisdictions, either as a matter of policy or legislation, prefer to state an age at which the child is regarded as capable of expressing her or his own views. The Convention, however, anticipates that this matter is determined on a case-by-case basis, since it refers to age and maturity, and for this reason requires an individual assessment of the capacity of the child.'[38]

B. Legislation Setting the Age of Autonomy

Applying the above framework to the case studies introduced at the outset of this chapter, at the ages of ten and eight, (the ages at which they were abducted); Sara, Aidan and Harris would each be considered to have reached the age of discernment in classical Islamic law. And whilst reaching this milestone would – under the historic rules – permit children a choice on which parent they want to live with, the classical Islamic law has been revised in many Islamic law countries. As a result of the reform, the age at which children have a voice in proceedings is delayed beyond the age suggested in the primary sources of Islamic law. The developments are attributable to the fact that the issue of custody is now fought from the perspective of the mother's fight for custody against the father, rather than the child's rights. Welchman explains:

> Developments in personal status laws in the region have tended generally to extend the period of custody normally assigned to a woman over her children following divorce beyond the age limits contemplated in the majority of [the traditional] rules. … The three new Gulf laws are part of more recent patterns in this direction. In the draft UAE codification approved by the cabinet in 2005, a provision ending the mother's custody over girls at 13 and boys at 11 provoked public condemnation by lawyers who had consulted on previous drafts and held these ages to be a curtailment of existing custody rights. The intervention appears to have had some impact: while the text of the law was passed maintained this position, it allows the court to extend a woman's custody until the male ward reaches puberty and the female marries. The UAE law allows the set extensions beyond these ages to be made by the court in consideration of the ward's interests.'[39]

It is only after this period of 'guaranteed' maternal custody that the child is given a choice between the parents if the legislation in the Islamic law country adheres to Shafi or Hanabali doctrines. Morocco is a good example of how this legislation affects the child's right to participate in decision-making. Prior to the reform, Moroccan custody law stipulated boys would remain living with the mother until age 12 and girls at age 15, after which they could elect between the parents.

[38] GC12 para 52.
[39] Welchman (2010) (n 27) 173–4.

Post-2004 reforms, in seeking to equalise the rights of girls and boys, Moroccan law stipulates both boys and girls can participate in proceedings and elect with which parent they wish to reside at age 15.[40] A decision was made to increase the age for boys, rather than decreasing the age of participation for girls to 12. Thus, while the domestic law in Islamic law countries now tends to delay the age at which a child can participate in decision-making, the delay is intended to serve the best interests of the child, to ensure the child remains for a longer period in the care of his or her primary carer. The developments in Islamic law appear to have allowed the child's rights to become subsumed with the custodial rights of the mother. There exists academic debate as to whether the child's rights can exist and be asserted in complete isolation from other 'relational rights' and this topic is examined further in chapter 5.

The reforms are illustrated in the example of the cases of Sara, Aidan and Harris. Rather than having a voice in proceedings at age seven, as would be the case in classical Islamic law, under Jordanian law, Sara is only able to choose between the parents on reaching 15 years of age.[41] In the case of Harris, Algerian law[42] grants the mother custody of male children only until age ten and of female children until they marry,[43] and so Harris aged ten at the time of proceedings would have a right to choose between his parents. The law in the UAE[44] affirms Aidan would have a choice in proceedings only upon reaching the age of puberty. While the term puberty also refers to physical changes, it is presumed that the phrase puberty is a legal trope rather than a biological fact,[45] and an assessment of Aidan's maturity would be undertaken by a judge rather than a medical professional.

For similar reasons, the age at which children can choose with which parent to reside is set at age 15 years in Egypt.[46] In Tunisia, children aged 12 or older have discretion.[47] In Kuwait, the mother retains the custody of a male child until he reaches puberty that is set as 15 years of age and a female child until she marries.[48] Under Qatari law,[49] the mother can retain the right of custody of a male child until that child is 13 years and a female child up to 15 years of age. The court may extend the mother's right of custody to 15 years for male children and until the child marries for female children, or decide who should be the custodian after investigating the child's wishes if it is in the best interests of the child.[50]

[40] 2004 Moroccan Family Code.

[41] *Jordanian Personal Status Law* (JPSL) Law No 36 of 2010, Art 170, 173.

[42] Article 65 of the 2005 Family Code; see also Concluding Observations Algeria CRC/C/DZA/CO/3-4 (18 July 2012) para 48–54.

[43] Concluding Observations Algeria ibid.

[44] Federal Law no 28 of 2005 on Personal Status.

[45] The term 'trope' adopted here is used by Emon and Khaliq (n 30).

[46] Law No 25 of 1929 Egypt Concerning Certain Personal Status Provisions, as amended by Law Nos 100/1985 and 2/2006, Art 20. Substituted by Law No 4/2005.

[47] Article 214 of the Family Code.

[48] Code of Personal Status of Kuwait, 1984, Art 189.

[49] Qatari Family Law, Law No 22/2006, Art 166.

[50] Ibid, Art 173.

In contrast, the legislation in some Islamic states does not specify a particular age, and in that situation, the judge has the discretion to assess the child's maturity. In Yemen, for example, children who are 'self-sufficient' can choose with which parent to live.[51] In Pakistan s 17 of the Guardian and Wards Act of 1890 specifies 'if the minor is old enough to form an intelligent preference, the Court may consider that preference.' The formerly colonised Malaysia adopts a similar model to Pakistan, except that it has a dual legal system, in which Islamic law applies for Muslim families and a civil law system[52] for individuals of other faiths living in Malaysia. The Islamic law legislation[53] provides 'the Shariah court shall have regard to the views of the child in matters pertaining to custody when the child attains the age where he or she can express an independent opinion. It further provides[54] that a child who has reached the age of discernment is given an option to choose either parent with whom he or she wants to live.

The ages prescribed in the legislation of the majority of Islamic law countries leave no discretion for a judge to decide if a child is mature earlier or later than the ages specified. This has drawbacks for children who consider themselves mature enough to make an independent decision earlier than the specified age, particularly as the child's stage of capacity is continually evolving.[55] In GC12 the Committee expands on the 'principle of evolving capacities':

> The more the child himself or herself knows, has experienced and understands, the more the parent, legal guardian or other persons legally responsible for the child have to transform direction and guidance into reminders and advice and later to an exchange on an equal footing. This transformation will not take place at a fixed point in a child's development, but will steadily increase as the child is encouraged to contribute her or his views.[56]

Lansdown also argues[57] that adults' interactions with children can affect the way in which the child's capacity develops. As the social context, the nature of the decision, the particular life experience of the child and the level of adult support will all affect the capacity of a child to understand the issues affecting them, and so the weight that must be given to children's views must reflect their level of understanding of the issues involved. The discussion illustrates that the child's competence does not develop uniformly according to rigid developmental stages, and so in

[51] Article 35 of Rights of the Child Act 2002 in Yemen; Concluding Observations (CRC/C/129/Add.2, 2003, para 55).

[52] The Law Reform (Marriage & Divorce) Act 1976 (LRA), which governs family matters of non-Muslims states that: 'In deciding in whose custody a child should be placed the paramount consideration shall be the welfare of the child and subject to this the court shall have regard (a) To the wishes of the parents of the child; and (b) To the wishes of the child, where he or she is of an age to express an independent opinion.' Cited in Che Soh (n 33) 62–67.

[53] Section 86(2)(b) of the Islamic Family (Federal Territories) Act 1984 (Amendment 2006) ('IFLA').

[54] Section 84(2) of IFLA.

[55] For discussion on this topic, see Sheila Varadan 'The Principle of Evolving Capacities under the UN Convention on the Rights of the Child' (2019) 27(2) *International Journal of Children's Rights* 306.

[56] GC12 para 84.

[57] Lansdown (2001) (n 15); Gerison Lansdown, *The Evolving Capacities of the Child* (UNICEF, 2005).

abduction situations, even very young children could be capable of understanding the implications of their decision.[58] So while Islamic law has increased the age at which children can make a choice, to serve what is presumed to be in the child's best interests, the change also has the effect of infringing upon the rights of children who would prefer to have a voice at an earlier stage in their development.

The fact that Islamic law countries adopt different scholarly interpretations of when children are deemed autonomous results in a situation where legislation entitles Harris to have a voice and a choice, whereas Sara, of the same age, is not legally entitled, and neither is Aidan. The difference in opportunity to participate based on age-related criteria highlights the jurisdictional differences of Islamic states, and in examining whether Hague accession by Islamic law countries will uphold the Article 12 rights of abducted children, it appears that the more uniform approach of the Hague Convention might enhance and standardise the approach to children's voice. Having examined the effect of the legislative provision in Islamic law countries, the following section reflects upon how the Islamic law provision applies in cases of an international nature.

C. Do Islamic Courts Listen to *Internationally Abducted* Children?

The Islamic law position is very different from the English legal system, where the child's views are one of several factors.[59] In an Islamic law situation, the child's voice is not *one* of the determining factors but rather *the only* determining factor. Giving absolute effect to the child's voice raises, however, the issue about whether the child's views will be listened to, by the Islamic courts, if the views are not the child's own, or the outcome may not be in the child's best interests? The Islamic system rationalises this position as it undertakes the best interests assessment before deciding to give the child a voice/choice, and if both parents are judged eligible custodians, the child can choose between the parents. So in participatory terms, the Islamic system adopts a 'gateway' type process. It excludes groups of children from participating in decision-making if both parents are not deemed suitable, but those children that are 'lucky' enough to be allowed to participate have complete autonomy to decide between the parents.

So, if we compare the two groups in categories, the influence an abducted child has over the outcome depends upon his or her mother's lifestyle choices. In category one, for example, the abducted child of (both) Muslim parents, having a mother who has not remarried and will live near the father will have complete autonomy to decide between the parents when reaching the age of autonomy prescribed in

[58] Priscilla Alderson and Virginia Morrow, *Ethics, Social Science Research and Consulting with Young People* (Barnardo's, 2004) 22.

[59] See Children Act 1989, s 1(3).

legislation. In category two, the abducted child who has a non-Muslim parent, a mother who has remarried or intends to return to the UK will have no voice or choice in abduction proceedings before the Islamic courts. The process of selecting which children can have a choice in abduction proceedings distinguishes between children based upon the Islamic law best interests of the child assessment and is justified on this basis, yet it has the effect of unfairly excluding specific groups of children from participating in proceedings.

Islamic law processes offer a complicated approach to children's participation, as the framework set out above on children's autonomy is only relevant to an abducted child if his or her mother is Muslim, has not remarried and agrees to live near the father. The law more effectively promotes children's participation in a domestic context, where the parents are both likely to be of the Islamic faith and live in close proximity. The approach is less effective for cross-border cases, as under no circumstances will the abducted child have a choice if the left-behind mother intends to travel back to the UK with the abducted child. The Islamic law approach to children's participation is non-existent, therefore, in cases of an international nature. The analysis at this stage suggests that Hague accession by Islamic law countries would advance the Article 12 right of abducted children.

The interview data analysed in the following section illustrates how the Article 12 CRC rights of abducted children actually transpire in practice.

D. Did the Islamic Courts Uphold Sara, Aidan and Harris's Article 12 Right to be Heard?

i. Sara

Sara is one of only two abductees from the sample of 54 children who were asked by the courts their views on where they would like to live after the abduction. Sara was taken to Jordan by her father but left in the care of her paternal family while her father went abroad to secure employment. The Islamic law court agreed to grant Sara's father custody, even though he was not physically present in the country and caring for her at that time. Sara explains how she thinks her views were influenced before she was due to meet with the court reporters:

> My uncle that day kept saying to me 'oh we're going to take you out to Pizza Hut and to bowl, we're going to buy you some clothes' and I was really excited about it, just for like to be able to get out. Then, later on, he called me into his room, and he said I want to let you know there are some people coming today from the court and if they ask you anything, say that you're really happy to be with your dad. I remember they made me change and brush my hair, and you know made me look as presentable as possible. I remember when they came, I think there were an Arabic lady and man, and they asked me a few questions, they didn't ask me as direct as are you happy, but they asked me like a few different questions. I remember the thing that they asked me which I found most difficult to answer was what do you day in your day and honestly, I remember at the

> time thinking I don't even know what to say to that because what do I do? Because there wasn't anything to do. I remember part of the hardest thing about it was just the fact that there was absolutely nothing to do. I didn't speak any Arabic at the time and all the TV was in Arabic, everyone was speaking in Arabic like all the time. There were loads of kids about all my cousins and stuff, but no one was really watching or looking after me.

Sara was promised a day out in return for informing the professionals ascertaining her views that she wished to remain living in Jordan with her father. At age ten, Sara was agreeable to this or was unduly influenced by the promise. Sara suggests that as a result of her uncle's influence, she did not express her views freely to the Islamic court, the requirement of which is an essential component of Article 12. The Committee expresses in GC12: '"Freely" means that the child must not be manipulated or subjected to undue influence or pressure. "Freely" is further intrinsically related to the child's "own" perspective: the child has the right to express her or his own views and not the views of others.'[60]

ii. Aidan

Aidan is the other of the two abductees who was asked his views by the court on where he would like to live after the abduction. Aidan was living with his father's family and was told by them that his father would be imprisoned if he chose to return to live with his mother. Aidan said when he spoke to the judge he felt he had no real choice as he wished to protect his father from imprisonment:

> The judge asked me if I would like to stay or go to my mum, but it was not really a free choice because at this moment my father was going to be in jail because of this story. And my [paternal] family and everyone told me if I go back to mum they will send my father to jail and I can never see him again. So I have to stay for many reasons, and when I will be 18, I can go where I want. So I didn't feel at this moment that I really had a choice."

iii. Harris

Neither the lawyers nor the court ascertained Harris's views about where he would like to live. Harris explains:

> I never went to any court regarding the matter. I was young and for the most part, oblivious to what was going on. I think the child doesn't know any other than what he is told, you know, the child accepts the situation, especially when the situation is given to them by their parents. Children are more easily manipulated into saying certain things. I don't know what I would have said if I had gone to court and been asked.

On further reflection, he adds:

> I think it would have been interesting for me if I was spoken to more about what's exactly going on and you know, but I wasn't really asked, I wasn't really told about what

[60] GC12 para 22.

was going on, like for me nobody really explained it to me. Maybe it would have had a different outcome, or maybe it wouldn't have been. Maybe then I would've wanted to go home [England], I don't know.

The interview data illustrates that in only a small proportion of abduction cases examined did the courts accommodate children's participation, and so the analysis is extended in the following section to reported cases heard by the courts in Islamic countries.

E. Do Courts in Islamic Countries Listen to Children in Reported Cases?

There is very little qualitative research available on the issue of children's participation before the Islamic courts;[61] the little available information emerges from Malaysia[62] and Pakistan.[63] The following section reviews this secondary literature against the two categories identified by Daly, that children should get to choose – if they wish – how they are involved in proceedings (process autonomy) and the outcome (outcome autonomy) unless it is likely that significant harm will arise from their wishes.[64]

i. Outcome Autonomy

The available case-law from Malaysia suggests the Malaysian Islamic law courts follow the traditional pre-15th Century Islamic law practices, where children are heard at the prescribed age of 'maturity', and the child's views carry significant weight.[65] The decision in the case of *Mohamed Koyamo* v *Sapura*[66] suggests that children are afforded the autonomy to determine the outcome of proceedings. In this case the father sought custody of his three children aged thirteen, twelve and nine. The court allowed the children the opportunity to choose which parent they wished to live with, and all three chose their mother. In *Maimunah bt Samir*

[61] For example in relation to Bangladesh, the CRC Committee is 'concerned about the lack of information regarding the practical implementation of the right of the child to express his or her views in judicial and administrative proceedings.' Concluding observations Bangladesh CRC/C/BGD/CO/5 (30 October 2015) para 32.

[62] Che Soh (n 33); Suzana Muhamad Said and Shamsuddin Suhor, 'International Parental Child Abduction in Malaysia: Foreign Custody Orders and Related Laws for Incoming Abductions' (2012) 101 *Pertanika J Soc Sei & Hum* 20; Abdul Hamid and others, 'The Applicability of the 1980 Hague Abduction Convention in Muslim Countries: Particular Reference to the Malaysian Position' (2018) 99 *Arab Law Quarterly* 32, 125.

[63] Shabnam Ishaque and Muhammad Mustafa Khan, 'The Best Interests of the Child: A Prevailing Consideration within Islamic Principles and a Governing Principle in Child Custody Cases in Pakistan' (2015) 78 *International Journal of Law, Policy and The Family* 29, 86–87.

[64] Daly (n 12).

[65] Che Soh (n 33) 62–67.

[66] [1407H] 5 *JH* (II) 352.

v Mohammad bin Embong[67] the fifteen-year-old child was allowed to choose to live with his mother, and the court decided the four-year-old sibling should also live with the mother until reaching the age at which to choose himself. Several other cases illustrate a similar approach by the Malaysian courts,[68] and the child's voice appears to be determinative in the Malaysian case-law available, suggesting adherence to the 'Influence' pillar of Lundy's model, which advocates children must know that what they say will have some influence on the outcome and that their views will be used respectfully. It is recognised that the cases considered are examples of cases where the child's best interests in Islamic law are met; the mother is Muslim, lives near the father and has not remarried. Notably, however, the available case-law suggests that children are given a choice in proceedings, regardless of the mother's religion or marital status. In the case of *Wan Abdul Aziz* v *Siti Aishah*, it transpires the Malaysian court paid greater regard to the views of the nine-year-old girl who wished to remain in her mother's care, than the fact that the mother had remarried at the time of the hearing.[69] The child was allowed to remain with the remarried mother, and a similar outcome was affirmed in the case of *Mohammed* v *Azizah*[70] and *Harun* v *Che Gayah*.[71]

Two further academic articles provide information on cases of cross-border parental abduction to and from Malaysia.[72] Unfortunately, the reports do not refer to whether the abducted children's views were ascertained during proceedings, and so a comparison of child participation between cases of a domestic and international nature cannot be undertaken. The cases cited also refer predominantly to the decisions of the civil courts in Malaysia and not the Islamic law courts. The only parental child abduction case of those reported which is decided by the Islamic (rather than the civil[73]) Malaysian courts is *In the marriage of Y&K Raja Bahrin*.[74] In this case, an Australian mother abducted her two children from Malaysia to Australia. The Muslim father re-abducted the children and was granted custody by the Islamic law court in Malaysia on the basis that the mother had remarried. The decision was founded upon the child's 'best interests' assessment in Islamic law, and since the mother was not deemed an eligible custodian, the children were not offered a choice between the parents, and so their views

[67] (1426H) XX *JH* (II) 270.

[68] *Marthias* v *Ahmad Sulaiman* and *Wan Mohd Kamil bin Wan Abdul Ghani* v *Rosliza @ Mazwani bt Mohamed Mustafa* (1427H) XXI *JH* (I) 135.

[69] (1977) 1 *JH* 50.

[70] (1979) 1 *JH* 79.

[71] [1980] 1 *JH* (I) 66.

[72] Said and Suhor (n 62); Hamid and others (n 62).

[73] The cases decided by the Malaysian civil courts illustrate that children are ordered to remain/return to the mother. See *Mahabir Prasad v Mahabir Prasad* [1982] 1 MLJ 189 where the case involved a non-Muslim family and so the Malaysian Civil Court had jurisdiction. The court ordered the children to remain with their abducting mother in India; similarly in *Herbert Thomas Small v Elizabeth Mary Small* (2006) 6 MLJ 372 the Malaysian Civil Court ordered the abducting father to return his children to Australia; in *Nicholas Tan Chye Seng v Au Gek Wee* (2013) 1 LNS 600 a Malaysian mother abducted the child to Singapore. The Malaysian Court ordered the child should be returned to Malaysia, but the orders have no effect in Singapore.

[74] (1986) 11 *The Family Law Report* 233.

were not ascertained. From the little case-law available, it appears that children's participation in a domestic Malaysian context can be positive, whereas, in an international abduction situation, the Islamic law court in Malaysia is unable to uphold the child's Article 12 CRC right to be heard as the best interests assessment under the Islamic law doctrine must prevail.

Of the brief information available on abduction cases to Pakistan, there is evidence of the child's views being given effect in the abduction case of *Louise Ann Fairley v Sajjad Ahmad Rana*.[75] In this case, the child abducted from Scotland to Pakistan was ordered to return to her mother's care in Scotland. The decision was later set aside by the Supreme Court of Pakistan,[76] based upon the fact that the lower court ignored the child's objections to return. The court heard from the child, Misbah,[77] who said she did not wish to return to the UK because her mother forbade her to practice her faith, gave her food forbidden to Muslims, and was living with a man outside of marriage. A settlement was mediated between the parties in which it was agreed Misbah was to remain with the father who would bear the costs of the mother's travel to regularly visit her in Pakistan. Misbah stayed in Pakistan until 2011 before returning to the UK, after which she is reported to have assisted in the production of a play about her abduction.[78]

The decisions of the Islamic courts appear to affirm the child's views are accorded weight in domestic cases and 'outcome autonomy' identified by Daly is observable.[79] This is not the case, however, in international parental abduction cases where there exists little evidence of children being ordered by the Islamic courts to return to a mother who is not habitually resident in the Islamic law country.

ii. Process Autonomy

Listening to children can only be determinative according to the children's rights-based approach when children have a choice in how their views are heard, which Daly refers to as 'process autonomy.' The available literature suggests the process by which children's views are ascertained in the Islamic law courts is directly by the judge, through a meeting with the child.[80] The direct approach has its advantages, as it allows the judge to hear the child's unfiltered views and ascertain if the child

[75] 113 PLD 2007 Supreme Court 292, cited in Ishaque and Khan (n 63).

[76] PLD 2007 Supreme Court 292.

[77] Ibid para 13–15.

[78] Jenny Morrison '*Revealed: The Story of an International Tug-of-Love Battle That Made Headlines Around the World*' (Daily Record 13.04.14) available at www.dailyrecord.co.uk/news/scottish-news/revealed-story-international-tug-of-love-battle-3408506.

[79] Notably the decisions by the Malaysian Civil Courts determine the child's welfare as is recognised in English law, as Malaysian Civil Law does not need to take account of the mother's religion, remarriage or habitual residence.

[80] Zakaria and others (n 31) 4813.

understands the implications of the choice being made. Stalford and Hollingsworth explain the direct approach has the potential to achieve more durable outcomes, fewer appeals, greater levels of compliance,[81] and less trauma.[82] Daly also stresses that a judicial meeting should be a right of children because many children "feel that the meeting is an opportunity not just to demystify the judicial process, but to argue the strength of their wishes."[83]

In the abduction/custody cases examined, there appears to be no formal process of the Islamic law courts to ascertain the child's views, and the process is left to the discretion of the judge. Professionals working in this area in Islamic law countries indicated that standard procedure was for the child to attend the hearing and inform the judge, if asked, which parent she or he chooses. In all of the 29 cases considered (involving 54 children), only Sara and Aidan were given an opportunity to express their views and, of the two, only Aidan had the opportunity to meet with the judge. The limited participation in the cases examined appears to be attributed to the fact that the left-behind parents in these cases were not judged to be eligible custodians, rendering the child with no voice in judicial proceedings. Information in the CRC Committee reports also indicates diverging practices. In the case of Iran, for example:[84]

> The Committee remains concerned with regard to respect for the views of the child in judicial decisions concerning custody or divorce and in administrative decisions when the child's view is only heard through the father or paternal grandfather or another appointed guardian and not from the child directly. The Committee recommends that the State party adopt and implement legislation recognising the right of the child to be heard in all relevant legal proceedings by establishing systems and procedures for social workers and courts to comply with the principle.

The fact that children abducted to Iran may have their voice relayed to the court through their abducting father is highly problematic. It is unclear whether children have a right to separate representation in Islamic custody/abduction law proceedings, there appears no information in the available literature and professionals interviewed for this project confirmed they did not know of any case in which the child received independent legal representation before the courts in Islamic law centres.[85] The processes described do not facilitate children's participation or conform to GC12 or Lundy's model, which also sets out that the child, should be granted 'space' when participating in proceedings. Space requires children to

[81] Particularly as return orders are difficult to enforce following an order. On enforcement see further Paul Beaumont and others (eds), *Cross-Border Litigation in Europe* (Hart Publishing, 2017); Paul Beaumont and others, 'Child Abduction: Recent Jurisprudence of the European Court of Human Rights' (2015) 64 *International and Comparative Law Quarterly* 39.

[82] For a detailed analysis of the evidence to this effect, see Daly (n 12).

[83] Ibid 258.

[84] Concluding Observations Iran CRC/C/IRN/CO/3-4 (14 March 2016) paras 27, 33–34, 41.

[85] Participants explained that children do receive independent representation in criminal and probate matters. See discussion on the information available on separate representation for children in the context of Hague proceedings below at IIID.

ideally be in an environment where they feel comfortable to express their views and also should not be obliged to express their views if this is against their wishes. The discussion earlier in the chapter illustrates that the legislation in Islamic law countries requires, if the parents are both eligible custodians, that the child must choose between the parents at a specified age. This feature of the legislation in Islamic law countries is contrary to what the UNCRC Committee recommends in GC12: 'expressing views is a choice for the child, not an obligation.'[86] The Committee reiterates this point in its dialogue with Islamic law countries, for example, it recommends Qatar must 'ensure that the opportunity of the child to express his or her opinion with regard to custody after divorce should be considered as a right and not an obligation.'[87] It appears from the case-law available to examine that Islamic law courts recognise and accommodate the fact that children have a right to express, or not express, a view.[88] Yet the Committee requires that the voluntary nature of participation is more explicitly expressed in legislation and this would also conform with Lundy's model and the pillars of 'space' and 'voice'. So that the environment in which children are asked if they wish to express a view must be sensitive to the pressure children might face if the legislation does not explicitly state that this is a choice for the child.

The pillar of 'voice' in Lundy's model focuses on the need to listen to children and put questions to them in a way that they can respond in their own voice. Another example of processes that do not conform to GC12 and Lundy's model is found in the example of a custody hearing in Malaysia. There is evidence that 'a five-man panel interviewed both children in chambers.'[89] The reason for the exorbitant judicial examination in this case is because the case involved children who were not originally Muslim, but whose father had decided to adopt the Islamic faith and convert his children also. Granted this is an unusual issue that does not fall easily into the legislative provisions, nonetheless the presence of five adults interviewing two siblings aged eight and eleven could be regarded as inappropriate by any measure. The children's wishes were listened to in this case, although it resulted in separating the siblings. The custody of the eight-year-old son was granted to the Muslim father and the eleven-year-old daughter, to the non-Muslim mother. The example highlights the variance in practice and illustrates the importance of guidance, such as that in Lundy's model, which requires an appropriate 'audience' for children participating in proceedings. Having reviewed the available case-law on proceedings before the Islamic law courts, the following section analyses collectively the data gathered of practices under Islamic custody/abduction law against the GC12 framework.

[86] GC12 para 16.

[87] Concluding Observations Qatar CRC/C/QAT/CO/3-4 (22 June 2017) para 26.

[88] See for example the Malaysian case in which the court decided custody based on the child's best interests, as the child did not wish to choose between the parents: *Nooranita bte Kamaruddin v Faiez bin Yeop Ahmad*. [1989] 2 *MLJ* cxxiv, (1990) 7 *JH* 52.

[89] Zakaria and others (n 31) 4813.

F. Is Domestic Law in Islamic Law Countries Compliant with the Guidance in General Comment 12?

The evidence illustrates there are practices in Islamic law countries which do satisfy *some* of the criteria of Lundy's model of children's participation and the broader CRC framework. The children's rights-based approach which adopts GC12 is also more specific than the CRC alone and so while some practices in Islamic law countries may conform to the expectations of the CRC, these still lack when measured against the standards developed under GC12. Thus while the pillar of 'influence', for example, may be positive, the fact that this good practice is not available to all children, and is reserved for only some children, means that it is a process that cannot claim to uphold the rights of abducted children. In the context of GC12, the CRC Committee proposes that children's participation should be effective, ethical and meaningful,[90] and to be so, requires States parties to adhere to five stages in implementing Article 12.[91]

The children that were asked for their views, Sara and Aidan, were not prepared as is recommended by GC12, *Preparation Stage (A)*. The practice of the Islamic law courts does not appear from the data to provide abducted children the option of how their views are ascertained and so does not appear to satisfy this stage. The practice of the Islamic law courts fares better in the GC12 recommendations at the *hearing stage (B)*. This stage requires that 'the context in which a child exercises her or his right to be heard has to be enabling and encouraging so that the child can be sure that the adult who is responsible for the hearing is willing to listen and seriously consider what the child has decided to communicate.'[92] While in theory, this format draws a parallel with how the child's views are listened to in proceedings before the courts in Islamic law countries, with children having the opportunity to meet with the judge, the data illustrates that in practice children are not always heard directly, they can be interviewed by up to five judges, or interviewed in the presence of, or through their legal guardians – even if the guardian is the abducting parent.

The discussion above explains that judicial discretion afforded by classical Islamic law was restricted by the introduction of inflexible codification of legislation. As a consequence, practice of the courts in Islamic law countries appears unsuccessful at the stage of *Assessment of the capacity of the child (C)*. This is because the legislation sets out the ages at which children are deemed to be mature enough to express a view, leaving little scope for the judiciary to undertake an individualised assessment as is prescribed by classical Islamic law and by the UN Committee.[93] In fact, the approach adopted by Islamic law countries is referred

[90] GC12 para 133.
[91] Ibid paras 40–47.
[92] GC12 para 42.
[93] GC12 para 52.

to by the Committee as arbitrary and discriminatory in its dialogue with Iran: 'The Committee remains concerned that article 1169 of the Civil Law relating to the custody of children after divorce prevents the court from taking into account the best interests of the child, and it reiterates that custody determined solely on the basis of a child's age is both arbitrary and discriminatory.'[94]

The practice of the courts in Islamic law countries also appears to fail at the stage of providing *feedback (D)* to the child, as Sara and Aidan were not given any feedback on their contribution to the proceedings.[95] The Committee explains: 'the decision-maker has to inform the child of the outcome of the process and explain how her or his views were considered. The feedback is a guarantee that the views of the child are not only heard as a formality but are taken seriously.'[96] While in theory, Islamic law does this, as the opinion of the mature child is acted upon, in the cases of cross-border parental abduction, the two children who were invited to share their views received no feedback on the outcome of proceedings. Abducted children in Islamic law countries do not have the opportunity of *redress (E)*, as the legislation in Islamic law countries falls short in providing children with complaint procedures and remedies when their right to be heard is disregarded.[97] It was argued in chapter two that children are largely invisible in the constitutions of Islamic law countries. A consequence of states failing to make reference to children in their constitutions is that processes are also then not established for children to seek redress.

It is identified in chapters 2 and 3 that Islamic law countries differ in how they respond to recommendations of the UNCRC Committee and how open they are to dialogue about interpreting Islamic law to conform to the CRC framework. A report by UNICEF explains:[98] 'The extent to which legislation reflects Islamic law or the legal traditions of colonial powers varies considerably from one country to another,[99] as does the willingness of the authorities to modify legislation to bring it into compliance with international human rights standards.' This is illustrated in an example from Morocco's Second Report to the Committee: 'the present orientation of the national legislation is to take into consideration the developments in Western society and to take appropriate measures to secure the basic principles of human rights …'[100] Morocco's response highlights that some Islamic law countries view the CRC framework as a 'Western' concept, and as is observed in chapter 2,

[94] Concluding Observations Iran (n 84) paras 27, 33–34.
[95] GC12 para 45.
[96] Ibid.
[97] Ibid para 46, see also Committee's General Comment No 5 (2003) *On General Measures of Implementation of the Convention on the Rights of the Child* para 24.
[98] Daniel O'Donnell, *The Right of the Child to be Heard: Children's Right to Have Their Views Taken Into Account and to Participate in Legal and Administrative Proceedings* (Innocenti Working Paper, UNICEF, 2009) 35.
[99] It is suggested that only three countries, Iran, Saudi Arabia and Sudan, fully recognise Islamic law as the official law of the land; Irshad Abdal-Haqq, 'Islamic Law: An Overview of its Origin and Elements' (2002, reprinted from 1996) *Journal of Islamic Law and Culture* 7 68–69.
[100] Second Report of Morocco CRC/C/93/Add.3 (2000) para 168.

not all states are willing to engage with the implementation of the reforms recommended by the CRC Committee. Morocco affirms it is willing, and this is why Morocco was the first Islamic law country to accede to the Hague Convention. Conversely, the approach of some other countries is to defend the way in which the custody legislation specifies age limits limiting children's legal capacity. Lebanon, for example, in its report to the Committee,[101] supports the prescribed age limits as being 'close to the stages into which childhood is divided by psychologists, education experts and sociologists.'[102] And indeed similar responses are seen across other, non-Muslim, States Parties.

The developments in children's Article 12 CRC rights are therefore linked very closely with the developments of children's rights more broadly in Islamic law countries. The dialogue between the Committee and Islamic law countries can be effective in developing the interpretation of children's Article 12 CRC rights. The example of the changes in Morocco illustrates that the interpretation of Islamic law can reflect societal developments *if* religious scholars and leaders allow. Thus over time, the Committee's efforts could serve to improve the landscape of children's participatory rights in Islamic law countries. The following section identifies the factors which the abductees felt affected their participatory rights, and illustrates why Islamic law countries should undertake to address the problematic legal regulation that affects children abducted to Islamic law countries.

G. Abductees' Views on Participation

The three themes on participation in proceedings that emerged from the interviews with abducted children are: (i) Children should have a choice. (ii) Children are made to feel powerless in the abduction situation. (iii) Children should be supported by the government to advance their Article 12 CRC rights. The discussions suggest, from the perspective of abducted children and the effect of Islamic custody law on their circumstances, that operating outside the Hague framework does not uphold the participatory rights of abducted children. Though Islamic law countries have relatively strong participatory processes, abducted children wishing to return to their home country are excluded from those deliberations. Accession to the Hague framework appears to be the only means by which to uphold the rights of abducted children in an Islamic law country context.

Nine of the ten abductees interviewed expressed that they should be asked during the proceedings which parent they wished to live with, and in which country. As Aliyah explains:

> I think it should be up to the child. I would have made a choice to come here [return to the UK], and I think it would have been better for me. But it could be a happy medium

[101] Second Report of Lebanon CRC/C/70/Add.8 (1998) paras 3, 12, 60–67.
[102] Ibid para 96.

> for the child to decide. Like during the school year I can stay with mum, but during the summer I can see dad, you know. You should give them [children] options, not just say 'you're going to stay here, and this is better for you!'

Only one abductee of the ten, Miriam, stated that children should not have a choice, 'I don't think that a child will know what's better for them.' Incidentally, this is the only one of the abductees interviewed who is a parent now herself. Miriam went on to say the age at which children should have a choice is:

> Maybe 16 or 18, it depends on the child. Because when you are a teenager, you want a parent who will let you do what you want. But when you are a child, I think you need your mother more. I don't think that a child could choose who he wants to live with. I think it depends on the parent's job, money, if they have a house or not, where and how the child is going to live. I didn't want anyone to ask me. I always thought if they did, the other parent would be upset. I always wished I lived like any other child, with both of them.

The abductees thought that rather than abducting the child, the parents should be less 'selfish.' Harris explains:

> children shouldn't be asked to choose between parents and the parents should be mature enough to come to an agreement with the child's best interests in mind. Although I know this does not always happen. After they have a child, they should think less selfishly.

Aliyah says

> twelve-year-olds know where they want to live. It's better to be able to support the child; they're not property they should be able to come back and forth between the parents. It's just selfish of a parent not have the child see the other parent; it's morally wrong in every way.

The abductees conveyed a strong sense of powerlessness, with adulthood, as Onora O'Neill suggests, being their only remedy.[103] Harris explains:

> That was my coping mechanism, to suppress it, I became very introvert, you know when I was young, very closed off because I wouldn't trust and wouldn't open up to people. Maybe those are all the results of the trauma. I had no power; there was nothing I could do you know, so there was no point in doing anything.

Aidan also explains:

> I think the best is to let the child live where he was living before [pre-abduction], so it doesn't change his whole life and habits. I don't remember the emotional aspect. I was just confused and didn't know what to think. Would it be better if I live here as they are telling me? Would it be better if I go home? That was the questions in my mind, so it was confusing. I tried to convince myself that it's better to live there [Islamic law country] because I was already there. It was easier and to convince myself that at the age of 18 I can go where I want.

[103] Onora O'Neill, *Having Children: Philosophical and Legal Reflections on Parenthood* (OUP, 1979).

The abductees felt that there was more that could have been done by the British government in ascertaining their views on where they wished to live after the abduction. Samir explains:

> my father didn't let anyone ask me what I wanted because he thinks I don't know what's right for me. If they cared about me, the government in England should work hard and make contact with me and ask what I want and what I need.

And Yasmin:

> I was born in England; I lived in England until I was seven and whether I liked it or not, I should have been in England. You know I could have had a really bad relationship with my mum, I could've hated her, but I still should've been in England, and I think my [UK] government should've helped more.

The views of abducted young people signify the failings of the law in upholding their Article 12 CRC rights, and those views are contextualised in the following section.

H. Abducted Children: Unheard

Islamic law grants mature children autonomy in decision-making within domestic custody disputes, however, the independence is not granted in an international abduction situation. The approach to children's participation is complicated, as the child only has a voice and a choice if both parents are regarded as equal custodians, and a left-behind mother agrees to live near the father. Which in the majority of case-studies examined, would require the left-behind mothers to relocate from the UK to the Islamic law country.

The sample studied suggests the practical reality of children's participation before the Islamic courts is far from what GC12 prescribes. On the rare occasion the views of children abducted to Islamic law countries are heard, abducted children are not afforded what Lundy describes as space, voice, audience, and influence.[104] Thus the positive approach to children's participation in domestic custody disputes is very different from the approach taken in cross-border abduction proceedings, simply because of the fact that the courts will never approve of the child returning to the UK, without the father's consent. The participatory rights of an abducted child under Islamic law – in cases of cross-border parental abduction – are therefore invisible as the court cannot give effect to the child's wishes as the child cannot be ordered to return to the UK.

The central question in this text is whether accession to the Hague convention by Islamic law countries will advance the rights of abducted children. Based on the evidence presented, the theory appears to be established, and Hague accession can only improve the situation for abducted children. Before being able to arrive at

[104] Lundy (2007) (n 20) 933–38.

this conclusion, however, the following section examines if the Hague Convention could uphold the Article 12 right of children abducted to Islamic law countries more consistently.

III. A Child's Right to *Participate*: Hague Proceedings

The Hague Convention specifically accommodates the child's right to object to return, and so has the scope, at least in theory, in which to hear the child's views and uphold the child's Article 12 CRC rights. Article 13(2) of the Hague Convention provides:

> The judicial or administrative authority may also refuse to order the return of the child if it finds that the child objects to being returned and has attained an age and degree of maturity at which it is appropriate to take account of its [the child's] views.

The phrasing of Article 13(2) illustrates, however, that the participatory rights of abducted children under Hague are limited to these narrowly prescribed circumstances.

The content of Article 13(2) of the Hague Convention was, as Beaumont and McLeavy explain, without doubt, the feature which most divided the delegates in 1980. This was because of concerns that 'the inclusion of any such provision would make the child the ultimate arbiter of the success of the abduction',[105] together with concerns that 'on the sole basis of the views of the child, a judicial authority could, by deciding on the non-return of a child, in fact, decide indirectly on custody issues.'[106] Further concerns drafters had about hearing the child in Hague proceedings arose from the very objections to children's participation in domestic disputes. That the child's views could conflict with their best interests[107] and children should not be made to take sides or worry about whether their views will remain confidential.[108] Also that the child could become subject to undue influence from the abductor, and 'courts would be able to manipulate the criteria to avoid making an order for return because an assessment of the child's wishes resembled an investigation into the merits of the custody issue.'[109] This viewpoint

[105] Reported by Paul Beaumont and Peter McEleavy, *The Hague Convention on International Child Abduction* (OUP, 1999) 177–180.

[106] Reported by Philipe Lortie and Frederic Breger, *The Child's Voice – 15 years later*, 4.

[107] Fiona Raitt, 'Hearing Children in Family Law Proceedings: Can Judges Make a Difference?' (2007) 19(2) *Child and Family Law Quarterly* 204, 213; Christine Piper, 'Assumptions about Children's Best Interests' (2000) 22(3) *Journal of Social Welfare and Family Law* 261.

[108] See Rhonda Bessner, *The Voice of the Child in Divorce, Custody and Access Proceedings* (Department of Justice, Canada, 2002); Pauline Tapp, 'Judges are Human Too: Conversations Between the Judge and a Child as a Means of Giving Effect to Section 6 of the Care of Children Act 2004' (2006) *New Zealand Law Review* 35; Barbara Atwood, 'The Child's Voice in Custody Litigation: An Empirical Survey and Suggestions for Reform' (2003) 45 *Arizona Law Review* 629.

[109] Beaumont and McEleavy (n 105) 177–180.

is illustrated in the reporting of the negotiations of Article 13(2) by the United States representative, Bodenheimer. She writes:

> Children's preferences are, of course, considered in hearings on the merits of the custody question. The return proceedings are not hearings on the merits. The exception places an inordinate burden of responsibility on children perhaps as young as six or seven years of age. It does so at a time when the children are fully dependent upon the person who abducted them and cannot help being influenced, if not pressured, by that person and perhaps other relatives. Permitting a child to block the return will make the child the ultimate judge of the abduction's success or failure. It is hoped that this exception will be eliminated and that the other exceptions will be sufficiently narrowed to preserve the objectives of the Convention.[110]

At the time of negotiations, there were 27 Members of the Hague Conference[111] as compared with 91 members today.[112] As a result, the text reflects some of the trends found in the domestic laws of the States sitting around the negotiation table. The content of Article 13(2) was still novel at the time, as legislation in most Western states did not oblige courts to consider the child's wishes in custody disputes.[113] The drafters, therefore, included the 'child objection defence' only because the Hague Convention applies to children up to the age of sixteen. The Convention's Explanatory Report highlights 'such a provision was necessary given the fact that the Convention applies, ratione personae, to all children under the age of sixteen. The fact must be acknowledged that it would be very difficult to accept that a child of, for example, fifteen years of age, should be returned against its will.'[114] The efforts by drafters to agree on a minimum age at which the views of the child could be taken into account failed because all the ages suggested seemed arbitrary.[115] It was, therefore, decided best to leave the application of Article 13(2) to the discretion of States.

The Hague Convention can be commended for including the opportunity for the child's views to be heard, prior to the enactment of the CRC. Though because the period was pre-CRC, the Hague Convention is not articulated in the language of a children's rights approach. So the Hague Convention only considers the child's voice if the abducting parent raises the child's objections to return as a defence.[116]

[110] Brigette Bodenheimer, 'The Hague Draft Convention on International Child Abduction' (1980) 14(2) *Family Law Quarterly* 110.

[111] Argentina, Australia, Austria, Belgium, Canada, Denmark, Egypt, Finland, France, Germany, Greece, Ireland, Israel, Italy, Japan, Luxembourg, Netherlands, Norway, Portugal, Spain, Suriname, Sweden, Switzerland, Turkey, the United Kingdom, the United States of America and Venezuela.

[112] See the status table of membership: www.hcch.net/en/instruments/conventions/status-table/?cid=29.

[113] Lortie and Breger (n 106) 3.

[114] See Elisa Perez-Vera, *Report on the 1980 Hague Child Abduction Convention* (Translation of The Permanent Bureau, 1981) para 30.

[115] Beaumont and McEleavy (n 105) 179–180.

[116] Note the situation differs with inter-EU abduction cases. In Regulation 2201/2003, the EU has adopted rules for intra-EU child abductions which build on The Hague Convention 1980 rules to reinforce the return remedy between the Member States. Article 11(2) Brussels II Revised stipulates

And so the child's views are not considered in cases where the abducting parent might agree to return the child once Hague proceedings are initiated. The child's limited participation is justified by the Hague Convention because it assumes that the child is to be heard by the courts of the child's habitual residence post-return, in which the child's Article 12 rights would be upheld. This is problematic, however, as the abducted child is not always given an opportunity to be heard in domestic proceedings post-return, particularly if proceedings are not initiated by the parents upon the child's return,[117] or the parents mediate an agreement amongst themselves.[118] This results in a situation where the child, if not heard in Hague proceedings, may not be heard at all. This approach to participation, therefore, does not comply with the child's Article 12 CRC right to be heard in *all* judicial proceedings in which she or he is affected. In order to interpret the Hague Convention so that it is compatible with the CRC, Schuz argues that the child's right to participation should not be restricted to Article 13(2) objections only, and the child should be given the opportunity to participate in proceedings regardless of whether he or she objects to return.[119]

The Hague Convention limits children's participation further as it presumes the abductor is capable of representing the child's interests, and so not only does this presumption serve to empower the abductor;[120] the court may not be aware of the child's objections to return.[121] McEleavy[122] notes the association of objections with the abductor may also create a negative impression in the mind of the court,[123] and the fact that Article 13(2) is classified as a 'defence' cannot be overlooked.[124]

the returning court is required to hear the child's views if the child is old enough to be heard. As a result, children will be given the opportunity to be heard in any return proceedings under the 1980 Convention between EU states and not only in proceedings limited to a defence under Article 13(2). As Islamic law countries are not part of the EU, this regulation will not apply to abductions to Islamic law countries and so is not explored here. For detailed commentary on the effect of Brussels II Revised, and how the Hague Convention's approach might be improved upon, see Helen Stalford, *Children and the European Union* (Hart Publishing, 2012) chapter 4; Ruth Lamont, 'Free Movement of Persons, Child Abduction and Relocation Within the European Union' (2012) 34(2) *Journal of Social Welfare and Family Law* 231, 234; note also that in practice, the research on the practical application of the Brussels regulation suggests children are not given the opportunity to be heard in most cases under that regulation either, and thus there appears to be a systematic flaw in upholding Article 12 rights; Paul Beaumont, Lara Walker and Jane Holliday, 'Not Heard and Not Returned: The Reality of Article 11(8) Proceedings' (2015) 2 *International Family Law* 124.

[117] If, for example, the abducting parent decides not to return with the child, or is imprisoned upon his or her return.

[118] Dan-Andrei Popescu, 'Mediation in Matters Concerning Parental Responsibility and International Child Abduction: Recognition and Enforcement of Agreements Concluded During Return Proceedings,' (2019) 2 *Studia Universitatis Babes-Bolyai Jurisprudentia* 22.

[119] Schuz (2013) (n 11) 373–87.

[120] Beaumont and McEleavy (n 105) 180–1.

[121] See the case of *Re F (Abduction: Child's wishes)* [2007] 2 FLR 697 in which it was suggested the abducting parent may not present the child's views for reasons of 'litigation strategy'.

[122] Peter McEleavy, 'Evaluating the Views of Abducted Children: Trends in Appellate Case-Law' (2008) 20 *Child & Fam L Q* 230.

[123] *Re D (Abduction: Rights of Custody)* [2006] UKHL 51, [2007] 1 FLR 961, para [58].

[124] See for example: *Zaffino v Zaffino* [2005] EWCA Civ 1012, [2006] 1 FLR 410, para [3]; *Re M (Children) (Abduction)* [2007] EWCA Civ 992, [2007] 3 FCR 564, para [1].

Article 13(2) of the Hague Convention is expressed as a defence, and not a right of the child, and perhaps if it was expressed as a right, the court might be inclined to engage more with what the child has to say. As McEleavy argues, while courts must be alert to situations where abductors have sought to manipulate and influence,[125] it is the interests of the child which are at stake within Article 13(2) and these risk being overlooked if they are conflated with the arguments presented by the abductor.[126] It appears that only separate representation for abducted children will address this flaw of the Hague Convention, and the obstacles to separate representation are discussed below (see D).

A. The Hague Convention Further Restricts Children's Participation Through Age-Related Assessments of Capacity

The views of the abducted children, Sara, Aidan and Harris, will also not be heard in Hague proceedings unless they have 'attained an age and degree of maturity at which it is appropriate to take account of its [the child's] views.' This feature of Article 13(2) of the Hague Convention mirrors Article 12 CRC as that too bases the right upon an assessment of the child's maturity: 'the views of the child being given due weight in accordance with the age and maturity of the child.'

The Hague Convention does not stipulate an age at which to hear the child's views and leaves the assessment of maturity to the discretion of Contracting States. The age at which children are heard in Hague proceedings in each of the Contracting States depends therefore on domestic practices. In most states, the age at which children are heard in domestic custody disputes is also the age at which they are heard in Hague proceedings, although there are exceptions such as in the Netherlands where children are heard at age 12 in domestic cases, but from age 6 in Hague Convention proceedings.[127]

The age at which children are considered 'mature' in non-Islamic parts of the world is also said to emerge from religious law. O'Donnell[128] identifies that Canon law in Europe maintained the Roman law concept that children under the age of 7 lack the ability to reason or take legal responsibility. Canon law also establishes the age of majority as 18 years but recognises capacity to testify in legal proceedings at the age of 14. The continued use of these age limits in many European countries and their former colonies is no doubt a legacy of Canon law. In Greece,[129]

[125] See comments of Balcombe LJ in *Re S (A Minor) (Abduction: Custody Rights)* [1993] Fam 242, para 252.

[126] In *Re T (Abduction: Child's Objections to Return)* [2000] 2 FLR 192 Ward LJ referred to the girl's Art 13 'defence', para 212.

[127] Annette Olland, 'The Voice of the Child in 1980 Hague Return Procedures in the Netherlands', *The Child's Voice – 15 Years Later*, 54.

[128] O'Donnell (n 98) 34–39.

[129] Karolina Zoi Andriakopoulou and Maria Louiza Andriakopoulou, 'The Voice of the Child in Hague Convention Proceedings in Greece', *The Child's Voice – 15 Years Later*, 34.

for example, the child can be heard from as young as 6, and in Italy[130] and Spain,[131] the child's views are heard from age 12. In Belgium, courts generally permit children 10 years or older to be heard. In France, children younger than 9 are not heard, with the exception of 6–8-year-olds who have older siblings.[132]

Like the courts in Islamic law countries, Belgian and French courts do not elaborate on the concept of maturity or 'discernment' in their case-law. Both jurisdictions generally refrain from a detailed assessment of the child's maturity and use biological age as a criterion to decide whether or not the child should be heard.[133] The approach also does not conform to the correct interpretation of Article 12, as the UNCRC Committee discourages States parties from introducing age limits either in law or in practice which would restrict the child's right to be heard. Beaumont and McEleavy, too, suggest that a child's objections to return should not be limited to mature children, and that 'any child capable of forming a view should be heard, directly or indirectly.'[134]

Both Sara and Aidan were aged ten at the time of proceedings, and so depending upon the country abducted to, it is likely, as English case-law indicates, their views would be considered in Hague Convention proceedings. Ward LJ commented in *Re T*[135] that he 'would not wish to venture any definition of maturity. Clearly, the child has to know what has happened to her and to understand there is a range of choice. A child may be mature enough for her views to be taken into account even though she may not have gained the level of maturity that she is fully emancipated from parental dependence and can claim autonomy of decision-making.' More specifically, Hale J, as she was then stated in *Re R (Abduction: Hague and European Conventions)*[136] that she would regard the chronological age of 10½ as normally being on the borderline.

In light of this guidance we can reflect on the fact that Harris was aged eight at the time of abduction proceedings, an age where several legal jurisdictions consider the child is not mature enough to express a view. GC12 recommends: 'States parties should presume that a child has the capacity to form her or his own views and recognize that she or he has the right to express them; it is not up to the child to first prove her or his capacity'.[137] There is some evidence from case-law which suggests Harris could be heard in Hague Convention proceedings. In *Re S (A Minor)*[138] the Court of Appeal accepted the objection of a 9-year-old girl

[130] Marzia Ghigliazza and Sara Luzzati, 'The Hearing of the Child in Civil Proceedings in Italy – Rules and Practice', *The Child's Voice – 15 Years Later*, 31.
[131] Christopher Lee, 'Listening to the Child's Voice in Spain', *The Child's Voice – 15 years later*, 37.
[132] Sara Lembrechts, 'Hearing Abducted Children in Court – A Comparative Point of View from Three Countries (Belgium, France & The Netherlands)', *The Child's Voice – 15 Years Later*, 28.
[133] Ibid 28.
[134] Beaumont and McEleavy (n 105) 201–2.
[135] [2000] 2 FLR 192, para 203.
[136] [1997] 1 FLR 663, para 667.
[137] GC12, para 20.
[138] [1993] 2 ALL ER 683.

who had the mental age of 12 and in *B v K (Child Abduction)*[139] the objections of a girl aged 8 and a boy aged 7 were held to justify a refusal to return. Moreover, in *Re M (Minors) (Abduction: Psychological Harm)*,[140] the views of brothers aged 9 and 8 were taken into account but with some hesitancy. Yet in *Re K (Abduction: Childs Objections)*[141] a child aged just under 8 was held on the facts not to be of an age and maturity in which it was appropriate to take account of her views. Lowe and Douglas,[142] however, affirm that children below the age of 10 or 11 are not generally considered by the courts to be sufficiently mature and this is affirmed in the 2015 survey of Hague Convention cases.[143] The survey found that the average age of an 'objecting child' in 2015 was 11 years with the lowest age being 4 years (this related to one application that also involved siblings aged 10 and 12). In 2008 the average age was found to be 10.7 years. In 2003 it was 11.3 years. The findings, however, only refer to applications in which a return application was actually refused. They do not include the number of applications in which the child objection defence was pleaded, or where the child objection defence was established but a return order was nevertheless made, nor is there any information on the number of applications in which the child was not heard at all.

B. The Overly-Complex Process of Hearing Children in Hague Convention Cases

The processes by which the views of abducted children are ascertained in the over 100 Hague Convention Contracting States vary significantly, depending upon domestic practices. In the Islamic law system, Aidan was heard by a judge, Sara by court welfare officers and Harris was not given the opportunity to express his views at all. In comparison, the Hague Conference acknowledges that there are as many practices on how to hear the views of the child as there are legal cultures and traditions.[144] There are also differing viewpoints on whether the child should be

[139] [1993] 1 FCR 382.
[140] [1997] 2 FLR 690 at 694.
[141] [1995] 1 FLR 977.
[142] Lowe, N et al, *Bromleys Family Law* (OUP, 2021) 861.
[143] Hague Survey (2015).
[144] In Italy the judge hears the child, in the presence of a psychologist. The hearing is recorded and the child must read and sign the record; Marzia Ghigliazza and Sara Luzzati, 'The Hearing of the Child in Civil Proceedings in Italy – Rules and Practice', *The Child's Voice – 15 Years Later*, 31; in Spain judges frequently interview children. However, children may also be interviewed by the child psychologist service linked to the court; Christopher Lee, 'Listening to the Child's Voice in Spain', *The Child's Voice – 15 Years Later*, 37; in Greece a child can only be represented by his or her parents, even in cases of parental child abduction. The legislation does not provide for the child to be made a ward of the court, nor does it provide for the child's independent representation before the courts. For a child to be heard the applicant parent must request this of the court and, if agreed, the child can be heard from aged six. Only the judge is present, and the judge does not have the benefit of any guidelines on how best to ascertain the child's views; Karolina Zoi Andriakopoulou and Maria Louiza Andriakopoulou, 'The Voice of the Child in Hague Convention Proceedings in Greece', *The Child's Voice – 15 Years Later*, 34.

heard directly by a judge or through a professional children's specialist. A recent global survey by Taylor and Freeman[145] found that there can be up to 17 different methods of ascertaining children's views in Hague Convention proceedings. The wide range of specialists involved to inform the legal process when a child's objections are raised include psychologists, family consultants, counsellors, social workers, guardians ad litem, children's officers, child protection officials and youth department workers.

In the English courts, Baroness Hale expresses in the case of *Re D*[146] three possible ways of hearing from the child: 1. Joining the child as a party to the proceedings with separate legal representation. 2. A face-to-face interview with the judge. 3. The report of an independent Cafcass officer[147] or other professional, who is skilled and experienced in interviewing children. Baroness Hale suggests of the three, direct meetings are better not only for the judge to hear first-hand an undiluted account of the child's views, but also to facilitate children's participation in proceedings affecting them.

Previously, as Baroness Hale explains, 'meetings between children and judges used to be commonplace, but the practice dwindled.'[148] It is suggested by senior judiciary deciding Hague cases in Australia[149] and Japan[150] that the practice dwindled as independent child experts are considered to be better trained than judges to ascertain the child's views because of their specialised training on interacting with children and their analysis based on their behavioural science expertise. The current practice in family proceedings in England and Wales is for children to participate in proceedings through sharing their views with a Cafcass officer, who as Raitt suggests, are 'gatekeepers' in the process of listening to children and effectually 'mediate children's participation.'[151] While the method of such professionals ascertaining the child's views is compliant with the text of Article 12 CRC, the CRC Committee has since suggested in GC12 that the direct approach, with judges meeting children, better upholds the child's right to participate in proceedings. The view is supported by research that suggests child welfare professionals 'gloss over', 'stifle' and 'filter out' children's voices.[152] This viewpoint is not limited

[145] Nicola Taylor and Marilyn Freeman, 'Outcomes for Objecting Children under the 1980 Convention', *The Child's Voice – 15 Years Later*, 11.

[146] In *re D (A Child) (Abduction: Rights of Custody)* [2007] 1 AC 619.

[147] The statutory body in England is CAFCASS (Children and Family Court Advisory and Support Service) and in Wales CAFCASS CYMRU.

[148] Baroness Hale, 'Child Abduction from the Child's Point of View', *The Child's Voice – 15 Years Later*, 42.

[149] Victoria Bennett, 'A Better Place for the Child in Return Proceedings under the 1980 Convention – A Perspective from Australia', *The Child's Voice – 15 Years Later*, 21.

[150] Tomoko Sawamura, 'Child's View in Return Proceedings – Practice of Japanese Courts', *The Child's Voice – 15 Years Later*, 25.

[151] Raitt (n 107) 204.

[152] Stalford, Hollingsworth and Gilmore (n 9) 4; Citing also Sally McNamee and others, 'Family Law and the Construction of Childhood in England and Wales' in Jim Goddard and others (eds), *The Politics of Childhood* (Palgrave Macmillan, 2005).

to the United Kingdom; several studies internationally[153] suggest children are unhappy with their views being misrepresented by report writers:

> Children have commented that they are not happy about the techniques employed by report writers, the lack of confidentiality, the feeling that their views have not properly been understood or taken seriously, and the filtering and reinterpretation by the report writer of what they have said. Children have no say in how their views are presented and have no opportunity to respond if they feel they have been misrepresented.[154]

Research highlights that in practice, children very rarely have the opportunity to meet with the judge.[155] The limitation to children's participation is compounded by the fact that there is discretion as to whether the judge wishes to meet the child. Hendrick notes 'Judicial attitudes towards seeing children differ significantly: not just from one area of the country to the other, but often between different courtrooms in the same court building. Many judges are reluctant to see children, while others are keen to do so. The UNCRC states that it is the child's right to be heard, but currently, whether a child gets to meet with the judge ultimately boils down to the temperament of the judge in question.'[156] The discretion judges have on whether or not they meet with a child can ultimately influence the outcome, as the Hague Convention grants the judiciary discretion to disregard the mature child's views. The evidence presented here suggests, as others have,[157] that abducted children should, therefore, be heard in every case, and not only in cases where the child's objection to return defence is raised.

C. The Hague Convention Grants the Judiciary Discretion to Disregard the Mature Child's Views

If the countries to which they were abducted had been party to the Hague Convention, Sara, Aidan and Harris could only have participated in proceedings if (i) their objections are raised by their abducting fathers, and (ii) the law in the country they are abducted to considers them of sufficient age and maturity.

[153] Patsy Henderson, 'To Heed the Child's Voice', (2000) *New Zealand Law Journal* 267, 268; Judith Cashmore 'Children's Participation in Family Law Matters' in Christine Hallet and Alan Prout (eds), *Hearing the Voices of Children: Social Policy for a New Century* (Routledge-Falmer, 2003) 164; Patrick Parkinson and Judith Cashmore, *The Voice of a Child in Family Law Disputes* (OUP, 2008) 149; Michelle Fernando and Nicola Ross, 'Stifled Voices: Hearing Children's Objections in Hague Child Abduction Convention Cases in Australia', (2018) 32(1) *Int J Law Policy Family* 93, 101.

[154] Fernando and Ross, ibid, 101.

[155] Kathryn Hollingsworth and Helen Stalford, 'Judging Parental Abduction: What Does It Mean to Adopt a Children's Rights-Based Approach?' in Gillian Douglas and others (eds), *International and National Perspectives on Child and Family Law Essays in Honour of Nigel Lowe* (Intersentia Publishers, 2018) chapter 9; See also Jemimah Hendrick, 'When Should the Judge and the Child Meet?' October [2011] *Fam Law* 1148; Raitt (n 107) 204; Beaumont, Walker and Holliday (n 116) suggests the courts also do not hear children in most cases under Brussels II Revised.

[156] Hendrick (n 155).

[157] Schuz (2013) (n 11).

The extent of their participation is further limited depending upon (iii) if they are given a choice of the process by which their views are ascertained. Once the children have surpassed these obstacles to participation, the Hague Convention further grants the judge discretion on how much weight to attach to the child's objections to return. As Baroness Hale explains:[158]

> The court is entitled to weigh in the balance the general policy considerations underlying the 1980 Convention against the interests of the child in the individual case. These include not only the swift return of abducted children but also comity between the Contracting States and respect for one another's judicial processes, as well as more general considerations of the child's rights and welfare.[159]

How judges approach the balance to be drawn between the child's objections and the Hague Convention's principles is the 'gateway test' articulated by Black LJ, as she then was, in *Re M (Republic of Ireland) (Child's Objections) (Joinder of Children to Appeal)*.[160] First, the test comprises of whether 'the child objects to being returned and has attained an age and degree of maturity at which it is appropriate to take account of his or her views.' At the second stage, the court must consider not only the nature and strength of the objections but a much wider range of considerations, including whether they are genuine and not influenced by the abducting parent, and whether the child's objections coincide with the child's welfare. If Aidan decided in Hague proceedings to continue objecting to returning, only the most strenuous of objections would be considered, a mere preference by Aidan to remain in the UAE would not be enough.[161] There are numerous case examples of children's objections being disregarded,[162] including where this has resulted in the child being forcibly returned by the police.[163] So as McEleavy argues, by balancing the child's views against the objectives of the Convention, 'there remains a very real prospect that Convention considerations will outweigh the child-centric considerations underpinning the finding of the defence.'[164]

The study by Hollingsworth and Stalford[165] of 30 child objection cases in Hague Convention proceedings reveals that Sara, Aidan and Harris will have

[158] Baroness Hale (n 148) 42.
[159] See also House of Lords, in *Re M (Children) (Abduction: Rights of Custody)* [2007] UKHL 55, [2008] 1 AC 1288, paras [42]–[43], [46]. See also discussion by Beaumont and McEleavy (n 105) 194.
[160] [2015] EWCA Civ 26.
[161] *Re R (A Minor: Abduction)* [1991] Fam 475, 475.
[162] *Re F (Hague Convention: Child's Objections)* [2006] FamCA 685; *Richards & Director-General, Department of Child Safety* [2007] FamCA 65; France, Cass Civ 16re 14/02/2006 (pourvoi no05-14646), [INCADAT cite: HC/E/FR 853]; Israel, Appl App Dist Ct 672/06, [INCADAT cite: HC/E/IL 885]; New Zealand, *White v Northumberland* [2006] NZFLR 1105; Scotland, *W vW* 2004 SC 63 IH (1 Div); Switzerland, 5P.3/2007/bnm; Bundesgericht, ll.Zivilabteilung, 13 February 2007, [INCADAT cite: HC/E/CH 894]; USA, *De Silva v Pitts* 481 F3d 1279 (10th Cir 2007)).
[163] See *M v B* [2016] EWHC 1657 (Fam); *Re M (Republic of Ireland) (Child's Objections) (Joinder of Children as Parties to Appeal)* [2015] EWCA Civ 26; and Israeli case FamA (Dist ta) 1167/99 *R v L* (unreported, 3 July 2000) [incadat cite: HC/E/IL 834].
[164] McEleavy (n 122).
[165] Hollingsworth and Stalford (n 155).

the additional evidential obstacle to demonstrate a high degree of independence from the views of their parents. For example, in *RB v DB*,[166] the judge rejected the validity of the children's views on the basis that they were too mature. The emphasis is wrongly placed upon the child to prove otherwise, rather than the judge, as their research highlights, 'interrogating further the views of the child, if necessary through appropriate expert intervention and assessment.'[167] In considering evidence of the impact of children's views on the judge's ultimate decision, in only a minority of cases they examine (8 out of the 30), did the child's objections make any difference to the outcome.[168] Based on this evaluation, any objections to returning raised by Sara, Aidan and Harris are unlikely to be granted any significant weight.

D. A Child-Centred Hague Convention Requires Separate Representation for the Child

This text argues, as others have, that the child's views can only be fairly presented through having the right to separate representation.[169] This would address the problem Baroness Hale highlights of children not knowing to phrase their views as an 'objection', as this affects the judge's ultimate decision on whether to treat the child's views as an objection rather than a mere preference:

> An adult on learning of the threshold test would be likely to present his evidence accordingly. If he did not want return to the State of habitual residence, he would be likely to frame this in terms of an objection. But we want to hear unaffected evidence about a child's wishes and feelings in her own words. Children will not necessarily use the language of objection or preference or mere unhappiness with the precision required by courts interpreting Article 13. But very often, a judge's refusal to return a child will be based on a strict analysis of the language used.[170]

This places the child on the evidential back foot, as Hollingsworth and Stalford[171] observe from their analysis of the case-law. And the problem is exacerbated through the use of intermediaries:

> The propensity of children to express their objections in persuasive terms depends heavily on the manner in which those views are elicited; namely how the child is questioned by intermediaries, and the circumstances surrounding those meetings. Indeed, CAFCASS officers in four of the thirty cases analysed were heavily criticised for failing to probe whether the child was objecting or simply expressing a preference, or to inform

[166] *RB v DB* [2015] EWHC 1817 (Fam), para [22].
[167] See, eg, *X v. Y, Z Police Force, A, B and C (by their Children's Guardian)* (2013) 1 FLR 1277; Hollingsworth and Stalford (n 155).
[168] Ibid.
[169] Schuz (2013) (n 11) 392.
[170] Baroness Hale (n 148) 43.
[171] Hollingsworth and Stalford (n 155).

the child of the importance of expressing their views in the unequivocal terms required for an objection.[172]

It is for this reason that there are calls for greater use of Independent Children's Lawyers and meetings between children and judges in Hague Convention cases.[173]

While the arguments given against separate representation include lack of necessity, delay, resources and the risk of harm to the child, the arguments are insufficient to withhold children the basic right to representation, because, without separate representation, the evidence suggests the child is unlikely to be heard and fairly represented.[174] To successfully articulate the requisite 'strength of feeling' when objecting to returning, Aidan, aged ten, would likely require independent representation. The representative would also be in a position to advise Aidan, independently, of whether or not his father is at risk of imprisonment. Whether or not Aidan would be entitled to independent representation depends again upon the law in the country to which he is abducted.[175]

Granting children independent legal representation is the only way to guarantee that the recommendations in GC12 are adhered to, particularly the 'redress' stage. Or the Hague Convention could go further still, as Schuz points out, and enable abducted children themselves to invoke the 1980 Convention, rather than being reliant on the parents to do so.[176] This could serve to improve how the Hague Convention upholds Article 12 rights of abducted children, as currently the statistics demonstrate that children's participation is limited. The review of Hague cases in 2015[177] illustrates that of the 2270 return applications in 76 Contracting States, 28 per cent were refused overall.[178] The survey recorded a total of 243 refusals

[172] For examples see Theis J in *MR v HS* [2015] EWHC 234 (Fam); Thorpe LJ in *Re D (Children)* [2011] EWCA Civ 1294.

[173] Fernando and Ross (n 153) 93.

[174] Elizabeth Pitman, 'Making the Interests of the Child Paramount: Representation For Children in the Hague Convention on the Civil Aspects of International Child Abduction' (2009) 17 *Cardozo Public Law, Policy & Ethics Journal* 515; Merle Weiner, 'Intolerable Situations and Counsel for Children: Following Switzerland's Example in Hague Abduction Cases' (2008) 58 *American University Law Review* 335.

[175] Professionals interviewed confirmed separate representation is not granted in Islamic family law proceedings. In contrast, the law in South Africa and Switzerland grants children representation, even though the Hague Convention does not stipulate this as a requirement (s 279 of the South African Children's Act 38 of 2005 and Art 9(3) of the Swiss Federal Act on International Child Abduction of 2007; see translation in Andreas Bucher, 'The New Swiss Federal Act on International Child Abduction' (2008) 4 *Journal of Private International Law* 139, 161–65)). It is reported that that there is a reluctance to allow children independent legal representation in England, New Zealand and Australia; Marilyn Freeman and Anne-Marie Hutchinson, 'Half Price for Children? The Voice of the Child and the Child's Fight for Party Status in Cases on International Child Abduction' (2007) 29 *International Family Law* 177; *Re L v H* [2009] EWHC 3074 (Fam); *In The Matter of M (A Child)* [2010] EWCA 178; Marilyn Freeman and Anne-Marie Hutchinson, 'Abduction and the Voice of the Child: *In re M*', [2008] *Int'l Fam L* 163.

[176] As is recommended by Schuz (2013) (n 11) 404.

[177] Hague Survey (2015).

[178] Reversing an upward trend compared with 34 per cent in 2008, 29 per cent in 2003 and 26 per cent in 1999.

(28 per cent), and in 185 of these, information was provided on the grounds relied upon. Of these 185 cases, the child objections defence comprised 27 cases (15 per cent of all refusals), lower than in previous years.[179] So far as individual States were concerned, Mexico had the highest proportion of 5 of the 11 refusals (45 per cent) based solely or in part upon the child's objections ground. Germany had the second highest number, 4 cases (19 per cent of all refusals). The number of cases in which the child's objection defence is accepted by the court is low, in only 27 of the 2270 cases surveyed that year. This is indicative of the degree to which the courts have, when determining a Hague Convention application, upheld the child's Article 12 CRC right to participate in proceedings, both to be heard and to be listened to.

E. Are Hague Practices Compliant with Article 12?

Children's participation in Hague cases should not be limited to Article 13(2) objection cases only,[180] because even if Sara, Aidan and Harris do not object to a return, they may wish to exercise their Article 12 CRC right to participate in Hague proceedings that will determine their future. Indeed, the very fact that for intra-EU abduction cases, the Hague Convention is improved upon, and children's views are to be heard in all cases,[181] offers up an immediate solution to the Hague Convention's inability to uphold the Article 12 rights of all children.[182] When both legal systems – Islamic and Hague – are compared alongside each other, and measured against the UNCRC Committee's guidelines in GC12, it transpires that children's participation in child abduction proceedings under both domestic Islamic law and the Hague Convention is far from ideal. In addressing this in a Hague Convention context, the Hague Conference issued guidance in 2020 advising national courts on how children's participation can be facilitated in Hague Convention proceedings, particularly where the child's views are to be ascertained with respect to an Article 13(1)(b) claim.[183] The document advises national courts on how children might be engaged in proceedings highlighting that the individual

[179] The 2015 finding is proportionally the lowest yet recorded for this exception. In 2008, 22 per cent (58 cases) of refusals were based upon the child's objections exception, 18 per cent (26 cases) in 2003 and 21 per cent (21 cases) in 1999.

[180] Claire Fenton-Glynn, 'Participation and Natural Justice: Children's Rights and Interests in Hague Abduction Proceedings' (2014) 9(1) *Journal of Comparative Law* 134.

[181] Article 11(2) Brussels II Revised Regulation 2201/2003 stipulates the returning court is required to hear the child's views if the child is old enough to be heard. As a result, children should be given the opportunity to be heard in any return proceedings under the 1980 Convention, and not only in proceedings limited to a defence under Article 13(2). For the effectiveness of this rule, see Lamont (n 116) 234.

[182] Though see (n 116) that comments on the ineffectiveness of the revised law.

[183] HCCH Convention of 25 October 1980 on the Civil Aspects of International Child Abduction – Part VI – Article 13(1)(b), available at https://assets.hcch.net/docs/e86d9f72-dc8d-46f3-b3bf-e102911c8532.pdf.

hearing the child's views should be qualified for the task, possessing knowledge of the Hague Convention and the way in which the exceptions to return operate. The guide invites courts to consider the appointment of separate representation for the child and to encourage the parties, the child's representative or appointed expert to inform the child of the ongoing process and possible consequences of the proceedings. This is to be undertaken in a 'timely and appropriate way' depending upon the child's age and maturity. Specific guidance issued by the Hague Conference on the importance of hearing children in proceedings, including where the Article 13(1)(b) exception is pleaded and the importance of separate representation for the child addresses some of the key criticism pointed at the Hague Convention. The guidance reflects the developments in children's rights since the Hague Convention was introduced and it is hoped that the Hague Conference's renewed recommendations will encourage national courts to give effect to the developments.

The UNCRC Committee's guidance in GC12 recommends (A) that the child must be given information about his or her right to express a view, and the option of communicating the view to the decision-maker directly or through a representative. 'She or he must be aware of the possible consequences of this choice.' The way in which the Hague Convention operates means that the child is very rarely given an option to select the process by which to convey his or her views, as most domestic processes offer one approach only. And in jurisdictions like the UK where alternative methods are possible, the discretion lies with the judge on whether or not he or she will meet with the abducted child.[184] In comparison, the process in Islamic law countries, while facilitating direct meetings with a judge, also does not offer a choice of alternative methods. GC12 further recommends that children are made aware of the consequences of their choice. It seems the children able to participate in Islamic Court proceedings are made aware their choice will be acted upon. By contrast, in Hague proceedings, though the process varies between states, in general, the child's views are *heard* in objection cases, yet the threshold is set high for *listening* to those objections.

On GC12 guidance (B), the Committee requires the context in which a child exercises her or his right to be heard 'has to be enabling and encouraging, so that the child can be sure that the adult who is responsible for the hearing is willing to listen and seriously consider what the child has decided to communicate.' In a Hague Convention context, it is questionable whether the judge is able to 'seriously consider' the child's views when studies illustrate that children are rarely heard in Hague Convention proceedings.[185] In the Islamic Court process, the child *once given* the opportunity to be heard can be confident his or her views will be listened

[184] *Guidelines for Judges Meeting Children who are subject to Family Proceedings* produced by the Family Justice Council and approved by the President of the Family Division, set out in *Family Court Practice* (LexisNexis, 2011) 2876, followed by *Guidelines in Relation to Children Giving Evidence in Family Proceedings* [2012] 2 FLR 456.

[185] Hollingsworth and Stalford (n 155); Fernando and Ross (n 153).

to, but whether the context can be 'enabling and encouraging' in cases where a five-man panel can interview children is questionable.

GC12's guidance (C) on assessing the capacity of the child is problematic under both legal frameworks, particularly concerning the age-related assumptions national legislation makes about children's capacity to make decisions in a parental abduction context. On guidance (D) information about the weight given to the views of the child (feedback), neither legal system provides a separate feedback meeting as recommended, although it is hoped that the Hague Conference's 2020 guidance will encourage national courts to engage children more meaningfully in Hague Convention proceedings. Neither legal framework fulfils guidance (E) which requires that legislation should provide children with complaint procedures and remedies when their right to be heard and given due weight is disregarded and violated. Children also do not have access to the appeals and complaints procedures that provide remedies for rights violations, unless they are represented separately in Hague proceedings.

The discussion identifies that neither legal framework entirely upholds the child's right to participate in abduction proceedings. The Hague Convention is marginally better in that it does not preclude children's participation based upon a best interests assessment. The main difference is that in the Hague model, the views of most objecting children are ascertained, but those views are only *listened* to if the views conform to the judge's assessment of the child's best interests. Conversely, the Islamic Court system undertakes the best interests assessment beforehand, and if both parents are judged to be eligible custodians, the child can choose between the parents. So, in participatory terms, the Hague model is somewhat more inclusive, as all objecting children should be 'heard', even though it might be considered 'tokenistic' participation. Whereas the Islamic Court system excludes groups of children from participating, but those that are allowed to participate have complete autonomy to decide.

Before arriving at a definitive conclusion, however, it will be helpful to identify how the three case studies would be resolved if decided under the Hague Convention.

F. Sara, Aidan and Harris's Participation in Hague Convention Proceedings

The children's views would be ascertained only if their abducting parents raise the Article 13(2) defence to return. If the objection is brought to the courts' attention, the children's views would be heard, but the weight that would be accorded to those views depends upon the child's age and the strength of his or her objections. The process by which their views are ascertained could differ depending upon the country abducted to; it is likely that in Islamic law countries, the judge would meet directly with the children to ascertain their views, rather than through an intermediary. Meeting the child alone, or at least without family members present, would assist the judge in identifying their true wishes, and perhaps also reassure Aidan about the situation of his father's imprisonment. At the age of eight, Harris's views would be ascertained only if it is domestic practice to hear from eight-year-olds in the country he was taken to by his abducting parent.

Both Sara and Aidan informed the adults asking, that they wished to remain in the Islamic law country. And based upon the position of children's autonomy and choice in Islamic law countries (subject to the Islamic law best interest's assessment) their voiced wishes were acted upon. Both Sara and Aidan, however, state that the views they expressed were not actually their true wishes and the result of undue influence. The influence over Sara's wishes was overt, whereas Aidan states his expressed views were genuine as at that time he believed remaining in the UAE would protect his father from imprisonment. The fact that the Hague Convention hears children, but does not always give any weight to the child's views, may serve these two children well in their circumstances since they both state they articulated to the court views which were not genuine.

The weight to be attributed to the views of Aidan and Sara is more unclear, as the objectives of the Convention (the policy of automatic return, comity between contracting states and judicial courtesy) would be balanced against their wishes.[186] The case-law and statistics illustrate that Sara, Aidan and Harris are likely to be returned unless they articulate very strong objections. A return order seems the likely outcome when compared with the example of Morocco, the only Islamic law country for which there is information on Hague Convention interpretation. The 2015 survey demonstrates children were returned by the Moroccan courts applying Hague more enthusiastically than any other state,[187] without Article 13(2) or indeed any of the exceptions to return being applied in all eight cases decided in Morocco. The Moroccan courts returned 87.5 per cent of abducted children, unlike other Hague states which returned children in only 65 per cent of cases.[188] Notwithstanding the ardent application of Hague's return policy, in view of the fact that domestic law in Islamic law countries does not give a voice to children whose mother is not Muslim, has remarried or will not live in the Islamic law country, the young people in the sample abducted to Islamic law countries would fare better under the Hague Convention framework than they would under domestic law.

[186] *Re M (Republic of Ireland) (Child's Objections) (Joinder of Children to Appeal)* [2015] EWCA Civ 26.

[187] Hague Survey (2015).

[188] Globally only 43 per cent of applications (compared with 87.5 per cent in Morocco) were decided in court. So of all the cases that proceeded to a court hearing, 65 per cent of those court decisions resulted in a judicial order for return. Similarly, there is no refusal to return children recorded by the Moroccan courts, whereas globally, 12 per cent of applications ended in a judicial refusal; Hague Survey (2015).

IV. Conclusion

The analysis affirms that children's participatory rights can be facilitated, albeit partially and under heavily prescribed conditions, through provisions of the Hague Convention. The difficulty in achieving a children's rights-based application of Hague Convention, however, is the construction of the provisions by the judiciary, rather than the law itself. Commitment to historical guidance[189] is one such obstacle,[190] and judges could develop their understanding of the children's rights-based approach to address this. It is possible that this may be improved through the accession of Islamic law countries to the Hague Convention.

The analysis undertaken in this chapter of the interplay between Hague and Islamic approaches to child participation leads to the observation that the Hague Convention could work well with the more participatory approach of Islamic states. Since Islamic courts are accustomed to listening to children in domestic custody cases, this method of participation can be extended to Hague Convention proceedings before the Islamic courts and could perhaps even serve to improve the Hague Convention's approach to children's participation in proceedings. The combination of an explicit participatory requirement in objection cases under the Hague Convention, coupled with more sympathetic and routine 'listening' in domestic Islamic law proceedings, could provide a stronger package of support for children in cross-border Islamic country abductions.

Accession by Islamic law countries to the Hague Convention offers new opportunity to revisit the currency of children's rights participation in Hague cases and could achieve a position where children benefit from the best of both legal processes. This analysis suggests that children's rights could be advanced if the Islamic courts apply the provisions of the Hague Convention and allow children to return irrespective of the mother's lifestyle choices, and at the same time, listen to the views of mature children. The approach could achieve an outcome that observes the children's rights-based approach and does away with the dated assumptions on the interests of children by the Islamic law Courts and capacities of children under the Hague Convention.

[189] Perez-Vera (n 114); Bodenheimer (n 110) 110.

[190] Matti Savolainen 'The Hague Convention on Child Abduction of 1980 and its Implementation in Finland', (1997) 66 *Nordic Journal of International Law* 131.

5

The Abducted Child's Right to Non-Discrimination

The focus of this chapter is on the right of the child to be protected from discrimination, the third of the four CRC General Principles. The chapter prioritises gender discrimination exclusively, as differences in treatment and experience on the basis of gender have arisen in one form or another throughout consideration of the data on parental abduction to Islamic law countries. Thus, to be faithful both to the empirical data and the underpinning principles of the CRC, it is an area that merits exploration.

The principle of non-discrimination is enshrined in Article 2 UNCRC 1989 and provides:

> 1. States Parties shall respect and ensure the rights set forth in the present Convention to each child within their jurisdiction without discrimination of any kind, irrespective of the child's or his or her parent's or legal guardian's race, colour, sex, language, religion, political or other opinion, national, ethnic or social origin, property, disability, birth or other status.
> 2. States Parties shall take all appropriate measures to ensure that the child is protected against all forms of discrimination or punishment based on the status, activities, expressed opinions, or beliefs of the child's parents, legal guardians, or family members.

Parental abduction to Islamic law countries is an inherently gendered phenomenon. Two types of gender discrimination emerge in the data: the impact of the law on girl abductees, and the impact of the law on left-behind mothers where fathers have abducted the child to an Islamic law country. Gender discrimination experienced by girl abductees sits more clearly within the framework of children's rights and Article 2 CRC. The second, discrimination experienced by left-behind mothers while not protected under the CRC framework, is pertinent because Article 2(1) seeks to protect children from discrimination targeted at the child, but also arising as a result of the discrimination experienced by the child's parent: 'irrespective of the child's or his or her parent's … sex.' The children's rights analysis will, therefore, encompass the gender discrimination experienced by mothers, but only in relation to how it impacts upon abducted children and affects the children's enjoyment of rights as protected by the CRC.

It will also be necessary to consider, in parts, some of the equality provisions available to adult females, as abducted girls are no longer protected by the CRC once they reach the age of 18, even though, as the evidence illustrates below, the abduction does not always end at age 18 for girls. The approach to assessing evidence concerning the right of abducted children to non-discrimination is therefore not as clear-cut as is the case with other CRC rights examined. So while the analysis of the non-discrimination right is a response to the data, this is an initial attempt at analysis through the children's rights lens and so necessarily raises as many questions as it answers.

The discussion in the preceding chapters highlights how gender discrimination manifests in the custody/abduction law in Islamic law countries. The law in Islamic law countries treats girls differently from boys in the age at which they are capacitous, their eligibility to choose with which parent to reside and their eligibility to participate in proceedings. The discussion in chapter 3 on best interests illustrates that abducted children are further affected by their mothers' ineligibility for custody because of her position as a woman, which resulted in the children's separation from their primary carer.

Gender further configures as a factor in the context of cross-border parental abduction in numerous ways that will be considered throughout the chapter. For example, the father is the abducting parent in the vast majority of the cases examined, in 26 of the 29 cases (89.65 per cent of the sample). And while mothers undertake the remaining three cases of abduction, it is noteworthy that domestic violence is reported to be a feature in two of those three cases. What is more, domestic violence is a feature in 25 of the 29 cases in the author's study (86.2 per cent) and is also reported by left-behind mothers to be one of the underlying causes for the abductions in the sample. Fathers abducted to regain custody of the children, to ensure the children were not exposed to the mother's new partners, and for the children to be raised in an Islamic environment. A controlling partner or parent has more authority and less restriction in an Islamic law country.[1] In this way, parental abduction, it seems from the data, is used to perpetuate and reassert control of the left-behind mother and the child.

The discussion in this chapter will more deeply examine how gender discrimination manifests in the custody/abduction law in Islamic law countries, in the legislative framing, procedural protocols and substantive outcomes for abducted children. This chapter aims to explore whether Hague accession might mitigate these entrenched inequalities. The analysis in this chapter will draw upon the remaining three of the ten case studies, those of Miriam, Aliyah and Ryan, to illustrate how gender discrimination manifests in the outcomes for abducted children.

[1] See the Welsh case of Amina Al-Jeffery, a 17-year-old taken to Saudi Arabia by her father because she 'kissed a guy'. She continued to be detained in her father's care in 2016, at the age of 21, when the matter came before the UK courts. The High Court ordered the father to return Amina to the UK. Amina's solicitors informed the court that she had run away to a refuge in Saudi Arabia, after which she was returned to her father and he was granted a parental care order from the Saudi courts for the purpose of caring and supervision. Mr Justice Holman ruled that the father must permit and facilitate the return of his daughter to the UK and could face contempt of court proceedings on his return to the UK if he failed to comply; Sarah Campbell, 'Amina Al-Jeffery: Locked up Woman Must Be Allowed Home' (BBC, 03.08.16).

This chapter begins by examining the legal framework on non-discrimination, identifying the protections available in the CRC and other human rights instruments. Part II then considers the interplay between gender discrimination, Islamic law and the abducted child and examines in more depth how gender discrimination features in the legislative framing and procedural protocols in Islamic law countries. Part II continues with an analysis of the evidence of gender discrimination in the outcomes for abducted children, looking closely at the effect of 'guardianship' provisions in Islamic law and how these can facilitate discriminatory practices.

The chapter will then proceed in part III to discuss the challenges in addressing gender discrimination which manifests in the law and legal processes in Islamic law countries, in a child abduction context. Part III will examine whether the challenges can be appropriately responded to through the lens of (a) the broader architecture of human rights and equality provisions (b) the cultural nature of the rights of abducted children, and (c) the relational nature of abducted children's rights. While this is an added layer to the examination in this chapter, it is a necessary approach to disentangle this complex area and engage with the relevant theoretical perspectives. The analysis builds upon the discussion in earlier chapters on the tension between children's rights and the operation of Islamic law in modern times, in a specific parental abduction context. The arguments are attended to as these are very relevant to the issue of the changing climate of parental abduction cases, with an acknowledgement that the majority of abductions under the Hague Convention framework are undertaken by mothers together with the new wave of Hague Convention accession by Islamic law countries.

Part IV of this chapter examines gender discrimination in the context of the Hague Convention, looking at whether the Hague framework can be a potential solution to address the challenges identified. It examines specifically how the English courts will respond to the gender discrimination in the law of Islamic law countries, where a child's return is sought under the Hague Convention to the Hague Islamic states of Morocco, Iraq, Pakistan and Tunisia. Finally, the chapter concludes with a reflection upon how the case studies of Miriam, Ryan and Aliyah would be determined if decided in Hague proceedings. The discussion assists in answering the principal question in this text of whether accession to the Hague Convention by Islamic law countries is likely to advance children's rights.

I. The Legal Framework on Non-Discrimination

The principle of non-discrimination is deep-rooted in human morality and is recognised legally as one of the fundamental principles of modern democracies.[2] The Second World War prompted concern for human rights protection and led to

[2] Samantha Besson, 'The Principle of Non-Discrimination in the Convention on the Rights of the Child.' (2005) 13 *International Journal of Children s Rights* 433, 434.

the principle being included in several international human rights instruments, including the 1948 Universal Declaration of Human Rights ('UDHR'),[3] the 1966 International Covenant on Civil and Political Rights ('ICCPR')[4] and the 1966 International Covenant on Economic, Social and Cultural Rights ('ICESCR'). In addition, the principle of equal rights is included in the 1945 Charter of the United Nations,[5] the 1981 United Nations Convention on the Elimination of All Forms of Discrimination against Women ('CEDAW'), and the European Convention on Human Rights ('ECHR'). Thus at the time the CRC was drafted, the principle was firmly established in international law.[6] The equality protections[7] extend to 'race, colour, sex, language, religion, political or other opinion, national or social origin, property, birth or other status'[8] and specifically refer to the non-discrimination protections in a legal context: 'All are equal before the law and are entitled without any discrimination to equal protection of the law.'[9]

The principle of non-discrimination is one of the most frequently protected norms of international human rights law[10] and the treaty protections extend to children.[11] Yet the right under most treaties cannot be invoked directly by individuals against the state or against other individuals. This is because states are

[3] Art 2 UDHR.

[4] Art 2 ICCPR.

[5] Warwick McKean, *Equality and Discrimination under International Law* (OUP, 1983) 277–83; Bertrand Ramcharan, 'Equality and Non-Discrimination' in Louis Henkin (ed), *The International Bill of Rights: The Covenant on Civil and Political Rights* (Columbia University Press, 1983) 249.

[6] Marit Skivenes and Karl Harald Søvig, *Child Rights and International Discrimination Law: Implementing Article 2 of the United Nations Convention on the Rights of the Child* (Routledge, 2019); Rachel Hodgkin and Peter Newell, *The Implementation Handbook for the Convention on the Rights of the Child* (UNICEF, 2002); Geraldine Van Bueren, *The International Law on the Rights of the Child* (Kluwer, 1995); L Hitch, 'Non-discrimination and the rights of the child. Article 2' (1989) 7 *New York University Law School Journal of Human Rights* 47; Lawrence LeBlanc, *The Convention on the Rights of the Child: United Nations Lawmaking on Human Rights* (University of Nebraska Press, 1995) ch 2; Sharon Detrick, *A Commentary on the United Nations Convention on the Rights of the Child* (Martinus Nijhoff, 1999); Sarah Muscroft, *Children's Rights: Equal Rights? Diversity, Difference and the Issue of Discrimination* (International Save the Children Alliance, 2000).

[7] The terms 'equality' and 'non-discrimination' are used in this analysis interchangeably.

[8] Arts 2 of the EDHR, ICCPR and Art 2 para 2 of the ICESCR. See also Art 14 ECHR and its Protocol 12 on the general prohibition of discrimination which extends the scope of Art 14 ECHR.

[9] Art 7 EDHR and Art 26 ICCPR.

[10] EW Vierdag, *The Concept of Discrimination in International Law, with Special Reference to Human Rights* (Martinus Nijhoff, 1973); Yoram Dinstein, 'Discrimination and International Human Rights, (1985) 15 *Israel Yearbook of Human Rights* 11–27; Anne Bayefsky, 'The Principle of Equality and Non Discrimination in International Law' (1990) 11 *Human Rights Law Journal* 1–34; Karl Josef Partsch, 'Discrimination' in *The European System for the Protection of Human Rights* (Martinus Nijhoff, 1993); Ian Brownlie, *Principles of Public International Law* (OUP, 2003) 578–80.

[11] Susan Marks and Andrew Clapham, 'Children' in *International Human Rights Lexicon* (OUP, 2005) 26; There are specific references to the child in Art 24 par 1 ICCPR which provides 'every child shall have, without any discrimination as to race, colour, sex, language, religion, national or social origin, property or birth, the right to such measures of protection as are required by his status as a minor, on the part of his family, society and the State'; also Art 10 par 3 ICESCR: Special measures of protection and assistance should be taken on behalf of all children and young persons without any discrimination for reasons of parentage or other conditions.

the addressees of human rights treaties – so enforcement is dependent upon implementation in the particular jurisdiction. This has a particular impact upon enforcement between private individuals given it is the state that owes the duty to rights bearers. Secondly, the non-discrimination principle is not a right in and of itself – it simply ensures all other rights are upheld without discrimination on the grounds of protected characteristics. Thus in the context of the CRC, the protections are mainly subordinate clauses that qualify other rights are upheld free of any discrimination, rather than prohibiting discrimination itself.[12] As the treaty protections are generally unenforceable, children are not sufficiently protected.

Likewise, as Van Bueren highlights, children can be doubly discriminated against: first, as children and, secondly, as members of a specific gender or group.[13] The double discrimination affects girls abducted to Islamic law countries, as we shall see in the data below. Article 2 CRC responds to this 'double jeopardy'[14] which the other international treaties identified above may not capture. A specific right of children to be protected from discrimination is therefore considered an essential addition to the non-discrimination framework.

A. Child-Specific Equality Provisions: Article 2 CRC

Article 2 affirms states parties are under a duty not to discriminate against children in their enjoyment of Convention rights. As a general principle of the CRC, Article 2 applies to the interpretation and application of the whole Convention and so requires that the other rights are not applied discriminatorily.[15] More specifically, the CRC is unique in that its Article 2 seeks to protect children from discrimination targeted at the child, but also any discrimination arising as a result of the child's family, such as gender discrimination against the mother (Article 2(1), as will be discussed below). While children can invoke the Article 2 CRC right, this is only possible, as is highlighted in chapter 2, if states have incorporated the CRC or other international treaty provisions into their domestic law. Islamic law countries, like the UK, are dualist states and, therefore, international treaties will require implementation.

The UNCRC Committee has not defined what it means by 'discrimination,' but a definition is provided by the UN Human Rights Committee. It explains discrimination as

> any distinction, exclusion, restriction or preference which is based on any ground such as race, colour, sex, language, religion, political or other opinion, national or social

[12] Bayefsky (n 10) 3–4; This is the case, for instance, of Art 2 par 2 ICCPR, Art 2 par 1 ICESCR, Art 2 UDHR and Art 14 ECHR. Though note the exception is found in Art 26 ICCPR, Art 14 ECHR and Art 1 Protocol 12 ECHR.

[13] Van Bueren (n 6) 39–40.

[14] Besson (n 2) 434.

[15] Muscroft (n 6) 27–8.

> origin, property, birth or other status and which has the purpose or effect of nullifying or impairing the recognition, enjoyment or exercise by all persons, on an equal footing, of all rights and freedoms.[16]

Bayefsky presents the working definition of the principle of non-discrimination as prohibiting treating differently similar situations without objective justification.[17]

II. Gender Discrimination, Islamic Law and the Abducted Child: A Conceptual and Contextual Analysis

The discussion in this section will illustrate how gender discrimination can manifest in the custody/abduction law in Islamic law countries, in the legislative framing, procedural protocols and substantive outcomes for abducted children.

A. Gender Discrimination in the Legislative Framing and Procedural Protocols

The discussion on the provisions in the preceding chapters 3 and 4 demonstrate the areas in which Islamic custody/abduction law discriminates between genders. Women, in their capacity as mothers, are discriminated against, compared to fathers. Children too are discriminated against in the way the law differentiates between girls and boys on children's: (i) age of capacity; (ii) participation in proceedings, and; (iii) entitlement to choose with which parent to live. Gender differentiation exists because of the historical determinations by the various schools of Islamic jurisprudence. The differences in jurisprudential opinion, as discussed in chapter 4, specified that the age at which girls were considered as mature and had the capacity to make decisions differed from boys. Boys were considered to have the capacity to decide with which parent they wish to reside at an earlier age, and some schools of jurisprudence held that girls should not be able to make a choice.[18] The limitation on the capacity of girls was justified in historical Islamic law because children's autonomy was inextricably linked to the

[16] Human Rights Committee *General Comment 18 on Non-Discrimination* HRI/GEN/I/Rev 5 (10/11/1989) reproduced in *Compilation of General Comments and General Recommendations adopted by Human Rights Treaty Bodies* HRI/GEN/1 (1992).

[17] Bayefsky (n 10) 11–24.

[18] It was established in chapter 4 that the differences between the schools of jurisprudence results in the legislation in Islamic law countries differing and thus some Islamic law countries have legislation that will discriminate against girls more so than other countries.

age at which girls were deemed ready for marriage. Emon and Khaliq, writing on the obstacles to Hague Convention accession by Islamic law countries, explain:[19]

> The Ḥanbalīs held that the father was best suited to uphold his daughter's interests at this transitional age because, as Ibn Qudāma claimed, a seven-year-old girl is potentially marriageable. Given that the legal doctrine on marriage designates her father as her guardian in setting a marriage, he ought also to exercise custodial authority when she reaches the minimum age of marriage. This link between the rules on marriage and guardianship fundamentally justified treating boys and girls differently with respect to exercising a choice over custodial authority: 'Analogizing her to the young boy is invalid because [the boy] does not need the custodial care and marital guardianship as she does.'[20]

They go on to explain:

> While we might find the marriage of seven-year-old girls preposterous, it would be anachronistic to impose that reading on Ibn Qudāma. Across different regions and traditions in the medieval period, it was common that girls were married at young ages, including in France and England.[21]

This line of reasoning is also undertaken by Rashid,[22] who explains the difference in treatment was justified in historic Islamic law as the father was considered the best person to educate the male child about adulthood. A female child who had reached the age of discernment was deemed to be ready for marriage and at this time she needed the father more than the mother because he is her guardian in marriage.[23] Islamic law requires a girl to be subject to male guardianship, even after reaching maturity, whereas guardianship over a boy ends when he is deemed mature. The Islamic law assessment of maturity was explained in chapter 4, as being either the age at which a child can cleanse himself or for some schools of Islamic jurisprudence, when the boy has reached puberty.

The historic law remains in place today and is applied in cases where children are abducted from the UK to Islamic law countries. Gender distinctions in the law will undoubtedly affect children abducted to Islamic law countries. And while boys abducted may not be directly discriminated against in domestic law in Islamic law countries, they can suffer indirectly because of the discrimination experienced by

[19] Anver Emon and Urfan Khaliq, *Private International Law, Islamic-law, and Cross-Border Child Abduction: A Historic-Legal Analysis* (Ontario, 2016) 53–54; Emon and Khaliq, *Jurisdictional Exceptionalisms: Islamic Law, International Law and Parental Child Abduction* (CUP, 2021).

[20] Ibn Qudāma, *al-Mughnī*, (Beirut, Mu'assasāt al-Ta'rīkh al-'Arabī, n.d.) 7, 615, cited in Emon and Khaliq (2016) ibid 58.

[21] See Fiona Harris Stoertz, 'Young Women in France and England, 1050-1300' (2001) 12 (4) *Journal of Women's History* 22–45, cited in Emon and Khaliq (2016) (n 19) 53–54.

[22] Khalil Abdur-Rashid, 'Islamic Custody Law as a Solution to Child Welfare Problems' (2008) 34 *M Ü İlahiyat Fakültesi Dergisi* 93, 102.

[23] See also Najibah Mohd Zin, 'How the Best Interests of the Child is Best Served in Islamic Law with Special Reference to its Application in the Malaysian Shariah Court,' (2005) 9 (1) *IKIM Law Journal* 338.

their mothers. The refusal to allow mothers custody because of gender discriminatory rules meant that all abducted children suffered by proxy, because of the forced detachment from their primary carers. The evidence in chapter 3 identifies the effect abducted young people say it had on them, at the time of the abduction and many years later.

B. Gender Discrimination in the Outcomes for Abducted Children

This section identifies the gender discrimination children experienced after being abducted from the UK to Islamic law countries. It is essential to recognise that the conditions for girls living in Islamic law countries differ from the situation of girls living in the UK. Thus the environment girls abducted from the UK are exposed to will inevitably differ. The UNCRC Committee's reporting process identifies several areas in which all girls (not just those abducted) are discriminated against explicitly in an Islamic country context: in family relations, the criminal justice system, property rights, compensation for physical injury,[24] inheritance and custody.[25] The Committee expresses concern at the lack of comprehensive legislation prohibiting all forms of discrimination and urges the repeal of legislation to eliminate all practices that discriminate against girls.[26]

The difference in treatment of girls from boys is not unique therefore to abducted children. Nonetheless, there are specific gendered features of Islamic law, namely 'guardianship' laws that can affect when the abduction comes to an end for abducted boys and girls. This feature of Islamic law is examined in detail to aid the understanding of how differently Islamic law treats abducted girls from boys.

i. The Effect of Guardianship on Abducted Children

Legal guardianship over children is recognised in many legal systems, including under English law. It was explained in chapter 3 that children in Islamic law countries are raised with the knowledge that the mother is responsible for the day-to-day care of the children and the father, as the legal guardian, is responsible for providing financially and making decisions about the children's education, travel and finances.[27] This arrangement continues even if the parents separate until

[24] Concluding Observations Iran CRC/C/IRN/CO/3-4 (14 March 2016) para 29–30.

[25] Ibid; Concluding Observations UAE CRC/C/ARE/CO/2 (30 October 2015) para 23; Concluding Observations Bahrain CRC/C/BHR/CO/4-6 (27 February 2019) paras 16–17, 33.

[26] Concluding Observations Bahrain ibid 3, 16–17; Concluding Observations UAE ibid 23–24; Concluding observations Pakistan CRC/C/PAK/CO/5 (11 July 2016) para 19; Concluding Observations Saudi Arabia CRC/C/SAU/CO/3-4 (25 October 2016) para 15–16.

[27] Lena-Maria Möller, 'An Enduring Relic: Family Law Reform and the Inflexibility of Wilaya' (2015) 63 *The American Journal of Comparative Law* 847, 910–11; An example of the law in Morocco is Morocco Law No 70.03 of 2004, articles 231, 238.

such time as boys are considered mature enough to make decisions themselves about their welfare and where they wish to live.[28] For girls, guardianship by the male head of the household continues indefinitely and transfers from the girl's father to her husband when she marries. The argument presented here is that legal guardianship that is reserved for one gender only, and extends beyond childhood, is classed as gender discrimination. The UNCRC Committee highlights that the obligatory male guardianship over girls in Islamic law countries is incompatible with the CRC. It 'conditions their enjoyment of most of the rights enshrined in the CRC, namely the rights to freedom of movement, access to justice, education, health-care services and identity documents, among others, upon the agreement of a male guardian.'[29]

The abducted girls in the sample who were unable to return from the Islamic law country as children continued to be subject to guardianship as they became adults, such as Miriam.[30] Miriam was abducted from England at age nine by her father, and the Libyan courts refused her return. As a female, Miriam is subject to the rules of guardianship in Libya and was unable to leave Libya on reaching adulthood, as she did not have her father's consent. Once Miriam was married, her husband became her legal guardian, and Miriam cannot leave Libya and return to the UK until her husband consents to the issuance of travel documentation and her travel. In this way, the abduction never comes to an end for abducted girls.

Unlike the girls, the boys abducted from the UK are free to travel as male adults. Many of the boys, particularly those able to retain a relationship with their left-behind parent, waited until age 18 and returned to the UK. A left-behind mother explains:

> Right from the beginning I always used to say I'm lucky because my children are boys and when they're 18 they can get out, and that's what they did. It was like a sentence, and 18 is the end. But with girls there was no end, it was an open sentence, you don't know when it was going to finish. And a lot of those girls never came back; I know quite a few that are still there, married with kids.[31]

Another left-behind mother explains how her daughter, who saw an opportunity to escape Libya, was returned to her father as a result of the law on guardianship:

> It wasn't that long ago when Britain went into Libya, the time when Ghaddafi was killed [2011].[32] My daughter wanted to come home, so she took the opportunity, and she got herself to the British Embassy in Libya before this Embassy was shut, as it was the last

[28] Note the interesting observation of O'Donnell, that while the rules appear arbitrary, the views of the wishes of adult duty-bearers are also of no relevance; Daniel O'Donnell, *The Right of the Child to be Heard: Children's Right to Have Their Views Taken Into Account and to Participate in Legal and Administrative Proceedings* (Innocenti Working Paper, UNICEF, 2009) 18.

[29] Concluding Observations Saudi Arabia (n 26).

[30] Participant 29C, interview 08/05/16 (on file with the author).

[31] Participant 07M, interview 16/06/16 (on file with the author).

[32] See media report at the time: Mark Mardell, 'Gaddafi Killed: A New Kind of US Foreign Policy Success' (BBC, 20.10.11).

> week they were sending in ships. She had to go pick it up [travel pass], so that was quite difficult for her, out on her own. She wasn't supposed to be going out, and there was a lot of trouble and fighting as well at the time. We were constantly keeping in contact with her, so I knew when she was on the boat, she was so scared but wanting to do it. She got on the boat, and a Libyan soldier took her off it because he recognised the name and knew the family. Her older brother was here [UK] on the phone talking to her, and so she gave the phone to the soldier. My son was trying to persuade him, saying 'why do you care? You don't even want to be in Libya, why do you care if my sister is leaving Libya?' This was all in Arabic, for ages. But they still took her off and rang her dad, and he came and picked her up. So that was awful for her, and you can imagine she was in a lot of trouble.[33]

The impact of guardianship is extensive and also affects boys, as is seen in the case study of Ryan,[34] who was inadvertently affected by the rules on guardianship imposed upon his step-mother. Ryan aged three and his sister aged two were abducted by their father from England to Iran. Ryan returned to England at age eight with his sister, father, step-mother and step-siblings. Ryan's father passed away when Ryan was aged ten. After his father's death, Ryan's stepmother was subject to the customary guardianship authority of her brother, even though she was living in England. Practice outside Islamic law countries is not unusual, as the CRC Committee observes:

> there is often continued adherence to the harmful practices by members of practising communities who have moved to destination countries. Social norms and cultural beliefs supporting these harmful practices persist and are at times emphasised by a community in an attempt to preserve their cultural identity in a new environment, particularly in destination countries where gender roles provide women and girls with greater personal freedom.[35]

As a widow in a foreign country, responsible for her four children and two of her late husband's, Ryan's step-mother was reliant on her brother for support. Ryan's step-uncle informed Ryan that as an adult male, Ryan was not permitted to live in the household with a woman to whom he was unrelated by blood, ie not within the prescribed kinship network under Islamic law. As a result, Ryan was again taken to Iran. He was separated from his siblings and the only parenting figure in his life. Conversely, as a female, Ryan's sister was allowed to remain living with her step-mother in England.

The individuals in Iran with supposed responsibility for Ryan did not know what to do with him, and so sent him to live in a Madrassa, a boarding facility in which children receive an Islamic education. Ryan was unhappy receiving the

[33] Participant 08M, interview 01/07/16 (on file with the author).

[34] Participant 30C, interview 17/03/16 (on file with the author).

[35] The Joint General Comment No 31 of the Committee on the Elimination of Discrimination against Women and No 18 of the Committee on the Rights of the Child on harmful practices CEDAW/C/GC/31-CRC/C/GC/18 (4th November 2014) para 17.

religious training and Ryan's concerns about the type of facility are also identified by the CRC Committee:

> The Committee is concerned that private madrasas are often used for child recruitment and military training by non-State armed groups. The Committee urges the State party to monitor registered and unregistered private madrasas, using adequate mechanisms, to prevent any possibility of abuse and exploitation. It also urges the State party to monitor non-State armed Groups and prohibit them from accessing educational facilities, and from protecting children from being exposed to recruitment and given military training by armed groups.[36]

The rules on guardianship of women and children are designed to control women but have a far-reaching impact on all children abducted to Islamic law countries; boys as well as girls. The overarching question in this analysis is whether Hague Convention accession by Islamic law countries will serve to advance children's rights more clearly than under domestic Islamic custody/abduction law. The impact of the rules on guardianship of girls/women highlights that the abducted child's Article 2 CRC rights to non-discrimination are not protected under the domestic law in Islamic law countries.

ii. Guardianship Laws can Facilitate Harmful Practice

The mandatory legal guardianship by males brings with it the duty to take responsibility and provide for the females of the family. The authority over women results in women being the compliant ones in the relationship, whether as an older daughter, wife or sister. This section illustrates how the nature of the relationship resulted in abducted girls adhering to their father's requests. The authority impacted upon the abducted girls as they became young women, too, even if they were not happy with the arrangement, such as requirements to cover their hair, in some cases to stop attending post-compulsory education and the refusal to allow the abducted girls to return to the UK. The data illustrates that most of the children abducted were able to retain some form of contact with their left-behind mother, whether through social media, telephone calls or visits by the mother to the Islamic law country. The link the abducted children retained with their life in the UK resulted in their questioning the authority over them, and the rules to which they had to conform.[37]

The cultural norm in the Islamic law countries such as the requirement of girls to cover their hair or to require a male guardian to accompany their travel was a 'culture shock' to the girls abducted at age nine and over, such as Miriam and Sara. Both Yasmin and Aliyah,[38] abducted at age seven to Jordan and the UAE, also learnt within the first couple of years that they would have to dress differently

[36] Concluding Observations Pakistan (n 26) 63–64.
[37] Participant 06M, interview 14/06/16 (on file with the author).
[38] Participant 33C, interview 01/06/16 (on file with the author).

from how they dressed in the UK. The CRC Committee recognises the hijab requirement for girls as young as seven years of age[39] and asserts that to ensure full respect for the equality of girls and boys states parties must stop imposing a dress code on girls.[40] The UN Committee for the CCPR protections affirms the dress requirement breaches several rights of women and girls.[41] Other cultural practices abducted children were exposed to, such as female genital mutilation, undue pressure to marry, and their father's polygamous marriages, are termed by the UNCRC Committee as 'harmful practices' in General Comment 18 ('GC18').[42] GC18 is issued jointly with the United Nations Committee on the Convention on the Elimination of Discrimination against Women ('CEDAW') and encourages States Parties to address gender discrimination in their respective states. The Committee explains:

> The Committees acknowledge that harmful practices affect adult women, both directly and due to the long-term impact of practices to which they were subjected to as girls. This General Comment, therefore, further elaborates the obligations of States parties to CEDAW with respect to the relevant provisions to eliminate harmful practices that affect the rights of women.[43]

The relationship between compulsory guardianship over girls and harmful practices is highlighted in the example of the guardian's right/duty to consent to the marriage of his ward/daughter. Under most Islamic schools of jurisprudence, the girl's guardian contracts her marriage.[44] Of the 30 girls abducted in sample of cases examined in the author's study, 20 remain living in the Islamic law country. Of these 20 abducted girls, 14 are now aged over 18, and all 14 have entered into an arranged marriage. In contrast, of the 24 boys abducted in the study, 11 remain living in the Islamic law country. Of these 11 abducted boys, five are now aged over 18, and none of the five is married. One left-behind mother whose daughters remain in Libya explains:

> they've gone from one tradition to the other because my daughters are all married so they've all got husbands to tell them what to do, what they can and can't do, so they kind of went from one controller to the next one.[45]

[39] Concluding Observations Iran (n 24) 49–50.

[40] Concluding Observations Saudi Arabia (n 26) 15–16.

[41] Art 26 on non-discrimination; Art 7 if corporal punishment is imposed to enforce such regulation. Art 9 when failure to comply is punished by arrest; Art 12 is also breached if liberty of movement is subject to such a constraint; Art 18 and 19 when women are subject to clothing requirements that are not in keeping with their religion or their right of self-expression; Art 27 when the clothing requirements conflict with the culture to which the woman can lay a claim; CCPR GC28: *Equality of Rights Between Men and Women* (Art. 3) CCPR/C/21/Rev.1/Add.10 (29/03/2000) adopted by the Human Rights Committee under Article 40, para 4 of the CCPR para 13.

[42] The Joint General Comment No 31 of the Committee on the Elimination of Discrimination against Women and No 18 of the Committee on the Rights of the Child on harmful practices CEDAW/C/GC/31-CRC/C/GC/18, (4th November 2014) para 7.

[43] Ibid paras 2 and 3.

[44] Hallie Ludsin, 'Relational Rights Masquerading as Individual Rights' (2008) 15 *Duke Journal of Gender Law & Policy* 195, 211.

[45] Participant 11M, interview 31/07/16 (on file with the author).

Some of the marriages were entered into as children, as another left-behind mother explains:

> My second daughter, she had an arranged marriage at the age of seventeen years, well I was horrified as you can imagine you know and she was married to an older man, and we knew nothing about the wedding until the actual day before the wedding.[46]

While the CRC does not explicitly refer to child marriage, the practice violates fundamental CRC principles, such as the right to life (Article 6), the right to health (Article 24), the right to be protected from harmful practices (Article 24) and the right to freedom from abuse and exploitation (Articles 19, 34, 39). In the author's study, some of the marriages were agreed to as a way out of the father's control. A left-behind mother explains:

> They never talk about what happened to them or how their life was, but I picked up little snippets. Because Fatmah was married off at a young age, I could see the others thought they would be better off married, as long as they were out of their father's control. I mean Amnah went off and married a stranger and Aishah went off and married a stranger. They didn't want to live with their father, so the only option for them was to get married.[47]

The system of guardianship and control of girls means that some abducted girls will agree to marriage under duress or undue influence. A left-behind mother whose daughter was abducted to Libya explained her fear of forced marriage for her abducted daughter:

> His [abductor's] mum got married when she was thirteen, and that's what they would have done with my daughter, she'd have been married off. My daughter is terrified of her father. While living in Libya, I knew of a girl who was speaking to a boy by text message and her brother found out. She was so frightened she threw herself off the top of a building and killed herself because she was frightened of her dad killing her. And this girl was twenty, old enough to get married. That's how terrified they are of their own family.[48]

Honour killings and forced marriage are also documented to be a problem in a report by the United States Government investigating cases of parental abduction to Saudi Arabia.[49] The report describes several instances of cases where girls abducted from the USA have been forced or coerced into a marriage after the abduction. Traditional Islamic law allows the guardian to consent to a child's marriage on behalf of the child.[50] The child can apply to the court to rescind the marriage once reaching puberty, but only if the marriage has not been consummated.[51]

[46] Participant 06M, interview 14/06/16 (on file with the author).
[47] Participant 06M, interview 14/06/16 (on file with the author).
[48] Participant 12M, interview 04/09/16 (on file with the author).
[49] USA Government, 'Investigation into Abductions of American Children to Saudi Arabia. Hearings before the Committee on Government Reform', House of Representatives, 107th Congress, second session (United States Government Publishing Office, 2002).
[50] Asaf Fyzee, *Outline of Muhammadan Law* (OUP, 1974) 208–209.
[51] Lynn Welchman, 'Capacity, Consent and Under-Age Marriage in Muslim Family Law' (2001) *Int'l Surv Fam L* 243.

While many Islamic law countries have set the minimum age of marriage past the age of puberty, the right to rescind a marriage consented to by the father remains within the legislative framework.[52]

The CRC Committee notes the increased prevalence of child marriages in Islamic law countries; this is despite legislation, which has increased the age of marriage in Pakistan, Bangladesh and Morocco.[53] In the Concluding Observations to Iran, the Committee states it 'is seriously concerned about reports of the increasing number of girls aged 10 and younger who are subjected to child and forced marriages to much older men.'[54] On Morocco, the Committee notes:

> early marriage is on the rise in the State party, and thousands of girls, some of them as young as 13 years, are married every year as a result of the extensive use of derogations from the law by family judges. The Committee is also seriously concerned about the widespread practice of forced marriage and girls committing suicide as a result of such marriages; the last reported cases having taken place in January and May 2014.[55]

The deaths occurred only weeks before the report was published.

While legislation seeks to deter child marriage, the legal framework in Islamic law countries continues to accommodate the option for judges to approve an application for the marriage of children.[56] In the Concluding Observations to Saudi Arabia, the CRC Committee expresses concern 'that judges frequently authorise the marriage of girls who have attained puberty. It also notes with deep concern that efforts to set a minimum age for marriage were successfully challenged in December 2014 by the highest-ranking religious leader, who declared being in favour of marriages involving girls as young as nine years old.'[57] Saudi Arabia has

[52] See examples of Pakistan and Bangladesh where the Dissolution of Muslim Marriage Act (1939) (as amended by the Muslim Family Law Ordinance 1961) provides a woman shall be entitled to obtain a decree for the dissolution of her marriage on the grounds that she had been given in marriage by her father or other guardian before she attained the age of 18 years, and she seeks to repudiate the marriage before attaining the age of nineteen years, provided that the marriage has not been consummated; cited in Javaid Rehman, 'Religion, Human Rights and the Rights of the Child: Complexities in Applying Sharia in Modern State Practices' (2011) 62 (2) *Northern Ireland Legal Quarterly* 153, 160–62.

[53] Though note the research by Ali, who finds that minimum age of marriage set in legislation in Pakistan is circumvented by other legislation. Sec 3 The Majority Act 1875 defines majority as having been attained at 18. The Act lists exceptions to this age, which includes the exception of 'personal law.' Thus for purposes of marriage the Islamic age of majority is accepted, which means when a girl menstruates and when a boy is capable of sexual intercourse. This can be as low as nine years for a girl. See Shaheen Sardar Ali, 'Rights of the Child under Islamic law and Laws of Pakistan. A thematic Overview' (2006) 1 *J Islamic St Prac Int'l L* 11; see also Abdullahi Ahmed An-Na'im, *Islamic Family Law in a Changing World: A Global Resource book* (Zed Books, 2002).

[54] Concluding Observations Iran (n 24) 59–60.

[55] Concluding Observations Morocco CRC/C/MAR/CO/3-4 (14 October 2014) para 42.

[56] On this topic see the work of Virginia Caputo, '"Too Young to Wed": Envisioning a "Generous Encounter" between Feminism and the Politics of Childhood' in Rachel Rosen and Katherine Twamley (eds), *Feminism and the Politics of Childhood: Friends or Foes?* (UCL Press, 2018) 201–217; Neha Jain 'Forced Marriage as a Crime against Humanity' (2008) 6(5) *Int Criminal Justice* 1013–32.

[57] Concluding Observations Saudi Arabia (n 26) 13–14; see similar recommendation in Concluding Observations Iran (n 24) 27; see also reference to judicial sanction of child marriages in the UAE by the CRC Committee, Concluding Observations UAE (n 25) 27.

therefore not set a lawful age, and Iranian law permits marriages for boys at 15 and 13 for girls.

The factors which a judge has to consider in approving an application for a child's marriage are set out in research by Prettitore.[58] Prettitore explains the necessity of the marriage is supposed to be evaluated by a court based on economic and social grounds. The need for the court's approval should amount to a true necessity, and the marriage should 'serve some interest of the minor.' Notwithstanding the requirements, in the study in Jordan, Prettitore observes that judges appear to rubber-stamp most applications for the marriage of a minor (between 86 and 93 per cent of all applications between 2007 and 2012).[59] The gendered element of child marriages is apparent in that 99 per cent of requests for approval of underage marriage made to courts in Jordan involved girls.

The cultural nature of child marriage is recognised by Prettitore, as he highlights the difficulty judges are faced with when presented with evidence by the child's parents that they do not have the financial means to care for a child. Some requests are made to spare the child from criminal prosecution for sex outside of marriage, which is a crime in both Jordan and Morocco. Having a child outside of marriage is also a crime in Morocco, as is having an abortion. In such cases, marriage may be socially preferable to criminal prosecution and the resulting shame on the family. Unmarried girls suspected to be involved in sexual relations are also at risk of honour crimes, whereby they are killed by family members to protect the family's honour. The fact that the killing is committed to protect the honour of the family is treated as a legitimate mitigating factor by the Islamic courts, lessening the length of imprisonment of convicted perpetrators. Prettitore highlights that this, too, is a factor in the court's assessment of whether marriage is in the child's best interests. A child may also inevitably be married as a victim of rape, as the law in Jordan allows a rapist to avoid prosecution if he agrees to marry his victim for at least five years. These social and cultural factors all feed into gender discrimination and the practice of child marriage in Islamic law countries. For the purpose of this analysis, there is no distinction in Islamic law for children abducted from other countries, and so the practices and norms identified by Prettitore are also imposed upon children abducted from the UK to Islamic law countries.

Ludsin identifies that the rules of marriage, to the extent they are protected by a constitution and the judiciary, not only treat girls/women as incompetent but give their guardians control over women's access to equality and autonomy rights, all of which maintain patriarchy and discrimination. The discriminatory law also requires wives to be obedient, and 'obedience is a husband's enforceable right.' Disobedience, whether by leaving home without permission, denying her husband

[58] Paul Scott Prettitore, 'Family Law Reform, Gender Equality, and Underage Marriage: A view from Morocco and Jordan' (2015) 13 (3) *The Review of Faith & International Affairs* 32.

[59] Ibid.

sexual relations or refusing to have children, results in a loss of the woman's right to financial maintenance. It also allows a man to 'discipline' his wife.[60] The modern-day application of the 'enforcement' of a guardian's rights is seen in the following example from the interview data of a left-behind mother who sought her daughter's return from the courts in the United Arab Emirates (UAE). The mother applied to the UAE courts for custody of her daughter. The father sought legal advice, and as a tactic in the hope she would leave the UAE and return to the UK, the father made use of the UAE laws on requiring wives to return to their husband's authority. As a ploy, the father initiated proceedings before the UAE court for his wife's 'return to the marital bed'. The left-behind mother explains:

> He'd applied to the Sharia court for my return to the marital bed. I had this court summons, and I had no idea what it meant. I turned up at the court, and I was informed that I wasn't a good wife. The judge was saying, 'you must go back to your husband, you must clean the house, you must be nice to your husband.' A lawyer then told me they're ordering you to go back home and sleep with your husband. I couldn't believe what was being requested.[61]

The example illustrates that the law in Islamic law countries can propagate gender discrimination, and the abduction of girls to Islamic law countries means that once abducted there they are unable to rely on protection from the State. Nor are the mothers protected when they travel to Islamic law countries hoping to litigate successfully for the abducted child's return.

The harmful practices of domestic violence and polygamy identified in GC18 also emerge in the data for the author's study. Allowing legal guardians to exert authority over girls/women resulted in them being subjected to domestic abuse. It is noteworthy that domestic violence against the mother is a feature in 25 of the 29 cases in the author's study (86.2 per cent). It is indistinguishable whether this high incidence is attributable to the fact that the Muslim fathers are applying their Islamic law right to address 'disobedience',[62] or whether the high incidence relates to the fact that domestic abuse is a feature in cases of parental abduction occurring in most parts of the world,[63] or that domestic abuse is a cause and consequence of family separation more generally. There is evidence in the author's study of abducted children also being subjected to domestic abuse, the incidence of which is also observed in other studies.[64] None of the ten abductees interviewed referred to domestic abuse in their interviews, but domestic abuse was reported

[60] Ludsin (n 44) 211–16.

[61] Participant 09M, interview 22/06/16 (on file with the author).

[62] Ludsin (n 44) 211–216.

[63] Domestic abuse was reported in more than 50 per cent of the parental abduction cases in two studies; Geoffrey Greif and Rebecca Hegar, *When Parents Kidnap: The Families Behind the Headlines* (The Free Press, 1993); C Hatcher and others, *Reunification of Missing Children: Training Manual* (US Department of Justice, 1993).

[64] Thalia Kruger, *International Child Abduction: The Inadequacies of the Law* (Hart Publishing, 2011) 63–64; Grief and Hegar ibid 285; Marilyn Freeman 'The Outcomes for Children Returned Following

concerning other abducted children in the sample during the interviews with left-behind mothers. One left-behind mother said:

> My eldest was sixteen by the time she'd come across my letters. The more she questioned her father, the more he was getting aggressive with her. It had come to the point that he's beaten her so badly he stabbed her. Because the British Embassy was back in Libya, she'd run away. They rang me and said we could keep her here in the Embassy, but we can't get her out of Libya because she can only leave on a Libyan passport. She couldn't stay away from her sisters, so she returned to the house.[65]

GC18 also identifies polygamy as a harmful practice that harms women and their children. The Committee recognises that though a large number of States parties have banned polygamy, it continues to be practised in some countries. It explains:

> The coexistence of statutory laws with religious, personal status and traditional customary laws and practices often contribute to the persistence of this practice. Constitutional and other provisions that protect the right to culture and religion, at times, have also been used to justify laws and practices that allow for polygamous unions.[66]

Polygamy emerges in the data in two ways. First, where the parents separated after the mother discovered the Muslim husband was also married in the Islamic law country, in the case of the abductee Ryan, for example, whose English mother knew nothing about Ryan's father's wife and children in Iran. Secondly, polygamy is highlighted in cases where left-behind mothers are only allowed to visit the abducted child if they continue with the pretence that they are still a family. As one left-behind mother explains:

> He'd remarried, and then he wanted me to stay in this house with him and his wife you know like that was a bit too difficult for me. Although I was divorced from him in this country [England], I wasn't divorced from him in that country [Libya]. So I was finding that all very uncomfortable being in the same house. He never actually divorced me and so in Libya, I'm still his wife really, so it did cause a lot of awkwardness. I mean his wife was never awful or unpleasant, but then she wouldn't be because that's not expected. So I found it very awkward and it was hard for the children. I didn't want to be anywhere near him, but at the same time, you have to do it to be with your children. Which is why the hardest bit was having to you know, do all the other bits that you have to do as a wife when you don't want to be anywhere near him.[67]

If Islamic family law, as discussed in chapter 3, did not preclude this mother's entitlement to custody because she wished to live in the UK with the children, she would not have to appease the abducting father to be allowed to visit the abducted children. The data evidences the broad spectrum of gender discrimination arising

an Abduction' (Reunite, 2003); Jeffrey Edleson and Taryn Lindhorst, 'Multiple Perspectives on Battered Mothers and their Children Fleeing to the United States for Safety: A Study of Hague Convention Cases' (National Institute of Justice, US Department of Justice, 2010).

[65] Participant 06M, interview 14/06/16 (on file with the author).

[66] GC18 para 24–27.

[67] Participant 08M, interview 01/07/16 (on file with the author).

from cases of abduction from the UK to Islamic law countries. The inequality is experienced by the abducted children, but also by their left-behind mothers. The mothers' attempts to be reunited with the abducted children resulted in their travel to the Islamic law country where they, too, become subject to the discriminatory laws. The gender discrimination encountered by abducted children as a result of the domestic legal provision in Islamic law countries breaches Article 2 CRC and, once again, points towards the Hague Convention as an alternative legal framework that could more effectively advance the rights of abducted children.

The challenge of trying to address gender discrimination in a child abduction context is the focus of the discussion in the following section.

III. The Challenge of Gender Discrimination in Cases of Parental Abduction

Addressing the gender discrimination which manifests in the legislative framing, procedural protocols and substantive outcomes for abducted girls presents considerable challenges. The analysis in this section will examine whether the challenges can be appropriately responded to through the lens of (a) the broader architecture of human rights and equality provisions, (b) the cultural nature of the rights of abducted children, and (c) the relational nature of abducted children's rights. The discussion will then progress to an analysis of whether these factors will potentially affect the Hague Convention application in Islamic law countries, in the following section IV.

A. The Broader Non-Discrimination Legal Framework

The discussion above highlights that there are limitations to Article 2 CRC, as it does not cover the rights of abducted children when gender discrimination and harmful practices extend beyond childhood. This is because many of the abducted girls in the sample remain within the Islamic law country after reaching adulthood,[68] and are no longer protected by the CRC provisions. Those abductees, such as Miriam, would have to look to CEDAW or the other international rights treaties such as Article 12 CCPR[69] to uphold their rights, depending upon whether the country they are abducted to is a signatory.

[68] Note from the discussion above in chapter 4, adulthood in Islamic law countries is not always prescribed at age 18, and in some countries is set at the age at which puberty is reached.

[69] Art 12 CCPR protects women's rights from the exercise of parental powers over adult daughters and marital powers over the wife. The provision also protects Miriam's right to seek protection from the law which prohibits her from travelling and the requirement of consent of her male guardian to the issuance of travel documents: CCPR GC28 (n 41) para 16.

The interaction between the different human rights treaties is, therefore, essential for children abducted to Islamic law countries. It is for this reason that the broader human rights architecture, the guidance on non-discrimination issued by the UN Committee on Human Rights overseeing CEDAW, the ICCPR, ICESCR, and the UDHR must also be drawn upon collaboratively to develop the best possible provision to respond to the gender discrimination in parental abduction law. Reference to the protections the abducted girls will have as women will also avoid what is described as the 'ghettoisation' of children's rights issues, where the discrimination of girls has gradually become a separate issue from that of women and hence has been addressed through different standards. While this may be positive from a children's rights approach, it does mean that gender-related measures can lack coherence when girls like Miriam pass the age of 18 years of age.[70] The collaborative approach of the Committee for the CRC and CEDAW in GC18 on harmful practices highlights the necessity of this approach. But it is argued that the CRC could do more to protect the rights of older girls. Loenen asserts that while the CRC Committee recognises the interplay between women's rights and children's rights, the Committee's references to women's rights are limited, primarily focused on the specific vulnerabilities of the girl child and the protection of mothers in their biological role.[71] Loenen proposes that the close connection between children's and women's rights warrants the CRC Committee to draw much more inspiration from the gender-based approach underlying CEDAW than it has so far, to improve the position of women and children to realise their rights fully.

B. The Cultural Nature of the Rights of Abducted Children

One of the challenges in responding to cases of parental child abduction to Islamic law countries is the reality of the differences in culture experienced by children abducted to Islamic law countries. Put simply, the outcomes for children abducted to Islamic law countries differ because the lives of the families in Islamic law countries differ from the lives of the children living in the UK, a point which will now be explored with reference to relevant literature and the data from the author's study.

When evaluating the right to non-discrimination of the abducted children in the sample, the fact cannot be ignored that the CRC imposes a universal and international framework on very different cultural regimes that exist within Islamic law countries. The CRC does not accommodate the boundaries between universal norms, respecting cultures and national sovereignty, which is why the CRC

[70] Hitch (n 6) 54; see also the application of the framework by Besson (n 2) 450–51.

[71] Titia Loenen, 'Towards an Integrated Approach to Intra-Family Relations under the CRC and CEDAW: Some Reflections' in Eva Brems and others (eds), *Children's Rights Law in the Global Human Rights Landscape: Isolation, Inspiration, Integration?* (Routledge, 2017) 173, 187.

can be limited as a framework. As An-Na'im argues, the CRC is premised on the assumption of universal normative consensus without distinctions on the grounds of race, gender religion, and so forth. The genuine normative universality may be something agreed by governments, but is a concept that is yet to be realised in concrete terms.[72] This is because, as he explains, there are significant differences among perceptions of how to raise children to uphold and live by specific values, depending upon the worldview and religious beliefs of parents and the cultural norms of their societies. What is important for Muslim parents to instil in their children will differ from Buddhists, Hindus and agnostic parents. Within each religious and cultural group, economic, educational and other differentials will influence parents' objectives and expectations for their children, thereby affecting child-rearing practices. An-Na'im observes that given the wide range of contextual specificity and cultural relativity between the regions of the world, normative universality on children's rights is difficult to achieve.[73]

The example of Saudi Arabia is illustrative of the point An-Na'im makes. Saudi Arabia ratified CEDAW in 2001 and is aware of its obligations to equality between genders. Islamic laws on guardianship are a relic from classical Islamic law when men provided for and accompanied women on long journeys.[74] Rather than seeking to address the laws to comply with CEDAW obligations, Saudi Arabia has instead developed the operation of the laws on women's travel in a modern-day form, through the creation of an 'app' called 'Absher,' owned and operated by the Saudi Kingdom's Interior Ministry. The app has been downloaded more than one million times and gives men the power to grant and rescind travel permission for women and to set up SMS alerts for when women use their passports.[75] The modern-day application of law developed hundreds of years ago highlights the power of entrenched cultural attitudes to override international agreement on the right to equality. Islamic law countries, including Saudi Arabia, have entered reservations against the CEDAW provisions that relate to the ability of women to travel freely[76] and so it is not a legal regulation that is likely to be reformed imminently. In the context of parental abduction, this will, of course, have a more significant impact on mothers travelling with their children, and will impact upon the girls abducted from the UK, more so than the boys. Not least by contributing to girls' perceptions of their future life opportunities and a general culture of coercive control of women, which will be observed and internalised by (male and female) abducted children.

[72] Abdullahi An-Na'im, *Muslims and Global Justice* (University of Pennsylvania Press, 2010) 164.

[73] Ibid 173.

[74] Judith E Tucker, *In the House of Law: Gender and Islamic law in Ottoman Syria and Palestine* (University of California Press, 2000) 138–41; Mahdi Zahraa and Normi Malek, 'The Concept of Custody in Islamic Law' (1998) 13 *Arab LQ* 155, 156–57.

[75] Maya Oppenheim 'Saudi Government's "Wife-Tracking" App Linked to Domestic Violence and Abusive Working Conditions, says Rights Group' (*The Independent*, 07.05.19).

[76] Though note the general reservation 'in case of contradiction between any term of the Convention and the norms of Islamic law, the Kingdom is not under obligation to observe the contradictory terms of the Convention'.

It is recognised that some Islamic law states have taken measures to address the discriminatory cultural practices prevalent in that country. The CRC Committee observes that the criminalisation by Islamic law countries of harmful practices such as child marriage, polygamy and FGM,[77] has had little effect, however, and the practices still occur.[78] Abducted girls in the sample of cases examined were exposed to the harmful practices because the practices are prevalent in the countries to which they were abducted. FGM, for example, was an issue in three of the 29 cases (10.34 per cent) in the sample. All three cases relate to Egypt, where the practice is more common than in other Islamic law countries.[79] In all three cases, the abducted girls were not subjected to FGM but were given the option to partake in the practice, this being the cultural norm in the region to which they were abducted. A left-behind mother whose daughters were abducted to Egypt aged eight and five explains:

> They came back in May 2013, and the dad did an undertaking to the High Court, he swore that she [eldest daughter] hadn't been circumcised. She won't talk to me about it but told the doctor they had booked the operation for her in Egypt. They [abducted sisters] were waiting for the person to come and do them next but became frightened when they could hear other girls screaming. My girls asked to cancel. Their dad's wife rang him in England, and he said it's up to the girls whether they want to be cut or not. She [the abducted child] told the doctor here [in England] she had wanted to be cut because in Egypt if you're cut, you get presents and have a party.[80]

The UNCRC Committee recognises gender discrimination and harmful practices persist because of the coexistence of statutory laws with religious, personal status and traditional customary laws. Constitutional and other provisions that protect the right to culture and religion, at times, have also been used to justify laws and practices.[81] So where does this leave the girls abducted from the UK to Islamic law countries? Are they to be protected by the CRC's universal ambitions, or can Islamic law countries apply the argument that the CRC must accommodate the practices and cultures within different parts of the world, of which one is gender discrimination?

The following section reflects upon whether gender discrimination should be tolerated as a cultural norm and therefore not subject to interference by 'Western' standards, particularly as this affects children which consequently affect children born and raised in that country as well as children abducted from other parts of the world. Consideration is given to whether the cultural nature of gender discrimination validates it as objective justification.

[77] For example by Art 663 of the Islamic Penal Code in Iran.

[78] GC18 24–27.

[79] Michael Jefferson, 'FGM/Cutting: Contextualising Recent Legal Developments' (2015) 79 (6) *The Journal of Criminal Law*; Amel Fahmy and others, 'Female Genital Mutilation/Cutting and Issues of Sexuality in Egypt' (2010) 18 (36) *Reproductive Health Matters* 181.

[80] Participant 13M, interview 10/09/16 (on file with the author).

[81] GC18 24–27.

i. Any Objective Justification for Gender Discrimination under the Equality Framework?

The principle of non-discrimination prohibits treating similar situations differently without objective justification.[82] The differentiation between girls and boys breaches Article 2 CRC and satisfies the definition of discrimination, a *difference of treatment of similar situations*, as the outcomes for abducted girls differ for boys abducted from the UK to Islamic law countries. The next question for this analysis, therefore, is whether the reason for cultural norms is a justified objection under international human rights law? Is the different treatment of girls/boys and men/women a positive action measure in place that discriminates on legitimate grounds?

Many of the practices identified are considered from the 'traditional, historical, religious or cultural attitudes' of people living in Islamic law countries.[83] As was discussed in chapter 2, most Islamic law countries have entered reservations against those articles of the CRC that conflict with Islamic law. According to a strict reading of the CRC commitments of Islamic law countries, therefore, they will not be in breach of Article 2 CRC. The argument is further complicated in a cultural context as the gender discrimination against women in Islamic custody law (ie preventing a mother from acquiring custody if she is not Muslim, remarries or does not live near the child's father) is intended to serve the best interests of the child in Islamic law.[84] Islamic law upholds the child's best interests, in a cultural context by ensuring the child can be supervised by his or her legal guardian, the child is raised in the Islamic faith and is not made to live in the household of a stepfather in which she or he may feel unwelcome.

The argument is circular, as Islamic law discriminates against women supposedly to serve the child's best interests. But the discrimination can lead to the separation of children from their primary carers, which also harms children. Thus, according to the Islamic law viewpoint, the only way to prevent this harm from occurring to children is for the mother to live near the father, not re-marry and to raise the child as a Muslim. The liberty and rights of the mother are obviously infringed compared with the father's rights and are likely to be cumbersome in a domestic Islamic country context, let alone for women habitually resident in the UK.[85]

In order to be considered as a valid objective distinction between genders, the difference in treatment must pursue a legitimate aim.[86] There must also be a

[82] Human Rights Committee GC18 on Non-Discrimination (n 16); see also working definition by Bayefsky (n 10) 11–24.

[83] CCPR GC 28 (n 41) para 13.

[84] Analysed in detail in chapter 3.

[85] See also commentary by Lamont who discusses how the process of upholding the rights of the abducted children can operate against the mother's rights; Ruth Lamont, 'Mainstreaming Gender into European Union Family Law? The Case of International Child Abduction and Brussels II Revised' (2011) 17 *European Law Journal* 366, 369–70.

[86] Bayefsky (n 10) 11–24.

reasonable relationship of proportionality between the means employed, and the aim sought to be achieved. Besson identifies three conditions for the proportionality test. The means must be appropriate to attain the aim sought, be a necessary means to do so and be the least restrictive means to reach that aim.[87] Applying these criteria, the reason for gender discrimination to supposedly promote the child's best interests is not a valid justification in the custody law. The child's best interests could also be served if the father moves to live near the mother. There are also examples in the data where the abducted father's remarriage affected the abducted children, yet historic Islamic law presumes that it is only the mother's remarriage that is potentially harmful to children. A left-behind mother describes how the abducting father's remarriage affected her abducted children:

> Within nine days of the abduction, my ex remarried. He didn't take my eldest boy [aged eight] to his new home, he only took the little one [aged two]. The eldest felt totally abandoned, he wasn't with either of his parents, he was with his grandmother, but she was a very old lady and they don't even like each other.[88]

The difference in the treatment of mothers is not legitimate or proportionate. The different treatment is premised on outdated assumptions which have a negative impact upon abducted children.

The CRC Committee explained in its General Discussion Day on the Girl Child that Islamic law countries have attempted to justify the different treatment of girls and boys because girls, they say, attain physical maturity earlier. This position is not accepted by the CRC Committee,[89] by academics,[90] or in this analysis. The evidence affirms that maturity cannot be identified simply as physical development; social and mental development must also be taken into account.[91] The fact that girls are considered old enough to marry at the age of thirteen, or even nine in some Islamic law countries, would mean they are no longer considered children and are therefore further deprived of the protections under the CRC.

While gender discrimination may form the 'traditional, historical, religious or cultural attitudes' of people living in Islamic law countries, it leads to inequality in the enjoyment of rights by girls and is not, according to the children's rights-based approach and the UNCRC Committee, justified in violating girls' and women's rights to equality before the law and equal enjoyment of all rights.[92] The existence of the reservations by Islamic law countries on the basis of cultural norms is not

[87] See also the application of the framework by Besson (n 2) 450–51.

[88] Participant 07M, interview 16/06/16 (on file with the author).

[89] CRC Committee, *General Discussion on the Girl Child*, UN Doc CRC/C/38 (21 January 1995) para 294.

[90] See Amina Wadud, *Qur'an and Women: Rereading the Sacred Text from a Woman's Perspective* (OUP, 1999); Fatima Mernissi, *The Veil and the Male Elite: A Feminist Interpretation of Women's Rights in Islamic Law* (Addison-Wesley, 1991); Ziba Mir Hosseini, *Islam and Gender* (Princeton University Press, 1999); Ayesha Chaudhry, *Domestic Violence and the Islamic Tradition* (OUP, 2014).

[91] Rehman (n 52) 160–2.

[92] Concluding Observations Saudi Arabia (n 26) 15–16; see also CCPR GC28 (n 41).

accepted by the CRC Committee,[93] and so culture norms are not a valid justification to fail to address the discrimination within the law.

The analysis highlights that there is the risk that if universal norms are not applied as a measure, and children's rights are adapted to the social environments in which children live, then children are at risk of 'cultural domination' within their own local cultures and communities. And whilst many cultural traditions are beneficial to children, the 'harmful practices' identified above are an example of those practices that are a concern, to the UNCRC Committee, left-behind parents and to the abductees themselves. Brando identifies that both universalist and embedded approaches to the CRC seek to protect children from the imposition of a dominant group's conception of good and justice when implementing children's rights. These both seek to protect from competing angles, however. A universal application of the CRC seeks to protect children from domination within the domestic sphere, such as the harmful practices discussed earlier in this chapter. In contrast, the deliberations on embeddedness and cultural relativism seek to protect children from domination occurring at the international level,[94] protecting children from 'Western imperialism' and 'colonial brainwashing.'[95] The published literature affirms the diversity of opinion on these two competing perspectives, highlighting that even within communities and cultures, individuals disagree with the views of dominant groups within their cultural environment.[96] The competing debates do little to assist abducted children and varying viewpoints emerge within the interview data collected for the author's study; from abducted children, abducting parents, left behind parents and a variety of professionals with experience of cases of parental abduction to Islamic law countries. In an attempt to bridge the competing perspectives, Brando builds on the suggestion of An-Na'im. An-Na'im argues that the definitions of universalism and embeddedness can become porous to one another, through diversifying internal discourses within each social setting (between the actors in each community) and diversifying cross-cultural dialogue amongst different social settings (across states).[97] Power dynamics within and across the cultural groups are identified as an obstacle to overcome in this endeavour and, in the same way, Brando identifies that the power dynamics between adults and children will undoubtedly impact the universalist and embedded approaches to upholding children's rights afforded by the CRC. Brando suggests that the only way in which to overcome this conflict is to directly engage children in the decision-making process, he observes 'by including

[93] GC18 13.

[94] Nico Brando, '"Universalism, embeddedness and domination": an analysis of the Convention on the Rights of the Child' 2019 (15) 3 *Journal of Global Ethics*, 270–86, 271.

[95] See discussion in this area by K, Valentin and L, Meinert, 'The adult North and the young South: Reflections on the Civilizing Mission of Children's Rights' 2009 (25) 3 *Anthropology Today*, 23–28.

[96] For discussion and examples see U Narayan, *Dislocating Cultures, Identities, Traditions and Third-World Feminism* (Routledge, 2007); see also WJ Talbott, *Which Rights Should be Universal?* (OUP, 2005).

[97] A An-Na'im, *Muslims and Global Justice* (Penn State University Press, 2010).

children directly in the decision-making process, the asymmetric power dynamic which pervades both purely universalist and embedded approaches, may be overcome.'[98] This viewpoint supports the premise of the analysis in this text which argues that that the adoption of a child rights approach is essential to responding to the issue of parental child abduction to Islamic law countries. The power dynamic between political leaders and the populations in Islamic law countries is recognised throughout the analysis and so, of course, the power dynamic between children and adults in the abduction situation is unsurmountable unless and until the child's Article 12 CRC right to be heard is respected in abduction proceedings.

Nothing in the data examined suggests there is either objective justification or a legitimate aim for subjecting abducted children and their mothers to gender discrimination. It is argued here that in the context of child abduction, even if a cultural relativist approach is adopted, it should not be forgotten that Miriam, Aliyah, Ryan and the other 51 abducted children in the sample were born and raised – up until the abduction – in the UK. And so, they should, arguably, be afforded the protection that prevails in the UK, since they did not choose to move to the Islamic law country and their abduction to the new country is deemed unlawful. The examination in this chapter illustrates that not only are the abductees' Article 11 CRC rights to be protected from parental abduction breached, but also that the children abducted were – and are still – subjected to gender discrimination in the Islamic law country, which they would be unlikely to experience in the UK had they not been abducted. Thus, in an international parental child abduction context, it is argued that only a universal interpretation of children's rights should apply.

ii. Islamic Law and Universal Rights

In an Islamic country context, An-Na'im argues that the paradox of normative universality can be mediated through processes of internal discourse and cross-cultural dialogue to broaden and deepen genuine and substantive consensus over the formulation interpretation and implementation of human rights norms.[99] He argues that it is possible to find authority for both liberal and conservative ideologies in the primary sources of Islamic law. It is his view that Muslims should choose a liberal interpretation of Islamic sources to make Islamic law amenable to modern international relations and human rights.[100] This view is opposed by other academics, who argue that 'repealing or changing a Koranic verse is solely the right of God, and there is no room for human involvement,' whilst offering the competing view that human rights are of Western origin and that Islam has its

[98] Brando (n 94) 281.

[99] An-Na'im (2010) (n 72) 173.

[100] Mashood Baderin (ed), *Islam and Human Rights: Selected Essays of Abdullahi An-Na'im* (Ashgate Publishing, 2010) 8.

own system of human rights.[101] An-Na'im dismisses opposing views as a form of cultural relativist opposition and proposes that the universality of human rights renders human rights immune to 'cultural relativism'.[102] He further argues that there is no need to revert to cultural relativism when examining the rights of girls/women, as classical Islamic law promoted the rights of women more favourably than in other legal systems until the nineteenth century.[103] Islam declared women as full legal persons with rights, for example, to share an inheritance, to hold and dispose of property, to have access to education and healthcare facilities, and to possess other civil and political rights before women were accorded those rights in other legal systems. Thus there is no reason why women's rights cannot be equalised in Islamic law countries in modern times.[104]

An-Na'im's argument is supported by others, who point out that the Islamic scriptures do not refer to the control of women,[105] and that gender discrimination is not attributable to the Islamic religion; rather, it is the subject of a patriarchal culture propagated by leaders in Islamic law countries.[106] Commentators highlight the misogynistic influences through religious interpretation and the privileges of male scholarship in religious teachings that result in the reluctance to reform Islamic law.[107] Part of this problem Farid ascribes to the fact that there is little discussion between Muslim scholars about women's rights.[108] She states that in the West, the Jewish and Christian feminist scholars are already well advanced in their criticism of male chauvinistic religious knowledge. The Hindu and Buddhist feminist scholars are also actively engaged in refuting male biases in their religions. But in the context of Islam, the 'women question' is still being addressed mostly by conservative male scholars who do not seem to wholeheartedly admit that in various parts of the Islamic world and different periods of history women have been denied rights given to them by Islam. Cesari[109] notes that most of the chief reformist thinkers derive from the countries of the Muslim world; it was there that they began their studies, and continue to maintain friendships and associations in their countries of origin. But it is easier for these thinkers to express certain ideas and methodologies in the West than in the Muslim world, for the obvious reason that the West makes specific provisions for the free expression of thought. Despite

[101] Niaz Shah, *Women, the Koran and International Human Rights Law* (Martinus Nijhoff, 2006) 11; Niaz Shah, 'A Woman's Human Rights in the Koran: An Interpretive Approach' (2006) 28 (4) *Human Rights Quarterly* 868.

[102] Baderin (n 100) 57.

[103] See Farid who discusses religious oppression of women who are regarded as responsible for the fall of Adam in Christianity and Judaism and as a temptress in Hinduism and Buddhism: Arifa Farid, *Muslim Woman in World Religions' Perspective* (The University of Karachi, 2006).

[104] Baderin (n 100) 269.

[105] Ali (n 53).

[106] See Wadud (n 90); Mernissi (n 90); Hosseini (n 90); Chaudhry (n 90).

[107] See further Fatima Mernisi, *Woman and Islam* (Basil Blackwell, 1991) 77.

[108] Farid (n 103).

[109] Jocelyn Cesari, *When Islam and Democracy Meet* (Palgrave Macmillan, 2004) 154, 180.

this, she is of the opinion Islamic practices are being revamped and secularised, and Islamic thought is at the peak of activity.

The fact that Islamic law allows reform of its provisions has led to assertions that Islamic law countries retain the guardianship provisions either out of choice, or because it is not an area of priority for reform.[110] There is evidence of some Islamic law countries attempting to reform laws that discriminate against women, based on the Islamic law principle that 'there is no doubt that rulings change along with the change of times.'[111] It is noteworthy, however, that even where there are clear attempts to reform the law of child custody, such as in Morocco, provisions subjecting girls and women to the guardianship framework are barely altered. In a comparative analysis of the position of the guardianship of women and older girls across several Islamic law countries, Möller attributes the impediments to reform as threefold:

> A patriarchal reading of pre-modern Islamic legal doctrine, the legislatures' preference to vest financial control in men, and, lastly, the outsourcing of guardianship from the larger body of codified family law, as can be witnessed in jurisdictions such as Bahrain, Qatar, and Iraq.[112]

The first two points are self-explanatory, the third is best explained by recognising that law-makers, whether deliberately or inadvertently, categorise the function of guardianship as property law instead of family law. Thus the aspect is overlooked during the process of custody reform, or it is deliberately ignored because decision-makers in a patriarchal society prefer control to be retained by men. Morocco, Tunisia and Algeria have reformed the law on guardianship so that mothers are now also allowed to be appointed as guardians of their children, but this is only on the father's death. The law prioritises a mother's guardianship over other paternal male relatives such as the grandfather, or an uncle, but not in the father's lifetime.[113]

Despite calls for universal application of rights, society's views on equality have an impact on how far and how quickly the discriminatory laws can be reformed, and how soon abducted children and their mothers can rely upon equality before the law. As Prettitore[114] observes, the social norms, both religious and non-religious, are restricting the ability of women to exercise their rights. General attitudes in

[110] Rehman (n 52); Abdullahi Ahmed An-Na'im, *Toward an Islamic Reformation of Civil Liberties in Human Rights and International Law* (Syracuse University Press, 1990).

[111] As stated by the Chief Justice of the Jordanian Shari'a Courts, Dr Hleil who notes that conditions of modern life had evolved, necessitating a reconsideration of personal status principles balanced with practicality, custom, and Shari'a law, cited by Prettitore (n 58) 33.

[112] Lena-Maria Möller, 'An Enduring Relic: Family Law Reform and the Inflexibility of Wilaya' (2015) 63 *The American Journal of Comparative Law* 847, 910; Imen Gallala-Arndt, 'Negotiating Parenthood in Muslim Countries: Changing Concepts and Perceptions' (2015) 63 *The American Journal of Comparative Law* 847.

[113] Decree No 05-02 of 2005, art 87 (Algeria); Law No 70.03 of 2004, arts 231, 238 (Morocco); Code of Personal Status, arts 154–155 (Tunisia); Möller (n 112) 910–11.

[114] Prettitore (n 58) 33–4.

Morocco and Jordan do not appear supportive of gender equality, especially among men. Only 16 per cent of Jordanian and 33 per cent of Moroccan male respondents to the World Values Survey considered equality of men and women as an essential part of democracy.[115] Numbers were slightly higher for Jordanian female respondents (19 per cent) compared to Jordanian men, but considerably higher for Moroccan women (60 per cent). Even after reforms, Jordanian and Moroccan law, therefore, remains discriminatory as it retains unequal grounds for accessing divorce, requirements for guardianship over women, and default legal custody of children in case of divorce. Gender distinctions in the law will undoubtedly affect children abducted to Islamic law countries. The impact will be particularly felt where girls are abducted from the UK (or other Western states), ie girls who are unlikely to encounter the subjugation if they had not been abducted. Moreover, even though abducted boys may not be directly discriminated against in domestic law in Islamic law countries, the abducted boys in the sample of cases examined suffered indirectly because of the discrimination experienced by their mothers.

The next challenge is to address the obstacle of gender discrimination through the use of relational theory, to consider the inequalities against mothers and children as an interrelated issue.

iii. Children's Rights are Relational to the Mother's Rights

Another obstacle to addressing cases of parental abduction to Islamic law countries is that parental abduction law considers the rights of children, but pays little regard to the rights of the primary carer who is, more often than not, the child's mother. The interrelated effect of gender discrimination on women and their children reinforces the premise of relational theory, which is that that the rights and interests of the two are one and the same.[116] The appropriateness of the relational approach in a parental abduction context will be examined in this section, beginning with a brief consideration of how relational theory could appear to conflict with some children's rights theories.

First, there are strong arguments as to why children's rights should not be conflated with the rights of a parent. The need to advocate children's rights independently is understandable, in light of historical developments in recognising and securing rights for children. Some children's rights advocates see a tension between children's rights and parental rights,[117] through a concern that attempting to strike a balance between the rights of children with the rights of the caregivers

[115] The World Values Survey ('WVS') consists of nationally representative surveys conducted in almost 100 countries which contain almost 90 per cent of the world's population, using a common questionnaire; Wave 6 data (2010–2014): WVS is a global network of social scientists studying changing values and their impact on social and political life, led by an international team of scholars in Austria: www.worldvaluessurvey.org/wvs.jsp.

[116] Jennifer Nedelsky, *Reconceiving Rights as Relationship* (1993) 1 *Review of Constitutional Studies* 1, 1–26.

[117] Dwyer argues that the correct thing to do is stay focused on the child; James Dwyer, *The Relationship Rights of Children* (Cambridge University Press, 2006) 130.

could serve to undermine the rights of the child.[118] Daly[119] strongly disagrees with the view that the interests of others should be given greater recognition in child welfare assessments.[120] While the Hague Convention regulation is not intended to assess the child's welfare, it does undertake a welfare assessment in cases where the child's circumstances must be considered before deciding whether the defences to return apply. Daly's approach, therefore, appears to conform to the aims of the Hague Convention, where the mother's rights are not supposed to be factored in the court's decision. Other academics express the value of children's relationships in upholding their rights[121] but highlight that safeguarding children within their relationships will serve the needs of adults more than children.[122] The distinction is made because, as Eva Brems argues,[123] there is an essential distinction between women's rights and children's rights, which lies in what can be considered to be the optimal balance between protection rights and autonomy rights. She argues that this balance is not the same for both groups. An example would be the situation identified in chapter 4, where advocacy for women's custodial rights in Islamic law countries has become conflated with the child's rights. A direct consequence of the battle for women's custody has resulted in limiting the child's right to participate in proceedings. The complexity is observed in Morocco's reforms, for example, where the age at which a mother can retain custody of the child increased from age 12 to age 15, which also means the child is unable to participate in proceedings until age 15, thereby limiting the child's Article 12 CRC rights.

Notwithstanding the strong children's rights-based arguments, there are also compelling reasons why relational theory should not be discounted in examining the rights of abducted children.[124] If we apply the theories of Katharine Bartlett,[125] Martha Milnrow[126] and Jennifer Nedelsky,[127] who evaluate the parent–child relationship, their application to the case of primary carer abductions is of relevance.

[118] Pamela Laufer-Ukeles, 'The Relational Rights of Children' (2016) 48 3 *Connecticut Law Review* 769.

[119] Aoife Daly, *Children, Autonomy and the Courts: Beyond the Right to be Heard* (Brill, 2017) 25.

[120] See argument of Martha Minow, 'Rights for the Next Generation: A Feminist Approach to Children's Rights' (1986) (1) 9 *Harv Women's L J* 19.

[121] Barbara Bennett Woodhouse, 'Hatching the Egg: A Child-Centred Perspective on Parents' Rights' (1993) 14 *Cardozo Law Review* 1747, 1815, 1841.

[122] Ibid.

[123] Eva Brems, 'Lesson's from Children's Rights from Women's Rights? Emancipation Rights as a Distinct Category of Human Rights' in Eva Brems and others (ed) *Children's Rights Law in the Global Human Rights Landscape: Isolation, Inspiration, Integration?* (Routledge, 2017) 95.

[124] Note that some academics have applied the relational argument also to the relationship between the guardian and ward in the marital context in Islamic law; Ludsin (n 44); Joseph Suad, 'Problematizing Gender and Relational Rights: Experiences from Lebanon Social Politics' (1994) 1 (3) *International Studies in Gender, State & Society* 271.

[125] See the work of Bartlett who characterises parental rights as responsibilities and obligations to children due to parent–child interdependency; Katharine Bartlett 'Re-Expressing Parenthood' (1988) 98 *Yale L J* 293, 297–98, 304–06, 315.

[126] Martha Minow, 'Forming Underneath Everything that Grows: Toward a History of Family Law' (1985) *Wis L Rev* 819, 894. She argues a body of family law that protects only the autonomous self fails to nurture the relationships between individuals that constitute families.

[127] Jennifer Nedelsky, *Law's Relations: A Relational Theory of Self, Autonomy and Law* (OUP, 2011) 3–5.

The relational theory would propose that primary carers and their abducted children are interdependent and that their choices and experiences are shaped by the relationships '(intimate, familial, community and societal)' within which they are embedded.[128] The child is in an inseparable, interdependent relationship with their primary carer, and the relational nature of children's lives cannot be ignored.[129] Relational theorists go as far as to argue that individualistic rights fundamentally miss the extent to which children's relationships with others allow them to become who they are – their identities, their capacities, their desires – through the relationships in which they participate.[130] The inter-dependent relationships have a number of consequences for the rights of abducted children. The relational theory would argue that an abducted child's right to have his or her best interests treated as a primary consideration, to participate in decision-making and to be protected from discrimination are inter-related with the rights of the primary carer, and the two should be evaluated together in parental abduction proceedings, not because the child's rights are not at the centre of the analysis, but because relational theory dictates that the child's rights cannot be realised without also understanding the primary carer's rights.

The data analysed in this text identifies that in the context of parental abduction to Islamic law countries, children's rights intimately link with women's rights,[131] and it is difficult to address one without addressing the other. The discriminatory custody legislation in Islamic law countries, as discussed in chapter 3, which applies in cases of parental abduction, has an impact on the abducted child as well as the left-behind mother. This point is also noted by Frances Olsen, who argues that women's role as primary caretakers of children gives them an interest in children's rights, but that this has resulted in their domination. Olsen refers to Morocco as an example and observes that the legal protection of children can be used as a basis for controlling women.[132] The challenges lie, she argues, in the way the law in Morocco treats children and how Moroccan law treats women by a woman's status as a mother. Welchman[133] supports this view, as do others who rely on evidence from empirical studies to suggest that men have used

[128] Helen Stalford, Kathryn Hollingsworth and Stephen Gilmore (eds), *Rewriting Children's Rights Judgments: From Academic Vision to New Practice* (Hart Publishing, 2017) 74–75.

[129] See Herring that states that the emphasis on autonomy in family law results in a focus on self-sufficiency and self-determination; Jonathan Herring, 'Relational Autonomy and Family Law' in Julie Wallbank and others (eds), *Rights Gender and Family Law* (Routledge, 2010) 259.

[130] Nedelsky asserts rights are broadly relational, and applies her theory to children; Nedelsky (1993) (n 116).

[131] Loenen (n 71) 173.

[132] See Francis Olsen, 'Children's Rights: Some Feminist Approaches to the UN Convention on the Rights of the Child' in Philip Alston and others (eds), *Children, Rights and the Law* (Clarendon Press, 1992); see also Frances Olsen, 'Children's Rights: Some Feminist Approaches to the UNCRC, (1992) 6 (1) *International Journal of Law, Policy and the Family* 192.

[133] Lynn Welchman, *Women and Muslim Family Laws in Arab States: A Comparative Overview of Textual Development and Advocacy* (Amsterdam University Press, 2007).

their custody rights in Islamic law to their advantage, such as to bargain spousal maintenance upon divorce.[134] Thus the law that favours fathers appears not to be applied to serve the child's interests but to serve the father's interests. The point is also observed in the analysis in this text, in chapter 3, which highlights that the rules preventing mothers from relocating with the child to another country were designed to uphold the child's interests, but appear to be used as a basis to control women.

It is on the basis of this intimate and inextricably linked relationship in the context of parental abduction to Islamic law countries, that this analysis suggests the conflation of rights is unavoidable. Children are affected by the discrimination directed at their mothers in Islamic custody legislation, and at the same time, women encounter gender discrimination in their role as mothers.[135] The CRC Committee makes the association of women's and children's rights in Islamic law countries in several ways. It makes this connection in the Concluding Observations for most Islamic law countries in the areas of family breakdown, domestic violence and the roles of women more generally.[136] For example, the CRC Committee also highlights the link noting that:

> insufficient measures have been taken to change the prevalent gender stereotypes concerning the tasks and roles of women in Oman. The Committee recommends the State party: (a) Adopt measures for changing mindsets and stereotypes regarding the roles of parents to encourage equal sharing of parental responsibilities. (b) Consider introducing reform to ensure that men and women, and boys and girls, have equal rights and responsibilities. (c) Abolish all provisions that discriminate against women and have a negative impact on their children, such as those that allow polygamy and (divorce) repudiation.[137]

The correlation is further established by the fact that the Committees of the CRC and CEDAW felt the necessity to jointly issue GC18 on the gender discrimination girls and women experience:

> The Committee on the Elimination of Discrimination against Women and the Committee on the Rights of the Child consistently note that harmful practices are

[134] Homa Hoodfar, 'Circumventing Legal Limitation: Mahr and Marriage Negotiation in Egyptian Low-Income Communities' in Homa Hoodfar (ed), *Shifting boundaries in marriage and divorce in Muslim communities* (Grabels, 1996) 125; Ziba Mir-Hosseini, *Marriage on Trial: A Study of Islamic Family Law, Iran and Morocco Compared*, 2nd edn (IB Tauris, 2000) 151; Lynn Welchman, *Beyond the Code: Muslim Family Law and the Shari'a Judiciary in the Palestinian West Bank* (Kluwer, 2000) 279; Annelies Moors, *Women, Property and Islam: Palestinian Experiences 1920–1990* (Cambridge, 1995) 211; Aharon Layish, *Women and Islamic law in a Non-Muslim state* (Jerusalem, 1975) 159.

[135] Note also the CCPR GC28 makes several references highlighting the connection between children's rights and women's rights, in addition to specifically referring to non-discrimination against the 'girl-child'; CCPR GC28 (n 41).

[136] See Concluding Observations Bahrain (n 25) 33; Concluding Observations Qatar CRC/C/QAT/CO/3-4 (22 June 2017) 26; Concluding Observations Oman CRC/C/OMN/CO/3-4 (14 March 2016) 43–44.

[137] Concluding Observations Oman ibid 43–44.

> deeply rooted in social attitudes according to which women and girls are regarded as inferior to men and boys based on stereotyped roles.[138]

The question this chapter seeks to resolve is to what extent child abduction law upholds the abducted child's right to equality before the law. The analysis demonstrates that gender discrimination in Islamic custody/abduction law is deep-rooted, and it raises the question of whether children's rights can be upheld in a legal framework that not only tolerates but actively promotes inequality. Can the power of entrenched cultural attitudes override international agreements on non-discrimination? And how will this affect children abducted to Islamic law countries and the left-behind mothers who travel to Islamic law countries to seek the child's return? Most Islamic law countries have become parties to CEDAW, which requires states to modify laws, customs and practices which constitute discrimination against women and to ensure equality of rights for women and men in a range of matters relating to marriage and the family. As with the CRC, CEDAW is subject to a high number of reservations from Islamic law countries, and the controversial nature of reservations entered by Islamic law countries arises from their generality.[139] Specifically, reservations have been made by different Islamic law countries to Articles 15 and 16 which guarantee equality of women with men before the law, including in legal capacity and at all stages of court proceedings. Other articles objected to include the law relating to the movement of persons and the freedom to choose their residence and domicile and the article requiring states to take all appropriate measures to eliminate discrimination against women in all matters relating to marriage and family relations. The reservations entered by Islamic law countries caused some controversy and in response CEDAW's Committee proposed the United Nations should 'undertake studies on the status of women under Islamic laws and customs and in particular on the status and equality of women in the family.'[140] The proposal resulted in allegations of 'cultural imperialism and religious intolerance' and warnings against 'using the Convention as a pretext for attacks on Islam.'[141] The General Assembly subsequently agreed

[138] Ibid 6.

[139] See Jennifer Riddle, 'Making CEDAW Universal: A Critique of CEDAW's Reservation Regime under Article 28 and the Effectiveness of the Reporting Process' (2002) *34 Geo Wash Int'l L Rev* 605, 627; Welchman (2007) (n 127) 34–36.

[140] During the CEDAW Committee's sixth meeting, it expressed concern about "the significant number of reservations that appeared to be incompatible with the object and purpose of the Convention': *Rep of the Comm on the Elimination of Discrimination against Women* A/42/38 (10th April 1987) 579–580. In 1993 the Vienna Conference on Human Rights called for the withdrawal of such reservations in its declaration. World Conference on Human Rights (14–25 June 1993) *Vienna Declaration and Programme of Action* A/CONF.157/23 (July 12, 1993) 26.

[141] Jane Connors, 'The Woman's Convention in the Muslim World' in Mai Yamani (ed), *Feminism and Islam* (Ithaca Press, 1996) 362.

that no further action is to be taken on the suggestion.[142] The Committee does, however, continue to seek information from Islamic law countries on progress towards the withdrawal of reservations.[143]

The reluctance of Islamic law countries to uphold the rights of women will, of course, have a more significant impact on the girls abducted from the UK, more so than the boys. The case studies cited throughout this analysis are illustrative of this point, and both abducted girls and boys will be affected by the gender discrimination experienced by their mothers. The CRC also protects children from this form of discrimination, which is directed at the parents, under Article 2(1) CRC. It provides: 'State Parties shall respect and ensure the rights set forth in the present Convention to each child within their jurisdiction without discrimination of any kind, irrespective of the child's *or his or her parent's* ..., sex'. Thus abducted children are protected by the CRC even where gender discrimination is directed at their mother.

The interrelated effect of gender discrimination on women and their children reinforces the premise of relational theory that the rights and interests of the two are the same. On this basis, when deciding cases of parental abduction, the courts should have to factor in any gender discrimination the mother is subject to by virtue of the operation of legal provisions. Though this approach is unlikely to be adopted by Islamic courts until the custody legislation is reformed, or the CRC is incorporated in the Constitutions of Islamic law countries, it is an approach the English courts have taken in cases of parental abduction by mothers *from* Islamic law countries.[144] In such cases, the effect of gender discrimination in the legislation in Islamic law countries has been considered by the English courts. In the 2015 case of *AR v AS*[145] the mother refused to return her child to Saudi Arabia as she alleged she was the victim of domestic abuse by the child's father as well as by her own family. The mother claimed she experienced pressure from her own family to conform to their expectations of duty and honour. The child, aged eight, expressed a wish to remain with his mother. The English court did not order the child's return to Saudi Arabia because of the impact the mother's fear and consequent reluctance

[142] Welchman (2007) (n 133).

[143] On changes by Libya and Algeria to the wording of reservations to the Convention, see Ann Elizabeth Mayer, 'Islamic Reservations to Human Rights Conventions' (1998) 15 *Recht van der Islam*; and see also Ann Elizabeth Mayer 'Rhetorical Strategies and Official Policies on Women's Rights: The Merits and Drawbacks of the New World Hypocrisy' in Mahnaz Afkhami (ed), *Faith and Freedom: Women's Human Rights in the Muslim World* (Syracuse University Press, 1995) 104, critiquing the positions of Egypt and Morocco. For a specific examination of Arab states before the CEDAW Committee see Ann Elizabeth Mayer 'Internationalizing the Conversation on Arab Women's Rights: Arab Countries Face the CEDAW Committee', in Yvonne Yazbeck Haddad and Barbara Freyer Stowasser (eds), *Islamic law and the Challenges of Modernity* (Walnut Creek, 2004) 133.

[144] See also *AB v AB* [2015] EWHC 2422 (Fam) concerning the laws in Algeria.

[145] [2015] EWHC 3440 (Fam).

to accompany the child would have upon him. The expert giving evidence recommended the child should not return to Saudi Arabia because of 'the power of his guardian (normally the child's father) to block the child's exit from that country.'[146] The English court explained:

> As a divorced woman she [the mother] would be subject to her father's authority and would customarily and in practice follow his injunctions, which might include that she should return to live at her family home; that she should not leave it save as permitted, and then only in the company of a close male relative; that she should not take up employment; that she should not travel within or outside Saudi Arabia without her father's permission; and, indeed, that she should surrender her child to the child's father's authority as the child's guardian.[147]

The power of the English court to order a child's return means that the court has an obligation to reflect upon the implications of its decision to return a child to an Islamic law regime. The broader implication of the decision is for the English courts to show sympathy for women/mothers and to endeavour to address the discrimination women encounter under the family law in Islamic law countries. The Hague Convention did not apply in the case of *AR v AS* as Saudi Arabia is not a Hague treaty partner with the UK. So it is noteworthy that the English courts may not have the same power to refuse a child's return based upon discrimination against the mother in a case decided under the Hague Convention, as the Hague Convention requires the automatic return of an abducted child.

In comparing with the Hague legal framework, it must be noted that while the text of the Hague Convention does not endorse discrimination on the grounds of gender, the Hague Convention does, however, defer in many respects to domestic law. The deference, therefore, results in different treatment and outcomes in situations with similar circumstances depending upon the State Party in question. Domestic variances would, for example, be observed in the extent to which children are allowed to participate in Hague proceedings. By deferring to domestic law in each of the member states, the Hague Convention may inadvertently subject the child to discriminatory treatment, particularly girls in Islamic law countries.

Another area of Hague application in which gender has become an issue is the abduction of children by their primary carers. In the study of cases of parental abduction from the UK to Islamic law countries, primary carer abductions comprise a small minority in the sample (comprising 10.35 per cent of cases). This is in stark contrast to data that confirms abductions between Hague states are predominantly undertaken by mothers. It is reported that mothers are the abducting parent in approximately 70 per cent of cases in the last survey.[148] The contrast

[146] Ibid para 8.
[147] Ibid para 22.
[148] Hague Survey (2015).

is noteworthy, and it will be interesting to monitor whether the representation of primary carer abductions changes with the recent accession of Islamic law states. The only data available on Hague-Islamic states (at the time of writing) is the survey of cases heard under the Hague Convention in 2015. The survey reports that mothers were the abducting parent in 62.5 per cent of Hague Convention cases *to* Morocco – and so abductions by primary carer mothers may become a trend for Islamic states too, if and when they accede to the Hague Convention.

a. Primary Carer Abductions

At the time the Hague Convention was drafted, the prevailing view was that abductions were undertaken by the parent not living with the child, usually the father.[149] The Convention was nonetheless drafted on the basis that it applies to either parent[150] and as Schuz explains

> when the abduction convention was drafted, gender was not an issue. Since abductors were assumed to be non-primary carers who were taking the law into their own hands after having lost a custody battle, it made little difference whether they were mothers or fathers, as the return would restore the child to the primary carer.[151]

The climate of parental abductions has altered in the last four decades, and there are now more mothers that abduct internationally, between Hague states, comprising approximately 70 per cent of cases.[152] The study by Kruger of Belgian cases further evidences this trend. In Kruger's sample of 667 cases to and from Belgium, the mother was the abductor in 65.2 per cent of cases. Kruger also refers to data from a parallel study undertaken in Hungary by Kek Vonal, in which 88.4 per cent of abductors were mothers.[153]

Under the Hague Conventions policy of automatic return, children are returned, irrespective of whether or not their primary carer abducts them, as this position upholds the child's right to maintain a relationship with both parents, pursuant to Article 9 CRC. A gendered difficulty under the Hague framework can arise, however, as a result of the fact that a non-resident parent has a right to veto removal

[149] Adair Dyer, 'A Report on International Child Abduction by One Parent ("Legal Kidnapping")' (The Hague Conference, 1978) 17–20; Elisa Perez-Vera, 'Report on the 1980 Hague Child Abduction Convention' (Translation of The Permanent Bureau, 1981) para 81; Paul Beaumont and Peter McEleavy, *The Hague Convention on International Child Abduction* (OUP, 1999) 8–9; see also studies in support of this view: M Agopian, *Parental Child Stealing* (Lexington Books, 1981) and D Finkelhor, G Hotaling and A Sedlak, 'Children Abducted by Family Members: A National Household Survey of Incidence and Episode Characteristics' (1990) 53 *Journal of Marriage and the Family*, 805–17, as referred to in Beaumont and McEleavy, *The Hague Convention on International Child Abduction* (OUP, 1999) 7.

[150] For discussion on this point see Maria Caterina Baruffi and Jayne Holliday, 'Child Abduction' in Paul Beaumont and Jayne Holliday (eds), *A Guide to Global Private International Law* (Hart Publishing, 2022).

[151] Rhona Schuz, *The Hague Child Abduction Convention* (Hart Publishing, 2013) 58.

[152] Hague Survey (2015).

[153] Kruger (n 64) 75.

of the child from the jurisdiction if that parent can demonstrate possessing 'rights of custody' as per Article 5 of the Hague Convention. Article 5 provides 'rights of custody shall include rights relating to the care of the person of the child and, in particular, the right to determine the child's place of residence'. The position was affirmed by the United States Supreme Court in the case of *Abbott v Abbott*[154] where it was held that the non-resident parent, the father in that case, was to be regarded as having 'rights of custody' in accordance with Article 5 of the Hague Convention where there was an order in place that prevented the parents from removing the child from Chile, the country in which the family were habitually resident.

Whilst the right is enforceable by either parent, regardless of gender, commentators have observed[155] that the gendered effect can be greater when a father's right to veto the child's removal from the jurisdiction is interpreted in Hague Convention proceedings as a custody right, which they argue does not accord with the premise of the Hague Convention. The dissenting opinion of Justice Steven, (with whom Thomas and Breyer JJ agree) in *Abbott* resonates with this view. Justice Stevens asserts: 'use of the Convention's return remedy under these circumstances is contrary to the Convention's text and purpose.'[156] A key point Justice Stevens presents is that Article 3 of the Hague Convention provides that the removal or retention of a child is 'wrongful', and in breach of the Convention, only when the removal 'is in breach of the rights of custody'. The fact that a removal may be 'wrongful' in the sense that it violates domestic law or violates only 'rights of access' does not make it 'wrongful' within the meaning of the Convention. Only when a removal is 'wrongful' under Article 3 can the parent who possesses custody rights make a request for the child's return through the Convention's automatic return mechanism. Justice Stevens argues that a parent without 'rights of custody,' therefore, does not have the power granted by Article 3 to compel the child's return and his rights are limited to those in Article 21 on access rights. Ultimately, he furthers the argument that the Hague Convention provides recourse for the non-custodial parent to exercise his right of access with the child and the Hague Convention does not provide the non-custodial parent the right to seek the child's return, in that case, from the United States to Chile.

Notwithstanding Justice Steven's minority opinion, Hague Convention jurisprudence establishes that the right of a non-custodial parent to veto the child's removal from the jurisdiction is to be regarded as a right of custody. Yet this does not alter the fact that automatic return under all circumstances can be problematic for mothers in particular because, as Lamont points out, the very reasons for the abduction, the needs of mothers raising children alone travelling for economic

[154] 560 US 1 (2010).

[155] Rhona Schuz, 'In Search of a Settled Interpretation of Article 12(2) of the Hague Child Abduction Convention' (2008) (20) 1 *Child & Family Law Quarterly* 64; Schuz (2013) (n 151) 58; see also the views of Sandy Anton, the chair of the Special Commission and Diplomatic Session responsible for drafting the Convention; Beaumont, P 'The Contribution of Alexander (Sandy) Anton to the Development of Private International Law' (2006) *Juridical Review* 1–28.

[156] 560 US 1 (2010) pp 1–2 (no para numbers provided in the published opinion).

and practical support from family or other networks, is itself gendered, as is the case of women fleeing domestic abuse.[157] The commitment to the process of automatic return has meant that in cases even where serious violence is alleged, children, and by implication their mothers, are returned.[158] Weiner[159] argues the Hague Convention perpetuates violence and contributes to gender subordination where victims are dissuaded from fleeing domestic abuse as a result of the Convention; blaming some courts for being unable to appreciate the connection between domestic violence against the parent and the psychological wellbeing of a child.[160] The summary nature of return applications means allegations of domestic violence are difficult to assess for reliability, and the lack of evidence indicates the focus remains on the mother's actions in removing the child, rather than on her motivations for doing so. Accordingly, Bucher[161] advocates for a softer application of the Convention when the abduction has been carried out by a primary carer and Freeman[162] has argued in cases of primary carer abductions, the child should always remain with the primary carer. The dissenting opinion of Judge Pinto de Albuquerque in *X v Latvia*[163] supports this view. He explains the sociological shift in Hague Convention cases, from a non-custodial abductor to a custodial abductor, usually the child's primary carer, calls for a purposive and evolutive interpretation of the Hague Convention. He further observes that a restrictive reading of the exceptions to return, based on an outdated, unilateral and over-simplistic assumption in favour of the left behind parent and which ignores the real situation of the child and his or her family and envisages a mere punitive approach to the abducting parent's conduct, will serve to defeat the aim of the Hague Convention, especially in the case of abduction by the child's primary caregiver. Such an interpretation of the Hague Convention would be at odds with the human rights and especially the Article 8 ECHR rights of the abducted child in Hague Convention proceedings. Such a viewpoint does, however, raise the issue of whether the rights

[157] Lamont (2011) (n 85) 369–70.

[158] Carol Bruch, 'The Unmet Needs of Domestic Violence Victims and their Children in Hague Abduction Convention cases' (2004) 38 *Family Law Quarterly* 529; Merle Weiner, 'International Child Abduction and the Escape from Domestic Violence' (2000) 69 *Fordham L Rev* 593, 637–39; Marilyn Freeman, 'Primary Carers and the Hague Child Abduction Convention' [2001] *IFL* 140; Roxanne Hoegger, 'What If She Leaves? Domestic Violence Cases Under the Hague Convention and the Insufficiency of the Undertakings Remedy' (2003) 18 *Berkeley Women's Law Journal* 181; Miranda Kaye, 'The Hague Convention and the Flight from Domestic Violence: How Women and Children Are Being Returned by Coach and Four', (1999) 13 *Int'l JL Pol'y & Fam* 191.

[159] Merle Weiner, 'The Potential and Challenges of Transnational Litigation for Feminists Concerned about Domestic Violence Here and Abroad' (2003) 11 *Journal of Gender, Social, Policy and the Law* 749, 799.

[160] Merle Weiner, 'Intolerable Situations and Counsel for Children: Following Switzerland's Example in Hague Abduction Cases' (2008) 58 *American University Law Review* 356.

[161] Andreas Bucher, 'The New Swiss Federal Act on International Child Abduction' (2008) 4 *Journal of Private International Law* 139.

[162] Freeman (2001) (n 158) 140; D Harris, 'Is the Strength of the Hague Convention on Child Abduction Being Diluted by the Courts? The English Perspective' (1999) 35 *International Legal Materials* 77.

[163] Application No 27853/09 Grand Chamber pages 45–46 (no paragraph number provided).

of the left-behind father will be disregarded and the impact this could have on the child.[164]

In cases of abduction by primary carers, relational theory avoids the idea of 'competing rights.' Advocates of the relational theory[165] argue that the primary carers' rights are directly relevant to discussing children's rights because the primary carer spends the majority of their time caring for children. And as Woodhouse argues, 'a truly child-centred perspective would also expose the fallacy that children can thrive while their caregivers struggle, or that the caregiver's needs can be severed from the child's.'[166] The discussion illustrates that it is difficult to disentangle the interests of children from the interests of their mothers, the interdependency is a reality, and as Laufer-Ukeles[167] suggests, recognising the interdependence is more important in supporting children's rights than symbolic gestures. Thus as Erica Burman[168] proposes, the relation between women's rights and children's rights should be approached as 'neither adversarial, nor equivalent, but as allied – albeit as necessarily structured in tension and contest.'

Stalford et al[169] develop relational theory in the context of the assessment by courts of children's autonomous decision-making. They explain that the relational approach has several consequences for children's autonomy. If children make choices that take account of the interests of others, it does not render that choice contrary to children's rights, provided that the judge engages in an examination of the relationship to ensure it is nourishing and not oppressive. They point out that a relational approach also allows the judge to recognise that children may need adult support to make decisions, but that this does not necessarily render the decision non-autonomous. The fact that a child is likely to be influenced to some degree by the primary carer's views is thus an inevitable part of the child's relationship with the primary carer. So when determining the abducted child's rights, can the court separate the child's rights and interests from their parents? The CRC Committee does not seem to think so in its analysis of the law in Islamic law countries, where it recognises the rights of children are in many respects intertwined with the rights of their mothers, in the context of parental responsibility, polygamy and divorce.[170] When deciding a case of abduction by a primary carer, the court should

[164] Beaumont and McEleavy (n 149) 262; see also the body of work on international relocation that recognises the effects of such determinations: M Hayes, 'Relocation Cases: Is The Court of Appeal Applying the Correct Principles?' [2006] CFLQ 351; J Herring and R Taylor, 'Relocating Relocation' [2006] CFLQ 517; F Judd QC and R George, 'International Relocation: Do We Stand Alone?' [2010] *Family Law* 63; S Gilmore, 'The Payne Saga: Precedent and Family Law Cases' [2011] *Family Law* 970; R George, 'Reviewing Relocation?' [2012] CFLQ 110; R George, *Relocation Disputes: Law and Practice in England and New Zealand* (Hart Publishing, 2014).

[165] Laufer-Ukeles (n 118) 774; Olsen (n 132).

[166] Woodhouse (n 121) 1815.

[167] Laufer-Ukeles (n 118) 774.

[168] Erica Burman, 'Beyond "Women vs. Children" or "WomenandChildren": Engendering Childhood and Reformulating Motherhood' (2008) 16 *International Journal of Children's Rights* 177.

[169] Stalford, Hollingsworth and Gilmore (n 128) 4–5.

[170] Concluding Observations Bahrain (n 25) 33; Concluding Observations Qatar (n 136) 26; Concluding Observations Oman (n 136) 43–44.

evaluate the child's relationship with the parent before deciding whether to order the child's return. Forcing return in a case where the abducting mother is unable to return, or will struggle in the requesting state, might uphold the child's independent Article 11 CRC rights, but when examined in the context of a relational right, this may not serve the child's interests or uphold the child's rights as is suggested by Freeman,[171] Weiner[172] and Bucher.[173]

Could 'positive discrimination' be applied in cases where the abducting parent is the child's sole primary carer (and the left-behind parent is not a joint carer of the child)? Would this be justified to uphold the child's rights, based upon the child's relationship with his or her primary carer? The following discussion on relational rights in this context examines whether the Hague Convention's policy of automatic return should be enforced in abductions by a primary carer. A mother having to travel overseas after the breakdown of the parents' relationship to seek familial or economic support or, for example, to flee domestic abuse, is unlikely to leave behind the child. Seeking the court's consent to relocate may not be a possibility if the mother cannot afford to litigate or does not wish to risk the court declining an application if the mother has no other means of survival. Can the rights of the child in this situation be considered independently of the mother's rights, particularly if a mother may have decided to move for the child's safety and security?

Different treatment of abductions by primary carers is possible if the view of the UN Human Rights Committee is adopted in the context of Hague proceedings.[174] It is possible to argue that primary carer abductions justify legitimate differentiation, and the distinction is reasonable and objective, as the aim is to achieve a purpose that is legitimate under the Convention. Besson identifies that objective justification might be provided as in the general case of discrimination as a positive action measure in the context of anti-discrimination protections.[175] The difference in treatment for primary carers must pursue a legitimate aim to be a justified distinction. Protecting children from the 'harmful effects' of parental abduction is one of the principal aims of the Hague Convention[176] and Article 11 CRC. Moreover the studies discussed above demonstrate that abducted children describe separation from their primary carer as causing them harm.[177] Accordingly, the differential treatment in the case of primary carer abductions could be argued as a justified distinction and of reasonable proportionality between the means employed and the aim sought to be achieved. The argument appears to have some validity, and attempts have been made to further this argument by some Hague Convention

[171] Freeman (2001) (n 158) 140.
[172] Weiner (2008) (n 160) 356.
[173] Bucher (2008) (n 161) 139.
[174] CCPR GC18 (n 41) 13.
[175] Besson (n 2) 450–51.
[176] See preamble to the Hague Convention.
[177] See discussion above at sec 3.III.C.

Contracting States. During a Hague Conference meeting, Switzerland proposed that a protocol is required to address the issue of primary carer abductions.[178] After consultation with states through a questionnaire, responses from States indicated diverging views, with some States opposed to such a protocol.[179] As a result, The Hague Conference has indicated that it will not develop a protocol for this purpose. A refusal by the Hague Conference to develop the text of the Convention, despite acknowledging that the category of abductions has changed since 1980, runs the risk that the Hague Convention may fail to appropriately respond to the very problem it seeks to address. Paradoxically, it would suffer from a similar setback to that identified in Islamic custody law – where the law is intended to uphold the interests and rights of all people particularly children – but because there is a reluctance by leaders to develop the archaic law as it could upset some groups, it results in a detrimental impact upon the very children it intends to protect. Without any positive action by the Hague Conference, it is a matter for domestic courts applying the Hague provisions to decide how to respond to primary carer abductions and how flexibly the defences to return can be used by the judiciary to respond to this issue.[180]

The discussion so far has demonstrated gender discrimination in the law is targeting women rather than children directly. Though we know from the CRC and CEDAW Committees and relational theory that harming the mother harms the child and harming the child harms the mother. Consideration needs to be given to how this can be overcome using the equality framework and this consideration will form the subject matter of the following section.

IV. Solutions to Gender Discrimination in Parental Child Abduction Law

The analysis above has demonstrated the gender discrimination that arises in legislation, procedures and outcomes in cases of parental abduction decided in Islamic law countries disadvantages the mother and abducted children. Conversely, the analysis of whether accession to the Hague Convention by Islamic law countries

[178] Consultations on the Desirability and Feasibility of a Protocol to the Hague Convention of 25 October 1980: Prelim Doc No 7 (Hague Conference, 2011) 4, available at www.hcch.net/upload/wop/abduct2011pd07e.pdf.

[179] Guide to Part II of the Sixth Meeting of the Special Commission and Consideration of the Desirability and Feasibility of Further Work in Connection with the 1980 and the 1996 Conventions: Prelim Doc No 13 (Hague Conference, 2011) available at www.hcch.net/upload/wop/abduct2012pd3_e.pdf.

[180] Switzerland has taken steps of its own. In 2007 The Swiss Parliament passed the Federal Act on International Child Abduction and the Hague Conventions on the Protection of Children and Adults. The Swiss Act provides guidance to Swiss courts about the phrase 'intolerable situation' in Article 13(1)(b) of the Hague Abduction Convention. The Swiss Act also directs courts to appoint representatives for children in Hague abduction proceedings.

will improve children's rights is more clearly established in relation to Article 2 CRC than the other CRC articles examined. The following section now turns to how the English courts will respond to the gender discrimination where a child's return is sought under the Hague Convention to an Islamic law country. With the accession of the Islamic law countries of Morocco, Iraq, Pakistan and Tunisia, this is a practical rather than a theoretical issue.

A. How Will the Hague Convention Respond to Gender Discrimination Established in Legislation?

In light of the UK's acceptance of Morocco's accession to the Hague Convention in 2016, the English courts may at some point be required to decide a Hague Convention case with Morocco. This analysis now examines whether the Hague Convention can address the obligation of Hague States to return abducted children to an Islamic law country if the return would breach the non-discrimination rights of an abducted child. The Article 20 defence under the Hague Convention is significant to the analysis. It stipulates: 'the return of the child may be refused if this would not be permitted by the fundamental principles of the requested state relating to the protection of human rights and fundamental freedoms.'

The discussion of how children's Article 2, 3 and 12 CRC rights are upheld in Morocco and indeed other Islamic law countries illustrates that children's rights are not upheld as the CRC intends, because a conservative rather than a liberal interpretation of Islamic law is applied according to An-Na'im. He argues that Islamic law countries can choose a liberal interpretation of Islamic law to make Islamic law amenable to modern international relations and human rights.[181] The current failure of Islamic law countries to uphold children's rights is problematic for English courts considering the return of an abducted child to Morocco under the Hague Convention. For ease of reference, let us consider a hypothetical case of Solomon, aged eight, abducted by his mother, Farida, *from* Morocco *to* England. Moroccan law does not permit Farida, as a mother, to relocate outside of Morocco with Solomon.[182] Can the English court, on this basis, refuse to return Solomon to Morocco, because Farida could be subject to discriminatory treatment before the Moroccan courts? Applying the Hague Convention Article 20 defence, Solomon's return may be refused by the English court where his return 'would not be permitted by the fundamental principles of the requested State relating to the protection of human rights and fundamental freedoms.'

[181] Baderin (n 100) 8.

[182] Article 179 of the 2004 Moroccan Family Code states 'permission shall not be granted until the judge has ascertained that such travel is temporary and that the child will be returned to Morocco.' Thus it is exceptionally difficult, if not impossible, for a mother to persuade the Islamic court that the child should be taken to live in another country.

So what is included within the UK's human rights framework of protection from discrimination? These are governed domestically by the Human Rights Act 1998 which implements the European Convention for the Protection of Human Rights and Fundamental Freedoms 1950 ('ECHR'). Article 14 ECHR protects the right not to be discriminated against on the grounds of gender, and although it does not provide a free-standing right to non-discrimination, it does require that Farida's rights such as those to family life (Article 8) and a fair hearing (Article 6) are secured without discrimination. Article 2 CRC is also relevant in this context, as it protects Solomon from discrimination directed at Farida. Moreover, the UK Supreme Court case of *ZH Tanzania*[183] makes it very clear that the CRC is a key instrument in determining the scope of Article 8 ECHR rights when a child is involved.

The discrimination in the legislative framework in Morocco will affect Farida's claim for custody. In such a situation, the English court may not feel it is appropriate to return Solomon to Morocco. This cause for concern is further strengthened by the fact that in deciding on whether to return Solomon, the English court is also bound by section 6 of the Human Rights Act 1998 which makes it unlawful for a court to act in a way that is incompatible with a person's rights under the ECHR. Farida could, therefore, argue that ordering Solomon's return to the Moroccan regime will deny her and Solomon's Article 8 ECHR right to family life together[184] and that she will not be protected from discrimination in the law. Both claims, if upheld, will breach the UK's principles on human rights and accordingly satisfies the threshold of the Article 20 defence.

B. Can the English Courts Apply Article 20 Based on Gender Discrimination in Islamic Country Legislation?

There are several reasons why the Article 20 defence may not be effective in Solomon's case. To begin with, the defence was only included within the Hague Convention as a way to appease those delegates that sought a 'public policy' clause in the Convention.[185] The inclusion of this type of clause, which could serve to exclude the participation of many States, was a contentious factor within the drafting process. Professor Adair Dyer (the then Deputy Secretary-General of the Hague Conference on Private International Law) explains:

> The Commission which drafted the Convention consistently refused to allow a general exception to the duty to return children based on 'public policy' or on the 'general

[183] *ZH (Tanzania) (FC) (Appellant) v Secretary of State for the Home Department (Respondent)* [2011] UKSC 4.

[184] See the case of *EM (Lebanon) v Secretary of State for the Home Department* [2008] UKHL 64 where this was argued in the context of asylum proceedings.

[185] Katarina Trimmings and Paul Beaumont, 'Article 20 of the 1980 Hague Abduction Convention' (2014) 88 9 *J Comp L* 66.

> principles of family law of the requested State' but, in extremis, in order to avoid a possible reservation based on the latter grounds, Article 20 was accepted.[186]

Secondly, the United Kingdom made the decision not to include Article 20 within the legislation incorporating the Hague Convention into domestic law, the Child Abduction Act 1984, and therefore it is questionable whether or not Farida could even claim Article 20 is applicable. Baroness Hale has indicated in *Re D (A Child) (Abduction: Rights of Custody)*[187] that Article 20 has now been given effect by the Human Rights Act 1998:

> By virtue of s 6 of the 1998 Act, it is unlawful for the court, as a public authority to act in a way which is incompatible with a person's European Convention rights. In this way, the court is bound to give effect to the European Convention rights in Hague Convention cases just as in any other. Article 20 of the Hague Convention has been given domestic effect by a different route.[188]

Thirdly, even though Farida might be entitled to raise the Article 20 defence, the strict criteria for the implementation of the defences have resulted in the use of Article 20 almost becoming extinct. This is by no means accidental: the Convention's Explanatory Report by Professor Perez-Vera emphasises the high threshold necessary for Article 20 to apply, to prevent the Convention from becoming a 'dead letter'.

> It will be necessary to show that the fundamental principles of the requested State concerning the subject matter of the Convention do not permit it; it will not be sufficient to show merely that return would be incompatible, even manifestly incompatible, with these principles.[189]

The caution in applying Article 20 is illustrated in the body of case law that has emerged over the last four decades.[190] The threshold is set extremely high, and the evidence suggests the guidance has been almost faithfully adhered to. Article 20 was not successfully applied in any case in the 1999 survey,[191] successful in only eight of 204 refusals in the 2008 survey (all by one court),[192] and in only two cases of 238 refusals in the 2017 review.[193]

[186] Adair Dyer, 'The Hague Convention on the Civil Aspects of International Child Abduction – Towards Global Cooperation its Successes and Failures' (1993) 1 *The International Journal of Children's Rights* 273.

[187] [2006] UKHL 51.

[188] *Re D (A Child) (Abduction: Rights of Custody)* [2006] UKHL 51, para 65, per Baroness Hale.

[189] Perez-Vera (n 149) para 31 and 34.

[190] For further discussion on this topic see Merle Weiner, 'Using Article 20' (2004) 38 *Fam L Q* 587, 622; Merle Weiner, 'Strengthening Article 20' (2005) *International Family Law Journal* 209; John Eekelaar, 'International Child Abduction by Parents' (1982) 32 *U Toronto L J* 281, 314; Trimmings and Beaumont (n 185).

[191] Nigel Lowe and others, 'A Statistical Analysis of Applications made in 1999 under the Hague Convention on the Civil Aspects of International Child Abduction' Preliminary Document No 3 (2001) 17 ('Hague Survey 1999').

[192] Nigel Lowe and others, 'A Statistical Analysis of Applications Made in 2003 under the Hague Convention on the Civil Aspects of International Child Abduction' Preliminary Document No 3 (2006) 39 ('Hague Survey 2003').

[193] Hague Survey (2015).

States that did incorporate Article 20 into domestic legislation, such as the United States, have also refused to accept an Article 20 claim. The United States has had the highest number of cases of parental abduction and yet because the threshold for Article 20 is so high in the United States, where the return must 'utterly shock the conscience of the court or offend all notions of due process',[194] Article 20 has not yet been successfully argued in *any* case in the United States. Its limited use is celebrated by many, including Professor Adair Dyer, the former Deputy Secretary-General of the Hague Conference on Private International Law: 'It is a matter for cautious satisfaction that, almost ten years after the Convention entered into force, no abductor has successfully invoked the provisions of Article 20. This follows the wishes of the Convention's Reporter, Professor Elisa Perez-Vera.'[195] Katarina Trimmings and Paul Beaumont writing on Article 20 share this viewpoint:[196]

> The analysis of the case law on Article 20 in States Party to the 1980 Convention that we were able to discover through our research reveals that it has relatively rarely been invoked and has rarely succeeded. This is a pleasing finding fully in line with the correct aspiration of the Explanatory Report to the 1980 Hague Abduction Convention that the 'application' of this provision should have a 'clearly exceptional nature'. Indeed, in several cases where a plea for non-return of a child based on Article 20 has succeeded in an individual case (for example, in Australia and Ireland) subsequent case law has cast doubt on the value of those cases as precedents.

Not all academics agree with this stance, however, and Weiner argues the Perez Vera Explanatory Report has disproportionately limited the application of Article 20, and that there was never any suggestion that Article 20 must remain exceptional if the world's understanding of human rights abuses expands.[197] As yet there is no reported case where the English courts have had to grapple with the issue of returning an abducted child under the Hague Convention to an Islamic law country. As no such case has yet arisen, this analysis undertakes an examination of the hypothetical example of Solomon, to evaluate which of the two possible approaches the English courts could adopt in Hague proceedings. Whether to order Solomon's return, in accordance with the automatic return policy, or refuse to return Solomon applying the Article 20 defence.

[194] *Sacramento v Lewis* 523 US 833 (1998); United States Department of State, *Hague International Child Abduction, Text and Legal Analysis* Public Notice 957, 51 Fed Reg 10494, 10510 (US Department of State, 1986).
[195] Dyer (1993) (n 186) 280.
[196] Trimmings and Beaumont (n 185) 88.
[197] Weiner, 'Using Article 20', (n 190) 587; Weiner, 'Strengthening Article 20' (n 190) 4.

C. To Return or Not to Return Solomon: Which is the Correct Children's Rights Interpretation?

The assumptions about gender discrimination are critiqued elsewhere in the context of culture, best interests and the universal application of rights.[198] The narrow scope in this analysis is, therefore, to undertake an examination of the options available to the English courts in accordance with the Hague Convention and a children's rights-based analysis.

i. Refuse Solomon's Return?

The use of Article 20 appears the only means by which to respond to a situation like Solomon's, where there is evidence before the English court on the discrimination Farida would encounter if Solomon is ordered to return. The use of Article 20 in this context was suggested by Beaumont and McEleavy in 1999, who stated that Article 20 might be of greater importance if the Convention succeeds in gaining accessions 'among countries which enforce laws or traditions found unacceptable in modern Western democracies.'[199] They do not refer specifically to Islamic law countries, but state 'there may be some merit in Article 20 being applied where the State of the child's habitual residence operates a total prohibition on the relocation of a sole custodian and child from the jurisdiction.'[200]

Would the court factor in the gender discrimination directed at Farida as engaging the Article 20 defence? While the Hague Convention's exceptions relate exclusively to only Solomon's welfare, the Article 20 public policy exception is wider and could include the consideration of Farida's rights before the Islamic courts.[201] The clearest example of how the English courts could respond to Solomon's abduction *from* Morocco under the Hague Convention is found in a statement by Baroness Hale in *Re J* [2005].[202] Baroness Hale considered obiter how a case concerning family law provision in Saudi Arabia would be determined if the

[198] For consideration of arguments relating to human rights in a cultural context see further Michael Freeman, 'The Morality of Cultural Pluralism' (1995) 3 *International Journal of Child Rights* 1–17; Rhona Schuz, 'The Relevance of Religious Law and Cultural Considerations in International Child Abduction Disputes' (2010) 12 *Journal of Law & Family Studies* 453, 491–92; Schuz (2013) (n 151) 366–67; Urfan Khaliq and James Young, 'Cultural Diversity, Human Rights and Inconsistency in the English Courts' (2001) 21 *Legal Studies* 192, 212.

[199] Beaumont and McEleavy (n 149) 175–76.

[200] Ibid 175; note the distinction in the USA-Israel abduction case of *Freier v Freier* 969 F Supp 436 (1996) where the Art 20 claim did not succeed as the mother had a right to appeal the decision to relocate to a secular court. This is not the case with Islamic law, as the legislation in Islamic law countries examined affirms the mother cannot relocate with the child without the father's consent.

[201] Eekelaar (n 190) 314.

[202] [2005] UKHL 40 at 45.

Hague Convention applied. Baroness Hale was of the view that the difference in treatment of the parents *would* permit the English court to apply Article 20, and refuse to order the return of the child:

> The importance of Article 20 is that it asks whether what might happen in the foreign country would be permitted under those fundamental principles were it to happen here. (It thus goes further than the principle under consideration in Ullah's case, which asks whether it is a breach of this country's obligations to send a person away to a country where his human rights may be violated.) In this country, it would not be acceptable to distinguish automatically between a father and mother in their relationship with their children. Non-discrimination between the sexes is a fundamental principle of our law. Were Article 20 of the Hague Convention to be incorporated, we would be entitled, though not obliged, to decline to return a child on that ground alone. If we were, therefore, to be applying the spirit of the Hague Convention in a non-Hague Convention case, there would be no reason not to apply the whole of the Hague Convention, including Article 20. Any discrimination in the foreign country which was contrary to Article 14 of the Human Rights Convention would allow, but not require, the court to refuse to return the child. This consideration serves to reinforce the view that the legal system in the foreign country cannot be irrelevant to the issue of summary return.[203]

So in the hypothetical scenario, the fact that Farida would be subject to discrimination under Islamic family law – as evidenced in chapters 3, 4 and 5 – would satisfy the Article 20 threshold as the discrimination encountered by Farida under Moroccan law is not permitted under English law. The threshold outlined by Baroness Hale would be met. Though the discrimination focuses upon Farida, Baroness Hale explains how the gender discrimination encountered by a returning mother could also affect the returning child and will engage the UNCRC.

> If those courts have no choice but to do what the father wishes so that the mother cannot ask them to decide with an open mind which country is best for the child then the English court must ask itself whether it is in the child's best interests to enable the dispute to be heard.[204]

Baroness Hale stated that the trial judge, in that abduction case, was wrong to leave out of account the absence of jurisdiction in the home country to enable the mother to bring the child back to England without the father's consent.[205]

ii. Alternatively, Ordering Solomon's Return Will Ensure the Hague Convention Can Operate Outside a European Context

The alternative option is for the English court to make an order for Solomon's return to Morocco. This approach prioritises Solomon's CRC rights to a relationship with

[203] Ibid.
[204] Ibid 39.
[205] Ibid 46.

both his parents,[206] the right to maintain his cultural identity,[207] the right to be protected from the adverse effects of cross-border parental abduction,[208] and the right to have his interests treated as a primary consideration.[209]

If the English courts do apply Article 20 and refuse the return of abducted children to Islamic law countries, it will have a profound effect on how the Hague Convention operates. The use of Article 20 would mean that children abducted *from* England *to* Islamic law countries, such as Miriam, Aliyah and Ryan, would be returned to England in Hague proceedings. Whereas children abducted *from* Islamic law countries *to* the UK would not be returned if abducted by their mother or if the abducted child is female. What this would mean for the Hague Convention is that it will fail to operate outside a European context.[210] A one-sided return is unlikely to be accepted by Islamic law countries, and this could serve to stall the operation of the Hague Convention in cases involving Islamic law countries.

As Baroness Hale stated in *Re J* [2005], the English court can still order Solomon's return under the Hague Convention, even if the Article 20 defence threshold is met. The court has the discretion to make the return order, even where one of the defences is demonstrated if the child's welfare will be served by ordering return.[211] As Baroness Hale explained: 'There are also bound to be many cases where the connection of the child and all the family with the other country is so strong that any difference between the legal systems here and there should carry little weight.'[212] The issue for the English court in Solomon's case is therefore not whether the Article 20 threshold is satisfied, but whether Article 20 should be allowed to act as a defence to return. The English court must weigh up whether a violation of Farida's right to be protected from gender discrimination is justified as proportionate when balanced against Solomon's rights. And also whether the harm caused by a refusal to return him to Morocco is greater than the harm caused to Farida (and consequently to Solomon), by ordering Solomon's return. Of course, the relational theory, if applied by the court, would determine that Solomon's interests and rights are intertwined with his mother's.

For a degree of certainty to remain within the law, the Hague Convention advocates the restrictive application of the defences and so arguably, on this basis, the correct application of Hague would be to order Solomon's return. While the custody law in Morocco may well discriminate against Farida by English law standards, custody will nevertheless be determined based upon Solomon's welfare needs as recognised by Moroccan society. The return would enable the custody dispute to be determined in Solomon's state of habitual residence, where Moroccan courts will apply the law that relates most closely to the family. The Moroccan courts can

[206] Pursuant to Art 9(1), 9(3), 10(2) CRC; and Art 8 ECHR.
[207] Art 8 CRC.
[208] Art 11 CRC.
[209] Art 3 CRC.
[210] Emon and Khaliq (2016) (n 19) 53–54.
[211] *Re J* [2005] UKHL 40 at 45.
[212] Baroness Hale, *Re J* at 39.

still be the appropriate forum from Solomon's viewpoint. The return would allow Solomon to retain a relationship with both parents in accordance with his CRC right, whereas a refusal to return Solomon could be inconsistent with his rights and interests as he would suffer the disadvantage of not being able to have contact with his father. A return would also satisfy the private international law principle of comity, reciprocity and judicial courtesy between contracting states,[213] which are a foundation of the Hague Convention.

This argument is strengthened, if the cultural relativist view is adopted, that Solomon and his mother would be returning to the culture and practices to which they are familiar, in which the gender discrimination is perhaps reconciled with the advantages Farida might benefit from in that society, such as being provided for and supported by Solomon's father.[214] Indeed the analysis above identifies only 19 per cent of Jordanian and 60 per cent of Moroccan women believe equality in the law is essential.[215] John Eekelaar[216] held the view that Article 20 should not apply in a case like Solomon's because family law 'in particular reflects different cultural patterns, and if the Convention is to operate successfully there must be mutual respect among states for these differences.' And so Solomon's 'future should normally be determined according to the cultural practices of the place of his habitual residence.' Eekelaar argued that Article 20 should not be applied in a situation like Solomon's unless Solomon himself was at risk of harm arising from the differences in family law, 'such as if the latter state operated a system of preferred custody rights in one parent' and in that situation the Article 13(1)(b) Hague exception would apply in any event, ie 'there is a grave risk that his return would expose Solomon to physical or psychological harm or otherwise place Solomon in an intolerable situation.' Based on Eekelaar's analysis, Farida's inability to relocate from Morocco would render the Article 13(1)(b) Hague Convention defence applicable and is sufficient enough to refuse a return, in which case Article 20 need not be applied.

In Schuz's analysis on the topic of human rights and cultural practices,[217] she makes a recommendation that falls short of the fact that Article 20 should be applied. Instead, she recommends a solution similar to Eekelaar:

> In the context of the Hague Convention, it is suggested that a pluralist approach to culture requires the exercise of caution and a careful balancing of the different interests and factors involved before refusing to return children on the basis of Article 20 in cases where the alleged breach of fundamental principles arises out of non-Western religious or cultural norms in the requesting state. The fact that mutual co-operation and reciprocity are so critical to achieving the objectives of the Hague Convention

[213] Joel Paul, 'Comity in International Law' (1991) 32 *Harvard Journal of International Law* 1; James Fawcett and Janeen Carruthers, *Cheshire, North and Fawcett, Private International Law* 14th edn (OUP, 2008) 36–37; Schuz (2013) (n 151) 126.

[214] The arguments are presented by Lynn Welchman, although she does not express an opinion on whether or not these are of an advantage or disadvantage to women and mothers.

[215] World Values Survey, cited in Prettitore (n 58) 33–34.

[216] Eekelaar (n 190).

[217] Schuz, 'Religious Law and Cultural Considerations' (2010) (n 198) 491–92.

> would seem to strengthen the arguments in favour of tolerance of cultural diversity and require a narrow interpretation of Article 20. However, where the breach of fundamental principles, results in a real risk of harm to the child, return should be refused under Article 13(1)(b).[218]

Such an interpretation is in keeping with the protections under Article 2 CRC, as the defence that allows a court to refuse a return based on the assessment that Solomon is at risk of harm, but it does not consider the effect on Farida.

Ultimately, it may be that Solomon's views sway the decision and thought must be given to the impact of his separation from his mother. If the views he conveys express a stronger connection to his life in Morocco more generally than his life in the United Kingdom with his mother, then any differences between the legal systems, as Baroness Hale highlighted, should carry little weight.[219] This approach would avoid the tension within the law that allows Farida's right to non-discrimination to supersede Solomon's rights, which is at odds with the aims of the Hague Convention. Nevertheless, based on the discussion on the child's voice in chapter 4, it cannot be assumed that Solomon's views will be heard or that his views will be given any weight.

iii. The Right to Non-Discrimination is an Unqualified Right

According to the child-rights based approach, Article 2 CRC is a general principle which underlies all other rights within the CRC. The right to non-discrimination could arguably supersede Solomon's Article 11 CRC right to be protected from the harms of parental abduction. This is particularly so if Solomon was a girl; Sara, for argument's sake, and Sara as a girl-child is at risk of gender discrimination if forced to return.

The academic opinion[220] seeks to uphold the Hague Convention's principles of comity and respecting judicial courtesy to a greater degree than the right to equality and defers to the use of Article 13(1)(b) in Solomon's situation, rather than invoking Article 20. It is suggested here, however, that such a viewpoint is not undertaken from the perspective of children's rights and does not conform to the children's rights-based approach. The evidence overwhelmingly points to gender discrimination in the legislation in Islamic law countries and the impact the discriminatory law has on abducted children. The evidence confirms that in abductions to Islamic law countries, mothers are denied custody, children are unable to participate in proceedings and many of the girls abducted are unable to return to the UK, even as adults. The gender discrimination cannot be ignored, and it is argued here that the children's rights-based approach would require that

[218] Note that this includes situations where the child will be harmed indirectly because of the physical abuse or persecution of the mother; Khaliq and Young (n 198) 221; Weiner, 'Strengthening Article 20' (n 190).

[219] Baroness Hale, *Re J* at 39.

[220] Eekelaar (n 190) Schuz, 'Religious Law and Cultural Considerations' (2010) (n 198) 491–92.

an abducted child is not returned to an Islamic law country if the state requesting return will impose a legal system in which the domestic courts have no choice but to discriminate against the girl-child and the abducting mother. Moreover, even in the case of an abducted boy, gender discrimination against the mother can be harmful to the boy-child, as is seen in the example of Ryan, and is protected under Article 2(1) CRC. The analysis throughout this chapter, on gender discrimination, harmful practices, the conflation of the child and mother's rights and the disparateness of abductions by primary carers all serve as evidence to support this evaluation.[221]

Despite only 19 per cent of Jordanian and 60 per cent of Moroccan women surveyed valuing equality in the law, the English courts cannot condone gender discrimination in the law. This analysis is more inclined to adopt the approach of Baroness Hale, who indicated the English courts are bound by their obligation to the principle of non-discrimination. On balancing the CRC's general principles and Solomon's right to have his best interests treated as a primary consideration, to participate in proceedings and to be protected from discrimination, it appears only his Article 12 CRC right to be heard would override the obligations of the English courts not to return. Solomon's views are, therefore, significant.

It is recognised that the popular opinion by Hague proponents is not to criticise the law in another State, as this could serve to impede the Hague Convention's operation. So it is likely that the courts will continue to respond to all such situations under the umbrella of the Article 13(1)(b) defence. The reason why courts may choose to do so is understandable; the child's return could be refused regardless of whether Article 13(1)(b) or Article 20 is applied and in this way, comity is upheld. Nevertheless, for the purposes of this children's right-based analysis, it is crucial to identify the discrimination for what it is – the gender discrimination advocated by the legislation in Islamic law countries satisfies the Article 20 Hague defence and also breaches Article 2 CRC.

a. How Likely Are the English Courts to Encounter Such a Case?

In the context of Islamic law countries that have acceded to the Hague Convention, thus far, the UK has only accepted Morocco's accession, which it accepted after a period of six years, becoming treaty partners in July 2016. Not all newly acceding states become treaty partners automatically; it is up to individual states to decide whether or not to enter into a reciprocal obligation with the state in returning

[221] The view taken in this text is that the only way in which the UK courts could make an order for the child's return in cases where the mother and child would be at risk of discriminatory treatment before the Islamic courts is with knowledge that the mother has also sought an application under asylum law for her and the child. Asylum law is outside the scope of discussion for this text, however, note the overlap with parental abduction cases; *EM (Lebanon) v Secretary of State for the Home Department* [2008] UKHL 64. A grant of asylum will overtake any return order under the 1980 Hague Convention and Solomon would not be returned; *FE v YE* [2017] EWHC 2165 (Fam); The position is confirmed by the UK Supreme Court in the case of *G v G* [2021] UKSC 9.

children. The way in which the Hague Convention arrangement works is that a newly acceding country is treated as offering to enter treaty relationships with all existing States Parties as well as any State that was a Hague Conference member in 1980 that thereafter ratifies.[222] Although the acceding country does not have the right to refuse treaty relationships with countries that previously acceded to the Hague Convention, it does have a right to accept or decline treaty obligations that are offered by later accessions. This complicated system means that any State that acceded after Morocco's accession in 2010 is an automatic treaty partner with Morocco. Those states will have to reconcile how they address the issue of gender discrimination within Moroccan law.

It is yet to be seen how the UK will respond to the accessions of Iraq, Pakistan and Tunisia. Pre-Brexit, like all other EU Member States (except Denmark), the UK did not have individual competence to decide whether to accept accessions, being bound by the revised Brussels II Regulation.[223] Instead, the decision is taken based upon unanimity in the Council of the European Union on the basis of a proposal from the EU Commission. Post-Brexit the UK once again has individual competence to decide whether or not to accept an accession and for which the UK Foreign, Commonwealth and Development Office will have sole responsibility. This will require the UK to evaluate the legal system of the newly acceding country.

Bruch recommends states should be careful to make sure that the standards of justice in a state are acceptable before accepting the accession since states cannot later question the standards of justice in that state's legal system in seeking to apply Article 20. The viewpoint may deter the UK from accepting accessions of Islamic law countries, but should not be a deterrent if the exception of Egypt is considered. Egypt is an Islamic law country and unlike other Islamic law countries, Egypt is entitled to ratify – rather than accede to – the Hague Convention, as it was a member of the Hague Conference at the time the Hague Convention was adopted.[224] Like other ratifying states, Egypt's ratification is automatically accepted by all states that have acceded to or ratified the Convention. Consequently, the discussion about whether or not states should accept the accessions of Islamic law countries will not apply to Egypt. And once Egypt ratifies, the UK will be in automatic reciprocal obligations with Egypt to return abducted children. The CRC Committee also criticises Egypt's legal system for subjecting girls to the system of guardianship, for condoning gender discrimination and harmful practices against girls.[225] It is therefore possible that the use of Article 20 could become more relevant in the future.

[222] Pursuant to Article 38 of the Hague Convention.

[223] See Opinion 1/13, EU:C:2014:2303, [2015] 2 FLR 1453.

[224] Article 37 of the Hague Convention provides that ratification is limited to those states who were members of the Hague Conference at the time of its 14th session.

[225] Concluding Observations Egypt CRC/C/15/Add.5 (18 February 1993); Concluding Observations Egypt CRC/C/15/Add.145 (21 February 2001); Concluding Observations Egypt CRC/C/EGY/CO/3-4 (July 2011) of which para 56 recommends 'The Committee recommends that the State party amend the Child Law (2008) so as to prohibit abduction of children, regardless of family kinship, and ensure appropriate penalties. The Committee urges the State party to consider ratifying or acceding to the 1980 Hague Convention and to ensure its incorporation into domestic legislation.'

It is argued here that the UK and other states should not be reluctant to accept the accessions of Islamic law countries, as Miriam, Aliyah, Ryan and the other 51 abducted children require the protection of the Hague Convention. At some point, at least when Egypt ratifies, all states will have to address the gender issue in the domestic law in Islamic law countries and so should not allow the disinclination to apply Article 20 to hinder accepting the accessions of Islamic law countries and entering into treaty obligation. Instead, States should accept the accessions of Islamic law countries and if need be apply Article 20 in accordance with the children's rights-based approach. Or if seeking to uphold comity with Islamic states, the courts should as a minimum adopt the relational approach and recognise that gender discrimination towards the mother is harmful to the child and therefore falls under the Article 13(1)(b) Hague Convention exception.

The following section will consider how the cases of Miriam, Ryan and Aliyah could be resolved under the Hague Convention.

V. How Will the Hague Convention Respond to the Cases of Miriam, Ryan and Aliyah?

If Hague proceedings were initiated, Miriam, Ryan and Aliyah are each likely to be returned to the UK, as none of the exceptions to return under Articles 12, 13 and 20 apply in their cases. If returned within the 12 months of abduction, in which Hague proceedings must be initiated, it is likely that Miriam would not have entered into marriage as a child, or been subject to the system of guardianship that prevents her from leaving Libya. Ryan is unlikely to have been forced to reside in a madrassa facility. And although Aliyah escaped from Jordan at age 13, she is also likely to have been returned to the UK at age seven. In answering the overarching question in this analysis, it appears from the investigation that accession to the Hague Convention by Islamic law countries would advance the Article 2 CRC rights of these abducted young people.

VI. Conclusion

This chapter commenced with the recognition that the examination on the right of abducted children to be protected from the effects of gender discrimination was not going to be 'clear-cut.' This was primarily because the CRC framework also protects children from discrimination experienced by their parents, and so the analysis would comprise a wider investigation and encompass a more extensive range of the empirical data. Also, as anticipated, the discussion has raised as many questions as it answers. The analysis has maintained a focus on the gender discrimination arising from the empirical data that impacts abducted children, the direct discrimination experienced by abducted girls and the effects on both abducted girls and boys of the gender discrimination experienced by their mothers. The gendered nature of parental abduction and the differential treatment of the parents in Islamic custody/abduction law has required examination of a number of theoretical perspectives, both relational and cultural, to attempt to make sense of how parental abduction law should respond to the gender discrimination identified. The study of the broader architecture of human rights and equality provisions, the cultural nature of the rights of abducted children, and the relational nature of abducted children's rights has illustrated that there appears to be no justified reason in the data analysed to accommodate gender discrimination within parental child abduction law.

Based on these findings, the analysis affirms that the legislation in the Islamic law countries examined does not uphold the Article 2 CRC right of abducted children and, in fact, as is evidenced by the data, serves to perpetuate the discrimination of girls and women. Article 2 CRC sufficiently captures any gender discrimination girl abductees are at risk of experiencing and in this regard the Hague framework can adequately address the abducted child's right to protection from gender discrimination through its exceptions to return under Articles 12, 13 and 20. In the context of gender discrimination experienced by the mother which impacts the abducted child, this too is protected under Article 2 CRC, but the protection is further bolstered by Article 20 of the Hague Convention. Thus, the accession to the Hague Convention by Islamic law countries will undoubtedly respect the rights of abducted children in this context. Yet it is up to Contracting States to decide when they will accept the accessions of Islamic law countries and extend these rights to children abducted from the UK to Iraq, Tunisia and Pakistan.

The only means by which the Article 2, 3 and 12 CRC rights of the child abducted to Islamic law countries would be upheld is through the implementation of the Hague legal framework. The advantage of accepting accessions by Islamic law countries for children should outweigh any concerns about the legal system of Islamic law countries. The situation of the 54 children abducted from the UK in this sample would be assisted through the Hague Convention. Concern about returning children to Islamic law countries would be addressed, if needed, through Article 20 or Article 13(1)(b). These exceptions to return are incorporated within the Hague Convention for a reason and so the consternation about their application should not be allowed to impede the rights of abducted children.

The following chapter brings the analysis to a close, through reviewing how parental abduction law measures against the children's rights indicators identified in chapter 1, examining the legal developments necessary to centralise the rights of abducted children and considering the future implications of this research.

6

Conclusion

Morocco's accession to the Hague Convention in 2010 presented an ideal opportunity to evaluate whether accession to the Hague Convention by Islamic law countries would advance children's rights. This analysis set out to achieve this aim by seeking answers to the following questions:

1. How does the legislation in Islamic law countries respond to cases of parental abduction from the UK?
2. What are the outcomes for children abducted from the UK to Islamic law countries?
3. Are children's rights upheld in domestic parental abduction law in Islamic law countries?
4. Do children abducted to Islamic law countries consider that the law upholds their rights?
5. Would accession to the Hague Convention by Islamic law countries improve outcomes for abducted children and advance their rights in comparison to the domestic Islamic law regime?

The three children's rights-based indicators adopted in this text[1] sought to analyse: (1) Whether or not the legislation responding to parental abduction (domestic Islamic law and the Hague Convention) upholds children's rights. (2) Whether the legislation grants the judiciary discretion to interpret parental abduction law in a manner consistent with children's rights. And (3) the developments in the law that are needed to centralise the rights of the child in a parental abduction context. This chapter will consider how the parental abduction law examined in this text measures against each of the three children's rights-based indicators, and then conclude by reflecting upon the future implications of this research.

[1] As explained in chapter 1, the specific children's rights-based indicators identified by Stalford and Hollingsworth are modified in this text to accommodate the Islamic law context. The adaptations to their model were necessary due to the limited accessibility of legal judgments/law reports. Thus instead of analysing the text of court judgments in accordance with their approach, this text focuses on the legislation in Islamic law countries; Kathryn Hollingsworth and Helen Stalford, 'Towards Children's Rights Judgments,' Chapter 3 in Helen Stalford, Kathryn Hollingsworth and Stephen Gilmore (eds), *Rewriting Children's Rights Judgments: From Academic Vision to New Practice* (Hart Publishing, 2017) 53–54.

I. Does the Legislation Responding to Parental Abduction Uphold Children's Rights?

The evidence collated in this analysis establishes that there are some similarities between the two legal processes examined, domestic law in Islamic law countries and the Hague Convention, in how they both satisfy and fail to uphold children's CRC rights to protect children from discrimination in the law (Article 2), for the child's best interests to be treated as a primary consideration by the court (Article 3) and for facilitation of the child's participation in proceedings (Article 12).

The analysis demonstrates that the problem with both legal frameworks in upholding the child's Article 3 CRC right is that procedurally both provisions are designed to consider and prioritise the interests of children as a homogenous group, rather than prioritising the interests and rights of the individual child. The Hague Convention presumes it is in the best interests of children that they return and Islamic law presumes that it is in the best interests of children that they live near the father. Applying presumptions as to what is deemed to be in the best interests of children results in a situation where both the Hague Convention and Islamic custody/abduction law can be criticised for overlooking the requirement to assess their impact on individual children. Thus while both legal frameworks strictly comply with the definition found within Article 3 CRC, from the threshold of a children's rights-based approach and General Comment No 14,[2] it would seem that neither legislative framework appropriately conveys the significance of the individual child's best interests. The way in which the Hague Convention is better from the perspective of children abducted to Islamic law countries, however, is through the use of its exceptions to return. Under closer scrutiny, domestic Islamic legislation sets out quite clearly what it presumes to be in the best interests of the child in domestic custody/abduction cases. The child's interests are pre-speculated, and while the law may be effective in a domestic setting, this is not the case when transposed to an international abduction context. In contrast, the Hague Convention at least allows for a best interests assessment to be undertaken in the courts of the child's habitual residence. And for some children, an interim best interests assessment occurs as part of the Hague proceedings if a defence to return is raised. The Islamic law courts did not uphold the Article 3 CRC rights for any of the ten young people in the case studies examined. The court could not undertake a best interests assessment as the criteria for the left-behind parent to be eligible for custody were not satisfied in any of the cases. All ten children were ordered to remain with the abducting parent in the Islamic law country as it was deemed to be in their best interests to continue living with a Muslim parent raised in an Islamic environment, irrespective of what the young people themselves consider to have

[2] On the Right of the Child to Have His or Her Best Interests Taken as a Primary Consideration CRC/C/GC/14 (2013).

been in their best interests. Left-behind mothers could have physical custody of the abducted child if they remained living in the Islamic law country, but in the vast majority of cases this was not practical because the mothers interviewed explained they would be unable to financially support themselves and their children living in the Islamic law country and would consequently become reliant on the abducting father. The analysis demonstrates, therefore, that it is better for abducted children that abduction proceedings occur under the Hague framework than under domestic legislation in Islamic law countries.

The findings illustrate that Islamic custody/abduction legislation is better at upholding children's Article 12 CRC rights. While abducted children in the sample did not have a choice in how their views were ascertained by the court, as is recommended by General Comment No. 12,[3] Islamic courts are well versed in listening to children's views in domestic custody cases. The problem with this positive feature of Islamic law is that the right is restricted to a domestic context, and so internationally abducted children have no voice in proceedings since it is presumed to be in the best interests of the abducted child to live near the father. In contrast, the Hague Convention specifies in its Article 12 that mature children can object to return and thus the Hague treaty appears to uphold the child's Article 12 CRC right. The analysis demonstrates, however, criticism of the way the right is interpreted in different Contracting States, because many courts do not give the child a choice on how their views are ascertained. The Hague Convention is further criticised as it grants the judiciary discretion to disregard the views of mature children, if the judge considers the child's views are not independent or if the judge decides to instead prioritise other objectives of the Hague Convention, such as comity between Contracting States and respect for one another's judicial processes.[4]

Suggestions for the Hague Convention to more clearly advance the child's Article 12 CRC right is to ensure the right to participate is facilitated in all Hague Convention proceedings and not limited to cases where the child 'objects' to a return under Article 12 of the Hague Convention. In addition, it is suggested in this text that the child should have a choice in how his or her views are ascertained, to be given an opportunity to meet with the judge in every case and for the judge to grant the child separate representation to ensure the child's interests and rights are independently argued before the court. Children's participation is an area identified as one where the interpretation of the Hague Convention may benefit from domestic processes in Islamic law countries, as the combination of the participatory requirement in objection cases under Hague, coupled with more routine 'listening' to children in domestic Islamic law proceedings, could provide a stronger package of support for children. Guidance issued by the Hague

[3] 'The Right of the Child to be Heard' CRC/C/GC/12 (2009).

[4] Baroness Hale, Child Abduction from the Child's Point of View, in *The Child's Voice – 15 Years Later*, 42; House of Lords, *In re M (Children) (Abduction: Rights of Custody)* [2007] UKHL 55, [2018] 1 AC 1288, paras 42–43, 46. See also discussion by Paul Beaumont and Peter McEleavy, *The Hague Convention on International Child Abduction* (OUP, 1999) 194.

Conference in 2020 recommends that courts should, where appropriate, ascertain the child's views with respect to a claim pertaining to the Article 13(1)(b) exception to return on the likelihood of harm to the child[5] and this could encourage courts in Contracting States to uphold the Article 12 CRC rights of abducted children to a greater extent than the current position.

The analysis further demonstrates that the legislation in Islamic law countries does not uphold the abducted child's Article 2 CRC right to be protected from gender discrimination. Girls abducted from the UK to Islamic law countries are treated differently from boys under domestic law in a number of ways, and most significantly are not allowed to leave the Islamic law country upon reaching age 18 without the abducting father's consent. The law in Islamic law countries treats girls differently from boys in the age at which they are capacious, their eligibility to choose with which parent they wish to reside and their eligibility to participate in proceedings. Abducted children, both boys and girls, are further affected by the gender discrimination directed at their mothers in the legislation on child custody in Islamic law countries. The effect of the discriminatory law was to separate the abducted children from their primary carers. This type of separation is considered harmful and nine of the ten abductees expressed in their interviews that they viewed the decision as 'denying' them a mother during their formative years.

The Hague Convention has also resulted, albeit inadvertently, in the separation of children from their primary carers. The premise of the Hague Convention is to address abduction by non-primary carers. At the time of drafting the Hague Convention, during the 1970s, it was fathers, rather than mothers who were regarded as most likely to abduct their child.[6] The climate of parental abductions has altered in the last four decades, however, and the evidence confirms there are now more mothers that abduct internationally between Hague states, comprising approximately 70 per cent of cases.[7] Under the Hague Convention's policy of automatic return, children should be returned to the country abducted from, irrespective of which parent abducts, as this position upholds the child's right to maintain a relationship with both parents, pursuant to Article 9 CRC. Automatic return under all circumstances is problematic for mothers raising children alone,[8] travelling for economic and practical support from family or other networks,

[5] *HCCH Convention of 25 October 1980 on the Civil Aspects of International Child Abduction* – Part VI – Article 13(1)(b) HCCH Publications available at https://assets.hcch.net/docs/225b44d3-5c6b-4a14-8f5b-57cb370c497f.pdf para 86–88.

[6] Adair Dyer, 'A Report on International Child Abduction by One Parent "Legal Kidnapping"' (The Hague Conference, 1978) 17–20; Elisa Perez-Vera, *Report on the 1980 Hague Child Abduction Convention* (Translation of The Permanent Bureau, 1981) para 81; Beaumont and McEleavy (1999) ibid 8–9.

[7] Hague Survey (2015).

[8] See the work of Freeman and Taylor who explore the challenges for the Hague Convention arising as a result of domestic abuse; Freeman, Marilyn and Taylor, Nicola, 'Domestic violence and child participation: contemporary challenges for the 1980 Hague child abduction convention', 2020 (42) 2 *Journal of Social Welfare and Family Law* 154–75.

or when fleeing domestic abuse.[9] And so it is argued by some[10] that the Hague Convention can perpetuate violence and contribute to gender subordination because some courts are unable to appreciate the connection between domestic violence against the parent and the psychological wellbeing of a child.[11] It is therefore suggested here that when deciding a case of abduction by a primary carer, the court should evaluate the child's relationship with the parent before deciding whether to order the child's return. Forcing return in a case where the abducting mother is unable to return, or will struggle in the requesting state, might uphold the child's independent Article 11 CRC right, but when examined in the context of a relational right, this may not serve the child's interests or uphold the child's rights. The judiciary has the discretion to undertake such considerations through more flexibly applying the defences to return.

The analysis affirms that the Hague framework upholds the Article 2 CRC rights of abducted children more clearly than domestic Islamic legislation and in some respects, the Hague Convention's Article 20 exception gives effect to Article 2 CRC. Conversely, domestic law in Islamic law countries does not uphold the Article 2 CRC right of abducted children as is evidenced by the data, and in fact, according to the CRC measure, perpetuates gender discrimination.

In sum, the evidence affirms the custody/abduction legislation in Islamic law countries does not uphold the Article 2, 3 and 12 CRC rights of the abducted child in the way that is envisaged by the CRC and the CRC Committee guidance found in General Comments 5, 12, 14 and 18. A comparative analysis identifies that although the Hague provisions are not flawless, the Hague legal framework gives greater effect to the CRC rights of the abducted child.

II. Does the Legislation Grant the Judiciary Discretion to Interpret Parental Abduction Law in a Manner Consistent With Children's Rights?

For hundreds of years, the judiciary in Islamic law countries had the discretion to interpret Islamic custody law in a manner consistent with children's welfare and rights. The rules were not codified and set out in legislation, and so decision-makers had the discretion to apply the regulations as appropriate in each case, based upon

[9] Ruth Lamont, 'Mainstreaming Gender into European Union Family Law? The Case of International Child Abduction and Brussels II Revised' (2011) 17 *European Law Journal* 366, 369–70.

[10] Merle Weiner, 'The Potential and Challenges of Transnational Litigation for Feminists Concerned about Domestic Violence Here and Abroad' (2003) 11 *Journal of Gender, Social, Policy and the Law* 749, 799.

[11] Merle Weiner, 'Intolerable Situations and Counsel for Children: Following Switzerland's Example in Hague Abduction Cases' (2008) 58 *American University Law Review* 356.

the individual circumstances of the child and family.[12] In the last 40–50 years, the common law rules have been fixed into legislation, however, and the discretion previously granted to decision-makers no longer exists.[13] What is more, the judiciary is required to apply the codified custody laws that were developed hundreds of years ago,[14] because, in many countries, no adaptations have been made to reflect changes in society and perceptions and experiences of childhood since the custody rulings were initially developed by Islamic law scholars.[15] The empirical data illustrates that in the cases examined the legislation is rigidly applied by the judiciary, even where the outcome results in gender discrimination, a failure of the individual child's best interests to be examined and the outcome serves to limit a child's participation in proceedings. The legislation in Islamic law countries does grant the judiciary discretion to uphold the right of children to be heard and be listened to, in accordance with Article 12 CRC and General Comment No 12.[16] The discretion is limited to domestic cases, however, and rarely extends to cases of an international nature, as it is presumed to be in children's best interests to live near the father. The judiciary, therefore, does not have the discretion to order that the child can return to the UK. In reflecting upon the second children's rights indicator, the evidence firmly concludes the abduction/custody legislation in Islamic law countries does not grant the judiciary discretion to interpret parental abduction law in a manner consistent with children's CRC rights.

In stark contrast, the Hague Convention is drafted to accommodate the legal processes in a vast number of member states and so is amenable to judicial construction. The analysis in the area of all three CRC rights affirms the Hague Convention grants the judiciary discretion to apply its provisions in a manner consistent with children's rights. The judiciary has the discretion to make determinations on wrongful removal, habitual residence and the exceptions to return[17] from the individual child's perspective. For example, when assessing the 'grave risk of harm' to a child in the event of a return, the child's interests can be treated as a primary consideration, in accordance with Article 3 CRC. This text argues,

[12] Ahmed Fekry Ibrahim, *Child Custody in Islamic Law: Theory and Practice in Egypt since the Sixteenth Century* (CUP, 2018) 6–8; Ahmed Fekry Ibrahim, 'The Best Interests of the Child in Premodern Islamic Juristic Discourse and Practice' (2015) 63 *The American Journal of Comparative Law* 859.

[13] See Nadjma Yassari (ed), *Changing God's Law: The Dynamics of Middle Eastern Family Law* (Routledge, 2016); Imen Gallala-Arndt, 'Negotiating Parenthood in Muslim Countries: Changing Concepts and Perceptions' (2015) 63 *The American Journal of Comparative Law* 847; Lynn Welchman, *Women and Muslim Family Laws in Arab States: A Comparative Overview of Textual Development and Advocacy* (Amsterdam University Press, 2007); Lynn Welchman, 'A Husband's Authority: Emerging Formulations in Muslim Family Law'(2011) 25 (1) *Int'l J L Pol'y & Fam* 1–23.

[14] Mahdi Zahraa and Normi Malek, 'The Concept of Custody in Islamic Law' (1998) 13 *Arab L Q* 155, 156–57; For further discussion of how the rules are applied in different countries, Welchman (2007) (n 13) 13.

[15] Welchman (2011) (n 13) 25.

[16] GC 12 (n 3).

[17] The exceptions to return that can be pleaded are found under Articles 12, 13 and 20 Hague Convention.

as others have,[18] that a child should not be returned in a case where the return will expose the child to a risk of harm, does not promote the child's interests and does not provide any real benefit for the child.

On the subject of children's participation, the Hague Convention's legislative framework further grants the judiciary discretion to interpret the Convention adopting a children's rights-based approach. The Hague Convention specifies that a mature child has the right to object to a return, but it defers to domestic law in allowing the judiciary discretion to decide the child's maturity and the independence of the child's views. The legislative discretion invokes a variety of approaches to children's participation in more than 100 different States that are a party to the treaty. Analysis of the case law and studies on children's involvement in Hague cases highlights children's participation in Hague proceedings is limited due to a lack of training for judges on interviewing children and in some cases a reluctance of the judiciary to meet children or even to consider the views of a child as mature and independent.[19] The discretion afforded to the judiciary under the Hague Convention means the judiciary can endeavour to facilitate more meaningful engagement of abducted children in decisions that directly affect the children. Children could be given a choice as to how their views are to be ascertained, and the opportunity to share those views directly with the judge should be an option. The judiciary also has discretion under the Hague framework to grant children separate legal representation to ensure the child's rights and interests are represented in proceedings. It is promising that the discretionary nature of the Hague Convention framework will apply in those Islamic law countries that have acceded to the Hague Convention.

III. What Developments in the Law are Needed to Centralise the Rights of the Child in a Parental Abduction Context?

The developments suggested in this chapter are influenced by a qualitative study, conducted to investigate the experiences of 29 families whose children were abducted from the UK to Islamic law countries. Although the sample is not vast, the participants' experiences provide a unique, personal insight into the legal problems abducted children and their left-behind parents encounter in cases of abduction from the UK to Islamic law countries. Based upon the analysis of the evidence gathered, the legal developments needed to centralise the rights of the child in a parental abduction context are: (i) For Islamic law countries to accede

[18] Rhona Schuz 'The Hague Child Abduction Convention and Children's Rights' (2002) 12 *Transnational Law & Contemporary Problems* 393, 449–52.

[19] Stalford, Hollingsworth and Gilmore (n 1).

to the Hague Convention. (ii) For the judiciary in Islamic law countries to apply the Hague Convention adopting a children's rights-based approach. (iii) Quicker acceptance by the UK of Islamic country accessions. (iv) Greater recognition in cases of primary carer abductions that any harm to the mother can also harm the child. (v) For governments to take greater action to resolve abduction cases pursuant to Article 11 CRC.

(i) *Islamic law countries to accede to the Hague Convention.* Experts in Islamic law have recently given time to the issue of the Hague Convention,[20] and since both the Hague Convention and Islamic custody law operate on a presumption of the best interests of the child, discussion ensues upon how the laws can be harmonised. While the manner in which domestic Islamic family law is currently applied appears incompatible with the aims of the CRC, or at least with subsequent guidance in CRC General Comments 5, 12, 14 and 18, the underlying principles of classical Islamic law are identified in the analysis above as being child-centred.

Kamaruddin[21] takes the view that Islamic law countries can be encouraged to accede to the Hague Convention. Accession she states is possible because while the primary sources of Islamic law are the same across the Islamic world; these are interpreted to varying degrees by different countries, often entwined with cultural norms, different legal backgrounds and social order which might be part of their colonial legacies and defined by the peculiarities of each of the jurisdictions.[22] Thus Islamic law countries, she argues, could be persuaded to adopt a more liberal interpretation of Islamic law. Kamaruddin suggests the Hague Conference can positively engage Islamic law countries to promote a sense of belonging which will achieve more 'buy-in' to the idea of a more inclusive international legal regime, which will involve identifying the values in Islamic traditions that agree with Hague's best practices, harmonising diverging principles, and drawing up common guidelines.[23] Hamid et al argue[24] that there is no glaring incompatibility between the underlying principles of the Convention and the basic tenets of Islamic law. Under the Hague Convention, the interests of abducted children are

[20] See Zaleha Kamaruddin, *Islamic Legal Perspectives on Cross-Border Family Disputes Involving Children* (Hague Conference in Private International Law, 2014); Shabnam Ishaque and Muhammad Mustafa Khan, 'The Best Interests of the Child: A Prevailing Consideration within Islamic Principles and a Governing Principle in Child Custody Cases in Pakistan' (2015) 78 *International Journal of Law, Policy and The Family* 29; Anver Emon and Urfan Khaliq, *Private International Law, Islamic-law, and Cross-Border Child Abduction A Historic-Legal Analysis* (Ontario, 2016); Emon and Khaliq *Jurisdictional Exceptionalisms: Islamic Law, International Law and Parental Child Abduction* (CUP, 2021); Mohammed Zaharuddin Zakaria and others, 'Children's Participation in Custody Disputes Involving Interfaith Parents' (2017) 23 *Advanced Science Letters* 4813; Abdul Hamid and others, 'The Applicability of the 1980 Hague Abduction Convention in Muslim Countries: Particular Reference to the Malaysian Position' (2018) 99 *Arab Law Quarterly* 32.

[21] Kamaruddin, ibid, ix, xix–xxi.

[22] Ibid.

[23] See Welchman who also identifies the concept of best interests resonates with Islamic law emphasis on the custody rules as protecting the rights of the child at different points of his or her life; Welchman (2007) (n 13) 141–42.

[24] Hamid (n 20) 125.

of paramount importance, and according to Islamic child custody law, the paramount consideration is the child's best interests. The greatest obstacle they identify is for Islamic States to overcome the issue of having to return abducted children to a non-Muslim country or a non-Muslim parent. They propose that Islamic States can reconcile this issue because Islamic law gives preference to the mother for custody of an infant child, and return under Hague facilitates the return of the abducted child to the custodial parent. While the philosophy behind the statement is accurate, the empirical data highlights that the mother's religion is a significant factor for the Islamic court in determining the best interests of the abducted child and the requirement is also a legislative constraint in many Islamic law countries. Thus, the type of judicial discretion they propose is only facilitated in Islamic law countries like Pakistan where the legislation grants the judiciary some scope to consider the child's interests. It may not be as straightforward in persuading all Islamic law countries, when taking into consideration the practice of the Islamic courts in the data examined.

Hamid et al highlight that there is a widespread misunderstanding in Islamic law countries that their domestic law must be revised to accede to the Hague Convention.[25] They suggest that Islamic law countries must be persuaded that the Hague Convention merely harmonises private international law, which means choosing the law of the state of habitual residence of the child as the applicable law for determining parental abduction cases. Emon and Khaliq advance these other suggestions, by asserting that harmonisation is not needed, they instead recommend a jurisdictional framework which Islamic law countries can adopt.[26] In explaining the operation of classical Islamic law, they argue that historical Islamic legal doctrine did address jurisdictional disputes as foreign matters. In dealing with a foreign matter, there were two options available to the Islamic court, to either reject or accept jurisdiction. The decision was historically based upon whether the parties were Muslim and whether the dispute occurred in the foreign or Islamic law country. Where jurisdiction was accepted, the court applied domestic (Islamic) law to decide the outcome of a case. Emon and Khaliq explain that the absence of a robust private international law regime resulted from an imperial logic that viewed the political other as an opponent or soon-to-be-subdued, rather than with the formal mutuality, equal status and respect that characterise international law today.[27]

To convey the jurisdictional rule into modern-day application, and to enable accession to the Hague Convention, Emon and Khaliq propose the creation of jurisdictional rules. The proposal will involve Islamic law countries legally recognising foreign parties and foreign law, exempting them from domestic Islamic law, and instead bringing them under a different regime. The framework could be

[25] Ibid.

[26] See Emon and Khaliq (2016) (n 20) 76–78.

[27] Ibid 10, 37–39, 55. Note whilst outside the scope of this analysis Emon and Khaliq also consider Islamic country accession to the Hague Convention of 19 October 1996 on Jurisdiction, Applicable Law, Recognition, Enforcement and Cooperation in Respect of Parental Responsibility and Measures for Protection.

adopted through legislative directives to the judiciary concerning cases in which a 'foreign element' is present. The proposal by Emon and Khaliq can accommodate the Hague Convention, without the need to reform existing custody law in Islamic law countries, which the discussion in chapters 2 and 3 illustrates could be an exceptionally drawn-out process. The proposals comply with Islamic law and thus leave very little room for Islamic law countries to ignore the interests of abducted children and the obligations under Article 11 CRC.

(ii) *The judiciary in Islamic law countries to apply the Hague Convention adopting a children's rights-based approach.* It is identified in preceding chapters that post-accession, a children's rights-based approach to applying the Hague Convention by Islamic courts is essential because if a state does not have a real commitment to children's rights, implementation of the Hague Convention by an Islamic law country will not necessarily achieve better outcomes for children. The Hague framework and Islamic law are both similar in that they are living instruments, which must develop along with societal changes and understanding of what is in the interests of the abducted child. The CRC Committee highlights the role of the judiciary in implementing a children's rights approach and recommends that judicial bodies should consider the impact of their decisions on children.[28] Stalford et al[29] also note the importance of the judiciary in advancing children's rights. They observe:

> It is a welcome development that the literature on the role of the judiciary in developing (rather than simply interpreting and applying) the law has turned its attention in the last two decades or so to their role in advancing children's rights. This work highlights the ultimate power of the judge to activate legal rights, particularly given children's limited ability to assert their rights through other democratic processes.[30]

The most feasible means by which this can be achieved is for the judiciary to give effect to the CRC's aims when interpreting and applying child abduction law. The analysis throughout the text highlights the areas in which the Hague Convention can improve its advancement of children's rights and on each of the CRC rights analysed, it is the judiciary that is identified as being in the best position to give effect to the aims of CRC in a child abduction context. The Hague Convention grants the judiciary the flexibility to interpret its provisions and so judges, once accepting of the children's rights-based approach, can readily give effect to its aims. (The specific actions that can be taken by the judiciary to implement a children's rights approach are discussed above at II).

The expertise of judges is essential for a children's rights compliant interpretation of the Hague Convention, and to achieve this, an effective measure has been to concentrate the number of courts within some Contracting States to hear

[28] CRC Committee, General Comment No 5: *General Measures of Implementation of the Convention on the Rights of the Child* CRC/GC/2003/5 para 12, 53.

[29] Stalford, Hollingsworth and Gilmore (n 1) 18–19.

[30] Ibid.

cross-border child abduction cases. Narrowing jurisdiction may assist the judiciary in Islamic law countries too, as it creates a process where fewer judges hear cases more regularly, so they can build on that knowledge and experience of specialised cases.[31] To increase familiarity, understanding, and expertise, 40 contracting states have limited jurisdiction to hear cases of parental child abduction to a small number of specialised courts.[32] This is intended to result in a situation where judges feel less hesitant towards hearing children, because they do it much more often, and this can facilitate greater participation opportunities for abducted children.[33] Hearing the child's objections and assessing where the child considers he or she is habitually resident requires a judge who is trained in such matters to weigh up and balance the child's wishes and recognise children as right's holders. The importance of training for judges to interpret the Hague framework in accordance with the CRC is recognised by the judiciary,[34] as well as by academics.[35]

Judicial training on the children's rights approach is disseminable through the 'International Hague Network of Judges.' The first network judges were appointed in 1998 to increase cooperation amongst the judiciary and the network is intended to provide knowledge to assist judges in Hague applications. Each jurisdiction designates one or more members of the judiciary as (a) a liaison with their Central Authority (b) between judges within their jurisdictions and (c) with other states parties.[36] Liaison judges are called upon, for example, to provide information upon the protective measures available for domestic violence victims when the court is ordering the return of an abducted child, but must also address safety concerns for an abducting mother.[37] Network judges, it is suggested here, could also be a

[31] For more detailed discussion on this issue, see Merle Weiner, 'Shrinking the Bench: Should United States Federal Courts Have Exclusive or Any Jurisdiction to Adjudicate ICARA Cases' (2014) 9 *J Comp L* 192, 252.

[32] *The Judges' Newsletter on International Child Protection* 20 (Hague Conference on International Law, 2013) 26.

[33] In 16 European countries where information is available, 8 countries concentrate jurisdiction, like in the Netherlands. 4 countries have found a middle ground (eg, Belgium) and in another 4 countries there is no concentration of jurisdiction at first instance level (eg, France); Sara Lembrechts, 'Hearing Abducted Children in Court – A comparative Point of View from Three Countries (Belgium, France & The Netherlands)', *The Child's Voice – 15 Years Later*, 28.

[34] For a judicial perspective, see Mr Justice MacDonald 'Hearing the Children's Objections – Some Perspectives from a Judge Hearing Cases in England and Wales' [2018] *International Family Law* 113.

[35] Rhona Schuz, *The Hague Child Abduction Convention* (Hart Publishing, 2013) 386–87; Beaumont and McEleavy, (1999) (n 4) 202; Thalia Kruger, *International Child Abduction: The Inadequacies of the Law* (Hart Publishing, 2011) 38.

[36] *Direct Judicial Communications: Emerging Guidance Regarding the Development of the International Hague Network of Judges and General Principles for Judicial Communications* (Hague Conference on Private International Law, 2013) available at https://assets.hcch.net/docs/62d073ca-eda0-494e-af66-2ddd368b7379.pdf.

[37] Note also the existence of European judicial networks which have also forged communication/co-operation between members of the judiciary working on cases of parental abduction; Ruth Lamont, 'Central Authorities and the European Judicial Network: Cross-Border Cooperation as a Mechanism for Advancing Children's Rights in Europe' in Ruth Lamont, Helen Stalford and Ingi Iusmen (eds) *The EU and the Global Protection of Children's Rights: Norms, Laws and Policy Dimensions* (Barbara Budrich, 2015) 77.

means through which to disseminate information and training on a children's rights application of the Hague Convention. Morocco has appointed two Hague liaison judges[38] who could aid the implementation of the Hague Convention in a children's rights compliant way, through receiving training and disseminating nationally.

The children's rights-based training may prove more effective for judges of the Islamic courts since they are new to implementing the Hague framework and so could be trained to adopt the children's rights approach as part of their training on Hague implementation from the outset, instead of having to adapt their approach, as may be the case with judges who have 40 years of experience in interpreting the Hague Convention in a particular way. The mass training of Islamic court judges on adopting a children's rights-based approach is realistic, in light of the fact that shortly after accession in 2010, 50 Moroccan judges received a training session on the practical operation of the Hague Convention by a French judge and the Hague Conference.[39] As part of the training, participants discussed the main judicial issues arising from the application of the Convention through hypothetical case studies.[40] The fact that Moroccan judges have subsequently ordered the child's return in seven of the eight cases heard by the Moroccan courts in 2015 could be indicative of the training the Moroccan judiciary received and could signify a need for guidance by the Hague Conference on adopting the children's rights approach to consider the case from the perspective of the abducted child, rather than prioritising comity with other contracting states. Moroccan judges also have access to a 206-page guide for judges on the implementation of Convention provisions.[41] The document highlights the priority of returning children to their country of habitual residence, irrespective of whether the abducting parent is the primary carer. The mother was indeed the abducting parent in 62.5 per cent of (five of the eight) cases decided in 2015 by the Moroccan Islamic courts applying the Hague Convention, and so it is unclear whether the orders for the children's return from Morocco in seven of the eight cases heard by the Moroccan courts in 2015 actually upheld the CRC rights of the children concerned.[42] The conferences and seminars held for judges to keep appraised of the developments in this area of law could be a means through which to reinforce the children's rights approach and the factors to be considered in cases of primary carer abductions (see (iv), below).

[38] At the time of writing these are the Honourable Judge Abdelouahed Jamali Iddrissi, President of Chamber, Supreme Court of Morocco and The Honourable Judge Zohra Fourat, Judge for Children, Court of First Instance of Benslimane; List of network judges available at https://assets.hcch.net/docs/665b2d56-6236-4125-9352-c22bb65bc375.pdf.

[39] Note that such training is already underway in all parts of the world, with the USA training judges in South America and Japan; Caitlin Bannon, 'The Hague Convention on the Civil Aspects of International Child Abduction: The Need for Mechanisms to Address Noncompliance' (2011) 21 *Boston College Third World Law Journal* 154.

[40] *Judge's Newsletter on International Child Protection* 31 (Hague Conference, Spring 2011) 34, available at https://assets.hcch.net/upload/spring2011e.pdf.

[41] James Garabolino, *Civil Aspects of International Child Abdcution: A Guide for Judges* (Federal Judicial Center, 2012) available at https://permanent.access.gpo.gov/gpo27181/hagueguide.pdf.

[42] Hague Survey (2015).

Specified children's rights-based training for Islamic court judges could also be undertaken through the Malta Judicial Conference on Cross-Frontier Family Law Issues referred to as the 'Malta Process.' The Malta Process is a meeting between judges and was first hosted by The Hague Conference in Malta in 2004 to begin dialogue between Hague member and non-member states. The conference aims to improve cooperation, promote accession, develop judicial networks,[43] and to agree on a common jurisdictional standard.[44] Several conferences have taken place and the number of participating Islamic states at each meeting has increased, comprising of the judiciary of non-Hague member states and other experts. The manner of the assemblies has progressed to informative seminars and networking events on issues that impact child abduction, such as judicial co-operation and networking, measures to prevent abduction, parental agreements, cross-border mediation in family matters and the exchange of information concerning the laws and practices of the different legal systems.[45]

It was agreed at the third Malta Conference that some practical accomplishments should also be achieved from the conferences. The Working Party on Mediation was thus established to promote the development of mediation structures, co-chaired by Canada and Pakistan. The Working Party has subsequently developed the 'Principles for the Establishment of Mediation Structures in the Context of the Malta Process.'[46] The mediation process seeks to establish a Central Contact Point for international family mediation in each country, to facilitate access to mediation and provide information on the local law. Contact Points have been established in Australia, France, Germany, Pakistan, Slovakia and the United States.[47] If fully implemented, the process will facilitate a point of contact in each Islamic law country, to collate data and could become a future Central Authority. Under Articles 6 and 7 of the Hague Convention, each contracting state is required to designate a Central Authority to discharge the duties imposed by the Convention, for example, to locate an abducted child, to secure the voluntary return of the child or arrange the facilitation of legal advice and representation. Creating a contact point in non-Hague States will serve as a location point at the

[43] Hans Van Loon, 'Legal diversity in a Flat, Crowded World: The Role of the Hague Conference' (2011) 39 (2) *International Journal of Legal Information* 1 176, 180–82.

[44] William Duncan, 'Purpose of the Malta Process', *The Judges' Newsletter* 16 (Spring 2010). 12; William Duncan 'Reflections on The Malta Process' in *A Commitment to Private International Law: Essays in Honour of Hans van Loon* (Intersentia, 2013).

[45] Fourth Malta Judicial Conference on Cross-Frontier Family Law Issues Hosted by the Government of Malta in Collaboration with the Hague Conference on Private International Law available at https://www.hcch.net/en/publications-and-studies/details4/?pid=6460&dtid=46.

[46] See Principles and Explanatory Memorandum on the Principles; *Mediation Guide to Good Practice under the Abduction Convention* (Hague Conference on Private International Law, 2012) 95–102 available at https://assets.hcch.net/upload/guide28mediation_en.pdf.

[47] Mobina Jaffer and Salma Ataullahjan, 'Challenges and International Mechanisms to Address Cross-Border Child Abduction: Report of the Standing Senate Committee on Human Rights' (Canadian Government, July 2015) 16, 278, available at https://sencanada.ca/content/sen/Committee/412/ridr/rep/rep13jul15-e.pdf.

very least, for left-behind parents to begin searching for their abducted child. Currently, no such office is designated in the Islamic law countries examined, and participants interviewed for this project explain that the information needed to locate their child and apply to the Islamic courts was extremely difficult to attain. One left-behind parent explains: 'there really aren't many institutional things you can use that would actually help you very much, it really becomes a private enterprise, you've got to do it on your own basically.'[48] The analysis in this text highlights a lack of institutions and organisations in Islamic law countries to implement a children's rights-based approach,[49] and so the creation of an office that acts as a contact point in abduction cases will prove purposeful. The office might in this way receive funds from the State, as a lack of resources to advance children's rights is also an obstacle identified by the CRC Committee.[50]

Training the judiciary to implement a children's rights-based approach in Hague cases is made more feasible with so many opportunities at the gatherings that already occur. Rossum,[51] who interviewed judicial participants attending the Malta Process, identifies that the most significant gain from the Malta Process does not lie in the official statements but in the discussions around actual cases which make clear where the lines of division lie. A judge told Rossum:

> Arabic judges, for example, may bluntly say that 'a Muslim father has a full right to abduct his child from a morally hazardous situation because the mother cohabits. So yes, they say, a court order from a European country will be disregarded.'[52]

The different legal perspectives identified during discussions illustrate that solutions are not easily found, but change can occur through informal exchange on how other legal jurisdictions respond to parental abduction. Since it is members of the judiciary who attend the Malta conferences, the dialogue could have a direct impact upon cross-border abduction cases decided by the Islamic courts. Change can be cultivated more readily by engaging the judiciary directly, rather than by awaiting governments to take the lead and reform legislation. The effect of this is seen in the statement of another judge interviewed by Rossum:

> What is important, however, is to meet people, to see faces. We liaison judges contact liaison judges in non-Treaty countries when necessary. We have met these judges at international meetings. Sometimes we can successfully mediate to get people talking again, or to have a situation looked into.[53]

Change in this way is implemented more effectively, at the grassroots level, which could serve to assist the judiciary in Islamic law countries to play a more

[48] Participant 03M, interview 19/04/16 (on file with the author).
[49] See particularly discussion in chapter 2.
[50] Concluding Observations Morocco CRC/c/MAR/CO/3-4 (14 October 2014).
[51] Wibo van Rossum, 'The Clash of Legal Cultures Over the "Best Interests of the Child" Principle in Cases of International Parental Child Abduction' (2010) 6 (2) *Utrecht Law Review* 33.
[52] Ibid 52–53.
[53] Ibid.

significant role in advancing the rights of abducted children. These very judges will be addressing abducting fathers in the Islamic courts, and the judge's views could be influential in persuading a father to agree for the child to return to the UK. Opposing the views of – rather than agreeing with – an abducting father is more likely when a judge has him or herself had an opportunity to reflect upon competing world views and differing approaches by judges in other parts of the world. The role of the judiciary in implementing change in Islamic law countries is recognised by academics,[54] the CRC Committee, in GC18[55] and the CRC Committee's comments in the Concluding Observations of Islamic law countries.[56]

(iii) *Quicker acceptance by the UK of Islamic country accessions.* As discussed in chapter 5, the hesitancy of Contracting States to accept the accessions of Islamic law countries denies children abducted to Islamic law countries the protection of the Hague Convention. Currently, the rights of children abducted from the UK to Iraq, Pakistan and Tunisia will not be protected under the Hague framework, despite those states having acceded to the Hague Convention.

The UK should use its best endeavours to extend the Hague protection to children abducted to Islamic law countries. The risk the English courts may have to uphold a claim of the Article 20 Hague Convention exception does not suffice in refusing to accept those accessions, particularly as other states have accepted accessions of Islamic law countries and subsequently entered into treaty obligations.[57] Hague Network Judges are available to provide information on the effect of the Islamic law on a particular child when courts are faced with a claim of Article 20 or Article 13(1)(b) of the Hague Convention, and this should alleviate some of the concern about acceptance of Islamic country accessions discussed in chapter 5.

(iv) *Greater recognition in cases of primary carer abductions that harm to the mother can also harm the child.* The analysis highlights that while the text of the Hague Convention is far from discriminatory, the effect of changing societal trends and the nature of the family has meant that the Hague Convention is now

[54] See also academic commentary that observes despite reforms, the judiciary prefer to adopt a conservative interpretation of Islamic law. See examples of Morocco, Afghanistan and Iraq; Hallie Ludsin, 'Relational Rights Masquerading as Individual Rights' (2008) 15 *Duke Journal of Gender Law & Policy* 195, 211; Stephanie Wilman Bordat and Saida Kouzzi, The Challenge of Implementing Morocco's New Personal Status Law, (2004) 2 (No 8) *Carnegie Endowment for International Peace Arab Reform Bulletin*; Laura Weingartner, 'Family Law and Reform in Morocco – The Mudawana: Modernist Islam and Women's Rights in the Code of Personal Status' (2005) 82 *University of Detroit Mercy Law Review* 687, 711.

[55] GC18 para 33–34, 42 and 54.

[56] See Concluding Observations Qatar CRC/C/QAT/CO/3-4 (22 June 2017) 24–25; Concluding Observations Bahrain CRC/C/BHR/CO/4-6 (27 February 2019) para 14, 16–17; Concluding Observations Iran CRC/C/IRN/CO/3-4 (14 March 2016) 29–30; Concluding Observations Pakistan CRC/C/PAK/CO/5 (11 July 2016) para 19; Concluding Observations Saudi Arabia CRC/C/SAU/CO/3-4 (25 October 2016) 15–16.

[57] Iraq is in treaty obligations with China, Japan, Argentina, Mexico, Serbia, Venezuela, Peru, Russia, Ukraine, Moldova, Chile New Zealand, Andora, Brazil, Georgia; Pakistan is in treaty obligations with New Zealand, Ukraine, Brazil, Argentina, Venezuela; Tunisia is in treaty obligations with Argentina, Brazil, China and Switzerland. See the Hague Convention Status Table available at https://www.hcch.net/en/instruments/conventions/status-table/?cid=24.

frequently applied to cases of primary carer abductions, even though this was not the Convention's aim when first developed.[58] The effect of the Hague Convention's policy of automatic return has the effect of separating children from their primary carers, or forcing the return of abducting mothers, often to a precarious situation without much needed financial and emotional support.[59] This analysis focuses on the individual rights of abducted children, but in undertaking that analysis, it produces evidence that in most cases, the rights of the abducted child are inseparable from the rights of their primary carers. The judiciary in Hague cases has often failed to make the connection between harm to the child and harm to the mother in cases of abductions by primary carers. While the children's rights approach, strictly speaking, may not see any distinction in cases of primary carer abductions, the evidence examined (in chapter 5) suggests the courts should give consideration to the impact this can have on the abducted child. Thus in accordance with relational theory and the guidance of the CRC Committee, the judiciary should, it is argued here, reflect upon that relationship when deciding the outcome of parental abduction cases. There is scope for the judiciary to do so under the Hague Convention when it is considering the exceptions to return (Articles 12 and 13 Hague Convention) and this would allow the situation of primary carer abductions to be addressed through the lens of children's rights. Judges could undertake the assessment from the perspective of the child and the significance the individual child places upon that relationship.

The proportion of primary carer abductions in the sample of cases studied in this analysis is lower compared with cases decided under the Hague Convention. In the author's study, the father was the abducting parent in 89.65 per cent of the cases examined involving Islamic law countries, whereas between Hague States, the survey of cases heard in 2015 highlights that mothers were the abducting parent in 70 per cent of cases.[60] The data available on the Islamic Hague state of Morocco is also suggestive of this trend, as 62.5 per cent of abductions to Morocco in 2015 were undertaken by mothers. The issue of primary carer abductions may therefore also become a feature for Islamic law countries acceding to the Hague Convention and so how the courts respond to cases of primary carer abductions could become an increasing concern.

(v) *For governments to take greater action to resolve abduction cases pursuant to Article 11 CRC.* Article 11 CRC requires States Parties to take measures to address parental child abduction. On the basis of the evidence analysed, this author advocates that until such time that Islamic law countries accede to the Hague Convention, governments must engage in a greater level of diplomatic intercession to further the Article 11 right of the abducted child. It is demonstrated in chapter 2 that any attempt to integrate a robust children's rights framework in a legal system (whether via Hague or other means) is dependent upon adults operating at the governmental

[58] See Dyer and Perez-Vera (n 6).
[59] See Lamont (n 9) and Weiner (n 10).
[60] Hague Survey (2015).

level to appropriately implement the CRC framework. The governmental responsibility could be extended to give effect to the Article 11 CRC aim to assist abducted children. The data in the author's study illustrates that the Islamic law courts did not order the return of abducted children to the UK without orders to do so by the rulers in the Islamic law countries. In only 3 of the 29 cases did the Islamic courts order the child's return to the left-behind mother, and authorised the child to leave the Islamic law country after approval by the country's rulers. The analysis suggests that more efforts are required between governments at the diplomatic level to assist abducted children, as this is currently the only means by which the courts will order the child's return, and the order is enforceable. The left-behind mothers in the three cases assert their claims to the court were unsuccessful until the UK government agreed to assist through diplomatic channels. One case involved negotiation with Libya, the other with Tunisia and the final with Egypt. These are rare outcomes for 3 of the 54 abducted children in the sample, since domestic law in Islamic law countries does not permit an order for the child's return to the UK, without the father's consent but was nevertheless approved by the state's rulers. This type of approval ensures the abducted child is allowed to exit the states' borders without the abducting father's agreement and safe passage is facilitated.

The interview data affirms the outcomes were dependent upon the involvement of a local Member of Parliament in the UK, the UK Foreign Minister and the nature of the Minister's relationship with the Islamic law country at that particular time.[61] The success is also dependent upon the diplomatic meetings taking place on other matters at that time, and the case of the abducted child is raised as a side issue as part of those other discussions.[62] The success is also very much dependent upon who is ruling the Islamic law country and what they seek in return.[63] The clandestine nature of this type of diplomatic support is documented academically[64] and in the public press.[65] The details illustrate that the courts in Islamic law

[61] Interview data on file with the author confirms the names of English MPs and rulers in Islamic law countries who have assisted left-behind parents, however direct quotations are not included to avoid participants becoming identifiable.

[62] Another example of this type of diplomacy in operation is seen in the widely reported cases of the British PhD student who was released after the UK's negotiations with the UAE, but see the delays in progress in the case of the British journalist detained in Iran: Richard Hall, 'Matthew Hedges: British Academic Released After Receiving Pardon for Spying Charges in UAE' (*The Guardian*, 26.11.18); Catherine Philip, 'Nazanin Zaghari-Ratcliffe's Husband Tells Boris Johnson to Accept Blame' (*The Times*, 24.08.19).

[63] See for example the 'terrorist-for-trade' allegation after the release of a Libyan terrorist from a British prison; Simon Johnson, 'Lockerbie Bomber: Jack Straw Admits Government Caved in to Libya' (*The Telegraph*, 31.08.09).

[64] For further detail on how state agents become involved with cross-border parental abduction disputes, see Kristin Haugevik, 'Parental Child Abduction and the State: Identity, Diplomacy and the Duty of Care' (2018) 13 *The Hague Journal of Diplomacy* 1–21; See also Kruger who notes in the Belgian data that 'some parents had contacted politicians, for instance by writing a letter, or the lawyer contacted a minister because she knew him. One of the interviewed parents thought that this contact really helped to speed up the return of her child;' Kruger (2011) (n 35) 153.

[65] Helen Pidd, 'How Colonel Gaddafi Helped to Get My Daughter Back' (*The Guardian*, 09.02.13; Helen Pidd and others, 'Abducted Atiya Anjum-Wilkinson Returns to UK From Pakistan' (*The Guardian*, 28.12.12).

countries are not independent of the state[66] and adhere to the instructions of the State's rulers. The situation appears very much a matter of luck and not law and is confirmed in research by Kruger who observes:

> embassies can try to assist in negotiating a solution, but in the absence of international legal rules, it is often difficult to resolve the case. The embassies' chances of success will depend on the experience of the staff at negotiation, the cooperation with local authorities, and the willingness of the parents to seek an amicable solution.[67]

The situation of the 3 children who were ordered to return by the Islamic courts can be compared with the other 51 abducted children in the sample. Of the 51 abducted children, 31 remain living in the Islamic law country (57.4 per cent) and 2 abductees aged 5 and 25 sadly passed away while still in the 'abduction' situation (3.7 per cent). Overall, 21 abductees returned to the UK (38.8 per cent). Of these 21 abducted children, 4 returned to the UK once aged 18 and over and the remaining 17 who returned were aged below 18 at the time of return. Opportunities for return varied. Of the 4 abductees that were aged over 18, 2 males could legally leave Libya as adults. The remaining 2 returnees were female; one returned with the abducting father's consent to attend university in the UK. The fourth, aged 19, was allowed by her abducting father to return to the UK after several unsuccessful attempts to escape Libya.

Of the 17 returnees aged below 18, 7 returned with the abducting father's agreement, 2 children escaped at the age of 14 and 15, and 2 were re-abducted by their left-behind mothers. Two children were able to return after the abducting father returned to the UK and later obliged with the High Court order for the children's return to England. One child returned as a result of family mediation.

The empirical data illustrates that without the abducting father's cooperation, it is only governmental involvement that can assist children abducted to Islamic law countries from the UK. The UK government could, therefore, undertake greater efforts to assist abducted children in protecting them from the harm of parental abduction, as is denoted by Article 11 CRC. Having reflected on potential developments in the law needed to centralise the rights of the child in parental abduction cases, the final section reflects upon the future implications of this research.

IV. Future Implications of the Research: Child Abduction Law as a Living Instrument

Understandably the world has evolved since the introduction of the Hague Convention four decades ago. Perceptions have changed, as have practices,

[66] Danny Boggs, 'Remarks on the 1980 Hague Convention on the Civil Aspects of International Child Abduction' (2000) 33 *N Y U J Int'l L & Pol* 43, 48, 47–48.

[67] Kruger (n 35) 152.

cultures, norms and recognition of rights. Mothers with custody are recognised as typical abductors, rather than the previously envisaged aggrieved father.[68] There is now wider acknowledgement of the varying forms of domestic violence, with an acceptance that fleeing from abusive partners may inadvertently result in parental abduction.[69] Many more children are born out of wedlock, resulting in the mother remaining independent and able to travel to live in another jurisdiction.[70] Migration patterns and marriage to individuals of different nationalities are much more commonplace,[71] and so as envisaged in 1980, the frequency of child abduction has increased.[72] Also, through the introduction of the CRC and related domestic provisions, children's rights are embedded in a way unrecognised in 1980. There is an increased emphasis on children's rights to maintain regular contact with both parents, to exercise and maintain their cultural identity, their right to access justice, to have their best interests considered paramount, and the right to participate in matters concerning their future. It is evident from the discussion on children's participation (chapter 4) and gender discrimination (chapter 5) that both these areas have also seen a shift in opinion in the past four decades.

The 40 years of developing case-law has incorporated some of the gradual changes in opinion and practices. Thorpe LJ in *Hunter v Murrow (Abduction: Rights of Custody)*[73] stated

> the Convention is a living instrument. Revision of the text as drafted and agreed in 1980 is simply impracticable, given that any revisions would have to be agreed upon among such a large body of Contracting States. Therefore, evolutions necessary to keep pace with social and other trends must be achieved by evolutions in interpretation and construction.

Thus, the reality of the situation is that any physical change to the Hague Convention, as with Islamic law, is slow and complex to achieve. Both the Hague Convention and Islamic custody law are identified as living instruments, which need to be developed along with the changing nature of parental abduction/custody situations. Without revisions being possible to the text, the only means by which this evolvement is possible is through the critical work of the judiciary.

[68] Dyer (1978) (n 6) 19–20.

[69] Merle Weiner, 'International Child Abduction and the Escape from Domestic Violence' (2000) 69 *Fordham L Rev* 593, 637–39; Miranda Kaye, 'The Hague Convention and the Flight from Domestic Violence: How Women and Children Are Being Returned by Coach and Four' (1999) 13 *Int'l J L Pol'y & Fam* 191.

[70] Helen Stalford, 'Crossing Boundaries: Reconciling Law, Cultures and Values in International Family Law Mediation' (2010) 2 *Journal of Social Welfare & Family Law* 32, 155, 163.

[71] Trevor Buck, *International Child Law* 3rd edn (Routledge, 2014) 277.

[72] See chapter one for detailed discussion; see also Alessandra Cancedda and others *Missing children in the European Union: Mapping, Data Collection and Statistics* (Luxembourg Publications Office of the European Union, 2013); Perez-Vera (1981) (n 6) para 24.

[73] [2005] EWCA Civ 976 para 30.

The research has highlighted the rights of children abducted to Islamic law countries are not upheld as intended by the CRC, or as is intended in classical Islamic law. Policies of piecemeal reform in Islamic law countries in the last five or six decades has resulted in the codification of common law rules into legislation, which has also resulted in the removal of judicial discretion that was a positive feature in classical Islamic law. The reforms are undertaken as a response to the aims of governments, encouragement from international law, such as the CRC, and through the insistence of the public in Islamic law countries.[74] Governments in some Islamic law countries have responded to demands for change, but little attention is paid to how the piecemeal reforms could affect individual children. The research presented in this text serves to highlight to Islamic law countries the effect of Islamic custody/abduction law on children and demonstrates that such results are not what is intended in the child-centred approach of classical Islamic law or the CRC. The evidence and its analysis in this text could further aid the discussions during the Malta Process and facilitate the discussions between policymakers to prioritise the focus on children's rights, rather than the jurisdictional differences and comity with nations that appear to have been the focus thus far.

From the perspective of abducted children, it must be borne in mind that separation of children from their primary carers is significantly shorter in abductions to Hague states than those to non-Hague states.[75] Thus the Convention can be regarded as a success, since before the Convention entered into force it was exceptionally difficult to recover a child abducted internationally by a parent.[76] The validity of this contention has arguably increased with the growing number of acceding states, particularly Islamic law States. So long as there are combined efforts on an international scale to adopt a children's rights-based approach in Hague cases, there is future hope for children abducted to Islamic law countries, which did not exist for Miriam and the other participants who currently remain in the Islamic law country. With the accession of Morocco, Iraq, Tunisia and Pakistan, future research examining how Hague cases are decided in Islamic law countries will prove invaluable.

[74] See discussion on the protests in Morocco relating to the reform of custody law: Giles Tremlett, 'Morocco Boosts Women's Rights' (*The Guardian*, 21.01.04).

[75] Janet Chiancone and others, *Issues In Resolving Cases of International Child Abduction by Parents* (United States Department of Justice, 2001) 5.

[76] Beaumont and McEleavy (n 6).

BIBLIOGRAPHY

Books and Book Chapters

Abiad, N, *Sharia, Muslim States and International Human Rights Treaty Obligations: A Comparative Study* (British Institute of International and Comparative Law, 2008).

Alderson, P and Morrow, V, *Ethics, Social Science Research and Consulting with Young People* (Barnardo's, 2004).

Ali, SS, 'Comparative Perspective of the Convention on the Rights of the Child and the Principles of Islamic Law: Law Reform and Children's Rights in Muslim Jurisdictions' in *UNICEF, Protecting the World's Children: Impact of the Convention on the Rights of the Child in Diverse Legal Systems* (Cambridge University Press, 2007).

—— and SS Khan, 'Evolving Conceptions of Children's Rights: Some Reflections on Muslim States' Engagement with the UN Convention on the Rights of the Child' in N Yassari and others (eds) *Parental Care and the Best Interests of the Child in Muslim Countries* (TMC Asser Press, 2017).

Alston, P (ed), *The Best Interests of the Child: Reconciling Culture and Human Rights* (Innocenti, 1994).

—— 'The Universal Declaration in a Era of Globalization' in B van der Heijden and B Tahzib-Lie (eds), *Reflections on the Universal Declaration of Human Rights: A Fiftieth Anniversary Anthology* (Martinus Nijhoff, 1998).

—— and J Tobin, *Laying the Foundations for Children's Rights* (UNICEF Innocenti Research Centre, 2005).

Amin, H, *Reunited in the Desert* (John Blake, 2008).

An-Na'im, AA, *Islamic Family Law in a Changing World: A Global Resource Book* (Zed Books, 2002).

—— *Muslims and Global Justice* (University of Pennsylvania Press, 2010).

—— *Toward an Islamic Reformation: Civil Liberties in Human Rights and International Law* (Syracuse University Press, 1990).

Baderin, M (ed), *Islam and Human Rights: Selected Essays of Abdullahi An-Na'im* (Ashgate Publishing, 2010).

Bahnassi, AF, 'Criminal Responsibility in Islamic Law' in Cherif Bassioni (ed), *The Islamic Criminal Justice System* (Oceana, 1982).

Barn, G and Franklin, A, 'Article 12 – Issues in Developing Children's Participation Rights' in Eugeen Verhellen (ed), *Monitoring Children's Rights* (Martinus Nijhoff, 1996).

Baruffi, Maria Caterina and Holliday, Jane, 'Child Abduction' in Paul Beaumont and Jayne Holliday (eds) *A Guide to Global Private International Law* (Hart Publishing, 2022).

Beaumont, P and McEleavy, P, *The Hague Convention on International Child Abduction* (OUP, 1999).

Beaumont, P and others (eds), *Cross-Border Litigation in Europe* (Hart Publishing, 2017).

Beazley, H and others, 'How Are the Human Rights of Children Related to Research Methodology?' in A Invernizzi and J Williams (eds) *The Human Rights of Children: From Visions to Implementation* (Ashgate Publishing, 2011).

Beitz, C, *The Idea of Human Rights* (OUP, 2009).

Bessell, B, *Research with Children: Thinking About Method and Methodology in Involving Children and Young People in Research* (ARACY and the NSW Commission for Children and Young People, 2009).

Bessner, R, *The Voice of the Child in Divorce, Custody and Access Proceedings* (Department of Justice, Canada, 2002).

Brannan, B, *Mixing Methods: Qualitative and Quantitative Research* (Aldershot, 1992).
Brems, E, 'Lessons from Children's Rights from Women's Rights? Emancipation Rights as a Distinct Category of Human Rights' in E Brems and others (eds), *Children's Rights Law in the Global Human Rights Landscape: Isolation, Inspiration, Integration?* (Routledge, 2017).
Brownlie, I, *Principles of Public International Law*, 6th edn (OUP, 2003).
Buck, T, *An Evaluation of the Long-term Effectiveness of Mediation in Cases of International Parental Child Abduction* (Reunite, 2012).
Cairns, L, 'Participation with Purpose' in John Davis and others, *Children, Young People and Social Inclusion: Participation for What?* (Policy Press, 2006).
Caputo, Virginia, '"Too Young to Wed": Envisioning a "Generous Encounter" between Feminism and the Politics of Childhood' in Rachel Rosen and Katherine Twamley (eds), *Feminism and the Politics of Childhood: Friends or Foes?* (UCL Press, 2018) 201–17.
Cashmore, J, 'Children's Participation in Family Law Matters' in C Hallet C and A Prout (eds), *Hearing the Voices of Children: Social Policy for a New Century* (Routledge-Falmer, 2003).
Cancedda, A and others, *Missing children in the European Union: Mapping, Data Collection and Statistics* (Luxembourg Publications, Office of the European Union, 2013).
Cesari, J, *When Islam and Democracy Meet* (Palgrave Macmillan, 2004).
Chaudhry, A, *Domestic Violence and the Islamic Tradition* (OUP, 2014).
Chiancone, J and others, *Issues In Resolving Cases of International Child Abduction by Parents* (United States Department of Justice, 2001).
Cohen, L and others, *Research Methods in Education* (Routledge, 2017).
Collins, TM, *The Monitoring of the Rights of the Child: A Children's Rights-Based Approach*, PhD Text (Queen Mary & Westfield College, University of London, 2007).
Connors, J, 'The Woman's Convention in the Muslim World' in Mai Yamani (ed), *Feminism and Islam* (Ithaca Press, 1996).
Couzens, M, 'The Contribution of the South African Constitutional Court to the Jurisprudential Developments of the Best Interests of the Child' in A Diduck and others (eds), *Reflections on Children, Family, Culture and Philosophy: Essays in Honour of Michael Freeman* (Brill, 2015).
Crossman, J, cited in K Charmaz, *Constructing Grounded Theory* (Sage, 2014).
Cuno, K and Desai, M (eds), *Family, Gender and Law in a Globalizing Middle East and South Asia* (Syracuse University Press, 2009).
Daly, A, *Children, Autonomy and the Courts* (Routledge, 2017).
Denzin, N (ed), *Sociological Methods: A Sourcebook* (Aldine Transaction Publishers, 2006).
Detrick, S (ed), *The United Nations Convention on the Rights of the Child* (Martinus Nijhoff, 1992) 238–248.
—— *A Commentary on the UN Convention on the Rights of the Child* (Martinus Nijhoff, 1999).
Donnelly, J, *International Human Rights* (Westview, 2007).
—— *Universal Human Rights in Theory and Practice* (Cornell University Press, 2003).
Duncan, W, 'Reflections on The Malta Process' in *A Commitment to Private International Law: Essays in Honour of Hans van Loon* (Intersentia, 2013).
Dworkin, R, *Taking Rights Seriously* (Harvard, 1978).
Dwyer, J, *The Relationship Rights of Children* (Cambridge University Press, 2006).
Edleson, J and Lindhorst, T, *Multiple Perspectives on Battered Mothers and their Children Fleeing to the United States for Safety: A Study of Hague Convention Cases* (National Institute of Justice, US Department of Justice, 2010).
Emon, A and Khaliq, U, *Private International Law, Islamic-law, and Cross-Border Child Abduction: A Historic-Legal Analysis* (Ontario, 2016).
—— 'Jurisdictional Exceptionalisms: Islamic Law, International Law and Parental Child Abduction' (CU, 2021).
Farid, A, *Muslim Woman in World Religions' Perspective* 2nd edn (The University of Karachi, 2006).
Fawcett, J and Carruthers, J, *Cheshire, North and Fawcett: Private International Law* 14th edn (OUP, 2008).

Fortin, J, *Children's Rights and the Developing Law* 2nd edn (Butterworths, 2003).
Freeman, M, 'Article 3: The Best Interests of the Child' in Andre Alen and others (eds), *Commentary on the United Nations Convention on the Rights of the Child* (Brill Nijhoff, 2007).
—— *Human Rights* (Polity, 2002).
—— *The Outcomes for Children Returned Following an Abduction* (Reunite, 2003).
—— *International Child Abduction: The Effects* (Reunite, 2006).
—— *Parental Child Abduction: The Long-Term Effects* (International Centre for Family Law, Policy, and Practice, 2014).
Fyzee, A, *Outline of Muhammadan Law* (OUP, 1974).
George, R, *Relocation Disputes: Law and Practice in England and New Zealand* (Hart Publishing, 2014).
Glesne, C, 'Research as Solidarity' in N Denzin N and M Giardina (eds), *Ethical Futures in Qualitative Research: Decolonizing the Politics of Knowledge* (Routledge, 2007).
Greif, G and Hegar, R, *When Parents Kidnap: The Families Behind the Headlines* (The Free Press, 1993).
Hantrais, L and Mangen, S (eds), *Cross-National Research Methods in the Social Sciences* (Pinter, 1998).
Hart, R, *Children's Participation: From Tokenism to Participation* (UNICEF, Florence, 1992).
Hatcher, C and others, *Reunification of Missing Children: Training Manual* (US Department of Justice, 1993).
Hedley, H, *The Modern Judge: Power, Responsibility and Society's Expectations* (LexisNexis, 2016).
Herring, J, 'Relational Autonomy and Family Law' in J Wallbank and others (eds), *Rights, Gender and Family Law* (Routledge, 2010).
Hodgkin, R and Newell, P, *The Implementation Handbook for the Convention on the Rights of the Child* (UNICEF, 2002).
Hollingsworth, K and Stalford, H, 'Judging Parental Abduction: What Does It Mean to Adopt a Children's Rights-Based Approach?' in Gillian Douglas and others (eds), *International and National Perspectives on Child and Family Law Essays in Honour of Nigel Lowe* (Intersentia, 2018).
Hollingsworth, K and Stalford, H, 'Towards Children's Rights Judgments' in *Rewriting Children's Rights Judgments: From Academic Vision to New Practice* (Hart Publishing, 2017).
Hoodfar, H, 'Circumventing Legal Limitation: Mahr and Marriage Negotiation in Egyptian Low-Income Communities' in Hoodfar H (ed), *Shifting boundaries in marriage and divorce in Muslim communities* (Grabels, 1996).
Hosseini, ZM, *Islam and Gender* (Princeton University Press, 1999).
Ibn Qudāma, *al-Mughnī*, (Beirut, Mu'assasāt al-Ta'rīkh al-'Arabī, n.d.) 7:615 cited in A Emon and U Khaliq, *Private International Law, Islamic-law, and Cross-Border Child Abduction: A Historico-Legal Analysis* (Ontario, 2016).
Ibrahim, AF, *Child Custody in Islamic Law: Theory and Practice in Egypt since the Sixteenth Century* (CUP, 2018).
Jaffer, M and Ataullahjan, S, *Challenges and International Mechanisms to Address Cross-Border Child Abduction: Report of the Standing Senate Committee on Human Rights* (Canadian Government, July 2015).
Klug, F, *Values for a Godless Age: The Story of the UKs New Bill of Rights* (Penguin, 2000).
Kohn, M (ed), *Cross-National Research in Sociology* (Sage, 1989).
Kruger, T, *International Child Abduction: The Inadequacies of the Law* (Hart Publishing, 2011).
Lamont, R, 'Central Authorities and the European Judicial Network: Cross-Border Cooperation as a Mechanism for Advancing Children's Rights in Europe' in R Lamont, H Stalford and I Iusmen (eds), *The EU and the Global Protection of Children's Rights: Norms, Laws and Policy Dimensions* (Barbara Budrich, 2015).
Lansdown, G, *Taking Part* (Institute for Public Policy Research, 1995).
—— *Promoting Children's Participation in Democratic Decision-Making* (UNICEF Innocenti Insight, 2001).
—— *The Evolving Capacities of the Child* (UNICEF, 2005).
—— *What's the Difference? Implications of a Child-focus in Rights-Based Programming* (Save the Children, 2005).

—— 'The Realisation of Children's Participation Rights' in Barry Percy-Smith and Nigel Thomas (eds), *A Handbook of Children and Young People's Participation: Perspectives from Theory and Practice* (Routledge, 2009).

Layish, A, *Women and Islamic law in a Non-Muslim State* (Jerusalem, 1975).

LeBlanc, L, *The Convention on the Rights of the Child: United Nations Lawmaking on Human Rights* (University of Nebraska Press, 1995).

Loenen, T, 'Towards an Integrated Approach to Intra-Family Relations under the CRC and CEDAW: Some Reflections' in E Brems and others (eds), *Children's Rights Law in the Global Human Rights Landscape: Isolation, Inspiration, Integration?* (Routledge, 2017).

Lowe, N et al, *Bromleys Family Law* 12th edn (OUP, 2021).

Lundy, L and McEvoy, L, *Getting it Right for Children: A Practitioners' Guide to Children's Rights Programming* (Save the Children, 2007).

—— and McEvoy, L, 'Childhood, the United Nations Convention on the Rights of the Child and Research: What Constitutes a Rights-Based Approach?' in M Freeman (ed), *Law and Childhood* (OUP, 2012).

Mahoney, J, *The Challenge of Human Rights: Origin, Development and Significance* (Blackwell, 2007).

Manara Network, *Country Profile of Morocco: A Review of the Implementation of the UN Convention on the Rights of the Child* (Save the Children Sweden, 2011).

Mann, C and Stewart, F, *Internet Communication and Qualitative Research: A Handbook for Researching Online* (Sage, 2000).

Marks, S and Clapham, A, 'Children' in *International Human Rights Lexicon* (OUP, 2005).

Mayer, AE, 'Rhetorical Strategies and Official Policies on Women's Rights: The Merits and Drawbacks of the New World Hypocrisy' in M Afkhami (ed), *Faith and Freedom: Women's Human Rights in the Muslim World* (Syracuse University Press, 1995).

—— 'Internationalizing the Conversation on Arab Women's Rights: Arab Countries Face the CEDAW Committee', in YY Haddad and BF Stowasser (eds), *Islamic law and the Challenges of Modernity* (Walnut Creek, 2004).

McKean, W, *Equality and Discrimination under International Law* (OUP, 1983).

McNamee, S and others, 'Family Law and the Construction of Childhood in England and Wales' in Jim Goddard and others (eds), *The Politics of Childhood* (Palgrave Macmillan, 2005).

Mernisi, F, *Woman and Islam* (Basil Blackwell, 1991).

—— *The Veil and the Male Elite: A Feminist Interpretation of Women's Rights in Islamic Law* (Addison-Wesley, 1991).

Mir-Hosseini, Z, *Marriage on Trial: A Study of Islamic Family Law, Iran and Morocco Compared* 2nd edn (IB Tauris, 2000).

—— and others (eds), *Men in Charge? Rethinking Authority in Muslim Legal Tradition* (One World Publications, 2015).

Mnookin, R, *In the Interests of Children: Advocacy, Law Reform and Public Policy* (WH Freeman, 1985).

Moors, A, *Women, Property and Islam: Palestinian Experiences 1920–1990* (Cambridge, 1995).

Muscroft, S, *Children 's Rights: Equal Rights? Diversity, Difference and the Issue of Discrimination* (International Save the Children Alliance, 2000).

Narayan, U, *Dislocating Cultures, Identities, Traditions and Third-World Feminism* (2007, Routledge, New York).

Nedelsky, J, *Law's Relations: A Relational Theory of Self, Autonomy and Law* (OUP, 2011).

Newiss, G and Traynor, MA, *Taken: A Study of Child Abduction in the UK* (PACT and the Child Exploitation Protection Centre, 2013).

O'Donnell, D, *The Right of the Child to be Heard: Children's Right to Have Their Views Taken Into Account and to Participate in Legal and Administrative Proceedings* (Innocenti Working Paper, UNICEF 2009).

O'Neill, Onora, *Having Children: Philosophical and Legal Reflections on Parenthood* (OUP, 1979).

Olsen F, 'Children's Rights: Some Feminist Approaches to the UN Convention on the Rights of the Child' in Philip Alston and others (eds), *Children, Rights and the Law* (Clarendon Press, 1992).

Parkinson, P and Cashmore, J, *The Voice of a Child in Family Law Disputes* (OUP, 2008).
Partsch, KJ, 'Discrimination' in *The European System for the Protection of Human Rights* (Martinus Nijhoff, 1993).
Paul, C and Kiesewetter, S, *Cross-Border Family Mediation: International Parental Child Abduction Custody and Access Cases* (Wolfgang Metzner Verlag, 2011).
Prout, A (ed), *The Future of Childhood: Towards the Interdisciplinary Study of Children* (Routledge, 2005).
Ramcharan, B, 'Equality and Non-Discrimination' in L Henkin (ed), *The International Bill of Rights: The Covenant on Civil and Political Rights* (Columbia University Press, 1983).
Roulston, K, *Reflective Interviewing: A Guide to Theory and Practice* (Sage, 2010).
Salime, Z, 'Revisiting the Debate on Family Law in Morocco: Context, Actors, and Discourse' in K Cuno and M Desai (eds), *Family, Gender and Law in a Globalizing Middle East and South Asia* (Syracuse University Press, 2009).
Schuz, R, *The Hague Child Abduction Convention* (Hart Publishing, 2013).
Shah, N, *Women, the Koran and International Human Rights Law* (Martinus Nijhoff, 2006).
Silverman, D, *Doing Qualitative Research: A Practical Handbook* (Sage, 1999).
Skivenes, M and Søvig, KH, *Child Rights and International Discrimination Law: Implementing Article 2 of the United Nations Convention on the Rights of the Child* (Routledge, 2019).
Stalford, H, 'Children's Rights under EU Family Law: Custody, Access and Parental Child Abduction' in *Children and the European Union: Rights, Welfare and Accountability* (Hart Publishing, 2012).
—— *Children and the European Union* (Hart Publishing, 2012).
—— 'The Broader Relevance of Features of Children's Rights Law: The "Best Interests of the Child" Principle' in E Brems and others (eds), *Children's Rights Law in the Global Human Rights Landscape: Isolation, Inspiration, Integration?* (Routledge, 2017).
Stalford, H, Hollingsworth, K and Gilmore, G, (eds), *Rewriting Children's Rights Judgments: From Academic Vision to New Practice* (Hart Publishing, 2017).
Standley, K, *Family Law* (Palgrave Macmillan, 2010).
Talbott, WJ, *Which Rights Should be Universal?* (OUP, 2005).
Theis, J, *Promoting Rights-Based Approaches: Experiences and Ideas From Asia and the Pacific* (Save the Children Stockholm, 2004).
Tobin, J, 'Understanding a Human Rights-Based Approach to Matters Involving Children: Conceptual Foundations and Strategic Considerations' in A Invernizzi and J Williams (eds), *The Human Rights of Children: From Visions to Implementation* (Ashgate, 2011).
Tobin, J, Lowe, N and Elliott, L, 'Article 11' in John Tobin (ed) *The UN Convention on the Rights of the Child: A Commentary* (Oxford University Press, 2019)
Tucker, JE, *In the House of Law: Gender and Islamic law in Ottoman Syria and Palestine* (University of California Press, 2000).
University of Antwerp, *Bouncing Back: The Wellbeing of Children in International Child Abduction Cases* (Missing Children Europe, 2017).
Van Bueren, G, *The International Law on the Rights of the Child* (Kluwer, 1995).
Veerman, P, *The Rights of the Child and the Changing Image of Childhood* (Martinus Nijhoff, 1992).
Vierdag, EW, *The Concept of Discrimination in International Law: With Special Reference to Human Rights* (Martinus Nijhoff, 1973).
Wadud, A, *Qur'an and Women: Rereading the Sacred Text from a Woman's Perspective* (OUP, 1999).
Wallerstein, J and Kelly, J, 'The Effects of Parental Divorce: The Adolescent Experience' in E Anthony and C Koupernik (eds), *The Child in His Family: Children At Psychiatric Risk* (Wiley, 1974).
Welchman, L, *Beyond the Code: Muslim Family Law and the Shari'a Judiciary in the Palestinian West Bank* (Kluwer, 2000).
—— *Women and Muslim Family Laws in Arab States: A Comparative Overview of Textual Development and Advocacy* (Amsterdam University Press, 2007).
Yassari, N (ed), *Changing God's Law: The Dynamics of Middle Eastern Family Law* (Routledge, 2016).

Yilmaz, I, 'Semi-Official Turkish Muslim Legal Pluralism: Encounters between Secular Official Law and Unofficial Shari'a' in A Possamai, J Richardson and B Tuner (ed) *The Sociology of Shari'a: Case Studies from Around the World* (Springer, 2015) 51–65.

Journal Articles

Abdal-Haqq, I, 'Islamic Law: An Overview of its Origin and Elements' (2002) *Journal of Islamic Law and Culture* 7.

Abdur-Rashid, K, 'Islamic Custody Law as a Solution to Child Welfare Problems' (2008) 93 *M Ü İlahiyat Fakültesi Dergisi* 34, 102.

Ackers, L, 'From "Best-Interests" to Participatory Rights – Children's Involvement in Family Migration Decisions' (2000) *Child and Family Law Quarterly* 167.

Alanen, L, (2010) 17(5) 'Taking Children's Rights Seriously' *Childhood* 5.

Ali, SS, 'Rights of the Child under Islamic Law and Laws of Pakistan: A Thematic Overview' (2006) 11 *J Islamic St Prac Int'l L* 1.

Anton, AE, 'The Hague Convention on International Child Abduction' (1981) 30 *Int'l & Comp LQ* 537, 543.

Atwood, B, 'The Child's Voice in Custody Litigation: An Empirical Survey and Suggestions for Reform' (2003) 45 *Arizona Law Review* 629.

Bannon, C, 'The Hague Convention on the Civil Aspects of International Child Abduction: The Need for Mechanisms to Address Noncompliance' (2011) *Boston College Third World Law Journal* 21.

Baron, N and Ling, R, 'Necessary Smileys and Useless Periods' (2011) 45(1-2) *Visible Language* 45.

Bartlett, K, 'Re-Expressing Parenthood' (1988) 98 *Yale LJ* 293, 297–98, 304–06, 315.

Bayefsky, A, 'The Principle of Equality and Non Discrimination in International Law' (1990) 11 *Human Rights Law Journal* 1–34.

Beaumont, P, 'The Contribution of Alexander (Sandy) Anton to the Development of Private International Law' (2006) *Juridical Review* 1–28.

—— 'The Jurisprudence of the European Court of Human Rights and the European Court of Justice on the Hague Convention on International Child Abduction' (2008) 335 *Hague Collected Courses* 9, 102.

—— and Trimmings, K, 'Article 20 of the 1980 Hague Abduction Convention' (2014) 88 9 *J Comp L* 66.

—— and Walker, L, 'Shifting The Balance Achieved by the Abduction Convention: The Contrasting Approaches of the European Court of Human Rights and the European Court of Justice' (2011) 2 7 *Journal of Private International Law* 231.

—— Walker, L and Holliday, J, 'Not Heard and Not Returned: The Reality of Article 11(8) Proceedings' (2015) 2 *International Family Law* 124.

—— et al, 'Child Abduction: Recent Jurisprudence of the European Court of Human Rights' (2015) *International and Comparative Law Quarterly* 39–63.

Besson, S, 'The Principle of Non-Discrimination in the Convention on the Rights of the Child' (2005) 13 *International Journal of Children s Rights* 433.

Bodenheimer, B, 'The Hague Draft Convention on International Child Abduction' (1980) 14 *Family Law Quarterly* 99.

Boggs, D, 'Remarks on the 1980 Hague Convention on the Civil Aspects of International Child Abduction' (2000) 33 *NYU J Int'l L & Pol* 43, 48.

Bordat, SW and Kouzzi, S, 'The Challenge of Implementing Morocco's New Personal Status Law' (2004) 2 (No 8) *Carnegie Endowment for International Peace Arab Reform Bulletin.*

Brando, N 'Universalism, embeddedness and domination: an analysis of the Convention on the Rights of the Child' 2019 (15) 3 *Journal of Global Ethics* 270–286.

Bruch, C, 'The Unmet Needs of Domestic Violence Victims and their Children in Hague Abduction Convention cases' (2004) 38 *Family Law Quarterly* 529.

Bucher, A, 'The New Swiss Federal Act on International Child Abduction' (2008) 4 *Journal of Private International Law* 139.
Burman, E, 'Beyond "Women vs. Children" or "womanandchildren": Engendering Childhood and Reformulating Motherhood' (2008) 16 *International Journal of Children's Rights* 177.
Dinstein, Y, 'Discrimination and International Human Rights' (1985) 15 *Israel Yearbook of Human Rights* 11–27.
Duncan, W, 'The International Family Law Lecture 2010: Is It Time For A Protocol?' (2010) 1 *Journal of Family Law and Practice* 4.
Dyer, A, 'The Contribution of the Hague Children's Conventions to the Protection of Human Rights' (2012) *International Family Law* 7.
—— 'The Hague Convention on the Civil Aspects of International Child Abduction – Towards Global Cooperation its Successes and Failures' (1993) 1 *The International Journal of Children's Rights* 273.
Eekelaar, J, 'International Child Abduction by Parents' (1982) 32 *U Toronto LJ* 281, 314.
—— 'The Emergence of Children's Rights' (1986) *Oxford Journal of Legal Studies* 161.
—— 'Judges and Citizens: Two Conceptions of Law' (2002) 22 (3) *Oxford Journal of Legal Studies* 497.
Fahmy, A and others, 'Female Genital Mutilation/Cutting and Issues of Sexuality in Egypt' (2010) (36) 18 *Reproductive Health Matters* 181.
Fekry Ibrahim, AF, 'The Best Interests of the Child in Premodern Islamic Juristic Discourse and Practice' (2015) 63 *The American Journal of Comparative Law* 859.
Fenton-Glynn, C, 'Participation and Natural Justice: Children's Rights and Interests in Hague Abduction Proceedings' (2014) (1) 9 *Journal of Comparative Law* 134.
Fernando, M and Ross, N, 'Stifled Voices: Hearing Children's Objections in Hague Child Abduction Convention Cases in Australia' (2018) 32 (1) *Int J Law Policy Family* 93.
Freeman, M, 'Primary Carers and the Hague Child Abduction Convention' [2001] *IFL* 140.
—— and Hutchinson, AM, 'Half Price for Children? The Voice of the Child and the Child's Fight for Party Status in Cases on International Child Abduction' (2007) 29 *International Family Law* 177.
—— 'Abduction and the Voice of the Child: *In re M*' [2008] *Int'l Fam L* 163.
—— 'When the 1980 Hague Child Abduction Convention Does Not Apply: The UK-Pakistan Protocol' [2009] September *IFL* 181.
—— and Taylor, Nicola, 'Domestic violence and child participation: contemporary challenges for the 1980 Hague child abduction convention' 2020 (42) 2 *Journal of Social Welfare and Family Law* 154–175.
—— 'The Morality of Cultural Pluralism' (1995) 3 *International Journal of Child Rights.*
—— 'Why it Remains Important to Take Children's Rights Seriously' (2007) 15(1) *International Journal of Children's Rights* 5–23.
Gallala-Arndt, I, 'Negotiating Parenthood in Muslim Countries: Changing Concepts and Perceptions' (2015) 63 *The American Journal of Comparative Law* 847.
Garrison, E, 'Children's Competence to Participate in Divorce Custody Decision-Making' (1991) 20 *Journal of Clinical Child Psychology* 78.
Gibbs, M and others, 'The Consequences of Parental Abduction: A Pilot Study with a Retrospective View from the Victim' (2013) 21(3) *The Family Journal.*
Gilmore, S, 'The Payne Saga: Precedent and Family Law Cases' [2011] *Family Law* 970.
George, R, 'Reviewing Relocation?' [2012] *CFLQ* 110.
Goolam, N, 'Formulation of the Best Interests Principle in Islamic Law' (Children's Rights International, 2005).
Green, M, 'What We Talk About When We Talk About Indicators: Current Approaches to Human Rights Measurement' (2001) 23 *Human Rights Quarterly* 1064.
Greif, G, 'A Parental Report on the Long-Term Consequences for Children of Abduction by the Other Parent' (2000) 31(1) *Child Psychiatry and Human Development* 59.
—— 'A Parental Report on the Long-Term Consequences for Children of Abduction by the Other Parent' *Child Psychiatry and Human Development* (2000) 31(1) 59.

—— 'The Long-Term Aftermath of Child Abduction: Two Case Studies and Implications for Family Therapy' (2009) 37*The American Journal of Family Therapy* 273.
—— 'Ambiguous Reunification: A Way for Social Workers to Conceptualize the Return of Children After Abduction and Other Separations' (2012) 93(4) *Families in Society: The Journal of Contemporary Social Services* 305–311.
—— and Hegar, R, 'Impact on Children of Abduction by a Parent: A Review of the Literature' (1992) 62(4) *American Journal of Orthopsychiatry* 599.
—— and Duane, D, 'Unresolved Loss: Issues in Working With Adults Whose Sibling Was Kidnapped Years Ago' (2007) 203 *American Journal of Family Therapy* 35.
Hamid, A and others, 'The Applicability of the 1980 Hague Abduction Convention in Muslim Countries: Particular Reference to the Malaysian Position' (2018) 32 *Arab Law Quarterly* 99.
Hantrais, L, 'Methodological Pluralism in International Comparative Research' (2014) 17 (2) *International Journal of Social Research Methodology* 133.
Harris, D, 'Is the Strength of the Hague Convention on Child Abduction Being Diluted by the courts? The English Perspective' (1999) 35 *International Legal Materials* 77.
Harris Stoertz, F, 'Young Women in France and England, 1050–1300' (2001) 12 (4) *Journal of Women's History* 22–45.
Hashmi, K, 'Religious Legal Traditions, Muslim States and the Convention on the Rights of the Child: An essay on the Relevant Documentation' (2007) 29 *HRQ* 194.
Haugevik, K, 'Parental Child Abduction and the State: Identity, Diplomacy and the Duty of Care' (2018) 13 *The Hague Journal of Diplomacy* 1–21.
Hayes, M, 'Relocation Cases: Is The Court of Appeal Applying the Correct Principles?' [2006] *CFLQ* 351.
Henderson, P, 'To Heed the Child's Voice' (2000) *New Zealand Law Journal* 267.
Hendrick, J, 'When Should the Judge and the Child Meet?' October [2011] *Fam Law* 1148.
Herring, J and Taylor, R, 'Relocating Relocation' [2006] *CFLQ* 517.
Hitch, L, 'Non-discrimination and the rights of the child: Article 2' (1989) 7 *New York University Law School Journal of Human Rights* 47.
Hoegger, R, 'What If She Leaves? Domestic Violence Cases Under the Hague Convention and the Insufficiency of the Undertakings Remedy' (2003) 18 *Berkeley Women's Law Journal* 181.
Ishaque, S and Khan, MM, 'The Best Interests of the Child: A Prevailing Consideration within Islamic Principles and a Governing Principle in Child Custody Cases in Pakistan' (2015) 29 *International Journal of Law, Policy and The Family* 78.
Jain, Neha 'Forced Marriage as a Crime against Humanity' (2008) 6(5) *Int Criminal Justice* 1013–32.
Jefferson, M, 'FGM/Cutting: Contextualising Recent Legal Developments' (2015) 79 (6) *The Journal of Criminal Law.*
Judd, F and George, R, 'International Relocation: Do We Stand Alone?' [2010] *Family Law* 63.
Kaye, M, 'The Hague Convention and the Flight from Domestic Violence: How Women and Children Are Being Returned by Coach and Four' (1999) 13 *Int'l JL Pol'y & Fam* 191.
Keller, H, 'Protecting the Best Interests of the Child: International Child Abduction and the European Court of Human Rights' (2015) 84 *Nordic Journal of International Law* 270.
Khaliq, U and Young, J, 'Cultural Diversity, Human Rights and Inconsistency in the English Courts' (2001) 21 *Legal Studies* 192.
Lamont, R, 'Habitual Residence and Brussels ll bis: Developing Concepts for European Private International.Family Law' (2007) 3 *Journal of Private International Law* 277.
—— 'Mainstreaming Gender into European Union Family Law? The Case of International Child Abduction and Brussels II Revised' 17 *European Law Journal* (2011) 366, 369–70.
—— 'Free Movement of Persons, Child Abduction and Relocation Within the European Union' (2012) 34(2) *Journal of Social Welfare and Family Law* 231.
Laufer-Ukeles, PL, 'The Relational Rights of Children' (2016) 48 3 *Connecticut Law Review* 769.
Ludsin, H, 'Relational Rights Masquerading as Individual Rights' (2008) 15 *Duke Journal of Gender Law & Policy* 195.

Lundy, L, '"Voice" is Not Enough: Conceptualising Article 12 of the United Nations Convention on the Rights of the Child' (2007) 33(6) *British Educational Research Journal* 927.
—— and McEvoy, L, 'Children's Rights and Research Processes: Assisting Children to (In)formed Views' (2012) 19(1) Childhood 116.
—— and others, 'The UN Convention on the Rights of the Child: A Study of Legal Implementation in 12 Countries' (UNICEF, Queens University Belfast, 2012).
MacDonald, the Honourable Mr Justice, 'Hearing the Children's Objections – Some Perspectives from a Judge Hearing Cases in England and Wales' [2018] *International Family Law* 113.
Mayer, AE, 'Islamic Reservations to Human Rights Conventions' (1998) 15 *Recht van der Islam*.
McEleavy, P, 'Evaluating the Views of Abducted Children: Trends in Appellate Case-Law' (2008) 20 *Child & Fam L Q* 230.
Minow, M, 'Forming Underneath Everything that Grows: Toward a History of Family Law' (1985) *Wis L Rev* 819.
—— 'Rights for the Next Generation: A Feminist Approach to Children's Rights' (1986) (1) 9 *Harv Women's LJ* 19.
Mol, C and Kruger, T, 'International Child Abduction and the Best Interests of the Child: An Analysis of Judicial Reasoning in Two Jurisdictions' (2018) 14 (3) *Journal of Private International Law* 421.
Mnookin, R, 'Child-Custody Adjudication: Judicial Functions in the Face of Indeterminacy' (1975) 39 *Law and Contemporary Problems* 226.
Möller, LM, 'An Enduring Relic: Family Law Reform and the Inflexibility of Wilaya' (2015) 63 *The American Journal of Comparative Law* 847, 910.
Ndanu, MC and Syombua, MJ, 'Mixed Methods Research: The Hidden Cracks of the Triangulation Design' (2015) 4 *General Education Journal* 46.
Nedelsky, J, 'Reconceiving Rights as Relationship' (1993) 1 *Review of Constitutional Studies* 1–26.
Olsen, F, 'Children's Rights: Some Feminist Approaches to the UNCRC' (1992) (1) 6 International Journal of Law, Policy and the Family 192.
Parker, S, 'The Best Interests of the Child: Principles and Problems' (1994) 8 *International Journal of Law, Policy and the Family* 26.
Paul, J, 'Comity in International Law' (1991) 32 *Harvard Journal of International Law* 1.
Piper, C, 'Assumptions about Children's Best Interests' (2000) 22(3) *Journal of Social Welfare and Family Law* 261.
Pitman, E, ' Making the Interests of the Child Paramount: Representation For Children in the Hague Convention on the Civil Aspects of International Child Abduction' (2009) 17 *Cardozo Public Law, Policy & Ethics Journal* 515.
Prettitore, PS, 'Family Law Reform, Gender Equality, and Underage Marriage: A view from Morocco and Jordan' (2015) (3) 13 *The Review of Faith & International Affairs* 32.
Rafiq, A, 'Child Custody in Classical Islamic Law and Laws of Contemporary Muslim World: An Analysis' (2014) (5) 4 *International Journal of Humanity and Social Science* 272.
Raitt, F, 'Hearing Children in Family Law Proceedings: Can Judges Make a Difference?' (2007) 19 (2) *Child and Family Law Quarterly* 204.
Redmond, M, 'Cultural and Ethical Challenges in Cross-National Research: Reflections on a European Union Study on Child and Youth Migration' (2003) (4) 2 *International Journal of Qualitative Methods* 2.
Rehman, J, 'Religion, Human Rights and the Rights of the Child: Complexities in Applying Sharia in Modern State Practices' (2011) 62 2 *Northern Ireland Legal Quarterly*, 153.
Riddle, J, 'Making CEDAW Universal: A Critique of CEDAW's Reservation Regime under Article 28 and the Effectiveness of the Reporting Process' (2002) 34 *Geo Wash Int'l L Rev* 605, 627.
Ryen, A, 'Exploring or Exporting: Qualitative Methods in Times of Globalisation' (2011) 14 (6) *International Journal of Social Research Methodology* 439.
Said, S and Suhor, S, 'International Parental Child Abduction in Malaysia: Foreign Custody Orders and Related Laws for Incoming Abductions' (2012) 20 *Pertanika J Soc Sci & Hum* 101.
Sagatun, I and Barrett, L, 'Parental Child Abduction: The Law, Family Dynamics, and Legal System Responses' (1990) 18 *Journal of Criminal Justice* 433.

Sampson, I, 'Religion and the Nigerian State: Situating the *de facto* and *de jure* frontiers of State–Religion Relations and its Implications For National Security' (2014) 3 (2) *Ox J Law Religion* 311.

Savolainen, M, 'The Hague Convention on Child Abduction of 1980 and its Implementation in Finland' (1997) 66 *Nordic Journal of International Law* 131.

Schiratzki, JL, 'Friends at Odds – Construing Habitual Residence for Children in Sweden and the United States' (2001) (3)15 *International Journal of Law, Policy and the Family* 4.

Schuz, R, 'The Hague Child Abduction Convention and Children's Rights' (2002) 12 *Transnational Law & Contemporary Problems* 393, 396–97.

—— 'In Search of a Settled Interpretation of Article 12(2) of the Hague Child Abduction Convention' (2008) 64 *Child & Family Law Quarterly* 34.

—— 'The Relevance of Religious Law and Cultural Considerations in International Child Abduction Disputes' (2010) 12 *Journal of Law & Family Studies* 453.

Senior, N and others, 'Child Snatching: A Case Report' (1982) 21 *J Amer Acad Child Psych* 579.

Shah, N, 'A Woman's Human Rights in the Koran: An Interpretive Approach' (2006) 28(4) *Human Rights Quarterly* 868.

Sheridan, V and Storch, K, 'Linking the Intercultural and Grounded Theory: Methodological Issues in Migration Research' (2009) 10(1) *Qualitative Social Research.*

Shier, H, 'Pathways to Participation: Openings, Opportunities and Obligations' (2001) 15(2) *Children & Society* 107.

Smart, C, 'From Children's Shoes to Children's Voices' (2002) 40(3) *Family Court Review* 307.

Soh, RC, 'Children's Participation in Custody and Access Proceedings' (2014) 22 *IIUMLJ* 53.

Stalford, H, 'Crossing Boundaries: Reconciling Law, Cultures and Values in International Family Law Mediation' (2010) 32(2) *Journal of Social Welfare & Family Law* 155.

Stephen, V and Lowe, N, 'Children's Welfare and Human Rights Under the 1980 Hague Abduction Convention – the Ruling in *Re E*' (2012) 34(1) Journal of Social Welfare and Family Law 133.

Suad, J, 'Problematizing Gender and Relational Rights: Experiences from Lebanon Social Politics' (1994) 1(3) *International Studies in Gender, State & Society* 271.

Tapp, P, 'Judges are Human Too: Conversations Between the Judge and a Child as a Means of Giving Effect to Section 6 of the Care of Children Act 2004' (2006) *New Zealand Law Review* 35.

Thomas, N, 'Towards a Theory of Children's Participation' (2007) 15(2) *International Journal of Children's Rights* 199.

Tobin, J, 'Increasingly Seen and Heard: The Constitutional Recognition of Children's Rights' (2005) 21:1 *South African Journal on Human Rights* 86.

—— 'Judging the Judges: Are They Adopting the Rights Approach in Matters Involving Children?' (2009) 33 *Melbourne University Law Review* 580.

Valentin, K and Meinert, L 'The adult North and the young South: Reflections on the Civilizing Mission of Children's Rights,' (2009) 25(3) *Anthropology Today* 23–28.

Van Loon, H, 'Legal diversity in a Flat, Crowded World: The Role of the Hague Conference' (2011) 39(2) *International Journal of Legal Information* 1, 176.

Van Rossum, W, 'The Clash of Legal Cultures Over the 'Best Interests of the Child' Principle in Cases of International Parental Child Abduction' (2010) 6(2) *Utrecht Law Review* 52–53.

Varadan, S, 'The Principle of Evolving Capacities under the UN Convention on the the Rights of the Child' (2019) 27(2) *International Journal of Children's Rights* 306.

Veerman, P, and Sand, C, 'Religion and Children's Rights' (1999) 7(4) *The International Journal of Children's Rights* 385.

Wallerstein, J and Tanke, T, 'To Move Or Not To Move: Psychological and Legal Considerations in the Relocation of Children Following Divorce' (1996) 30 *Family Law Quarterly* 305.

Warshak, R, 'Payoffs and Pitfalls of Listening to Children' (2003) 52 *Family Relations* 373.

Weiner, M, 'International Child Abduction and the Escape from Domestic Violence' (2000) 69 *Fordham L Rev* 593, 637.

—— 'The Potential and Challenges of Transnational Litigation for Feminists Concerned about Domestic Violence Here and Abroad' (2003) 11 *Journal of Gender, Social, Policy and the Law* 749.

—— 'Using Article 20' (2004) 38 *Fam LQ* 587, 622.
—— 'Strengthening Article 20' (2005) *International Family Law Journal* 209.
—— 'Intolerable Situations and Counsel for Children: Following Switzerland's Example in Hague Abduction Cases' (2008) 58 *American University Law Review* 356.
—— 'Shrinking the Bench: Should United States Federal Courts Have Exclusive or Any Jurisdiction to Adjudicate ICARA Cases' (2014) 9 *J Comp L* 192, 252.
Weingartner, L, 'Family Law and Reform in Morocco – The Mudawana: Modernist Islam and Women's Rights in the Code of Personal Status' (2005) 687 *University of Detroit Mercy Law Review* 82.
Welchman, L, 'Capacity, Consent and Under-Age Marriage in Muslim Family Law' (2001) *Int'l Surv Fam L* 243.
—— 'First Time Codification in Three Gulf States' (2010) *Int'l Surv Fam L* 163, 173–74.
—— 'A Husband's Authority: Emerging Formulations in Muslim Family Law' (2011) *Int'l JL Pol'y & Fam* 25.
Willman Bordat, S and Kouzzi, S, 'The Challenge of Implementing Morocco's New Personal Status Law', (2004) 2 (No 8) *Carnegie Endowment for International Peace Arab Reform Bulletin.*
Wilson, N, 'The Ears of the Child in Family Proceedings' (2007) September *Family Law* 808.
Wolfe, K, 'A Tale of Two States: Success and Failures of the 1980 Hague Convention on the Civil Aspects of International Child Abduction in the United States and Germany' (2000) 33 *New York University Journal of International Law and Politics* 317.
Woodhouse, BB, 'Hatching the Egg: A Child-Centred Perspective on Parents' Rights' (1993) 14 *Cardozo Law Review* 1747.
Zaharuddin Zakaria, MZ and others, 'Children's Participation in Custody Disputes Involving Interfaith Parents' (2017) Vol 23 *Advanced Science Letters* 4813.
Zahraa, M and Malek, N, 'The Concept of Custody in Islamic Law' (1998) 13 *Arab LQ* 155.
Zermatten, J, 'The Best Interests of the Child Principle: Literal Analysis and Function' (2010) 18 *International Journal of Children's Rights* 483.
Zin, NM, 'How the Best Interests of the Child is Best Served in Islamic Law with Special Reference to its Application in the Malaysian Shariah Court,' (2005) 9(1) *IKIM Law Journal* 338.

Reports

A Toolkit on Child Rights Programming (Save the Children Denmark, 2005).
Guidelines for Judges Meeting Children who are subject to Family Proceedings (Family Court Practice, 2011) 2876.
Guidelines in Relation to Children Giving Evidence in Family Proceedings [2012] 2 FLR 456.
Confirmation of the UK's acceptance of Morocco's Hague Convention accession: Opinion 1/13, EU:C:2014:2303, [2015] 2 FLR 1453.
Legislative History of the Convention on the Rights of the Child (Vol 1, Office of the United Nations High Commissioner for Human Rights, 2007), available at www.ohchr.org/Documents/Publications/LegislativeHistorycrc1en.pdf.
President's Guidance to Judges on the Implementation of the UK–Pakistan Judicial Protocol on Child Contact and Abduction (Reunite, 2004).
Report of the Committee on the Elimination of Discrimination against Women A/42/38 (10th April 1987).
Tunisian Family Law, (British Embassy, Tunis, 2019) 15, available at assets.publishing.service.gov.uk/government/uploads/system/uploads/attachment_data/file/797548/Tunisian_Family_Law_-_Print_Version_Final_Document.pdf.
Law Commission, Simplification of Criminal Law: Kidnapping and Related Offences (Law Com No 355, 2014).

Garabolino, J, 'Civil Aspects of International Child Abduction: A Guide for Judges (Federal Judicial Center, 2012) available at https://permanent.access.gpo.gov/gpo27181/hagueguide.pdf.

UNICEF, A Child Rights-Based Approach: Seven Principles Grounded in the UN Convention on the Rights of the Child.

United Nations, Statement of Common Understanding on a Human Rights-Based Approach to Development Co-operation (United Nations, 2003).

United Nations, Human Development Report (OUP 2000).

United States Government, 'Investigation into Abductions of American Children to Saudi Arabia. Hearings before the Committee on Government Reform', House of Representatives, 107th Congress, Second session (United States Government Publishing Office, 2002).

United States Department of State, 'Hague International Child Abduction, Text and Legal Analysis Public Notice 957', 51 Fed Reg 10494, 10510 (US Department of State, 1986).

Vienna Declaration and Programme of Action A/CONF.157/23 (July 12, 1993).

World Conference on Human Rights (14–25 June 1993).

Newspapers/Media

'Appeal to Find Abducted Daughter' (25.01.13) *Yorkshire Evening Post*, available at www.yorkshirepost.co.uk/news/crime/video-leeds-mum-launches-worldwide-appeal-find-daughter-5-1872845.

'Father Jailed for Abducting Six-Year-Old Daughter – Girl Now "Kept Prisoner" in a School in Punjab' (07.12.15) *Leicester Mercury*, available at mercury1536.rssing.com/chan-42040450/all_p39.html.

'Father Who Held Abducted Daughter in Pakistan For Three Years Ordered to Stay In Jail' (14.01.13) *Evening Standard*, available at www.standard.co.uk/news/crime/father-who-held-abducted-daughter-in-pakistan-for-three-years-ordered-to-stay-in-jail-8451519.html.

Campbell, S, 'Amina Al-Jeffery: Locked up Woman Must Be Allowed Home' (03.08.16) BBC, available at www.bbc.co.uk/news/uk-wales-south-west-wales-36955248.

Gibb, F, 'Judges Using Contempt of Court Laws to Punish Parents Who Abduct Children' (02.09.17) *The Times*.

Grimmer, D, 'Abduction torment of Norwich mum' (Easton Daily Press, 03.11.10) available at: Abduction torment of Norwich mum | Eastern Daily Press (edp24.co.uk)

Hall, R, 'Matthew Hedges: British Academic Released After Receiving Pardon for Spying Charges in UAE' (26.11.18) *The Independent*, available at https://www.independent.co.uk/news/world/middle-east/matthew-hedges-pardoned-uae-spying-dubai-jailed-clemency-case-latest-a8651671.html.

Johnson, S, 'Lockerbie Bomber: Jack Straw Admits Government Caved in to Libya' (31.08.09) *The Telegraph*, available at https://www.telegraph.co.uk/news/uknews/terrorism-in-the-uk/6116029/Lockerbie-bomber-Jack-Straw-admits-Government-caved-in-to-Libya.html.

Keegan, S, 'Dad Jailed for Kidnapping Daughter from her Mother and Taking her to Libya' (10.11.14) *Mirror*, available at www.mirror.co.uk/news/uk-news/dad-jailed-kidnapping-daughter-mother-4605929.

Mardell, M, 'Gaddafi Killed: A New Kind of US Foreign Policy Success' (20.10.11) BBC, available at https://www.bbc.co.uk/news/world-us-canada-15393497.

Miles, P, 'Father Jailed for Seven Years after Abducting his Two Children' (05.09.14) *Slough Express*, available at www.sloughexpress.co.uk/news/slough/70485/Father-jailed-for-seven-years-after.html.

Morrison, J, 'Revealed: The Story of an International Tug-of-Love Battle That Made Headlines Around the World' (13.04.14) *Daily Record*, available at www.dailyrecord.co.uk/news/scottish-news/revealed-story-international-tug-of-love-battle-3408506.

Nimmo, J, 'Man Jailed For Taking Son to Turkey in Custody Row' (24.05.2014) *Oxford Mail*, available at www.oxfordmail.co.uk/news/yourtown/oxford/11234491.Man_jailed_for_taking_son_to_Turkey_in_custody_row/.

Oppenheim, M, 'Saudi Government's "Wife-Tracking" App Linked to Domestic Violence and Abusive Working Conditions, says Rights Group' (07.05.19) *The Independent*, available at www.independent.co.uk/news/world/middle-east/saudi-arabia-absher-app-wife-tracking-human-rights-middle-east-a8903376.html.

Philip, C, 'Nazanin Zaghari-Ratcliffe's Husband Tells Boris Johnson to Accept Blame' (24.08.19) *The Times*, available at https://www.thetimes.co.uk/article/nazanin-zaghari-ratcliffe-s-husband-tells-boris-johnson-to-accept-blame-jhbbpfrvh.

Pidd, H and others, 'Abducted Atiya Anjum-Wilkinson Returns to UK from Pakistan' (28.12.2012) *The Guardian*, available at www.theguardian.com/world/2012/dec/28/abducted-atiya-wilkinson-return-pakistan.

Pidd, H, 'How Colonel Gaddafi Helped to Get My Daughter Back (09.02.2013) *The Guardian*, available at https://www.theguardian.com/lifeandstyle/2013/feb/09/gaddafi-helped-get-abducted-daughter-home.

Rees, J, 'Cardiff Mum's Plea After Daughter Abducted By Dad In 2012' (25.09.18) BBC, available at www.bbc.co.uk/news/uk-wales-45601290.

Simmonds, M, 'New FCO figures Show Parental Child Abduction cases on the Rise' (12 December 2013) Foreign and Commonwealth Office.

Stowe Family Law, 'Judge Empties Courtroom so Warring Parents Can Talk in Private' (21.12.16) *Stowe Family Law*.

Tremlett, G, 'Morocco Boosts Women's Rights' (21.01.04) *The Guardian*, available at www.theguardian.com/world/2004/jan/21/gender.gilestremlett.

Williams, K, 'Mum Breaks Down in Tears after Being Jailed For Abducting Her Daughter' (04.06.19) *Daily Post*, available at www.dailypost.co.uk/news/north-wales-news/mum-breaks-down-tears-after-16375254.

Websites

Child Notice Morocco (UNICEF, 2015) available at www.unicef.nl/media/4646666/cn-marokkoeng-def.pdf, 17.

Morocco's 2011 Constitution, English Translation of the Constitution, available at www.constituteproject.org/constitution/Morocco_2011.pdf.

Survey created for this project, available at https://nyaqub.wordpress.com/take-the-brief-survey/.

YouTube video created for this project, available at https://youtu.be/y9oq85FExrU.

Recruitment video embedded into website created for this project, available at https://nyaqub.wordpress.com/watch-the-video/.

Status table of Hague Convention Membership, available at www.hcch.net/en/instruments/conventions/status-table/?cid=29.

Survey of Islamic family law, available at www.law.emory.edu/ifl/.

UK Foreign and Commonwealth Office Freedom of Information Act Request 2014, available at www.gov.uk/government/uploads/system/uploads/attachment_data/file/382997/FOI_ref_0851_parental_child_abduction.pdf.

UK Foreign and Commonwealth Office Freedom of Information Act Request 2016, available at assets.publishing.service.gov.uk/government/uploads/system/uploads/attachment_data/file/540319/FOI_0503-16_International_parental_child_abduction_-_India___Pakistan.pdf.

UK Foreign and Commonwealth Office Consular data by country, available at www.gov.uk/government/collections/consular-data.

United States Parental Child Abduction Annual Report (United States Department of State, Bureau of Consular Affairs, 2016) available at https://travel.state.gov/content/dam/childabduction/complianceReports/2016%20IPCA%20Report%20-%20Final%20(July%2011).pdf.

Wave 6 data (2010–2014) World Values Survey. available at www.worldvaluessurvey.org/wvs.jsp.

UNCRC Documents

UNCRC, 'Reservations, Declarations and Objections Relating to the Convention on the Rights of the Child – Note by the Secretary-General', CRC/C/2/Rev.3 (11 July 1994).
CRC Committee, 'General Discussion on the Girl Child', UN Doc CRC/C/38 (21 January 1995).

General Comments

General Comment No 5: General Measures of Implementation of the Convention on the Rights of the Child CRC/GC/2003/5.
General Comment No 12: The Right of the Child to be Heard, CRC/C/GC/12 (20 July 2009).
General Comment No 14: On the Right of the Child to Have His or Her Best Interests Taken as a Primary Consideration CRC/C/GC/14 (2013).
General Comment No 18: Non-Discrimination HRI/GEN/I/Rev 5 (10/11/1989) reproduced in Compilation of General Comments and General Recommendations adopted by Human Rights Treaty Bodies HRI/GEN/1 (1992).
General Comment No 28: International Covenant on Civil and Political Rights 1966: Equality of Rights Between Men and Women CCPR/C/21/Rev 1/Add 10 (29/03/2000).
The Joint General Comment No 31 of the Committee on the Elimination of Discrimination against Women and No 18 of the Committee on the Rights of the Child on harmful practices CEDAW/C/GC/31-CRC/C/GC/18 (4 November 2014).

Country Reports Submitted to the CRC Committee

Morocco First Report CRC/C/28/Add.1 (1995).
Morocco Second Report CRC/C/93/Add.3 (2000).
Lebanon Second Report CRC/C/70/Add.8 (1998).
Yemen Third report (CRC/C/129/Add.2 (2003).
Morocco Third and Fourth Periodic Reports (CRC/C/MAR/3-4) (2013).

CRC Committee Concluding Observations

Algeria Concluding Observations CRC/C/DZA/CO/3-4 (18 July 2012).
Bahrain Concluding Observations CRC/C/BHR/CO/4-6 (27 February 2019).
Bangladesh Concluding observations (CRC/C/BGD/CO/5 (30 October 2015).
Djibouti Concluding Observations CRC/C/15/Add131 (28 June 2000).
Egypt Concluding Observations CRC/C/15/Add.145 (21 February 2001).
Egypt Concluding Observations CRC/C/EGY/CO/3-4 (15 July 2011).
Egypt Concluding Observations CRC/C/15/Add.5 (18 February 1993).
Iran Concluding Observations CRC/C/IRN/CO/3-4 (14 March 2016).
Morocco Concluding Observations CRC/C/15/Add. 211,4 (10 July 2003).
Morocco Concluding Observations CRC/c/MAR/CO/3-4 (14 October 2014).
Oman Concluding Observations CRC/C/OMN/CO/3-4 (14 March 2016).
Pakistan Concluding Observations CRC/C/PAK/CO/5 (11 July 2016).
Qatar Concluding Observations CRC/C/QAT/CO/3-4 (22 June 2017).
Saudi Arabia Concluding Observations CRC/C/15/Add148 (26 January 2001).

Saudi Arabia Concluding Observations CRC/C/SAU/CO/3-4 (25 October 2016).
Syrian Arab Republic Concluding Observations CRC/C/15/Add212 (10 July 2003).
UAE Concluding Observations CRC/C/ARE/CO/2 (30 October 2015).

Publications by the Hague Conference on Private International Law

Andriakopoulou, KZ and Andriakopoulou ML, 'The Voice of the Child in Hague Convention Proceedings in Greece' in *The Child's Voice – 15 years later. The Judge's Newsletter on International Child Protection* (Hague Conference on Private International Law, 2018) 22.

Bennett, V, 'A Better Place for the Child in Return Proceedings under the 1980 Convention – A Perspective from Australia' in *The Child's Voice – 15 years later: The Judge's Newsletter on International Child Protection* (Hague Conference on Private International Law, 2018) 22.

Conclusions and Recommendations of the Special Commission of March 1979, 15–17, available at www.hcch.net/en/publications-and-studies/details4/?pid=3121.

Consultations on the Desirability and Feasibility of a Protocol to the Hague Convention of 25 October 1980: Prelim Doc No 7 (Hague Conference, 2011) 4, available at www.hcch.net/upload/wop/abduct2011pd07e.pdf.

Direct Judicial Communications: Emerging Guidance Regarding the Development of the International Hague Network of Judges and General Principles for Judicial Communications (Hague Conference on Private International Law, 2013) available at https://assets.hcch.net/docs/62d073ca-eda0-494e-af66-2ddd368b7379.pdf.

Duncan, W, 'Purpose of the Malta Process' *The Judges' Newsletter 16* (Spring 2010) 12.

Dyer, A, 'A Report on International Child Abduction by One Parent 'Legal Kidnapping' (The Hague Conference, 1978).

Emon, A and Khaliq, U, 'Islamic Law, Private International Law & Cross-Border Child Abduction' (Hague Conference in Private International Law, 2014).

Fourth Malta Judicial Conference on Cross-Frontier Family Law Issues Hosted by the Government of Malta in Collaboration with the Hague Conference on Private International Law.

Marzia Ghigliazza and Sara Luzzati 'The Hearing of the Child in Civil Proceedings in Italy – Rules and Practice' in *The Child's Voice – 15 years later: The Judge's Newsletter on International Child Protection* (Hague Conference on Private International Law, 2018) 22.

Gosselain C, 'Child Abduction and Transfrontier Access: Bilateral Conventions and Islamic States' (Hague Conference, Permanent Bureau, Preliminary Document No 7, 2002) available at www.hcch.net/upload/abd2002_pd7e.pdf.

Guide to Part II of the Sixth Meeting of the Special Commission and Consideration of the Desirability and Feasibility of Further Work in Connection with the 1980 and the 1996 Conventions: Prelim Doc No 13 (Hague Conference, 2011) available at www.hcch.net/upload/wop/abduct2012pd3_e.pdf.

Hale, B, 'Child Abduction from the Child's Point of View' in *The Child's Voice – 15 years later: The Judge's Newsletter on International Child Protection* (Hague Conference on Private International Law, 2018) 22.

HCCH, Report on the Fifth Meeting of the Special Commission to Review the Operation of the Hague Conventions (March 2007) available at www.hcch.net/upload/wop/ abd_2006_rpt-e.pdf.

HCCH Convention of 25 October 1980 on the Civil Aspects of International Child Abduction – Part VI – Article 13(1)(b) (HCCH Publications) available at https://assets.hcch.net/docs/225b44d3-5c6b-4a14-8f5b-57cb370c497f.pdf.

Judge's Newsletter on International Child Protection 31 (Hague Conference, Spring 2011) 34 available at https://assets.hcch.net/upload/spring2011e.pdf.

Kamaruddin, K, 'Islamic Legal Perspectives on Cross-Border Family Disputes Involving Children' (Hague Conference in Private International Law, 2014) available at www.hcch.net/en/publications-and-studies/details4/?pid=6172.

Lee, C, 'Listening to the Child's Voice in Spain' in *The Child's Voice – 15 years later: The Judge's Newsletter on International Child Protection* (Hague Conference on Private International Law, 2018) 22.

Lembrechts, S, 'Hearing Abducted Children in Court – A Comparative Point of View from Three Countries (Belgium, France & The Netherlands)' in *The Child's Voice – 15 years later: The Judge's Newsletter on International Child Protection* (Hague Conference on Private International Law, 2018) 22.

List of network judges available at https://assets.hcch.net/docs/18eb8d6c-593b-4996-9c5c-19e4590ac66d.pdf.

Lortie, P and Breger, F, in *The Child's Voice – 15 years later. The Judge's Newsletter on International Child Protection* (Hague Conference on Private International Law, 2018) 22.

Lowe, N and Stephens, V, 'A Statistical Analysis of Applications Made in 2015 Under the Hague Convention of 25 October 1980 on the Civil Aspects of International Child Abduction – Global Report' (Hague Conference, 2017).

—— and others, 'A Statistical Analysis of Applications made in 1999 under the Hague Convention on the Civil Aspects of International Child Abduction' Preliminary Document No 3 (2001).

—— and others, 'A Statistical Analysis of Applications Made in 2003 under the Hague Convention on the Civil Aspects of International Child Abduction' Preliminary Document No 3 (2006) 39.

Olland, A, 'The Voice of the Child in 1980 Hague Return Procedures in the Netherlands' in *The Child's Voice – 15 years later: The Judge's Newsletter on International Child Protection* (Hague Conference on Private International Law, 2018) 22.

Pérez-Vera, E, 'Report on the 1980 Hague Child Abduction Convention' (Translation of The Permanent Bureau, 1981).

Principles and Explanatory Memorandum on the Principles: Mediation Guide to Good Practice under the Abduction Convention (Hague Conference on Private International Law, 2012) available at https://assets.hcch.net/upload/guide28mediation_en.pdf.

Sawamura, T, 'Child's View in Return Proceedings – Practice of Japanese Courts' in *The Child's Voice – 15 years later: The Judge's Newsletter on International Child Protection* (Hague Conference on Private International Law, 2018) 22.

See the Hague Convention Status Table available at www.hcch.net/en/instruments/conventions/status-table/?cid=24.

Taylor, N and Freeman, M, 'Outcomes for Objecting Children under the 1980 Convention' in *The Child's Voice – 15 years later: The Judge's Newsletter on International Child Protection* (Hague Conference on Private International Law, 2018) 22.

The Judges' Newsletter on International Child Protection 20 (Hague Conference on International Law, 2013).

INDEX

www.ingramcontent.com/pod-product-compliance
Ingram Content Group UK Ltd.
Pitfield, Milton Keynes, MK11 3LW, UK
UKHW020806290926
15470UKWH00003B/995

9 781509 939114